Duff Green

Facts and Suggestions

Biographical, historical, financial and political, addressed to the People of the

United States

Duff Green

Facts and Suggestions
Biographical, historical, financial and political, addressed to the People of the United States

ISBN/EAN: 9783337074906

Printed in Europe, USA, Canada, Australia, Japan

Cover: Foto ©ninafisch / pixelio.de

More available books at **www.hansebooks.com**

CONTENTS.

THE chief purpose of this volume is to state, briefly, the origin and progress of the conflict of interest and of opinion which superinduced the late civil war; that a knowledge of the past may have its proper influence on the future. If, as I believe, the organization of a sectional Northern party, for the purpose of a corrupt, sectional, political control of the government, in violation of the fundamental principles of the Constitution, necessarily led to the organization of a Southern party, in defence of the interest and principles which it was the purpose of that Northern party to assail and subvert;—then, if the civil war was the consequence of that conflict, the censure should rest on the men, who, by organizing a sectional Northern party for the purpose of aggression, compelled the counter organization of a Southern party in defence of the rights, interests, and principles thus assailed; and the fact that Mr. Lincoln was elected by less than a majority of votes given, and that, availing themselves of the power of the Federal government thus accidentally obtained, that Northern party, not content with the emancipation of Southern slaves, now seek to deprive the Southern States of the political rights guaranteed to them by the Constitution, and would enforce alterations of the Constitution, because they know that without such alterations they cannot retain the political control of the government, makes it the duty of the whole people to inquire into the motives which actuate that minority, who, having thus brought upon the country the calamity of civil war, are exerting their influence to prevent the restoration of peace. One purpose of this volume is to demonstrate that it is the duty of the whole country to harmonize in a common effort to restore the Union, on the basis of our common interests, and with this view I have endeavored to demonstrate that a wise use of the public credit, stimulating our industrial progress, as, by an abundant and cheap currency, we may do, will enable us successfully to compete with all other rival nations, in the markets of the world, and especially in the markets of the Pacific and of Asia. For the competition, in the progress of civilization, in commerce and finance, is not between the North and the South, as rival and opposing interests, but it is between the North and the South united, under a common government, organized as one people, for the promotion of their common welfare, happiness, and prosperity, and for the protection of their common rights and interests, as those rights and interests may be affected by the industrial competition or the financial or political measures and policy of foreign nations.

I would appeal to the working men, and urge them to unite their influence in support of an early restoration of the constitutional rights of the people of the Southern states, because the laboring men can, if they will, give peace and prosperity to the whole country, and thus, and thus only, give to themselves constant and profitable employment. " A fair day's wages for a fair day's work."

To the ladies of the United States, I would say, that the people of the South are compelled to contribute their proportionate part of the fund appropriated by the Federal government for the maintenance of the widows and orphans of Federal soldiers. We have accepted the terms of peace, and intend cheerfully and in good faith to comply ; but we have our own suffering poor—the war has made orphans for whose relief the Federal Congress has provided no fund, and for the maintenance and support of whom it is a gracious privilege to be enabled to contribute. May I not ask you to aid me in doing this ?

A large part of this volume was dictated to and written by my daughters while I was lying on a bed of sickness, and having given to them the whole proceeds of the sales, beyond the cost of printing, with the understanding that they will give one half of the sums, thus to be realized, to a fund to be applied by female societies in aid of the maintenance and education of female orphans in the Southern states, I would appeal to the ladies in the North and in the South to aid them in obtaining contributions to this fund.

Packages will be made up at the American Industrial Agency, 42 Broadway, New York, and forwarded by Adams & Co.'s Express, and the American Express Company, who have both agreed to convey such packages free of charge. All orders and communications should be addressed to the American Industrial Agency, 42 Broadway, New York, who are charged with the gratuitous superintendence of the publication.

DUFF GREEN.

CHAPTER I.

INTRODUCTORY.

AT no period of the world has the history of mankind been marked with incidents more interesting than during the last hundred years. Of these, among the most important, are the Independence of the American colonies, the adoption of the Federal Constitution, and the progress of the United States—embracing the issues which resulted in the late conflict of arms, and upon the adjustment of which depend not only our own future welfare and prosperity, but our relations to the other people of the earth.

Although an humble citizen, it has been my lot to be acquainted, personally and intimately, with the men who have for many years controlled the measures and policy of the United States; and hoping that a candid statement of facts, within my own knowledge, explanatory of the history of the past, may tend to allay the bitterness of sectional feeling, and to create that unity of interest and of opinion, which, if we are to live under one government, it is our incumbent duty to maintain, I am encouraged to write a review of the past; and inasmuch as the value of my statements as to the motives and conduct of others, will depend much upon the estimate which the public may place upon my own, and as the history of my own life is so intimately connected with that of the government and of the men of whom I must write, I trust that the generous reader will excuse the egotism, which seems indispensable in a narrative of events, in which I myself took part, and the chief merit of which narrative depends upon my personal knowledge of the facts of which I write.

MAN'S DUTY.

Why man, as created by God, was permitted to eat the forbidden fruit, and as a consequence was driven from Paradise, are mysteries hidden in the inscrutable will of the Creator—we all know that he is a sinner, and as such is subject to pain and death, yet few, if any there be, unenlightened by revelation, and the faith and hope which that imparts, can reconcile the dispensations of God's providence with the natural instincts of goodness, justice and mercy ("for the carnal mind is enmity against God"). Yet, to the humble, subdued Christian, who believes that whom God loveth he chasteneth, and who sees in the afflictions of men and of nations, the exercise of his power and the indications of his purpose, there is nothing in the calamity which has befallen this country, great as are the afflictions which it brings, which should make us despair. I, for one, feel that I should be reconciled to the destiny which has befallen us, and more zealous and earnest in the faithful discharge of the duties incumbent upon me as a man, a parent, a citizen, and a Christian; and I feel that in reference to my own antecedents and personal and political training, it is not only my privilege, but my duty, to aid in giving that direction to pending political issues, which will best promote the restoration of peace, and the organization of a national sentiment, which will tend to unite the North and the South, in a common effort for the promotion of our common interests, by a proper and kindly adjustment of all sectional issues, the tendency of which may be to prevent that union and concert of action which are indispensable to the proper discharge of the duties incumbent upon us whom the Almighty has endowed with blessings, temporal and spiritual, such as he has given to no other people.

THE REWARD OF LABOR.

" In the beginning God created the heavens and the earth, and said, Let the earth bring forth grass, the herb yielding seed, and the fruit-tree yielding fruit after his kind, whose seed is in itself upon the earth, and it was so."

And after man's transgression, He said unto Adam, " Because thou hast hearkened unto the voice of thy wife, and hast eaten of the tree of which I commanded thee, saying, Thou shalt not eat of it ; cursed is the ground for thy sake ; in sorrow shalt thou eat of it all the days of thy life ; thorns also and thistles shall it bring forth to thee ; and thou shalt eat the herb of the field. In the sweat of thy face shalt thou eat bread, till thou return unto the ground ; for out of it wast thou taken ; for dust thou art, and unto dust shalt thou return."

To labor is, therefore, the condition upon which man is permitted to live, and we find that although the grass and the herb yield their seed, and the fruit-tree yields its fruit, they are sub-ject to the influence of climate and of seasons, in accordance with the laws, which indicate the will and the purposes of the Creator. For He hath said, " While the earth remaineth, seedtime and harvest, and cold and heat, and summer and winter, and day and night, shall not cease."

As bread is indispensable to man's existence, and as the only means of obtaining it is by labor, it follows that he who complies with the condition imposed by the Creator, is entitled to the benefits which are promised as the reward of his compliance.

THE PURPOSE OF GOVERNMENT.

This is the natural right of man, for the protection of which, as their numbers increased, it became necessary to organize governments, the purpose and objects of which should be the protection of life and of property, which is the reward of labor.

BABEL—THE CONFUSION OF LANGUAGES.

We are told that " the whole earth was of one language and of one speech. And it came to pass, as they journeyed from the east, that they found a plain in the land of Shinar ; and they dwelt there. And they said, one to another, Go to, let us make brick, and burn them thoroughly, and they had brick for stone, and slime had they for mortar. And they said, Go to, let us build us a city, *and a tower whose top may reach unto heaven ; and let us make us a name, lest we be scattered abroad upon the face of the whole earth.* And the Lord came down to see the city and the tower, which the children of men builded. And the Lord said, Behold, the people is one, and they have all one language ; and this they begin to do ; and now nothing will be restrained from them, which they have imagined to do ; Go to, let us go down, and there confound their language, that they may not understand one another's speech. So the Lord scattered them abroad from thence upon the face of all the earth ; and they left off to build the city. Therefore is the name of it called Babel ; because the Lord did there confound the language of all the earth ; and from thence did the Lord scatter them abroad upon all the face of the earth."

THE JEWISH SLAVES INCOMPETENT TO OR-GANIZE A FREE GOVERNMENT.

What was written aforetime was written for our learning. The character, the will, and the purposes of God, are indicated in the Holy Scriptures. His promise, that the seed of the woman should bruise the serpent's head, was renewed to Abram, to Isaac, and to Jacob, and fulfilled in the birth and crucifixion of the Saviour. The Jews were a chosen people ; yet Joseph was sold as a slave by his brethren, and the Israelites were in bondage four hundred years, and *although He required that those who had been thus enslaved, and were therefore unfit depositaries of civil liberty, should wander in the wilderness until they perished,* and he had created a people, educated and trained under his special guidance and instruction, qualified to organize a government, in which the rights of persons and of property were defined and protected ; and although this people, thus cared for, like our first parents, rebelled against God, and as a punishment were carried into captivity, they were permitted to rebuild their temple and maintain their nationality until Christ, upon the cross, said, "IT IS FINISHED." Then the great purpose of the national organization of the Jews being accomplished, the

Romans were permitted to run a ploughshare over the foundations of the temple, and they, as a *people*, were scattered throughout the earth, as witnesses of the truth of revelation. Where is there a country on the face of the globe, in which these living witnesses, marked with characteristics which all persons recognize, are not to be found ? Do we not meet them in every street, in every village ? What do these truths indicate, as the duty of a Christian people ?

OUR DUTY AS A CHRISTIAN PEOPLE.

We find that when, after his resurrection, having made himself known to his disciples, the Saviour's last words, as he ascended to the Father, were, "Go ye and preach the gospel to all nations."

I have prayerfully studied, that I might ascertain, and earnestly endeavored to discharge, my duty in all the relations of life, and especially as a man and a Christian statesman. In the contemplation of the bounteous providence of God, I have realized the weighty responsibility resting on the United States, as a people. I have compared our vast extent of territory, the vast deposits of mineral wealth, the abundance and extraordinary distribution of water-powers, the peculiar products of our climate, the fertility of our soil, and the intelligent and enterprise of our people, with the condition and progress of other nations, and I have seen, or thought I saw, that as commerce must precede civilization, and as civilization must precede Christianity, we must become a manufacturing, that we may become a commercial people. For commerce is the medium through which civilization and Christianity are dispensed to the heathen world ; and, deeply impressed with this truth, I have labored for many years to arouse the federal and state governments to the necessity of such a regulation of our commerce with foreign nations as will protect the value of our currency, and thus prevent the constant recurrence of the monetary revulsions, which were, and ever will be, the inevitable consequence of the control, which the Bank of England has heretofore been permitted to have over the quantity and value of our currency. For it will be seen that under our regulation of commerce, that bank, and not our Congress, has regulated the value of our money and of our property, thus limiting and restraining the proper discharge of our duty as a Christian people.

MANY NATIONS, WHY.

No one can doubt that it was the purpose of God, in the confusion of languages and in scattering abroad on the face of all the earth those who had said, *"Go to, let us build us a city, and a tower whose top may reach unto heaven,"* not only to rebuke their arrogance and presumption, but to break them up into many different nationalities, and thus create those sectional national interests which constitute the peculiar characteristics of separate independent governments, including the right of individual persons and of property which it is the duty of such governments to foster and protect.

It becomes the duty of statesmen, therefore, to consider, what are the relations which the individuals constituting their separate communities bear to each other, and to their respective governments, and what are the relations which each of these separate governments bears to the rest of mankind. These necessarily embrace all the rights of persons and of property.

COMMUNITY OF NATIONS.

Few, very few of our statesmen realize the fact that we are one of a community of nations. They have been so absorbed with party politics and the conflicts of personal ambition and individual interests, that few of them have studied, as they should have studied, the bearing which the monetary systems and commercial policy of foreign nations have had upon the separate interests and prosperity of the United States. It must, therefore, be seen that in treating of our public policy it is indispensable that we should take into the account our relations with the other peoples of the earth, and especially to consider the fact that the great issue between the more civilized nations of the earth, who use machinery and have thus increased the productive power of their industry, creating thereby a large surplus beyond their home consumption, is how they can command the markets of the less civilized nations who do not use machinery, and are yet the consumers of machine-made goods. The people of Europe, and especially of Great Britain, use machinery, and are enabled to create a large surplus. The people of Africa, South America, India, and China, do not use machinery—they exchange raw agricultural products for European machine-made goods.

DIVISION OF LABOR.

It has been argued that under the general welfare clause of our constitution Congress has power to impose duties for the protection of domestic industry and this construction of the powers of the government and negro slavery have been made the chief sources of the sectional conflict between the North and the South. The question of slavery has been disposed of by the war, and the sum now requisite to pay the interest on the public debt and provide for an economical administration of our public affairs is so great, that the question of protection of domestic industry is lost in the necessity of maintaining the public faith. Instead of an increase, the domestic industry must now demand a reduction of taxation. The question for statesmen now, therefore, is, how can we lessen the burden of the public debt? Coupled with this is the kindred question : how can we provide for and increase the rewards of labor ? The time once was when the United States were comparatively free from debt, and the local demand for agricultural produce, caused by migration to the new states, was such that in the Northwest and in the South the cultivation of the soil gave a more profitable employment for labor than manufactures ; that is, labor in Illinois and Georgia could make better wages by producing wheat and cotton than by spinning thread. But as the population has increased, the greater number of persons engaged in the production of wheat and of cotton has so augmented the supply beyond the foreign as well as the home demand, that an appropriate division of labor so as to obtain constant employment and the best compensation has become indispensable. The time once was when a free trade in provisions would have greatly benefited the Northwest because England could then consume the surplus, which the Northwest could then spare. But that time has passed. We can now produce so much more than England can consume, that we are compelled to find a market elsewhere. As the value of our surplus produce will necessarily be taxed with the cost of sending it to the consumer, it can require no argument to demonstrate that the profits of the producer will be greater if we can so distribute our labor as to create a home market equal to the consumption of our surplus. A wise people should profit not only by their own experience, but by that of others.

Our relative condition being changed, our measures and policy should conform to the present and the future, rather than to the past—and yet a review and careful analysis of the past is indispensable to a proper estimate of the present or the future, and it is therefore that I write.

CHAPTER II.

PERSONAL NARRATIVE.

MY paternal great-grandfather, Robert Green, left seven sons, William, Robert, Duff, John, Nicholas, James, and Moses. He, with his cousin Sir William Duff and a Mr. Hite, were, as I have frequently heard my father say, joint owners of large tracts of choice land, some situated on James river, some near Fredericksburg, and others in the valley of the Shenandoah. Sir William was unmarried, and dying left his interest in these lands to his cousin, whose seven sons were all married, and many of their descendants now remain in that part of Virginia. My grandfather, Duff Green, married first a Miss Barbour, who died leaving a son and daughter, John and Elizabeth. He then married a sister of Col. Lewis Willis, of Fredericksburg. She was a cousin of Gen. Washington, and nearly related by marriage with the Lewises, the Henrys, and Lees, of Virginia. My grandfather died before the Revolution. My grandmother had three sons, Willis, Henry, and William, and one daughter, Eleanor. My father, William, the youngest son, was a volunteer in the army of the Revolution, and, when fifteen years of age, was with Morgan in the battle of the Cowpens.

As the eldest son, John, was heir, and, under the law of inheritance, as it then was, took the greater part of the property, the three younger brothers, through the influence of friends and relatives of the family, made contracts to locate land warrants in Kentucky. Under this arrangement Willis and Henry went to Kentucky, soon after the termination of the war, leaving my father in charge of his mother and sister. Willis was elected a delegate from Kentucky to the legislature of Virginia, and was appointed register of the land office. He then relinquished his interest in the land-warrants to his brothers and sister. Henry, having made his locations, returned to Virginia, sickened, and died. This made it necessary that my father should remove to Kentucky, taking his mother and sister with him. My aunt soon thereafter married John Smith.

My maternal grandfather was Markham Marshall, who married Ann Bailey. They resided on the Shenandoah until my mother, who was their second child, was about ten years of age. He removed to Kentucky in the fall of 1779, and settled near the Knob lick, in Lincoln county. My father, after his marriage, resided in Woodford county, until I, his eldest child, was about fourteen years old, when he removed to a large tract of land on the Cumberland river, in Wayne county. When I was about six years of age, I was sent to a neighborhood school. Most of the scholars were the children of my father's tenants, or of persons holding lands under an adverse title. Humphrey Marshall, my mother's cousin, was my father's counsel, and Henry Clay opposed to him. Mr. Marshall had married his cousin, the eldest sister of the chief justice; and she and my mother were intimate friends. He had been a senator in Congress from Kentucky, and voted for Jay's treaty, which was bitterly denounced by Mr. Clay and others. As party politics were of absorbing interest, and the political feeling was aggravated by the pending litigation, the prejudice thus created had, doubtless, its influence upon the estimate which I afterwards formed of Mr. Clay's conduct and character.

My father was much from home. I was the eldest child—three years the eldest. I was the companion of my mother. I read to her the history of Greece, of Rome, and of England. I also read to her Plutarch, with other miscellaneous books. Mrs. Humphrey Marshall gave me the use of books from her library, and upon my returning them, examined me upon what I had read. When I was fourteen years of age, I had studied, as they were taught in our country schools, arithmetic, geography, and English grammar, and had read the first books of Virgil in Latin.

TEACH SCHOOL.

When my father removed to Wayne, there was no school near his residence. Mr. Priestly, who had been teaching in Baltimore, was induced to remove to Danville, and I was placed in his school, where I was eighteen months. I reviewed my lessons in geography, and read Virgil, Cæsar, Horace, and Cicero, in Latin. Finding that my sisters and younger brother had no other instruction but such as my mother could give them, I induced my father to permit me to remain at home and teach them. I devoted four years to this duty, prosecuting my own studies as best I could. During the last of these four years I took a few additional scholars, and having earned

enough to buy me a watch, a horse, bridle, and saddle, a suit of "Sunday-clothes," and ten dollars in money, I tendered my services to the trustees of a school in Elizabethtown, Hardin county, which were accepted, with the understanding that in case of war with England, I should be at liberty to

JOIN THE ARMY.

William P. Duval, then a member of Congress, afterward the governor of Florida, had raised a volunteer company of six months' men, of whom ten had been my schoolmates. They formed a mess, with the understanding that I would join them in case of their receiving marching orders. On the 15th of August, 1812, the day on which I was twenty-one years of age, I was mustered into the service of the United States, at Jeffersonville, by General Harrison. Several of our company had special letters of introduction to him, and he imprudently appealed to us, in a public address, complimenting us upon our standing and character, and invoking us to become an example of order and discipline for the army. The effect was, to excite the envy, jealousy, and ill-will of the other companies.

INFLUENCE OF MY MOTHER.

My parents were both members of the Baptist church. My mother was my companion and friend. Her intelligent comment on the lessons in history which I read to her, and upon the events of the war of the Revolution, and her description of frontier life, did much to form my character. She had a happy faculty of illustrating her advice by appropriate anecdotes. One has often recurred to me, and has been useful in my subsequent intercourse with the world. Among the residents in the fort, in which my grandfather's family lived, was a Mr. Miller and his wife. He was a quarrelsome, passionate man, and part of his nose had been bitten off in a fight. He was called, *Nosey* Miller. One day he and his wife were quarrelling, using unkind language, greatly to the annoyance of their neighbors, when an old servant woman appealed to her mistress, saying, "Missis, missis, dar is a rope thrown over de house, an you is on one side an master is on tother, both pullin ; now, you just let go your eend, an go round tother side an take holt long with master, and see how soon it come over." What a lesson in domestic and social life ! Often, often have I remembered and profited by the old servant's advice ! How much in public and in private life depends upon our holding the right end of the rope !

THE TRUTH OF THE SCRIPTURES.

While at school in Woodford, a young Mr. Vawter, one of the elder scholars, commenting on the Holy Scriptures, said that the Bible was the work of priestcraft, written as a system of morals, by persons selected by one of the Roman Emperors. He denied its truth and divine inspiration. Such was my respect for my parents, and such my unwillingness to wound my mother's feelings, that I dared not let them know what I had heard, much less did I communicate to them the impression which his remarks had made upon my mind. The idea that the Scriptures were the work of man—a fable—that the responsibility for, and the punishment of, sin were imaginary, was a relief.

PROMISE NOT TO LEARN TO PLAY CARDS.

When I was leaving home to go to school in Danville, after I had taken leave of my mother and my sisters and brothers, my father walked with me to the stile, and, as I was about to get on my horse, he said, "My son, you are leaving me to enter the world, and before you go I have one request to make, and wish you to promise that you will faithfully comply with it." I said, "I know you will not ask what I should not perform, and I therefore promise." He replied, "When I was of your age, I was very fond of playing cards, and, had I not become a member of the church, I should probably have become a professed gambler. I wish you to promise me that you will never learn to play cards." I unhesitatingly gave the pledge. Several of my class-mates were much older than I. They boarded with Judge Bridges, a son-in-law of General Adair, who lived between my uncle's, where I lived, and the school-house. They were fond of playing cards, which was the subject of frequent conversation. Upon one occasion, school having been dismissed earlier than usual, I was prevailed upon to stop with them. We had scarcely entered their room when cards were produced, and I was urged to take a seat with them and learn to play. I thought of my father—I remembered my pledge. I was prompted to tell them why I could not play, but a false pride prevented my doing so. I took a seat at the table, I took the cards in my hand, but before I had taken my first lesson I heard my father's voice in the hall. I threw down the cards, I sprang from my seat, I upset the table, and, as I ran down stairs renewed my pledge that I never would learn to play cards, and I never did learn. I did not know or suppose that he was within sixty miles of me. He was on his way to Frankfort in great haste, to see the register of the

FACTS AND SUGGESTIONS,

BIOGRAPHICAL,

HISTORICAL, FINANCIAL AND POLITICAL,

ADDRESSED TO THE

PEOPLE OF THE UNITED STATES.

BY DUFF GREEN.

———————

NEW YORK:
RICHARDSON & CO., 540 BROADWAY.
LIPPINCOTT & CO., PHILADELPHIA.
1866.

land office. He stopped at my uncle's for his dinner, and there heard that the register, who was also a son-in-law of General Adair, was then on a visit to Judge Bridges, and came to inquire for him, without the remotest idea of seeing me. The incident, however, connected with the influence of my early training, made a deep and lasting impression on my mind.

BECOME CONVINCED OF THE TRUTH OF DIVINE REVELATION.

Upon my return home from Danville, I again appropriated a part of my time to the reading and study of history My attention was arrested by the following remarks of Rollin, upon

THE TRANSLATION OF THE BIBLE.

" The tumult of the wars which a diversity of interest had kindled among the successors of Alexander throughout the whole extent of their territories, did not prevent Ptolemy Philadelphus from devoting his utmost attention to the noble library which he had founded in Alexandria, wherein he deposited the most valuable and curious books he was capable of collecting from all parts of the world. This prince, being informed that the Jews possessed a work which contained the laws of Moses and the history of that people, formed the design of having it translated out of the Hebrew language into Greek, in order to enrich his library with that performance. To accomplish this design, it became necessary for him to address himself to the high priest of the Jewish nation; but the affair happened to be attended with great difficulty. There was at that time a very considerable number of Jews in Egypt, who had been reduced to a state of slavery by Ptolemy Soter, during the invasion of Judea in his time; and it was represented to the king, that there would be no probability of obtaining from that people either a copy or a faithful translation of their law, while he suffered such a number of their countrymen to continue in their present servitude. Ptolemy, who always acted with the utmost generosity, and was extremely solicitous to enlarge his library, did not hesitate a moment, but issued a decree for restoring all the Jewish slaves in his dominions to their liberty; with orders to his treasurer to pay twenty drams a head to their masters for their ransom. The sum expended on this occasion amounted to four hundred talents (three hundred thousand dollars), whence it appears that one hundred and twenty thousand Jews recovered their freedom. The king then gave orders for discharging the children born in slavery, with their mothers; and the sum employed for that purpose amounted to above half the former.

" These advantageous preliminaries gave Ptolemy hopes that he should easily obtain his request from the high priest, whose name was Eleazer. He had sent embassadors to that pontiff, with a very obliging letter on his part, accompanied with magnificent presents. The embassadors were received at Jerusalem with all imaginable honors, and the king's request was granted with the greatest joy. Upon which they returned to Alexandria with an authentic copy of the Mosaic law, written in letters of gold, given them by the high priest himself, with six elders of each tribe, that is to say, seventy-two in the whole; and they were authorized to translate that copy into the Greek language.

" The king was desirous of seeing these deputies, and proposed to each of them a different question, in order to make a trial of their capacity. He was satisfied with their answers, in which great wisdom appeared, and loaded them with presents, and other marks of his friendship. The elders were then conducted to the Isle of Pharos, and lodged in a house prepared for their reception, where they were plentifully supplied with all necessary accommodations. *They applied* themselves to their work without losing time, and, in seventy-two days, completed the volume which is commonly called the Septuagint version. The whole was afterward read and approved in the presence of the king, who particularly admired the wisdom of the laws of Moses, and dismissed the seventy-two deputies with extremely magnificent presents; part of which were for themselves, others for the high priest, and the remainder for the temple."

I read further in Rollin, as to

THE FALL OF BABYLON.

"God Almighty was pleased not only to cause the captivity which his people were to suffer at Babylon to be foretold a long time before it came to pass, but likewise to set down the exact number of years it was to last. The term he fixed for it was seventy years, after which he promised he would deliver them by bringing a remarkable and irretrievable destruction upon the city of Babylon, the place of their bondage and confinement. 'And these nations shall serve the King of Babylon seventy years.'—Jer. xxv. 11."

I turned to the prophecy and find the following:

"Therefore, thus saith the Lord of Hosts: Because ye have not heard my words, ... Behold, I will send and take all the families of the north, saith the Lord, and Nebuchadnezzar, the king of Babylon, my servant, and will bring them against this land. . . . . . And this whole land shall be a desolation and an astonishment; and these nations shall serve the king of Babylon seventy years. And it shall come to pass, when seventy years are accomplished, that I will punish the king of Babylon and that nation, saith the Lord, for their iniquity, and the land of the Chaldeans; and will make it a perpetual desolation."

I read further, and I found that Rollin says of

CYRUS, KING OF PERSIA.

"In the first of these seven years, precisely, expired the seventieth year of the Babylonish captivity, when Cyrus published the famous edict whereby the Jews were permitted to return to Jerusalem. There is no question but this edict was obtained by the care and solicitations of Daniel, who possessed great influence at court. That

he might the more effectually induce the king to grant him this request, he showed him undoubtedly the prophecies of Isaiah, wherein, above two hundred years before his birth, he was marked out by name as a prince appointed by God to be a great conqueror, and to reduce a multitude of nations under his dominions; and, at the same time to be the deliverer of the captive Jews, by ordering their temple to be rebuilt, and Jerusalem and Judea to be repossessed by their ancient inhabitants."

And I turned to the forty-fourth and forty-fifth chapters of Isaiah, and saw that the prophet had said of the

REBUILDING OF THE TEMPLE.

"Sing, O ye heavens; for the Lord hath done it: shout, ye lower parts of the earth; break forth into singing, ye mountains and forests, and every tree therein; for the Lord hath redeemed Jacob, and glorified himself in Israel. . . . . That saith of Cyrus, He is my shepherd, and shall perform all my pleasure: *even saying to Jerusalem, Thou shalt be built; and to the temple, Thy foundation shall be laid.* Thus saith the Lord to his anointed, to Cyrus, whose right hand I have holden to subdue nations before him. . . . . And I will give thee the treasures of darkness, and hidden riches of secret places, that thou mayest know that I the Lord, *which call thee by thy name,* am the God of Israel. For Jacob my servant's sake, and Israel mine elect, *I have called thee by thy name:* I have surnamed thee though thou hast not known me."

I turned to Ezra, and read the following

VERIFICATION OF THIS PROPHECY.

"Now, in the first year of Cyrus, king of Persia (that the word of the Lord, by the mouth of Jeremiah, might be fulfilled), the Lord stirred up the spirit of Cyrus, the king of Persia, that he made a proclamation throughout all his kingdom, and put it also in writing, saying, Thus saith Cyrus, king of Persia, The Lord God of heaven hath given me all the kingdoms of the earth, *and he hath charged me to build him a house at Jerusalem, which is in Judah. Who is there among you of all his people? his God be with him, and let him go up to Jerusalem, which is in Judah, and build the house of the Lord God of Israel (He is the God), which is in Jerusalem.* And whosoever remaineth in any place where he sojourneth, let the men of his place help him with silver and with gold, and with goods and with beasts, besides the free-will-offering, for the house of God that is in Jerusalem. Then rose up the chief of the fathers of Judah and Benjamin, and the priests, and the Levites, and all them whose spirit God had raised to go up to build the house of the Lord which is in Jerusalem. And all they that were about them strengthened their hands with vessels of silver, with gold, with goods, and with beasts, and with precious things, besides all that was willingly offered. Also Cyrus the king brought forth the vessels of the house of the Lord, which Nebuchadnezzar had brought forth out of Jerusalem, and put them in the house of his gods; even those did Cyrus, king of Persia, bring forth by the hand of Mithredath, the treasurer, and numbered them unto Sheshbazzar, the prince of Judah."

CONVICTION, FAITH, AND HOPE.

Here was proof—conclusive proof—of the divine inspiration. I could no longer doubt. The Scriptures were the word of God. I was in despair. I had refused to believe. I had refused to see or to hear the truth. My conviction was deep and severe. I tried to pray. I wrestled with the spirit; and the way of life and salvation through a crucified Redeemer was made manifest. I had gone to a secluded place some distance from the house. I wished to make my joy known to my parents. I hastened, but before I reached them, I was assailed by doubts, fearful doubts, but I would not, I could not, relinquish my hope or my joy. My father saw me coming. He sprang from his seat and ran to meet me. He clasped me

to his bosom. My mother, my dear mother, wept for joy, and I was happy. Reader, the faith and hope thus given to me in tender youth, remains with me and sustains and encourages me now in the feebleness of age. I believe that there is a merciful, kind, and good God, who, superintends and in mercy, by his special providence, controls the affairs of men and of nations, and that while he chasteneth he will protect and provide for his people to whom he will become reconciled, through his loving-kindness; and hence should we trust him, and strive to know his will, and labor unceasingly to discharge our duty to him and to each other.

POLITICS AND RELIGION.

As the events of which it is my purpose to write are chiefly political, and as there are many persons who have a vague impression that there is something in politics incompatible with religion, or something in religion incompatible with politics, and that therefore religion and politics should not be blended, it may be proper, in the peculiar circumstances in which this country is now placed, to say that, while I admit that Christ's kingdom is not of this world, we, as men, have our relations to temporal as well as spiritual matters, and that as a good government is the greatest of temporal blessings, it is no less our duty, as Christian men, to resist Satan's influence in the affairs of state, than to resist it in the government of the church; and that inasmuch as that the name and religion of Christ have been invoked, and it is apparent are still further to be used as a means of the oppression and desolation of the Southern states, I would invoke the Christian faith and hopes of the whole people in support of the great principles which constitute the foundation of our system of government, by demonstrating, as I believe I can do, that it is our duty to unite, as one people, in support of the measures and public policy which foster and protect American interests, as distinguished from those of all other peoples and governments ; and that dark and mysterious as the ways of Providence may seem, the great sin of the North and of the South has been an adherence to individual men, as leaders of party combinations, and a disregard of the great principles of civil and religious liberty—that we have substituted the dictation of selfish political combinations of corrupt party leaders, as indicated in their manifestoes, in party platforms, for the letter and spirit of our written constitution ; and hence, while I unmask the selfish and personal motives which have governed the conduct of leading public men, and thus trace to its source the cause which has spread gloom and despondency over the South, I would revive and confirm the hopes of that suffering people, by restoring their faith and confidence in the goodness and mercy and loving-kindness of God, who assuredly will, at the same time, subdue the wrath of their enemies, and give efficiency to the sympathy and support of their friends. But to resume my personal narrative.

CHAPTER III.

PERSONAL NARRATIVE.

OUR regiment, under the command of Colonel Wilcox, marched to Vincennes. I had a large school in Elizabethtown, and, by way of recreation, organized the boys into a company, and frequently drilled them, and after we reached Vincennes, it was proposed, and I, although a private, regularly drilled my own company. News reached us that the Indians under Tecumseh had attacked Fort Harrison, having defeated the Rangers. There was a panic, and, soon thereafter, firing was heard at the lower end of the town, and the women and children fled in great alarm to a small fort. One of my mess was sick ; we had placed him in a hotel, and I was his nurse. He was in a profuse perspiration. I loaded his gun, and having placed it by his bedside, told him I must join my company, but that he must remain in bed. As I ran to the camp I found the regiment forming in front of their camp-fires, on the bank of the river. I gave the word to put out the fires, and meeting the officer of the day, suggested the propriety of forming near a large picket fortification which had been erected by General Harrison. He replied, "Will you give the word, and move the regiment there ?" I took the command, and having placed the regiment, fell back to my place in my own company. It proved to be a false alarm. But a force of some fifteen hundred of the territorial militia, in addition to our regiment, was soon organized and marched to the relief of

FORT HARRISON.

There was a deficiency of transportation, and we were compelled to leave our surplus clothing and carry seven days' rations in our knapsacks, with the understanding that supplies would be forwarded after us. The Indians had burned the block-house which contained the provisions, and the only source of supply was a cornfield in the prairie, distant about five miles. The day after we reached the fort, news came to us that the wagons, having supplies, had been attacked by the Indians, the escort defeated, and the provisions destroyed. This proved that the enemy were between us and the settlements, in what force we did not know, but all admitted that the greater part of the army should return, and yet a part should remain to defend the fort. The whole army were formed in line ; I happened to be on the extreme right. All the general and field officers, with General Taylor, then a captain, commencing on the extreme left, marched in front of the whole line, with music, appealing to the respective commands for volunteers to remain and defend the fort. No one knew when we could hope for a supply of food, except the corn standing in the field, five miles distant, and no one volunteered. When they reached the extreme right they halted in front of my company. Under the influence of the moment, I stepped forward, and said, "Colonel Wilcox, your regiment volunteers." Startled, he said, tartly, "Who authorized you, sir, to volunteer my regiment?" I replied, "It appears that some of us should remain to protect the fort. All must admit that the territorial troops should go to the protection of their families—there is, therefore, no person to remain but your regiment, and as I take it for granted that every man in your regiment came here to do his duty, I assume that you will volunteer." And without waiting for a reply, I wheeled, and said in a voice to be heard by the whole regiment, "Volunteers, shoulder arms." My own company promptly obeyed. I ran along the line and repeated the command. The whole regiment having shouldered arms, I said, "Volunteers, one pace in front, march." My own company stepped forth, I made them dress by the right and again ran along the line, saying, "Dress by the right, boys, dress by the right." I then, standing midway the regiment, said, "Attention, volunteers; order arms." I then walked up to where the officers were all yet on horseback, silent spectators. I made a bow to Colonel Wilcox, and, without saying a word, took my place in the ranks. The regiment, including Colonel Wilcox, remained. When, after his election as President, I called with a friend, who introduced me to General Taylor, he said: "Oh, sir, I knew General Green long before you did." I replied, "I did not suppose that you would recollect me." He said, "I will never forget that you volunteered your regiment to remain at Fort Harrison."

COMMAND A SCOUT.

The territorial troops left us, and next day, Captain Quigley, the officer of the day, came to me and said, "I wish you to take a scout of twenty men and explore the opposite side of the river." I replied, "I am but a private." "I know that," said he, "but, nevertheless, I wish you to command the scout." Twenty volunteers, and among them a lieutenant, were immediately organized, and upon the opposite bank of the river we found a beaten Indian trail, and in the edge of a branch we saw the fresh tracks of Indian spies, in which the water was yet muddy. After providing against surprise, we followed the trail up the river, until we came to a creek in which the Indians had concealed a number of canoes, and ascertained that their principal encampment was on the east side of the river. It was then late, I had that morning baked in the ashes, without salt, my last morsel of flour, into a cake not larger than a ship biscuit. I halted the scout and said, "We will take our dinner, and then return." "Yes," said one, "if we had anything to eat." "Well," said I, "let us each see what we have." My ash cake was all. I divided it into twenty-one pieces, and each man took his piece. Never was bread better disposed of. We next day explored the eastern side of the river, found and examined the old encampment, and being satisfied that the Indians were no longer in force in that neighborhood, the men were permitted to hunt, and those who had eaten part of my ash cake often, very often, sent me part of the game which they had killed. As Captain Duval was brigade inspector, and Ensign Harrison the paymaster of our regiment, the command of the company devolved upon Lieutenant Murray, and he and all the non-commissioned officers united in a request that I should take charge of the company as orderly, and the proper discharge of my duties detained me in camp. I was rigid but just in my discipline, and was rewarded by the confidence, good-will, and cheerful obedience of every man in the company.

A MESSMATE RESOLVES TO QUIT SWEARING.

While in camp, one of my mess, who had been my classmate at school, said to me, "Green, do you know that you have cured me of swearing?" I replied, "I am glad to know it; but how so?" He said, "You never swear, and no one doubts your word. I was always calling God to testify the truth of what I said, thus admitting that I was unworthy of belief without a witness to vouch for me. I have resolved that I will swear no more."

THE SICK SOLDIERS.

As we had no food but the corn without salt, the command suffered very much from diarrhœa, and as we had no assurance of receiving supplies, the colonel determined to fall back upon Vincennes. We brought corn from the field and prepared food for the march. I was second in command, and consequently the rear of the left flanking company. We started early in the morning, and soon thereafter two of the company gave out and lay by the wayside to die. I took their knapsacks, and aided them, and encouraged them to hope that, as the army would be detained at a creek, they could overtake their friends. We did overtake them, and were met there by General Hopkins with some three thousand volunteers, who had come to our aid. We were soon surrounded

by friends; the sick were cared for, and I was permitted to organize a few volunteers, who purchased horses and went with the mounted men as an independent command. The Indians burnt the prairies, and we were compelled to return to the fort, where I rejoined my company. The mounted men returned to Kentucky. General Hopkins marched with three regiments to Tippecanoe. Here a scout of sixty-two men, of whom I was one, under the command of Colonel Miller, were led into an ambuscade, and sixteen were killed—including Lieut. Murray, of my company—and seven wounded. I was then elected to command the company. I was soon after detailed, and returned to Vincennes in charge of a detachment of sick. Here I was myself taken sick, and, but for the care with which I was nursed by the mother and sister of John Scott, of Missouri, and one of my company whom, at his request, I detailed for that duty, the chance for my recovery would have been very much against me. When I returned with the mounted men, the sick came to Vincennes, where my nurse was made a hospital steward, and on that account was enabled to render me the more efficient aid. Here again did a kind Providence reward me most abundantly for a simple act of kindness. I refer to the fact as illustrating a great truth, confirmed by the frequent recurring incidents of a long life. He who, in kindness, faithfully discharges his duty to others, hath not only the hopes and the rewards of the life to come, but of this. How often has some slight favor done for another—and it has been in my power to do many—been more than repaid to me and mine. Gentle reader, remember that Christian charity, kind words, and kind actions, are among the best investments we can make, whether for this world or the next.

RETURN HOME.

When my health was sufficiently recruited, my nurse suggested that, as the time of service would expire in a few days, and I could get permission for him to go with me, we had better precede the returning troops. On the first day after leaving Vincennes, he exchanged his gun for a pony. He said, "Now you can ride." When we were about to separate in Louisville, he was much affected, and, holding my hand, said, "You do not know me." I replied, "I know you as my kind nurse, to whose care I probably owe my life." He said, "Do you remember one who had laid down on the roadside to die, and you took his knapsack and aided him to overtake the army?" I replied, "I did not recognize you, although I remember the incident." "I," said he, "knew you, and thought you would die, and determined to render you all the aid I could." And faithfully did he do so.

MY DOG LION.

During the last four years which I remained with my parents, I was in the habit of frequently hunting squirrels and turkeys. Lion, my faithful dog, was my constant companion. On my return, he had crossed the river and met me at least two miles from the house. He seemed as if he had come to meet me. No one was with him. He repeatedly sprang upon my horse, and continued the demonstration of his joy until I was surrounded by the family, and then, placing his head upon the door-sill, by the expression of his eye and the wagging of his tail, indicated that he participated to the full in the common joy. Dear old Lion; my mind's eye sees thee now, and I well remember thy kind, confiding, loving, happy look.

RESUME MY SCHOOL.

I found that the trustees had refused to employ another teacher, and, after a short visit to my parents, I again took charge of the school, prosecuting, at the same time, the study of medicine. On the 26th November, 1813, I

MARRIED

Lucretia Maria Edwards, of whose parents Mr. Wirt, in an obituary notice, said:

OBITUARY OF BENJAMIN EDWARDS.

"Died on the 13th of November, 1826, at his residence in Elkton, Todd county, Kentucky, Benjamin Edwards, in the seventy-fourth year of his age, and the fifty-sixth of his Christian life. His venerable consort, Mrs. Margaret Edwards, after a union of more than fifty years, had preceded him to the grave about three months before. They both resigned this world with that perfect composure and full assurance of future happiness which religion alone can inspire, and left behind them a numerous and respectable family of children and their descendants to imitate their virtues and to deplore their loss. Mr. Edwards was a native of Stafford county, Virginia; and before he became of age, he intermarried with Margaret, the daughter of Ninian Beall, of Montgomery county, Maryland, and resided, for nearly twenty-five years, on his farm of Mount Pleasant, about nine miles above the court-house of that county. His pursuits were those of agriculture and merchandise, which he conducted with industry and irreproachable integrity. He had not the advantage of a classical education, but nature had given him a mind of extraordinary force and comprehension, and a moral character of uncommon elevation and energy. He was one of nature's great men ; and it had stamped this character most strikingly on his countenance and person. He was large and well-formed ; his countenance strongly marked with intelligence and benevolence ; his steps and movements uncommonly dignified and commanding, and in his whole action there was an easy, unaffected, natural gracefulness which proclaimed the gentleman and the man of feeling in a manner not to be mistaken. Though his manners were highly prepossessing, conciliatory, and kind, yet such was the dignity that surrounded him, and the respect with which he impressed all who approached him, that no man ever dreamed of using irreverent liberty or indulging a thoughtless levity in his presence. His colloquial powers were unrivalled in any company in which the writer of this article ever saw him. He had a manly and melodious voice, a natural fluency and eloquence that never hesitated, the most striking originality and vigor of thought, the aptest and happiest illustration drawn from objects of nature around him, and an accuracy and integrity of judgment which have never been surpassed, on the subjects which called for his decision. He had supplied the deficiencies of youthful education by careful reading, and had acquired a correct style which was yet marked with the native strength and originality of his thoughts, and he conversed with great power even on subjects of literature, taste, and science ; and many have been the flippant scholars and collegians, who, after the interchange of a few remarks, have felt themselves rebuked by his superior mind, and learned to listen with instinctive reverence and delight. He had made himself an excellent historian, both in ancient and modern history ; and to his children and their young companions (of whom the writer was one), with whom he always took pleasure in conversing, he was one of the most instructive companions whom the kindness of Providence could have sent them. Though always pious, there was nothing austere, obtrusive, or revolting, in his religion ; and in his domestic circle he would often indulge himself with great playfulness, and with the most successful humor ; yet no occasion was ever lost of instilling into them pure and honorable, and lofty sentiments and principles, and kindling in them the flame of patriotic and virtuous emulation, holding up to them, with great eloquence, the examples of ancient patriots, orators, and statesmen, with whom he was as much enamored as if he were still in his youth. He rose to considerable distinction before he left Maryland, which was about thirty years ago. He represented the county of Montgomery for several years in the state legislature ; was a member of the state convention which ratified the Federal Constitution, and afterwards a member of Congress for the district in which he lived. Though nature had made him an orator of high order, he was restrained by his unconquerable diffidence from hazarding himself often in public debate. He spoke but rarely, and then only on local subjects, when forced forward by a high sense of duty ; yet on one of these occasions, in the assembly of Maryland, with so much force did he strike the house, that the late Samuel Chase, and several others of the most competent judges of eloquence in that body, crossed the floor of the house to congratulate him, and to assure him that it rested with himself to become one of the most distinguished speakers of the age. But he was restrained by diffidence from profiting by this suggestion, and a man who may be justly pronounced to have been one of nature's happiest efforts, has now passed away, to be forgotten by the world. Never will he be forgotten by the grateful heart from which this humble tribute flows ; nor that excellent woman, who was the fit and happy counterpart of so extraordinary a man. They were both an honor to their species, ornaments to the church to which they belonged, and are now among the spirits of the blessed who surround the throne on high.

"WILLIAM WIRT."

BECOME A COUNTRY MERCHANT.

Shortly after my marriage, Mr. John Helm, came to me and said, "You have been very kind to my son. He has profited much by your example and instruction. I wish to place him in a store with you. You have married my brother's wife's sister. He is an old experienced merchant. I have ten thousand dollars, which I wish to lend you as your part of the capital in a partnership with him. He will advance a like sum and go to the East and buy the goods, with the understanding that you will take charge of the store, and when my son is old enough, he is to become a partner. I became a country merchant. My partner went to Philadelphia to make our purchases, but being a prudent man, and knowing that the effect of peace would be to reduce prices, he loaned out to others a large part of our funds.

Our profits on that investment were small. A lady who came to Kentucky, from Philadelphia, in 1816, refused to purchase a piece of muslin, saying that the price was too high. I examined our private mark, and told her the cost was some twenty-five per cent. more than I had asked. She said, reprovingly, "It is very hard to go to heaven from behind a counter." The suspended banks had not then resumed specie payments, and yet the loss, caused by the reduction of prices was a severe lesson in political economy to be followed by another much more severe shortly thereafter.

SURVEY LANDS IN MISSOURI.

In the fall of 1816, I obtained a large contract for surveying public lands on the south side of the Missouri river, above Booneville. Many of the inhabitants were yet living in forts and block-houses. Before my return to St. Louis, Colonel Cooper, then an old man, who had been in command of the militia at Boon's lick, requested me to write to the governor a letter, to be signed by him, resigning his command. I did so. After I reached St. Louis, Governor Clark told me that he was apprehensive that as soon as the migration to that section had sufficiently increased the white population, the old settlers, whose property had been destroyed, and whose relatives had been killed by the Indians, would provoke an Indian war, and that it was his wish to appoint some one in the place of Colonel Cooper, who would have the nerve to preserve peace ; and that from what he had heard of my character, he wished to appoint me. I told him that I was then on my way to Philadelphia, and did not know when I could return. He said that he would reserve the commission for me.

PURCHASE GOODS FOR RENÉ PAUL AND GUARANTEE PAYMENT.

My brother-in-law, Governor Edwards, had advanced thirty thousand dollars to René Paul, as a partner in a store in St. Louis, and it was agreed between them that I should purchase in the name of Paul, in Baltimore and Philadelphia, sixty thousand dollars worth of goods, one half of which were to be given by Paul in payment of the advances made to him.

After I had made the purchase, and the goods were packed, the merchants in Philadelphia ascertained that his brother, then residing in Baltimore, had also made large purchases in Paul's name, and said that they were unwilling for the goods, I had bought of them, to be delivered to Paul without a guarantee of payment; and I agreed that if Paul did not, upon my reaching St. Louis, give a satisfactory guarantee, I would retain the goods and sell them and make payment. When I reached St. Louis the market was overstocked, and Paul, having an ample supply through his brother's purchases, insisted that I had given the guarantee without his authority, and demanded that I should keep the goods, giving him security for payment, which I did. The detention in St. Louis made it so late in the season that I was met, at St. Charles, by ice, and compelled to remain there during the winter. I therefore did not reach my destination (Chariton) until next spring. Desiring to make payment on the goods as soon as funds could be realized on them, I left a store in St. Charles, and divided the remainder between stores at Franklin and Chariton. Wishing to make prompt sales, I asked prices so much below those charged by others, that my stores were crowded with customers. The consequence was, ill feeling on the part of other merchants, who could not sell at the same prices.

APPOINTMENT AS MILITIA COLONEL.

Frederic Bates was the secretary of the territory, and as the tendency there, as elsewhere, was to organize political parties, the discontents were represented by him and a few of his personal friends. Upon reaching St. Louis, on my return, Governor Clark gave me my commission, saying that there had been numerous applicants, and that as he was going to Kentucky, and Mr. Bates would become the acting governor, and would probably appoint some one else during his absence, he wished to make the appointment then, although my family had not yet reached the county, which then embraced all that part of the territory west of Leuter lick. Early in the spring I ordered the battalion and regimental musters. As the county was so large, and the migration to that section during the preceding twelve months had been great, there were twenty or more avowed candidates for the legislature, and the disappointed candidates for promotion in the militia, united with the irritated rival merchants, and the whole of the candidates for the legislature, in denouncing my appointment by Governor Clark, as an act of favoritism, insulting to the resident population; alleging that the commission had been held back until the governor could import a colonel from Kentucky. As most of the candidates were newcomers, and Colonel Cooper was the patriarch of that "settlement," he was selected as the candidate for the senate without opposition, and he and all the candidates for the house of representatives united in making the repeal of the act authorizing the governor to appoint the militia officers, the issue before the people.

OPPOSITION—HOW MET.

Matters went so far that meetings were held, a committee organized, and a regular protest against my appointment published as the basis of the canvass. My name, actions, and character, were made the subjects of unkind comments, and so great a prejudice was excited against me that my agent in Franklin closed my store, and wrote to me at Chariton most despondingly. I resolved to meet the crisis. The battalion muster was to take place at Franklin, the seat of the excitement, on the day after the next. I put on my uniform, and rode to Franklin in full-dress on the next day. The next morning, a Mr. Tompkins, one of the leaders in the movement against me, made an effort to provoke a personal quarrel. I told him that my purpose was to reply to their protest before the parade that day, and that I would meet him there. Some one whispered to me that the lieutenant-colonel was parading the battalion at Fort Hempstead. I immediately mounted my horse and rode to the parade-ground. I directed the lieutenant-colonel to perform some evolution. He could not give the word. I said, "If you will permit me, I will

TAKE THE COMMAND."

I looked along the line and did not see a single person whom I knew, save a lieutenant, whom I had known in Kentucky. I called him, and said, "Can I rely on you?" He replied, "You can, sir." I said, "Can you detail a guard of twelve men on whom you can rely?" He said, "I can." I then said, "Detail them." He did so,

and marched them in front of the parade. I said, "Load your guns with ball." They did so. I then said to the lieutenant, "Detail a good fugleman." He did so. I then said, "Attention the parade! I am told that many persons in this battalion have united in a protest against my appointment as your colonel, and that some have pledged themselves not to obey my orders as such. The governor, in the exercise of his legitimate authority, has given me the appointment. I do not come before you now to apologize or explain, but to discharge my duty as your commanding officer, and to enforce obedience, and, therefore, if any one in the ranks dares to disobey my orders I will put him under guard." I then, after taking them through the manual exercise, gave the word for several evolutions, when, a shower coming on, I handed over the command to Colonel Hickman, who dismissed the parade.

APPEAL TO THE PEOPLE.

After the rain, I got upon a large stump and called the attention of the battalion. They all collected before me. I took the printed remonstrance. I read it, and replied to, and commented upon it. I proved that my appointment had been made by the governor in the proper exercise of his official duty. To the charge that I had been imported for the purpose, and appointed to the exclusion of the other aspirants, I showed that while most of the many aspirants were in their forts, or else in Kentucky, I had surveyed the country which was then occupied by Indian hunting parties, and that I had resolved to remove to the county, and was on my way for my family when the appointment was tendered to me; and explained the cause of my delay in coming. In reply to the personal remarks which had been made against me, I pointed to the motives and conduct of my accusers, one of whom, a Mr. Benson threatened that if I used his name, he would drag me from the stump and cowhide me. He had been an aspirant, and when I came to speak of him, he came rushing through the crowd with a whip in his hand. I saw him coming. I drew my sword, poised myself on the stump, and would, if he had come near enough, have endeavored to cut off his head. He saw my purpose, threw up both hands and retreated. When I came to speak of

COLONEL COOPER.

And his letter, he came before me much excited and said, " Do not use my name, for if you do, I will drag you from that stump." I stopped speaking ; I looked him sternly in the eye, until I saw that he faltered, and I then said, " Colonel Cooper, you are the patriarch of this settlement. You have grown gray in the confidence and respect of those who know you. You are here, surrounded by your friends and my enemies, who, to flatter your vanity, and use your name and influence to my injury, have tendered you a nomination for the senate, and you have no opposition. I am a young man, just entering into life—my character has been assailed by a wicked combination, and it is necessary that I should use your name in my defence. You know that what I am going to say is true, and no threats or violence shall prevent my using your name, and stating the facts as they are." A Mr. Hancock, Colonel Cooper's brother in law, here said, "Go on, sir, I'll stand by you." I continued addressing the colonel. " It has been charged that you did not request me to write your letter of resignation. You know that you did come to me and request me to write, and that I wrote precisely the words which you wished to be written." He quietly took a seat outside of the crowd, and did not speak in reply. Two of the committee, who had published the remonstrance, replied to me. I then said : " Gentlemen, you have now heard me in reply to my accusers, you have heard their response to my reply. Under the circumstances you cannot expect me to resign the command, and I would not resign if every one in the regiment were to request me to do so. But I claim that an expression of your opinion is no less due to yourselves than to me, and it is therefore my wish that you should say whether you are willing that I should continue in the command of the regiment. Therefore, all of you who wish me to command will please move to the right, while those who are opposed, if there are any, will please go to the left.

THE BATTALION APPROVE MY APPOINTMENT.

The men threw up their hats, and, moving in a body to the right, shouted, " Hurra, hurra for our colonel." Even Benson went with them. Seeing him, I said, " Mr. Benson, you don't belong to that crowd ; please go to the left." He said, " The men did not understand you." I replied, " Gentlemen, Mr. Benson thinks you do not know which is to the right and which is to the left ; to satisfy him that it is he who is in the wrong, I renew the proposition, and respectfully request all those who wish me to command this regiment to move to my left, leaving Mr. Benson where he is." With a shout for "Our colonel," the whole mass moved to the left. My triumph was complete—opposition to me ceased—my popularity and influence were established, as indicated by my election as a member of the convention which made the state constitution, and then as a member of the house of representatives and of the state senate.

I have given this account thus in detail, partly because it is an illustration of the force and power of truth ; and of the generous sympathy, with right and justice, on the part of the people, which has been a ruling principle of my life, and because it tends to explain the state of parties as then organized in the territory, and especially my relations to Colonel Benton, whose malevolent influence, as it will hereafter be seen, has contributed so much to the disasters which have fallen upon this country.

COL. BENTON AND JAMES CRUTCHER.

Colonel Miller, of Hardin county, commanded one of the regiments which were with me at Tippecanoe. Crutcher and Wintersmith were merchants in Elizabethtown. After the return of the regiment, Crutcher induced the paymaster to resign, and he (Crutcher) was appointed. His partner came to Washington, drew the funds, and paid them for goods. Instead of paying the money which he had received, he required the soldiers to take a large part or the whole in goods. He became a candidate for Congress. I wrote and published a handbill censuring his conduct ; and as he and Thomas Speed, of Bardstown, his competitor, had a series of appointments at which they made speeches, I attended several of the meetings, and enforced my charges against Crutcher from the stump. Mr. Speed was elected. The canvass was exciting and very bitter. When I reached St. Louis, in 1816, as I entered the hotel, I met Benton in the door, and the likeness to Crutcher was such that I started as if I had met an enemy. My instincts of distrust were then so much excited that although I afterward voted for him as a candidate for the United States Senate, I always felt a conviction that he was a dangerous, unreliable man, against whose machinations I should ever be on my guard.

HOW AND WHY HE WAS MADE A SENATOR.

Am I asked why, with such an instinct of his character, I voted for him ? The answer is, that he was the editor of an influential paper ; that, in the division of parties, he sustained Governor Clark ; that he opposed the Missouri restriction ; and that, upon the organization of the state government, a seat in the United States Senate was allotted to him as a reward for his partisan services, and that, reluctantly yielding to party influence, I gave a party vote.

My experience is that man is selfish, that he is more under the influence of animosity than of friendship, and that passion and prejudice control his judgment and his conduct ; that the tendency of party organization is to subordinate the masses to the governing influence of a few party leaders, who are thus enabled to substitute party platforms for the written constitution, and gratify their personal animosities in disregard of the public interest and of the principles of public liberty. I have, therefore, always endeavored to regulate my own conduct, and to judge of the motives and conduct of others, by the test of truth, right, and justice. It was resentment, jealousy, hatred against the Creator, which prompted Satan to tempt Eve. It was jealousy, hatred, resentment, disappointed ambition, which brought upon us a civil war. It is my purpose to trace the working of these evil passions, that, by unmasking their idols, I may wean the people from their idolatry.

THE INDIANS.

The Sac and Fox Indians, who then resided on both sides of the Mississippi, near Rock Island, were in the habit of hunting on the Missouri, and, returning home in the spring, they stole horses from the frontier settlements. I sent for their chiefs, and, after explaining to them that I would hold them responsible, and that, if they could not prevent the young men from stealing horses, I would require them to appoint chiefs who could prevent it, they pledged themselves that there should be no further cause of complaint. The Iowas, who resided on the Chariton, were restrained in the same way, with like favorable results. And I am satisfied, from my own experience, that all our Indian wars may be traced to some misconduct on the part of the whites, or to mismanagement of government agents. I have risen from my bed at night, and, with no other guide but the stars and my general knowledge of the country, without even a pathway, I have been, the next morning at sunrise, thirty miles from my home, and intercepted an armed mob moving upon an Indian village, under the command of one of the old settlers, whose brother had, during the war, been killed by the Indians. The pretence was that the Indians had stolen a horse—the purpose was to avenge the wrongs which the Indians had previously committed. I called a council, and, by pledging myself that I would go to the village and, by a talk with the chief and warriors, prevent any further depredations, they were induced to return. I went to the village, and explained to the Indians that I was their friend ; that it was better for them to live in peace. I obtained their confidence, and not only prevented depredations on the whites, but I induced the tribes who had been at war to live in peace with each other. There was no conflict with the Indians so long as I was in command on that frontier.

ELECTED A MEMBER OF THE MISSOURI CONVENTION.

Congress having passed the act authorizing Missouri to organize a state government, I was a candidate for the convention, and then wrote and published my first political essay, in which I vindicated the institution of African slavery, and denied the power of Congress to impose the restriction. Young as I then was, my address was extensively published, and favorably noticed, in some of the leading republican papers, and especially by the Richmond Enquirer. I was elected, and took an active part in the convention, and there took my first lesson as to the distribution of party patronage. The candidates for the several judicial appointments wished to so restrict the power of the legislature, by a constitutional provision, that the salaries of the judges should never be *less* than three thousand dollars. I voted in the negative, and the clause was defeated. General Rector, the surveyor-general, had been personally kind to me, and under a pressing appeal made through him I was induced, against my own judgment, to reconsider the measure, and it was adopted. As a member of the committee on printing, I had given offence to one of the candidates for patronage, and my vote was made the pretence for a bitter criticism, which, on the day of the election of the members of the legislature, was distributed at most, if not all, the election precincts. The effect was to defeat my election by a few votes. One of the members elected died before the meeting of the legislature. I replied to the publication, and was elected by a large majority

THE MISSOURI COMPROMISE — MR. CLAY — THE BANK.

When the bill authorizing Missouri to organize a state government was before Congress, Mr. Clay was the Speaker of the House of Representatives. Maine applied for admission at the same time. Ninian Edwards and Jesse B. Thomas were the Senators, and Daniel P. Cook was the member from Illinois. Crawford, Adams, and Calhoun, were then prominent aspirants for the presidency, and all were members of Mr. Monroe's cabinet. Thomas was the active partisan of Crawford, Cook of Adams, and Edwards of Calhoun. Edwards was a slave owner, and most decidedly opposed to the restriction; Cook was his son-in-law, and among the most zealous advocates of it. Fearing that Thomas might be induced to unite with Cook, Mr. Edwards prepared an amendment, uniting Maine and Missouri in the same bill, and also the amendment known as the compromise line of 36° 30′, and gave them to Thomas on whose motion they were adopted. The constitution of Missouri contained a clause, which made it the duty of the legislature to pass laws preventing the migration of free negroes and mulattoes to the state. The pressure for money created through the Bank of the United States, had rendered the bank unpopular in the Southern and Western states, and Ohio, under the lead of Charles Hammond, had imposed a heavy tax, and levied on the branch at Chillicothe. Mr. Clay was induced to resign his seat as speaker, and when Congress met he was in Ohio, in charge of a negotiation with Hammond. In the meantime, the National Gazette, of Philadelphia, the organ of the bank, took the ground that free negroes and mulattoes were citizens of the United States, and as such were entitled to all the rights and privileges of citizens, and made a question against the admission of our Senators and member to their seats. Mr. Sargeant, the lawyer of the bank, and the leading member from Pennsylvania, took the same ground in Congress, and John W. Taylor, of New York, was elected Speaker as an opponent to the admission of Missouri. The opposition was kept up in the House, until Mr. Clay had converted Charles Hammond, from a bitter opponent of the bank and of Henry Clay, into a warm partisan of both, and, having obtained a concession that the bank was authorized to establish branches in the states, without the consent of the states, came to Washington and resumed his seat as a member of the House. The bank wishing to prevent any further discussion of her power to establish branches, and Mr. Clay, seeking popularity as a candidate for the presidency, the partisans of the bank saw that, as Mr. Clay was thus identified with the bank, to give him the credit of compromising the Missouri question, would tend to prevent discussion or comment on the arrangement which he had made at Chillicothe, and therefore they united in support of a resolution, offered by Mr. Clay, providing that the Senators and Representative from Missouri, should be permitted to take their seats upon condition that the legislature of Missouri should, by a solemn act, declare that the constitution of the state should not be so construed as to authorize the legislature to pass any act which would deprive any citizen of the United States of the rights to which they may be entitled under the Constitution of the United States; or, in other words, Mr. Clay's compromise was that the legislature of Missouri should by a solemn act declare that, inasmuch as they are required to take an oath to support the Constitution of the United States, they would not pass an act which may be a violation of the oath they had taken.

COL. BENTON'S ATTEMPT TO GET A CAUCUS NOMINATION OF MR. CLAY.

In December, 1823, I was a member of the state senate. Colonel Benton had sold the St. Louis Inquirer to a Mr. Ford. The legislature were in session at St. Charles. Benton was a relative and active partisan of Mr. Clay. He came to St. Charles, and Ford came to me and said that Benton's purpose was to get a caucus nomination of Mr. Clay, and urged me to unite in the support of Mr. Clay, saying that my position was such in the state that if I would but identify myself with Mr. Clay's friends, there was nothing in their power to grant that I might not command. The caucus met. I opposed the nomination, and notified Colonel Benton that if he was in St. Charles when the senate met the next day, I would introduce a resolution for a committee to inquire why, instead of being in Washington attending to his duties as a Senator, he was in St. Charles, seeking to obtain the electoral vote of Missouri as so much capital to be disposed of by him in the political market. I defeated the nomination, and Colonel Benton left St. Charles before the senate met the next day.

BECOME AN EDITOR.

In the latter part of December, I purchased the St. Louis Inquirer, and supported the election of General Jackson. Mr. Clay and his friends became satisfied that he could not be elected by the electors, and made extraordinary efforts to get sufficient votes to place him as one of the three, from whom the House of Representatives would elect one. Benton came back to Missouri and canvassed the state for Mr. Clay. Wherever he went he found my paper urging the election of General Jackson. We carried the southern district against Mr. Clay, but his half-brother (Watkins) was a returning-officer, and suppressed the return. It was urged by Mr. Clay and his prominent friends that, if one of the three having the greatest number of votes, he would be elected by the House of Representatives, and inasmuch as that might depend upon a single vote, Benton and the other partisans of Mr. Clay induced the legislature to declare the election of electors illegal, and gave the three votes of Missouri for Mr. Clay. At the same time a leading friend of Mr. Clay was at Albany negotiating for part of the vote of New York !

ELECTION OF JOHN QUINCY ADAMS.

There was no choice by the electors. General Jackson, Mr. Adams, and Mr. Crawford, were the three who having received the greater number of votes, were returned to the House, and Mr. Adams was elected; Mr. Clay, Mr. Cook, of Illinois, and Mr. Scott, of Missouri, voting for him.

It so happened that as the attorney for parties having large claims against the government for Indian depredations, I reached Washington a few days after the election, and it was deemed of so much importance to secure the influence of my press, that Mr. Cook and Mr. Scott were deputed to make the arrangement.

My wife's cousin and John Quincy Adams had married sisters. My personal influence, sustained by my press, was such, that Benton, fearing that I would become his competitor for the Senate, had made Mr. Clay's vote for Mr. Adams a pretence for the conciliation of General Jackson, who had driven him from Tennessee as a personal enemy; and it was urged that by uniting with the friends of Clay and Adams, and thus securing their support, aided as I would be by the control of the federal patronage which was tendered to me, contributing so much as I could do to the success and permanence in power of the new party, there was nothing in the power of the government to give which I might not confidently expect to receive.

"INTRIGUE, BARGAIN, AND MANAGEMENT."

Mr. Clay's partisans during the canvas had urged his pretensions upon the ground that he was the representative and friend of the West and of Western interests, and that Mr. Adams was unfriendly to the interests and prosperity of the West; and yet he endeavored to justify his vote upon the ground that Mr. Adams was more favorable to the West than General Jackson. I saw that the tendency of the coalition between Clay and Adams was to strengthen the sectional anti-slavery party, by introducing the tariff and internal improvements as parts of their system of measures. High duties to create a large surplus revenue, to be expended by a log-rolling, sectional, corrupt party majority in Congress; high duties for the benefit of Eastern manufacturers, and a large surplus revenue to build turnpike roads in the Northwest and Western States. I saw that the ten millions of dollars appropriated as a sinking fund would soon pay off the national debt, and that, therefore, instead of increasing the duties, they should be reduced.

CHAPTER IV.

THE COALITION.

DURING the preceding summer, Mr. Clay's Central Committee had issued a circular, in which they said:

"And let them [the people] remember that, after the choice of electors once takes place, their voice will no more be heard in the contest. ALL WILL BE CARRIED BY INFLUENCE AND INTRIGUE, BARGAIN AND MANAGEMENT. He who has the most extensive means of influence, and will promise the most favors, will have the best prospect of success; and the nation will receive the President, not from the pure hands of the people, but from a CLUB OF POLITICAL MANAGERS AND INTRIGUERS."

And believing that the prediction of Mr. Clay's committee had been verified by the election of Mr. Adams, and that the inevitable tendency of the "INTRIGUE, BARGAIN, AND MANAGEMENT," between Messrs. Adams and Clay, would be to

ORGANIZE A CORRUPT NORTHERN PARTY,

Predicated upon a deliberate purpose of plundering and oppressing the South, and that the inevitable consequence would be a counter-organization of the South in defence of the rights and interests of the South, and that the sectional conflict would necessarily endanger the peace and perpetuity of the Union; and, therefore, tempting as the inducements were, I refused to unite in support of the coalition.

GENERAL JACKSON.

While then in Washington, I became personally acquainted with General Jackson, and on my return to St. Louis, travelled in company with him as far as Louisville. He then urged me to remove to Washington and take charge of a paper opposed to the re-election of Mr. Adams. I had established the first line of stages west of the Mississippi. I had a profitable contract for carrying the mail. I had placed the line under the charge of trustworthy partners who paid me a large fixed income. I had a valuable business as an attorney. I was the editor and proprietor of a leading paper, giving me considerable profit, and I was investing my income in and adjoining the city of St. Louis. I had a young and interesting family, and my social and political position was second to that of no man in the state. I had refused to exchange my position for a seat in the Senate of the United States, and I did not consent to become the editor of a party paper in Washington. But the next year I came to Washington on professional business.

PURCHASE OF THE UNITED STATES TELEGRAPH.

It so happened that I boarded in the same house with Mr. Agg, the editor of the Washington Journal, then the acknowledged organ of Mr. Adams. Having leisure I wrote several articles which were adopted by Mr. Meehan, the editor and proprietor of the Telegraph, and published as editorials.

3

One morning, while at breakfast, I read in the Journal a reply, assuming that I was the writer, and assailing me personally with scurrilous abuse. Agg sat opposite to me at the table, and his look and manner were offensive. I arose from the table and went directly to Mr. Meehan's office and asked him for what price he would sell me his paper. He named the price, and I drew a check for the money. I went back to St. Louis. I sold my property in and near the city, at a great sacrifice. I relinquished my profession. I sold my paper. I afterwards sold my line of stages and mail contract, and concentrated my resources and my energies to defeat the re-election of Mr. Adams, by demonstrating that his election was, as foretold by Mr. Clay's Kentucky committee, the result of BARGAIN, INTRIGUE, AND MANAGEMENT, between Mr. Clay and Mr. Adams, and by defeating his re-election, prevent that sectional northern party organization, which, by restoring the FEDERAL party to power, would endanger the peace and perpetuity of the Union.

I was not an adventurer, purchased by promises of plunder or patronage—I was a devotee, sacrificing my own private interests in the effort to maintain the rights of the people, and to assert and enforce the responsibility of their public servants.

Among other property sold at a nominal price, for funds to purchase and support a free press in Washington, were one square, then in the heart of the city, and two hundred and fifty arpens of land adjoining Choteau's pond on the south, which I am told is now in city lots of great value. Had I remained in St. Louis investing, as was my purpose, my surplus earnings in lands in and adjoining the city, I would have been, long ere this, one of the most wealthy men in this country. I acted under a sense of public duty, and now refer to the sacrifice as one of the incidents which strengthen my claim upon the public confidence.

REMOVE TO WASHINGTON.

Having hastily, and consequently at a great sacrifice, arranged my business in Missouri, I came with my wife, four children, and a few family servants, to Kentucky. When we reached Hopkinsville we heard of the death of my mother-in-law, and upon reaching Elkton we found my father-in-law so ill that Mrs. Green preferred to remain with him, and that I should precede her to Washington to make arrangements for housekeeping. Her father survived but a few weeks. She nursed him until his death, and then, accompanied by one of her nephews, came in a carriage to Washington.

I had two brothers-in-law living in Russellville, and, wishing to see General Jackson before I came to Washington, I came that far on my way to Nashville. The next morning the stage took up another passenger, who was also going to Nashville. He was scarcely seated before he said, "Duff Green has come to town." "Ah," said I, "what of him?" "Why," said he, "he is going to Washington to abuse Mr. Clay." Finding that he was disposed to be communicative, I encouraged him to talk, and was much more than usually polite to him. When we reached Nashville, one of the Nashville committee, who had been notified of my coming, asked the driver if General Green was in the stage. Upon my replying in the affirmative, I was received and welcomed by the committee and others who had met at the hotel for the purpose. My fellow-traveller, as soon as he could well do so, came to me and said, " I owe you an apology." " For what ?" said I. He replied, " I did not know who you were, or I never would have talked to you as I did to-day." I said, " I am aware of that, and therefore your comments gave me no offence." " You are not," said he, " the man I thought you were, and you must send me your paper, and I will do all I can to aid you." He became a valuable correspondent.

GENERAL JACKSON—JOHN POPE—WM. T. BARRY—AMOS KENDALL.

I spent a day with General Jackson at the Hermitage, and, when leaving him for Nashville, he rode with me to his gate ; he held my hand, and having again said that he was much gratified at my having purchased the Telegraph, and renewed his promise of friendship and personal regard, he concluded, by way of encouragement, saying, " Truth is mighty and will prevail."

From the Hermitage I went to visit my own father, intending to call on Mr. Monroe, who had married one of the daughters of General Adair. The chief purpose of my visit to General Jackson was to ascertain whether I could aid in restoring friendly relations between him and General Adair. I saw Mr. Monroe, and enlisted his co-operation ; I then went to Louisville. Worden Pope told me that Mr. Kendall, the editor of the Argus, was much inclined to support the election of General Jackson, and advised me

to go to Frankfort to see him. When I reached Frankfort, Mr. Kendall was sick. I saw Judge Bibb, who advised me to go to Lexington and see Judge Barry, who had been a candidate on Mr. Clay's electoral ticket. I found him hesitating, and apprehensive that John Pope, who was the brother-in-law of Mr. Adams, and who, during the canvass, had sustained General Jackson as against Mr. Clay, and had taken a decided part against the new court, of which Mr. Barry was a judge, would unite with the partisans of Mr. Clay, and that their influence in the state would preponderate. As Mr. Pope happened to be in Lexington, I invited him and Judge Barry to dine with me, and, a mutual understanding of concert and co-operation having been agreed upon, Judge Barry went with me to see Colonel Richard M. Johnson, who told us that he had had a confidential conversation with Mr. Kendall, who had borrowed fifteen hundred dollars from Mr. Clay as the executor of Morrison, and that the Argus would oppose the re-election of Mr. Adams, as soon as Mr. Kendall could arrange for funds to pay Mr. Clay. I thereupon authorized Colonel Johnson to say to him, that I would advance the fifteen hundred dollars, which I did. Mr. Kendall had been an active and confidential friend of Mr. Clay, and, as such, had taken an active part against the election of Mr. Adams. He and the Argus became warmly enlisted in support of the election of General Jackson, and were influential auxiliaries in that eventful contest.

CHAPTER V.

THE ANTI-SLAVERY CONSPIRACY.

IN 1816, Daniel Pope Cook, who had studied law with Judge Pope, of Illinois, upon the recommendation of Ninian Edwards, my brother-in-law, then a Senator in Congress, was appointed by Mr. Monroe bearer of despatches to notify Mr Adams, then our minister in London, of his appointment as Secretary of State. He brought me a letter of introduction, and told me that, being in delicate health, his purpose was to try the effect of a sea voyage, intending, upon his return, to remove to the South I saw him in Washington city in October, 1817, when he told me that Mr. Adams had satisfied him that the migration to the north of the Ohio would be so great that the anti-slavery party would soon obtain the political control of this country; and that, under the advice of Mr. Adams, he had abandoned the idea of going South to practise law, and would go back to Illinois, with a a view of becoming a candidate for Congress for the purpose of agitating the slavery question. He said that he had already commenced the agitation, and gave me a pamphlet containing two letters, which he had addressed to Mr. Monroe, and published in Meade's Register.

The following is a quotation from

MR. COOK'S SECOND LETTER.

"A great similarity in manners, habits, and mode of thinking, must be preserved, as the strongest cement of our Union and safeguard of our tranquillity. But slavery destroys this similarity in each of those particulars. Idleness, with its train of vices, will ultimately become habitual to the slaveholder, while the necessity of industry will secure the virtue of the other. The love of equality will be the predominant principle of the one, while a familiarity with domestic power—I may say, tyranny—will beget a love of distinction, a love of aristocracy, in the other. This circumstance, added to the difference of climate, will tend much, as has already been witnessed, to estrange the Southern from the Northern people. In the South, the people are more under the influence of feeling than in the North; they are, consequently, more hasty in their deliberations. In the North they are a more cool and calculating people, and are more apt to view things through the medium of interest. Hence there is, from the difference in climate, a dissimilarity in the construction of their minds; and the adventitious circumstance of slavery will increase this difference. The motto of a republic should be 'PEACE.' But a people who are under no necessity of pursuing habits of industry, will naturally acquire a taste for war. Hence the people of the South, where slavery prevails, will be more ready to embark in a war than those of the North, and 'Hartford Conventions'—more baleful in their results than that which has already been experienced—will be as frequently repeated as we are engaged in war.

"Slavery is confined to particular states, and they must, therefore, remain in a narrower compass than the white population. By this means, their number will increase in those sections of the country, so as ultimately to exceed that of the whites. In this state of things, when they shall have been enlightened by one solitary ray of knowledge—when their own numbers shall be known to them and which we cannot conceal from them—like the stream that has been feebly dammed, they will rise in the majesty of their strength, and burst those chains with which they are bound; and like the deluge which leaves desolation behind it, their progress will be known by their ravages. This cannot be looked upon as mere speculation. 'Tis the ordinary course of nature. It was by that grand operation of nature, that we became free and independent ourselves. And if we place the same fetters on the works of nature, may we not fairly expect she will make the same exertion to throw them off? We were favored by Heaven in our Revolutionary struggle—and believing ourselves injured, we even appealed to the Divinity to aid and assist us—we were fighting for our natural rights; those rights which we believed the God of Nature intended 'all' should 'equally' enjoy. To that appeal the Heavens bowed propitiously and the tyrant's scourge was no longer allowed to be visited upon us. With this recent example of the justice of Heaven before us, can we, with any well-founded hope of escaping a similar visitation of Divine justice, expect to go on, inflicting more unwarrantable oppressions upon others than were inflicted upon us? No! the ways of Heaven are alike, are unalterable, and for us they will not swerve from their altered course. In the Revolution we were unable to achieve our freedom without foreign assistance—and so sweet was the name of liberty—so musical did it sound in the ears of foreigners, that they rallied around our standard, and offered up their lives as a voluntary sacrifice at the altar of that goddess under whose banners they were fighting. And when the manacles of slavery shall become intolerable to these people, and they shall be found bleeding in the cause of freedom—will not the same flame, which then warmed the trans-Atlantic bosom, again shed its genial warmth upon them, and invite them to rally around their sable standard? So long as the same cause will produce the same effect, so long may this be expected.

"Let us now dwell for a moment on the effect which Algerine captivity has had on the civilized world—for holding in captivity and slavery, the subjects of Christian powers. Has not the united resentment of all Christian nations been levelled against them? Have they not had to withstand the thunder of civilized warfare, for those gross and flagrant impositions? And yet we, we who have acted a distinguished part in punishing this outrage, are daily inflicting it upon almost millions. Americans, look at this picture! does it not arouse your sensibility and wound your high-blown pride? Does it not disturb you in your daily occupations, and haunt your midnight dreams? Or, are you callous to the feelings of humanity and deaf to the voice of justice?

"When that secret monitor, which dwells in every bosom, shall call us to an account for our conduct, for this outrage upon the rights of humanity, unless the feelings are steeled against remorse and compunction, their poignant shafts will be levelled against us, and all the joys of life must be embittered.

"But this is not all, let those states which have imbrued their hands in the blood of their fellow-beings, for attempting to throw off the galling yoke of slavery, put on the weeds of mourning. Let them make atonement by the emancipation of those whose meekness and forbearance have shielded them against a future accountability for similar iniquity. Apply not that odious epithet of 'insurgent,' of 'rebel,' of 'traitor,' to the man who strives to gain his liberty; remember that it was but yesterday that you were in the same predicament—and yet your venerable Congress declared you 'free,' and no longer subject to the disgraceful epithet of 'traitor to your country.' Who is a traitor? Not the man who is bound in the iron chains of slavery, and strives to break his fetters! Not the man who is actuated by the noblest feeling of our nature to secure his happiness and his freedom. But it is he who, from ambitious or malignant motives, aims at the destruction of social happiness, by raising the hostile hand against that government which protects him, and to which he owes his allegiance.

"But can a government be said to protect a people which it enslaves? and can they be said to owe allegiance to that government which enslaves them? If so, away with such protection, and with such allegiance. They are terms indefinite and inapplicable to the social state.

"It is to be hoped that, through your influence, the general government will take some measures preparatory to the completion of this work, and that individuals and the state governments will ultimately complete it.

                 "D. P. C.

"WASHINGTON, *September* 14, 1817."

It will be seen that letters were

THE TEXT FOR THE SLAVERY AGITATION; That in them Mr. Cook drew a disparaging picture of Southern society, of the habits, education, and general character of the Southern people; that he boldly declared the right of the slaves to rebel and make war on their masters! He said: "Let those states which have imbrued their hands in the blood of their fellow-beings, for attempting to throw off the galling yoke of slavery, put on the weeds of mourning. Let them make atonement by the emancipation of those whose meekness and forbearance have shielded them against a future accountability for similar iniquity." Here we see Mr. Cook, under the prompting of John Quincy Adams, as far back as 1817, openly asserting that the "meekness and forbearance" of our slaves would shield them from "a future accountability" for imbruing their hands in the blood of their masters! Startle not, reader! These letters, avowedly published under the promptings of John Quincy Adams, then Secretary of State

of the United States, as the text for the organization of a party, for the purpose of giving the political control of our government to the federal party, then openly asserted the broad doctrines afterward avowed by the British government in the case of the murder of the crew of the Creole by insurgent slaves, viz.: that a slave may rightfully do whatever may be necessary to obtain his freedom, and that hence if the murder of the crew was necessary to enable the slaves to get command of the ship, then the slaves, so committing murder, ought not to be punished. Hear John Quincy Adams, speaking through Mr. Cook, on the 14th of September, 1817: "Apply not the odious epithet of insurgent, of rebel, of traitor, to the man who strives to gain his liberty." He exclaims: "Who is a traitor?" and replies, "Not the man who is bound in the iron chains of slavery and strives to break his fetters! Not the man who is actuated by the noblest feelings of our nature, to secure his happiness and his freedom. Can a government be said to protect a people which it enslaves? and can they be said to owe allegiance to that government which enslaves them? If so, away with such protection and with such allegiance." Mr. Cook did go to Illinois, was elected to Congress, and took a leading part in support of the Missouri restriction. He, in the meantime, had married a daughter of Governor Edwards, who was then a Senator in Congress, and took an active and decided part against the restriction.

RUFUS KING'S AVOWAL.

After his return home, I asked Mr. Edwards how it was that he, a slaveholder, and so much opposed to the restriction, a Senator from the state, so much older than and the father-in-law of Mr. Cook, could not control him? His reply was, that Mr. Cook was a young man of fine talents and great ambition; that he had become much attached to Mr. Adams, and had identified his hopes of future political promotion with the election of Mr. Adams to the Presidency, and that he, although his father-in-law, had no right to dictate to or control him. He further said, that he had messed with Rufus King, then a Senator from New York; that they had conversed freely on the subject, and that Mr. King had told him that the federal party looked to the agitation of the slavery question as the certain means of regaining political power; and that so confident were they of success that a son of Rufus King had gone to Ohio and a son of Alexander Hamilton had gone to Illinois to be in position to avail themselves of it. I am thus enabled to trace back as far as 1817, the deliberate purpose of organizing the anti-slavery party as a sectional political influence, whereby the federal party, under the leadership of John Quincy Adams, had then resolved to array the North against the South, and thus create a sectional Northern majority, which, by that sectional organization, could and would govern the North and South! I saw that it was no regard for the rights of the slave—no sympathy for the condition of the negro—which stimulated their zeal, but a thirst for power, regardless of the letter or the spirit of the Constitution, which I feared would embitter the South against the North and endanger, if it did not dissolve, the Union. To prevent this, I have made many sacrifices, personal, social, political, and pecuniary.

CHAPTER VI.

THE MONARCHISTS.

IT will be seen that the votes of Mr. Clay, of Kentucky, Cook of Illinois, and Scott of Missouri, each of whom represented states opposed to the election of Mr. Adams, put in issue:

1. The motives which led them to disregard the will of their constituents; and

2. The character and purposes of the party to be organized under the auspices of the coalition between Messrs. Clay and Adams.

Believing, as I do, that the late civil war was the bitter fruit of the sectional organization of the federal party of the North, and that their pretence of a desire to benefit the African is but a mask to cover their purpose of enslaving the white man, by the centralization of a corrupt, irresponsible power in the federal government, in open violation of the fundamental principles of the Constitution, I turn to the history of the past, and trace the connection between the old federal party, whom it was the avowed purpose, as declared by Rufus King, to reinstate in power, and the radical party who now control the legislation of Congress.

WHO WERE THE MONARCHISTS?

Who were the leaders of the old federal party, and what were their avowed and well-ascertained principles? and what was the form of government which they wished to establish?

We are at no loss for the names of the leaders, nor for the form of government which they proposed to organize. Alexander Hamilton and John Adams were the representative men of that party.

ALEXANDER HAMILTON'S PLAN.

The plan for a government proposed by Alexander Hamilton was as follows:

1. The supreme legislative power of the United States of America to be vested in two different bodies of men; the one to be called the assembly, the other the senate, who, together, shall form the legislature of the United States, with power to pass all laws whatsoever, subject to the negative hereafter mentioned.

2. The assembly to consist of persons elected by the people, to serve for three years.

3. The senate to consist of persons elected to serve during good behavior. Their election to be made by electors chosen for that purpose by the people—in order to this the state to be divided into election districts. On the death, removal, or resignation of any senator his place to be filled out of the district from which he came.

4. The supreme executive authority of the United States to be vested in a governor, to be elected during good

behavior, the election to be made by electors chosen by the people, in the election districts aforesaid; the authorities and functions to be as follows: To have a negative upon all laws about to be passed and the execution of all laws passed; to have the direction of war when authorized or begun; to have, with the advice and consent of the senate, the power of making all treaties; to have the sole appointment of the heads or chief officers of finance and foreign affairs; to have the nomination of all other officers, ambassadors to foreign nations included, subject to the approbation or rejection of the senate; to have power of pardoning all offences except treason, which he shall not pardon without the approbation of the senate.

5. On the death, resignation, or removal of the governor, his authorities to be exercised by the president of the senate till a successor be appointed.

6. The senate to have the sole power of declaring war, the power of advising and approving all treaties, the power of approving and rejecting all appointments of officers, except the heads or chiefs of departments, finance, war, and foreign affairs.

7. The supreme judicial authority of the United States to be vested in judges, to hold their offices during good behavior, with adequate and permanent salaries; the court to have original jurisdiction in all cases of capture, and an appellate jurisdiction in all causes in which the revenues of the general government or the citizens of foreign nations are concerned.

8. The legislature of the United States to have power to institute courts in each state, for the determination of all matters of general concern.

9. Governors, senators, and all officers of the United States, to be liable to impeachment for corrupt conduct, and, upon conviction, to be removed from office, and disqualified for holding any office of public trust and profit; and all impeachments to be tried by a court, to consist of the chief or judge of the superior court of law of each state, provided such judge hold his place during good behavior, and have a permanent salary.

10. All laws of the particular states, contrary to the Constitution or laws of the United States, to be utterly void; and the better to prevent such laws being passed, the governor or president of each state shall be appointed by the general government, and shall have a negative upon the laws about to be passed in the state of which he is governor or president.

11. No state to have any force, land or naval, and the militia to be under the sole and exclusive direction of the United States, the officers of which to be appointed and commissioned by them."

Such was the plan of Alexander Hamilton.

CHAPTER VII.

JOHN ADAMS A MONARCHIST, AND WHY.

THE plan of John Adams was given in a work published immediately before the adoption of the Federal Constitution, from which the following are extracts :

GENTLEMEN AND COMMON PEOPLE.

"The people in all nations are naturally divided into two sorts, the gentlemen and the simple men, a word which is here chosen to signify the common people. By the common people we mean laborers, mechanics, husbandmen, and merchants in general, who pursue their occupations and industry without any knowledge in liberal arts and sciences, or in anything but their own trades and pursuits." See vol. 3, p. 458.

WHY CHILDREN OF ILLUSTRIOUS FAMILIES ARE PREFERRED.

"It must be acknowledged in every state —Massachusetts for example—there are inequalities which God and nature have planted there, and which no human legislature can ever eradicate." "Inequality of birth. Let no man be surprised that this species of inequality is introduced here. Let the page of history be quoted where any nation, ancient or modern, civilized or savage, is mentioned among whom no difference was made between the citizens on account of their extractions. The children of illustrious families have generally greater advantages of education, and earlier opportunities to be acquainted with public characters and informed of public affairs than those of meaner ones, or even those in middle life ; and, what is more than all, an habitual national veneration for their names and the character of their ancestors, described in history, or coming down by tradition, removes them further from vulgar jealousy and popular envy, and secures them, in some degree, the favor, the affection, and respect of the public." See vol. 1, pages 109–19.

"The son of a wise and virtuous father finds the world about him, sometimes, as much as he is disposed himself, to honor the memory of his father; to congratulate him as the successor of his estate ; and to compliment him with election to the places he held." Same vol., p. 116.

POOR PEOPLE SHOULD WORK, AND SHOULD HAVE A KING.

"The distinctions of poor and rich are as necessary in states of considerable extent (such as the United States) as labor and good government ; the poor are destined to labor, and the rich, by the advantages of education, independence, and leisure, are qualified for superior stations." Same vol., p. 360.

"It has been the common people, then, and not the gentlemen who have established simple monarchies, all over the world." See vol. 3, p. 451.

"It is the true policy of the common people to place the whole executive power in the hands of one man." Vol. 3, p. 460.

"By kings and kingly power is meant the executive power in a single person." See vol 3, p. 461.

"The people themselves, if uncontrolled, will never long tolerate a freedom of inquiry, debate, or writing ; their idols must not be reflected on, nor their schemes and actions scanned, upon pain of popular vengeance, which is not less terrible than despots or sovereign senators." Vol. 3, p. 326.

COMMON PEOPLE CORRUPT, AND THEREFORE A NOBILITY MUST AND WILL EXIST.

"The whole history of Rome shows that corruption began with the people sooner than the senate." Vol. 3, p. 327.

"Sobriety, abstinence, and severity, were never remarkable characteristics of democracy, or the democratic branch or mixture in any constitution. They have oftener been the characteristics of aristocracy and oligarchy." "Athens, in particular, was never conspicuous for these qualities; but, on the contrary, from the first to the last of her democratic constitution, levity, gayety, inconstancy, dissipation, intemperance, debauchery, and a dissolution of manners, were the prevailing characteristics of the whole nation." Same vol., p. 344.

"Powerful and crafty underminers have nowhere such rare sport as in a simple democracy, or single popular assembly. Nowhere, not in the completest despotisms, does human nature show itself so completely depraved; so nearly approaching an equal mixture of brutality and devilishism, as in the last stages of such a democracy, and in the beginning of despotism, which always succeeds it." Same, vol. 2, p. 329.

"Every passion and prejudice of every voter will be applied to, every flattery and menace, every trick and bribe that can be bestowed and will be accepted, will be used, and what is horrible to think of, that candidate or that agent who has fewest scruples, who will propagate lies and slander with most confidence and secrecy, who will wheedle, flatter, and cajole; who will debauch the people by treats, feasts, and diversions, with the least hesitation, and bribe with the most impudent front which can consist with hypocritical concealment, will draw in tools and worm out enemies the fastest—unsullied honors, sterling integrity, real virtue, will stand a very unequal chance. When vice, folly, impudence, and knavery, have carried an election one year, they will acquire in the course of it fresh influence and power to succeed the next!" Vol. 3, p. 275.

"A nobility must and will exist." "Descent from certain parents and inheritance of certain houses, lands and other visible objects [titles] will eternally have such an influence over the affections and imaginations of the people, as no arts and institutions will control; time will come, if it is not now, that these circumstances will have more influence over great numbers of minds than any considerations of virtue and talents, and whatever influences numbers, is of great moment in popular governments and in all elections." Vol. 3, p. 377.

HEREDITARY FIRST MAGISTRATES AND SENATORS.

"There is not in the whole Roman history so happy a period as this under their kings; the nation was formed, their morality, their religion, their maxims, their government, were all established under their kings—the nation was defended against numerous warlike nations of enemies; in short, Rome was never so well governed or so happy." Vol. 3, p. 305.

"I only contend that the English constitution is, in theory, the most stupendous fabric of human invention." Vol. 1, p. 70.

"In future ages, if the present states become a great nation, their own feelings and good sense will dictate to them what to do; they may make transitions to a nearer resemblance of the British constitution." Same, p. 71.

"It [the aristocracy] is a body of men which contains the greatest collection of virtue and character in a free government; is the brightest ornament and glory of the nation; and may always be made the greatest blessing of society, if it be judiciously managed in the constitution." Same vol., p. 116.

"This hazardous experiment [election of their first magistrate] the Americans have tried, and if elections are soberly made, it may answer very well; but if parties, factions, drunkenness, bribes, armies, and delirium come in, as they always have done, sooner or later, to embroil and decide everything, the people must again have recourse to conventions, and find a remedy for this 'hazardous experiment.' Neither philosophy nor policy has yet discovered any other cure than by prolonging the duration of the first magistrate and senators. The evil may be lessened and postponed by elections for longer periods of years till they become for life; and if this is not found an adequate remedy, there will remain no other but to make them hereditary. The delicacy or the dread of unpopularity that should induce any man to conceal this important truth from the full view of the people, would be a weakness if not a vice." Vol. 3, p. 296.

"Mankind have universally discovered that chance was preferable to a corrupt choice, and have trusted Providence rather than themselves. First magistrates and senators had better be made hereditary at once, than that the people should be universally debauched and bribed." Vol. 3, p. 283.

CHAPTER VIII.

JOHN Q. ADAMS' PLAN OF MAKING THE GOVERNMENT A MONARCHY.

THESE extracts show that Hamilton and Adams, the acknowledged leaders of the federal party, were monarchists—that both were opposed to an elective government ; that Mr. Adams believed that the "people of all nations are naturally divided into two sorts, the gentlemen and the simple men," a term used by him to designate "the common people, the laborers, mechanics, husbandmen, and merchants ;" that "there are inequalities that God and nature planted in every state, which no legislature can ever eradicate ;" that "the children of illustrious families" are further removed from "popular envy" and "vulgar jealousy ;" that "the poor are destined to labor, and the rich, by advantages of education, independence, and leisure, are qualified for superior stations ;" that "it is the true policy of the common people to place the whole executive power in the hands of one man," and that "by kings and kingly power is meant the executive power in a single person," and that the American people, "would not be happy without an hereditary chief magistrate and senate, or at least for life." And I call the special attention of the reader to the fact, that in his letter of the 21st of February, 1804, to Wm. Cunningham, the elder Adams said : "I have always been of opinion, that in popular governments the people will always choose their officers from the most ancient and respectable families." "The more democratical the government, the more universal has been the practice. If a family which has been high in office, and splendid in wealth, falls into decay from profligacy, folly, vice, or misfortune, they generally turn democrats, and court the lowest of the people with an ardor, an art, a skill, and consequently with a success, which no vulgar democrat can attain. If such families are numerous, they commonly divide. Some adhere to one party, some to another ; so that whichever prevails, the country still finds itself governed by them ;" and connect this with the fact, that in the spring of 1807, Mr. John Q. Adams, in a conversation with political friends, deplored "the fearful progress of the democratic party and of its principles, and declared that he had long meditated the subject, and had become convinced that the only method by which the democratic party could be destroyed was by joining with it, and urging it on with the utmost energy to the completion of its views, whereby the result would prove so ridiculous and so ruinous to the country, that the people would be led to despise the principles, and to condemn the effects of democratic policy ; and then," said he, "*we can have a form of government better suited to the genius and disposition of our country than our present Constitution.*"

PRETENDS TO TURN DEMOCRAT AND CHARGES THE FEDERALISTS WITH TREASON.

I beg the reader to connect with this the further fact, that during the next session of Congress Mr. Adams, being a Senator, was riding in the same carriage with Gov. Giles of Virginia, and became very serious, seeming weighed down with care, at length told Gov. Giles he had a matter of great importance, which he thought it his duty to relate to Mr. Jefferson, then President, but did not know how to approach him, and desired Mr. Giles to make the communication; the latter encouraged him to do it himself; and also that, during the canvass in 1828, Mr. Jefferson wrote a letter, which he authorized to be published, in which he gave the purport of the communication which Mr. Adams did make to him. In the National Intelligencer of the 21st of October, 1828, is an article published by authority of Mr. Adams, as explanatory of the charges then made against the federalists of New England, which not only admits his interview with Mr. Giles and Mr. Jefferson, but admits that, in 1808, he wrote to Mr. Giles and other members of Congress, and that, commenting upon the measures and purposes of the leaders of the federal party of Massachusetts of that day, he said (I use his own words as given in the Intelligencer): "He [Mr. Adams] urged that a continuance of the embargo much longer would certainly be met by forcible resistance, supported by the legislature, and probably by the judiciary of the state. That, to quell that resistance, if force should be resorted to by the government, it would produce a civil war, and that in that event he had no doubt the leaders of the party would secure the co-operation with them, of Great

Britain; that their object was, and had been for several years, the dissolution of the Union and the establishment of a separate confederacy. He knew this from unequivocal evidence, although not proveable in a court of law; and that in case of a civil war, the aid of Great Britain to effect that purpose would be as surely resorted to as it would be indispensably necessary to the design."

Mr. Adams, in a subsequent notice, reiterates the same charge, and says: "This design [of dissolving the Union and forming a new confederacy under the auspices and protection of Great Britain] had been formed in the winter of 1803 and 1804, immediately after, and as a consequence of, the acquisition of Louisiana;" and adds:

"That project, I repeat, had gone to the length of fixing upon a military leader for its execution, and although the circumstances of the times never admitted of its execution, nor even of its full development, I had yet no doubt (in 1808 and 1809), and have no doubt at this time (30th December, 1828), that it is the key to all the great movements of these leaders of the federal party in New England from that time forward till its final catastrophe in the Hartford Convention."

JOHN QUINCY ADAMS' PRETENDED CONVERSION A FRAUD.

The elder Adams, in his letter to Cunningham, of December, 1808, says:

"I may mention to you, in confidence, that considerable pains have been taken to persuade your friend John Quincy Adams to consent to be run by the republicans. Yet he is utterly averse to it, and so am I, for many reasons, among which are: 1st. The office, though a precious stone, is but a carbuncle shining in the dark. 2d. It is a state of perfect slavery. The drudgery of it is extremely oppressive. 3d. *The compensation is not a living for a common gentleman.* 4th. He must resign his professorship. 5th. He must renounce his practice at the bar. 6th. He must stand in competition with Mr. Lincoln, who would divide the republican interest and certainly prevent the election of either. 7th. *It would produce an eternal separation between him and the federalists, at least that part of them who now constitute the absolute oligarchy.*"

Connect with these facts the toast of his relative, Josiah Quincy, "Those who fell with the first Adams will rise with the second," and that soon after his appointment as Secretary of State he gave the public printing to the Boston Centinel, and that as soon as he became President he gave the mission to England to Rufus King, and no one can doubt the purpose of the disclosures made to Mr. Giles and to Mr. Jefferson—nor can any one doubt his thirst for power, or his fellowship with the monarchists.

CHAPTER IX.

THE BOSTON FEDERALISTS A BRITISH DISUNION PARTY.

DOES any one ask further proof that the federal abolition party of Boston is a disunion, British party? If so, I refer them to the following extracts from the message of the President of the United States (Mr. Madison) to Congress, communicating the disclosures made by John Henry, the agent employed by the Governor-General of Canada, etc., on a political mission to the United States.

[Extract from John Henry's memorial to Lord Liverpool of the 13th of June, 1811.]

"Soon after the affair of the Chesapeake frigate, when his Majesty's Governor-General of British America had reason to believe that the two countries would be involved in a war, and had submitted to his Majesty's ministers the arrangements of the English party in the United States for an efficient resistance to the general government, which would probably terminate in a separation of the Northern states from the general confederacy, he applied to the undersigned to undertake a mission to Boston where the whole concerns of the opposition were managed. The object of the mission was to promote and encourage the federal party to resist the measures of the general government; to offer assurances of aid and support from his Majesty's government of Canada, and to open a communication between the leading men engaged in that opposition, and the Governor-General upon such a footing as circumstances might suggest; and finally, to render the plans then in contemplation subservient to the views of his Majesty's government."

[Extract of a letter from John Henry to Sir James Craig, Governor-General of British America, dated March 7, 1809.]

"SIR: I have already given a decided opinion that a declaration of war is not to be expected; but, contrary to all reasonable calculation, should the Congress possess spirit and independence enough to place their popularity in jeopardy by so strong a measure, the legislature of Massachusetts will give the tone to the neighboring states, will *declare itself permanent* until a new election of members; invite a congress, to be composed of delegates from the federal states, and erect a separate government for their common defence and common interest."

[Extract from the same to the same, dated Boston, March 20, 1809.]

"Since the plan of an organized opposition to the projects of Mr. Jefferson was put into operation the whole of the New England states have transferred their political power to his political enemies, and the reason that he has still so many adherents is, that those who consider the only true policy of America to consist in the cultivation of peace, have still great confidence, that nothing can force him (or his successor who acts up to his system, or rather by it) to consent to war.

"A war attempted without the concurrence of both parties, and the general consent of the Northern states, which constitute the bone and muscle of the country, must commence without hopes and end in disgrace. *It should, therefore, be the peculiar care of Great Britain to foster division between the North and the South, and by succeeding in this she may carry into effect her own projects in Europe, with a total disregard of the resentments of the democrats on this continent.*

THE RADICALS ARE MONARCHISTS AND DISUNIONISTS.

If there be any who doubt that the radicals in the present Congress are monarchists, and that their purpose is to perpetuate a military despotism, further proof will be given as I progress.

THE DISUNION PARTY.

The Boston Centinel was the organ of the old federal party, and in its issue of December 10, 1814, that paper said:

"We must demand that no new states with feelings and sentiments foreign to our own, shall be cut out of the distant wilds and admitted into the Union. . . . . . Those who startle at the danger of a separation, tell us that the soil of New England is hard, sterile, &c. Do these men forget what national energy can do for a people? Have they not read of Holland? Do they not remember that it threw off the yoke of Spain (our Virginia), and that its chapels became churches, and its poor men's cottages princes' palaces?"

Again, on the 17th of December, 1814, it said:

"Our course is so easy and plain, that I know not how the most timid can pause at the entrance upon it. It gives us the start of the Southern states; finds employments for our impoverished mechanics, brings revenue to our treasury, spreads activity and wealth through the country. A peace with England for a single year would bring every state east of Virginia into our confederacy. A strict neutrality will give only temporary relief. It leaves government to make peace for us, and with that peace, such as it will be, it holds us in its power. We will then be too late to demand alterations in the representations and security to our rights as the only condition upon which we will adhere to the Union.

"It is said that to make a treaty of commerce with the enemy is to violate the Constitution and sever the Union? Are they

not both already destroyed? Or in what stage of existence would we be should we declare a neutrality, or even withhold taxes and men? Let us leave it to the schools to put this question to rest, while we are guarding the honor and independence of New England.

"By a commercial treaty with England which shall provide for the admission of such states as may wish to come into it, and which shall prohibit England from making a treaty with the South and West, which does not grant us at least equal privileges with herself, our commerce will be secured, our standing in the nation raised to its proper level. If peace leaves us at the mercy of the Western states, we may dream of freedom, but we shall be in bonds.

"We must no longer suffer our liberties to be made the sport of theorists, the subject of speculation of men of cold hearts and muddy understandings; neither allow that region of the West, which was a wilderness when New England wrought the independence of America, to wrest from us those blessings which we permitted them to share."

THE BOSTON FEDERALISTS AND THE HARTFORD CONVENTION DISUNIONISTS.

Mr. Monroe, then President of the United States, in a letter to Mr. Jefferson, dated Washington, May, 1820, brings down this conspiracy to a later date. Mr. Monroe, writing on the subject of the Florida treaty, says:

[Extract from a letter from Mr. Monroe to Mr. Jefferson, dated Washington, May, 1820.]

"DEAR SIR: I have received your letter of the 14th, containing a very interesting view of the late treaty with Spain, and of the proceedings respecting it here. If the concurrence involved in it nothing more than a question between the United States and Spain, or between them and the colonies, I should entirely concur in your view of the subject. I am satisfied that we might regulate it in every circumstance as we thought just, and without war; that we might take Florida as an indemnity, and Texas for some trifle, as an equivalent. Spain must soon be expelled from this continent; and with any new government which may be formed in Mexico, it would be easy to arrange the boundary in the wilderness so as to include as much territory on our side as we might desire. No European power could prevent this, if so disposed. But the difficulty does not proceed from these sources. It is altogether internal, and of the most distressing nature and dangerous tendency. You were apprized by me, on your return from Europe, of the true character of the negotiation which took place in 1785 and 1786, with the minister of Spain, for shutting up the mouth of the Mississippi, a knowledge of which might have been derived, in part, from the secret journal of Congress, which then came into your hands. That was not a question with Spain in reality, but one among ourselves, in which her pretensions were brought forward in aid of the policy of the party at the head of that project. It was an effort to give such a shape to our Union as would secure the dominion over it to its eastern section. It was expected that dismemberment by the Alleghany mountains would follow the occlusion of the river, if it was not desired; though the latter was then and still is my opinion. The Union then consisted of eight navigating and commercial states, with five productive, holding slaves; and, had the river been shut up, and dismemberment ensued, the division would always have been the same. At that time Boston ruled the four New England states, and a popular orator in Faneuil Hall ruled Boston. Jay's object was to make New York a New England state, which he avowed on his return from Europe, to the dissatisfaction of many in that state, whose prejudices had been excited in the Revolutionary war, by the contest between New York and those states, respecting interfering grants in Vermont. It was foreseen by those persons that if the Mississippi should be opened, and new states should be established on its waters, the population would be drawn thither, the number of productive states be proportionately increased, and their hope of do-

minion on that contracted sectional scale be destroyed. It was to prevent this that that project was formed. Happily it failed; and since then our career in an opposite direction has been rapid and wonderful. The river has been opened, and all the territory dependent on it acquired. Eight states have already been admitted into the Union in that quarter; a ninth is on the point of entering, and a tenth provided for, exclusive of Florida. This march to greatness has been seen with profound regret by those in the policy suggested; but it has been impelled by causes over which they have no control. Several attempts have been made to impede it; among which the Hartford convention in the late war, and the proposition to restrict Missouri, are the most distinguished. The latter measure contemplated an arrangement on the distinction, solely between slaveholding and non-slaveholding states; presuming that, on that basis only, such a division might be founded as would destroy, by perpetual excitement, the usual effects proceeding from difference of climate, the produce of the soil, the prosperity and circumstances of the people, and marshal the states differing in that circumstance in unceasing opposition and hostility with each other. To what account this project, had it succeeded to the extent contemplated, might have been turned, I cannot say. Certain, however, it is, that since 1786, I have not seen so violent and persevering a struggle, and on the part of some of the leaders in the project, for a purpose so unmasked and dangerous. They did not hesitate to avow that it was a contest for power only; disclaiming the pretext of liberty, humanity, &c. It was also manifest that they were willing to risk the Union on the measure, if, indeed, as in that relating to the Mississippi, dismemberment, was not the principal object. You know how this affair terminated, as I presume you likewise do, that complete success was prevented by the patriotic devotion of several members of the non-slaveholding states, who preferred the sacrifice of themselves at home to a violation of the obvious principles of the Constitution and the risk of the Union.'

CHAPTER X.

FURTHER PROOF THAT THE RADICALS ARE BRITISH MONARCHISTS.

IN the preface to Mr. M. Carey's Olive Branch, second edition, page 6, he says:

"It cannot be any longer doubted that there exists a conspiracy in New England among a few of the most influential and wealthy citizens to effect a dissolution of the Union at every hazard, and to form a separate confederacy. This has been asserted by some of our citizens for years and strenuously denied by others, deceived by the mask the conspirators wore, and their hollow professions. But it requires more than Bœotian stupidity and dullness to hesitate on the subject, after the late extraordinary movements, which cannot possibly have any other object. It is eighteen years since the dangerous project was promulgated. [In a series of essays published under the signature of Pelham, in "The Connecticut Courant," 1796.] From that period to the present it is not one hour out of view. And unholy and pernicious as was the end, the means were at least as unholy and pernicious. Falsehood, deception, and calumny, in turn have been called in to aid the design," &c.

I quote further from Mr. Carey's Olive Branch. He says:

"For eight years, the most unceasing efforts have been used to poison the minds of the people of New England toward, and to alienate them from, their fellow-citizens of the Southern states. The people of the latter section have been portrayed as demons incarnate, and destitute of all the qualities that dignify and adorn human nature! Nothing can exceed the violence of these caricatures, some of which would have suited the ferocious inhabitants of New England, rather than a civilized or polished nation." Page 253.

And commenting upon the publications of Pelham, he says:

"The unholy and demoniac spirit that inspired the writer of the above vile libel has been from that hour to the present (vide speeches of radicals in the present Congress) incessantly employed to excite hostility between the different sections of the Union. To such horrible length has this spirit been carried, that many paragraphs have continually appeared in the Boston papers, intended and calculated to excite the negroes of the Southern states to rise and massacre their masters. This will undoubtedly appear incredible to the reader; it is nevertheless sacredly true. It is a species of turpitude and baseness of which the world has few examples!" Page 254.

Mr. Carey further says:

"I am tired of this exposure; I sicken for the honor of the human species. What idea must the world form of the arrogance of the pretensions of the one side [Eastern states], and on the other, of the folly and weakness of the rest of the Union, to have so long suffered them to pass without exposure and detection. The naked fact is, that the demagogues in the Eastern states, not satisfied with deriving all the benefits from the Southern states, which they could from so many wealthy colonies, with making princely fortunes by the carriage and transportation of their bulky and valuable productions, and supplying them with their own manufactures, and the manufactures and productions of Europe and the East and West Indies to an enormous amount, and at an immense profit—have uniformly treated them with outrage, insult, and injury." Page 269.

"I repeat it, and hope the solemn truth will be borne in constant remembrance, that the Southern states are virtually colonies to those states whose demagogues have never ceased slandering and persecuting them." Page 280.

UNQUESTIONABLE PROOF THAT THE BOSTON MONARCHISTS ARE DISUNIONISTS.

The Centinel was not only the organ of the old federal, monarchical party, under the reign of the elder Adams, and of the "British party" in 1809, and of the Hartford convention, 1814, but it was the organ of the same party in 1825, under the leadership of John Quincy Adams, who, as soon as he became Secretary of State, made the Centinel his official organ, and as soon as he was elected President appointed Rufus King our resident minister in London.

SUMNER AND DISUNION.

Does any one pretend to deny the identity of that party with the present radical Congress? If there be any such I refer them to the proceedings of a meeting held in Worcester, Mass., just before the war, as given in the publications at the time:

"Mr. Higginson now took the floor. He dissented from Mr. Garrison's tribute to Mr. Bird for his courage in standing on the convention platform. It was a thing to be proud of, to be grateful for, that one had been permitted to stand there, or to sign his name to the call of the convention. The day will come back to Worcester when the meeting of this convention will be considered the proudest day in her history. There was no Union upon which those who were in convention could stand, unless it was disunion. He did not realize, until after he had signed the call, now near the people of Massachusetts were to disunion. As for the Constitution, it meant nothing, or it might mean anything. Mr. Higginson

passed to talk of Charles Sumner. He had a talk with the Senator in Athenæum hall, in Boston, last week, and when he asked him if, when he got back to Washington, he would reiterate his words against slavery, Mr. Sumner replied, 'Reiterate, reiterate. If when I get back to Washington, I make the speech I expect to make, it will be like fourth proof brandy to molasses and water.' When asked what result he expected from it, he replied, 'I expect to be shot; there is nothing else left for them to do.' 'Good God!' exclaimed Mr. Higginson, 'and has it come to this—the foremost statesman in all the land to be answered with a bullet because he has spoken the truth.' He spoke despairingly of the prospects of the republican party. It was a futile expectation that the party would recover in 1860. There are no hopes for them. According to Mr. Banks, the last election decided the politics of the United States for the next thirty years; and according to Senator Wilson, defeat in 1856 would place the party beyond resuscitation. The democratic party know that this position was the true one. Mr. Higginson continued: 'Disunion is not a desire merely—it is a destiny—it is the destiny of this nation. It was needful that we should exhaust the political power of the North to prepare the people of the North for disunion. The free soil power have performed that work, and now begins our destiny. It is coming, and, in God's name, let it come quickly.'

"William Lloyd Garrison spoke for an hour, and was listened to with great attention, and was frequently applauded.

"After some remarks by the chairman, Wendell Phillips spoke at some length. The Hutchinsons sang, and at six o'clock the convention adjourned till 7:30 to Brinley hall.

"8:15 P. M.—Wendell Phillips is speaking in Brinley hall. No steps have yet been taken to dissolve the Union.

"The business committee submitted the following resolutions:

"*Resolved,* That the meeting of a state disunion convention, attended by men of various parties and affinities, gives occasion for a new statement of principles and a new platform of action.

"*Resolved*, That the cardinal American principle is now, as always, liberty; while the prominent fact is now, as always, slavery.

"*Resolved*, That the conflict between this principle of liberty and this fact of slavery has been the whole history of the nation for fifty years; while the only result of this conflict has thus far been to strengthen both parties and prepare the way for a yet more desperate struggle.

"*Resolved*, That in this emergency we can expect little or nothing from the South itself, because it too is sinking deeper into barbarism every year;

"Nor from a supreme court which is always ready to invent new securities for slaveholders;

"Nor from a President elected almost solely by Southern votes;

"Nor from a Senate which is permanently controlled by the slave power;

"Nor from a new House of Representatives which, in spite of our agitation, will be more pro-slavery than the present one, though the present one has at length granted all which slavery asked;.

"Nor from political action, as now conducted. For the republican leaders and press freely admitted, in public and private, that the election of Fremont was, politically speaking, 'the last hope of freedom,' and even could the North cast a united vote in 1860, the South has before it four years of annexation previous to that time.

"*Resolved*, That the fundamental difference between mere political agitation and the action we propose, is this—that the one requires the acquiescence of the slave power, and the other only its opposition.

"*Resolved*, That the necessity for disunion is written in the whole existing character and condition of the two sections of the country—in their social organization, education, habits, and laws—in the dangers of our white citizens in Kansas, and of our colored ones in Boston—in the wounds of Charles Sumner and the laurels of his assailant—and no government on earth was ever strong enough to hold together such opposing forces.

"*Resolved*, That this movement does not seek merely disunion, but the more perfect union of the free states by the expulsion of the slave states from the confederation, in which they have ever been an element of discord, danger, and disgrace.

"*Resolved*, That it is not probable that the ultimate severance of the Union will be an act of deliberation or discussion, but that a long period of deliberation and discussion must precede it, and this we meet to begin.

"*Resolved*, That henceforward, instead of regarding it as an objection to any system of policy, that it will lead to the separation of the states, we will proclaim that to be the highest of all recommendations, and the grateful proof of statesmanship; and will support, politically, or otherwise, such men and measures as appear to tend most to this result.

"*Resolved*, That by the repeated confession of Northern and Southern statesmen, 'the existence of the Union is the chief guarantee of slavery;' and that the despots of the whole world have everything to fear, and the slaves of the whole world everything to hope, from its destruction, and the rise of a free Northern republic.

"*Resolved*, That the sooner the separation takes place the more peaceful it will be; but that peace or war is a secondary consideration, in view of our present perils. Slavery must be conquered, 'peaceably if we can, forcibly if we must.'"

CHAPTER XI.

ANTI-SLAVERY CONSPIRACY.

THE identity of names, and of the declared purposes of the radical leaders, with men who are thus proved to be a British party in America—their warfare upon the South—their unscrupulous abuse of power — and their avowed purpose to subvert the previous government, by so changing the Constitution as to make it conform to the *monarchy* which they prefer, identify them as the traitors who were in treaty with the British agent Henry. He said, in 1809, that "The legislature of Massachusetts will give the tone to the neighboring states, will declare itself permanent until a new election of members, invite a congress to be composed of delegates from the federal states, *and erect* a separate government for their common defence and common interest," and in proof of the truth of what he wrote, and of the treasonable purposes of his Boston associates, we need do no more than refer to the Hartford convention, and the warfare they waged upon Mr Madison, the Constitution and the Union in 1814—their plan was then, as the radical plan now is, to declare themselves permanently in power. Then they were allied with England, and their measures and principles were so much identified with the purposes and interests of England, that Henry, the confidential agent of England, called them "*the English party in the United States.*"

I would call the attention of the reader to the following extract from one of Henry's letters. He said : "*It should therefore be the peculiar care of Great Britain to foster division between the North and the South, and by succeeding in this, she may carry into effect* HER OWN PROJECTS IN EUROPE, *with a total disregard of the resentments of the* DEMOCRATS *of this country.*"

We are at no loss to determine what were the "PROJECTS," which it was then the purpose of England to carry into effect in Europe. Their purpose was to establish the maritime and commercial supremacy of England, and to make the Boston monarchists aid in the accomplishment of that purpose, by stimulating them to make war upon the interests and welfare of the South.

WHY ENGLAND WAS OPPOSED TO AFRICAN SLAVERY.

By the 16th article of the treaty of Utrecht, in 1713, England confirmed the contract between the English Guinea Company and the king of Spain, whereby that company gave to Spain two hundred thousand crowns, and to Spain and *England*, each, one quarter share of the profits for the privilege of importing slaves into the Spanish American provinces, and yet, in 1817, she gave to Spain *two millions of dollars to abolish the slave trade!* The motive for this change of policy was explained by Wilberforce, who, in the debate in the House of Commons on this treaty, said : "I cannot but think that the grant to Spain will be more than repaid to Great Britain in commercial advantages, *by the opening of a great continent to British industry*—an object which will be entirely defeated if the slave trade is to be carried on by Spain. Our commercial connection with Africa will much more than repay us for any pecuniary sacrifices of this kind. I myself will live to see Great Britain deriving the greatest advantages from its intercourse with Africa."

THE DUKE OF WELLINGTON,

In the debate on the corn laws in 1842, said:

" I am sure no man regrets more than I do that commerce or manufactures should be depressed; but I believe, if the corn laws were repealed to-morrow not a yard of cloth or a pound of iron more would be sold in any part of Europe, or of the world, *over which this country does not exercise a control.* My lords, the greatest number of European nations, and of the nations of the globe, have adopted measures for the encouragement of home manufactures. These measures were not taken, as stated by some, in consequence of the English corn laws. They are attributable to the example of this country. They had their rise in the spectacle which this country exhibited during the late war, and in the great and noble exertions by which her power and strength were displayed on every occasion. Those who contemplated those exertions, as well as those who were relieved and assisted by them, thought they might as well follow the example of our power, of our industry and our system of commerce. They have followed our example, and have established among themselves manufactures, and given a stimulus to their commerce."

LORD PALMERSTON,

In the debate on the state of the country, on the 6th July, 1842, having explained that the markets of France and Germany were closed to British manfactures, said :

" I therefore look to more distant regions for *future prosperity.* We must look to the rising nation which inhabits the North American continent. There we are met by our corn laws, and, until we alter these, we will be crippled in our commercial intercourse. We must also look to South America. There again we are met by heavy duties on sugar, and, until these are modified, we cannot expect to carry on commerce with South America to the extent it is possible. *We must look again to* AFRICA, *and we must look especially to* INDIA *and to* CHINA."

And why must Great Britain look to AFRICA, and especially to INDIA and to CHINA, for her future prosperity ? Is it not because, to use the words of the Duke of Wellington, *Africa,* and *India* and *China,* are under the " *control*" of England ? And how has she exercised her control ? Let us see. I quote from the Edinburgh Review of 1825 :

BRITISH COLONIAL POLICY.

" The act of 1650, passed by the Republican Parliament, laid the foundation of the monopoly system, by confining the import and export trade to the colonies exclusively to British or colony-built ships. But the famous Navigation Act of 1660 (12 Charles II., cap. 18) went much farther. It enacted that certain specified articles, the produce of the colonies, and since well known in commerce as enumerated articles, should not be exported directly from the colonies to any foreign country; but that they should first be sent to Britain, and there unladen (the words are, *laid upon the shore*), before they could be forwarded to their final destination. Sugar, molasses, ginger, fustic, tobacco, cotton, and indigo, were originally enumerated; and the list was subsequently enlarged by the addition of coffee, hides and skins, iron, corn, &c. . . . . But the insatiable rapacity of monopoly was not to be satisfied with compelling the colonists to *sell* their produce exclusively in the English markets. It was next thought advisable that they should be obliged to *buy* such foreign articles as they might stand in need of, exclusively from the merchants and manufacturers of England. For this purpose it was enacted, in 1663, that no commodity of the growth, production, or manufacture of Europe shall be imported into the plantations, but such as are laden and put on board in England, Wales, or Berwick-upon-Tweed, and in English-built shipping, whereof the master and three fourths of the crew are English. . . . . It was also a leading principle in the system of colonial policy, adopted as well by England as by the other European nations, to discourage all attempts to manufacture such articles in the colonies as could be provided for them by the mother-country. The history of our colonial system is full of attempts of this sort; and so essential was the principle deemed, to the idea of a colony, that even Lord Chatham did not hesitate to declare, in his place in Parliament, that the British colonists in North America, had NO RIGHT *to manufacture even a nail for a horseshoe!* And when such were the enactments made by the legislature, and such the avowed sentiments of a great parliamentary leader and a friend to the colonies, we need not be surprised at a declaration of a late Lord Sheffield, who did no more indeed than express the decided opinion of all the merchants and politicians of his time, when he affirmed thus : ' *The* ONLY *use of American colonies or West India islands is the* MONOPOLY *of their consumption and of the carriage of their produce.'* . . . . Were it not for the perverse and most injurious regulations to which this system has given rise, we might supply ourselves with sugar from the East Indies or South America for a great deal less than it now costs to buy it from the West India planters. This is a much more serious loss than is generally supposed. Sugar has become a necessary, equally indispensable to the poor and the rich. The quantity of West India sugar annually consumed in Great Britain may, we believe, be taken on an average at about three hundred and eighty million pounds weight. And it has been repeatedly shown, that a reduction of the duties on sugar from the East

Indies and South America to the same level with those laid on West India sugar, would enable us to obtain as good sugar for 4½d. per pound as now costs 6d.; but taking the difference at only 1d. per pound, it would make, on the above-mentioned quantity, a saving of no less than £1,583,000 ($7,915,000) a year. . . . . Not only, however, do we exclude the sugars of the Dutch colonies, Brazil, and Louisiana, but we actually lay 10s. a cwt. of higher duties on the sugar imported from our own dominions in the East Indies than on that which is imported from the West. Not satisfied with giving the West India planters a monopoly of the home market against foreigners, we have given them a monopoly against our own subjects in the East. It is impossible to speak too strongly in condemnation of this arrangement—not that we mean to insinuate that the East Indies have any right whatever to be more favorably treated than the West Indies; but we contend that they have as clear and undoubted right to be as favorably treated. To attempt to enrich the latter, by preventing the former from bringing their produce to our market, or by loading it with higher duties, is not only to prefer the interests of *one million,* and those—we do not say it disparagingly of the planters—mostly slaves, to the interests of *one hundred millions* of subjects; but it is totally inconsistent with, and subversive of, every principle of impartial justice and sound policy. It is said, however, that slavery exists in Hindostan as well as in Jamaica, and that by reducing the duties on East India sugar and facilitating its cultivation, by allowing Europeans to purchase and farm lands, we should not get rid of the evils of slavery, but would be merely substituting the produce of one species of slave labor for another. Now, admitting for a moment that this statement is well founded, still it is certain, from the cheapness of free labor in Hindostan, no slaves ever have been, or ever can be, imported into that country. And hence it is obvious that by substituting the sugars of the East for those of the West, we should neither add to the number, nor deteriorate the condition of the existing slave population in our dominions, while we should save above a million and a half in the purchase of one of the principal necessaries of life, at the same time that we subverted a system of monopoly and laid the *foundation of a new and extensive intercourse with India—a market which may be enlarged to almost any conceivable extent.*" (*See Edinburgh Review for* 1825.)

I would entreat the reader to note and consider the facts disclosed by the extracts given above, as connected with other known facts. The Duke of Wellington tells us that the repeal of the corn laws would not enable Great Britain to sell a yard of cloth or a pound of iron more in any part of Europe or of the world, over which Great Britain does *not exercise a control,* and why? Because the greatest number of European nations, and of the nations of the globe, have adopted measures for the encouragement of home manufactures. And Lord Palmerston told us, that being no longer able to sell to the other European nations, they were compelled to look to Africa, and especially to India and to China, for a market for their surplus manufactures.

The extract from the Edinburgh Review shows us the purpose and the manner in which England has used her power in the countries over which she has had a "control," and explains why she emancipated her West India slaves. When England was engaged in the slave trade, with a view to increase the profits, and thus stimulate the trade in African slaves, she gave to the West India proprietors a monopoly of the supply of the home market in the shape of discriminating duties favoring West India produce, and that monopoly was continued until the competition of the other European nations compelled England to look to Africa,

India, and China, to use the words of Lord Palmerston, for "future prosperity." And the fact that having the same power to emancipate her slaves in Hindostan, that she had to emancipate the slaves in the West Indies, and that she has not yet, and does not propose, to emancipate her East India slaves, is conclusive to show that the one hundred millions of dollars, which she gave to the West India proprietors, under pretence of compensating them for the emancipation of their slaves, was, in truth, given as compensation for the repeal of the discriminating duties which gave them a monopoly of the supply of the home market with West India produce; and no one can believe otherwise than that the inducement was, as in the case of the sum paid to Spain for abolishing the African slave trade, the "commercial advantages" to be obtained by exchanging a market of one million, mostly slaves of West India consumers, for the markets of Africa, India, and China, where there are more than seven hundred millions of consumers, over the greater part of whom Great Britain exercises a control, more or less direct.

EFFECT OF EMANCIPATION IN THE WEST INDIES.

In confirmation of this view, I again refer to the debates in the British Parliament. In the debate on the condition of the West Indies in 1842, Lord Stanley, then a member of the government, said, that on sixty-two sugar estates, from the 1st January, 1841, to December, the actual loss was nine hundred and eighty-three thousand dollars on an outlay of twelve hundred and fifty thousand, and the London Times, commenting on this speech, said that the result of abolition in the West Indies was the ruin or approaching ruin of the planter, who was thus compelled to incur a clear loss of three fourths of the sum expended in the cultivation of his estate; and added: "The abolition act is fairly sweeping away a whole class of men who thought themselves in possession of comfortable, perhaps handsome incomes; annihilating, or at least rendering unavailing to its owners, the whole mass of the English West India Islands, and compelling them to hand over their entire property, on the most ruinous terms, to another race—a race, too, which has obtained its purchase money out of the pockets of the present owners during the two or three last years, which will have completed their ruin," and then admitted that the inevitable consequence of the abolition act was to convert the West India Islands into "black colonies, because the white man is not suited to labor in that climate, and cannot resist its terrible diseases."

And the London Courier of April 23, 1842, said:

"The Tay steamer brought an immense quantity of correspondence and papers which have been long accumulating at the various islands. Jamaica apparently continues in a disturbed state, *which is mainly attributable to the growing demoralization of the negro population.* The attention of the enlightened portion of the inhabitants had been drawn to this fact, and means were being devised to ameliorate the evil if possible. Commercial affairs continued in a very embarrassed condition; and it was doubted if some property, which was advertised for sale under a late bankruptcy, would find purchasers. It is mentioned, with regret, that the event had been caused by keeping up these very estates."

SIR ROBERT PEEL ON EMANCIPATION.

Such were the inducements to, and such were the results of, British West India emancipation; and yet, on a

petition addressed to the House of Commons in 1842, praying for an equalization of the duties on foreign and colonial sugars, which asserted that, by comparing the average gazette price of Muscovado sugar with Brazilian in 1840, the people of the United Kingdom paid the sum of $24,789,365 more for colonial than the average price of Brazilian sugar. Sir Robert Peel, then the head of the government, said:

"To open our markets to the sugars of Cuba and Brazil will detract from the high character which this country [England] has acquired, in its efforts and sacrifices to put down the slave trade. . . . . . I hold in my hand a letter from an intelligent naval officer, who, speaking of the state of feeling in Cuba, says that he understands there is a strong feeling prevailing on the subject of emancipation, and that the consequence is much embarrassment and mistrust among the proprietors. This is in Cuba where slavery exists in its most unmitigated form; and when we consider that such feelings exist in that island, let us ask ourselves, if they are not likely to prevail also in the Brazils, where the system is less rigid? And more than all, are they not likely to prevail with great, very great force among the intelligent and enlightened people of the United States? . . . . . . We are in peculiar circumstances. Our efforts on the coast of Africa may be described as failures. [Oh, oh!] I refer to those two vessels which were sent out last year, and whose expedition has closed without success. [An ironical hear hear!] Yes, but great importance has been attached to that expedition."

He then referred to the position of France, the refusal, under the protest of General Cass, to ratify the Quintuple treaty, and of the importance of preserving a high character for disinterestedness (?), urged that this could not be done if they repealed the duty on Cuban and Brazilian sugar, and proceeded:

"What I say is, make the attempt—try to get concessions from those from whom we get our supply. You may depend on it, there is a growing conviction among the people of those countries that slavery is not unaccompanied by great dangers. In Cuba, in the United States, in the Brazils, there is a ferment on the subject of slavery, which is spreading, and will spread. Some from humane and benevolent motives —some on account of interested fears—begin to look at the great example we have set, and have begun to look at the consequences which may result from that example nearer home. It is impossible to look to the discussions in the United States, and especially to the conflicts between the Northern and Southern states, without seeing that slavery in that nation stands on a precarious footing."

FREE LABOR CANNOT COMPETE WITH SLAVE LABOR.

Why did Sir Robert Peel oppose the repeal of the discriminating duties on Cuban and Brazilian sugars, upon the ground that, by continuing those duties, Cuba, Brazil, and the United States, could be induced to emancipate their slaves, and how was England to be benefited by the emancipation of our slaves? He gave the answer. The Duke of Wellington had said that the repeal of her corn-laws would not enable England to sell a yard of cloth or a pound of iron more in any country over which England did not exercise a control; and Lord Palmerston had said that, being no longer able to sell to European countries, England must look to Africa, and especially to India and China, for her "future prosperity." It is apparent that the "prosperity" to be derived from Africa, India, and China, depends upon the ability of Africa, India, and China, to pay for the manufactures which it was the purpose of England to sell; and it is equally apparent that Africa, India,

and China, could not pay for British manufactures unless Great Britain would receive their agricultural produce in payment. We have seen that the estimate of the Edinburgh Review in 1825 was, that the repeal of the monopoly given to the West India planters, to enable them to purchase African slaves—when England was a slave trader—would open a market in India, which might be "enlarged to almost any conceivable extent."

EFFECT OF THE WEST INDIA EMANCIPATION ON THE EAST INDIES.

Now, what are the facts? The acts emancipating the West India slaves, modifying the West India monopoly, and opening the trade of the East Indies to British commerce, all passed in 1835. In 1814, India sent to England 1,266,608 pieces of cotton goods, made without the use of improved machinery. In 1837, England sent to India 64,212,633 pieces of cotton goods, the product of her improved machinery! and, having the control over the commerce of India, she imposed a duty of twenty per cent. on India goods sent to England, and of *three* per cent. only on British goods sent to India. The result was, that in the town of Daca alone, where two hundred thousand persons had been employed in the manufacture of cotton goods, the entire population was reduced in one year to about thirty thousand, whole families having perished for want of food, and many thousands more perished by famine than were emancipated in the West Indies. The governor-general of India, in his report, said:

"The sympathy of the court is deeply excited by the report of the board of trade, exhibiting the gloomy picture of the effects of a commercial revolution, productive of so much suffering to numerous classes in India, and hardly to be paralleled in the history of commerce."

WHY THIS FAMINE IN INDIA?

Sir Robert Peel gave the answer. He said :

"*I have my doubts if a colony, in which slavery has been abolished by law, can, at present, enter into successful competition with a district in which the system continues to exist. . . . .* The honorable member for Montrose announced his wish to maintain our colonial dependencies, but said that his object is to see each colony paying for itself. I apprehend that the proposal of the honorable and learned member for Bath, to admit to an unlimited competition with slave-possessing colonies, is not the way to insure that object. The honorable member has said that if the weavers of Lancashire were asked what benefit they derived from the duty on foreign sugar, they would answer—'None.' But I put it to the honorable member, whether that is the test by which any great question affecting the country is to be decided? If I ask a Lancashire weaver, what benefit he derives from Jamaica, and his reply is—'none,' ought that to induce me to abandon my measure? Is the honorable gentleman prepared to test the advantages derived from our connection with India in the same manner? or should we abandon our colonial dependencies altogether, upon the assurance of a distressed weaver of Lancashire, that he is not aware that any benefit is conferred upon the country by our dependencies? If that is the principle of the honorable gentleman, it is quite clear, that in order to conform to it, we must resolve ourselves into the narrow limits of our own resources, and try what England can do against the world, after having abandoned all those dependencies which she has established to her glory."

COMMENT—ENGLAND AND NAPOLEON.

We have seen that, to use the words of the Duke of Wellington and Lord Palmerston, the other European nations having established for themselves a system of manufactures and of commerce, England is compelled to look to Africa, and especially to India and China, for her "future prosperity." We have seen that the effect of the introduction of her machine-made goods into India was such that the governor-general, in his comment on the report of the board of trade of India, said, that it exhibited "the gloomy picture of the effects of a commercial revolution, productive of so much suffering to numerous classes in India, and hardly to be paralleled in the history of commerce," and that Sir Robert Peel urged the continuance of the discriminating duty on Cuban and Brazilian sugars, because he hoped, by tendering the repeal of that duty as an inducement, he could prevail on Cuba and Brazil to emancipate their slaves, and that then the United States, for fear of the consequences, would emancipate ours. We have seen that Sir Robert said that he was unwilling to repeal the duty on slave-grown sugar, because he had ascertained that "a colony in which slavery had been abolished by law could not successfully compete with a district in which the system continues to exist," and we know that for more than two hundred and fifty years Great Britain has been increasing her dominions and extending her power and commerce in India—that, as a means of maintaining her own supremacy, it has been "the peculiar care of Great Britain to foster division between" the local governments and people in India, that she may so excite local prejudice and sectional feeling, as that her influence, consisting of native troops, led by British officers, aided by a few, very few, British auxiliaries, became the preponderating, governing power. We know that the commerce of India has enriched the several nations, who have possessed the "control" of it, from the days of Solomon—the Portuguese, the Dutch, the French, and the English. We know that the traditionary policy of Russia, from the days of Catharine, has been to seize upon Constantinople and the Dardanelles as the gate to the commerce of India, and that to prevent this, the ruling policy of England was to interpose the countervailing power of Austria and Turkey. For this, her royal princes and princesses have intermarried with the petty princes of Germany—for this she made war on France and the elder Napoleon—for this she organized the holy alliance, and having aided to restore the Bourbons, finding that she could better "carry into effect her own projects in Europe," she aided in placing upon the throne of France the present emperor, and was thus enabled to use the power of France in the Crimea and in China, as she had used the power and resources of Russia and Germany at Waterloo, to confirm, increase, and perpetuate her power and dominion in India. Every intelligent observer of passing events must see that this union and concert between France and England is the result of the far-seeing and ever-vigilant commercial policy of England, and that the purpose of both England and France is to organize a European combination which, their jealous rivalry prompts them to believe, is necessary to prevent the preponderance of American wealth, power, and influence, among the nations of the earth. In proof of this truth, a few pertinent extracts are submitted:

MR. COBDEN—ENGLAND AND AMERICA COMPARED.

In a pamphlet published by Mr. Cobden, in 1835, he said:

"We are upon the verge of a novel combination of commercial necessities that will altogether change the relation in which we have hitherto stood with our colonies; we call them necessities, because they will be forced upon us, not from conviction of the wisdom of such changes, but by the irresistible march of events. The New World is destined to become the arbiter of the commercial policy of the Old. . . . .

"It is to the industry, the economy, and peaceful policy of America, and not to the growth of Russia, that our statesmen and politicians of whatever creed ought to direct their most anxious study; for it is by these and not by the efforts of barbarian force that the power and greatness of England are in danger of being superseded; yes, by the successful rivalry of America shall we, in all probability, be placed second in the rank of nations."

"We allude to the danger in which we are placed of being overshadowed by the commercial and naval ascendency of the United States. It has been through the peaceful victories of mercantile traffic, and not by the force of arms, that modern states have yielded to the supremacy of more successful nations; thus the power and civilization of maritime Italy succumbed to Spain and Portugal; these again were superceded by the more industrious traders of Holland, who, in their turn, sank into insignificance *before the gigantic growth of the* MANUFACTURING *industry of Great Britain;* and the latter power now sees in America a competitor, in every respect calculated to contend with advantage for the sceptre of naval and commercial dominion. Whether we view the rapid advance of the United States during the last forty years in respect to population or wealth, it is equally unparalleled in any country, and making no allowance for the probable increase of emigration from Europe, will, in seventy years from this time, that is, during the lifetime of individuals now arrived at maturity, exceed one hundred millions. These circumstances demonstrate the rapid tendency toward a superiority as far as numbers go, but we apprehend that in respect to the comparison of our commercial prospects with those of America, the position of Great Britain does not, according to the facts which we have to state, wear a more flattering aspect. . . . . This republican people present the only example of past, as we believe it will prove of future history, in which a nation has honorably discharged its public debt. . . . . The results may be seen, not only in the unparalleled advances of wealth and civilization at home, but in the fact that we have just demonstrated, and which we doubt not will surprise most of our readers, that even the foreign commerce of this people is as great or greater than our own."

ENGLAND DEPENDENT ON AMERICA FOR RAW PRODUCTS.

This was in 1835, and shows that this far-seeing British statesman then foresaw that "by the successful rivalry of America," England would "be placed *second* in the rank of nations," and bearing this fact in mind, I would call the attention of the reader to the following extracts from the same pamphlet:

"*Bearing in mind that the supply of the raw material of nearly one half of our exports is derived from a country that threatens to eclipse us by its rival greatness,* we cannot, while viewing the relative positions of England and the United States at this moment, avoid recurring to the somewhat parallel cases of Holland and Great Britain, *before the latter became a manufacturing state;* when the Dutchman purchased the wool of this country and sold it to us again in the form of cloth. Like as the latter nation became at a subsequent period, we are now overwhelmed with debt, contracted in wars or the acquisition of colonies; while America, free from all burdens as we were

at the former epoch, is prepared to take up, with far greater advantage, the fabrication of their own cotton, than we did of our wool. The Americans possess a quicker mechanical genius than even ourselves. Such again was the case of our ancestors in comparison with the Dutch (as witness their patents and improvements for which we are indebted to individuals of that country) in mechanics, such as spinning, engraving, &c. We gave additional speed to our ships, by improving upon the naval architecture of the Dutch, and the similitude again applies to the superiority which, in comparison with British models, the Americans have, for all the purposes of activity and economy, imparted to their vessels."

FRANCE IN ACCORD WITH ENGLAND.

It will be seen that in 1835, Mr. Cobden laid great stress upon the fact that England was indebted for the "supply of the raw material of nearly one half of her exports," to a country which even then threatened to eclipse her by its rival greatness, and, looking to her previous and subsequent measures and policy, who can fail to see that her contemporaneous emancipation of her West India slaves, repeal of the West India monopoly, modification of the charter, and abrogation of the monopolies of the East India Company, were all and each intended to relieve her of her dependence upon her great commercial rival for a supply of the raw material, so essential to her maritime and commercial supremacy, and who so blind as not to see, in the fact that from that time she has been an abolitionist in Boston and a freetrader in Charleston, a deliberate and matured purpose of substituting the raw products of India for those of America? And who that has noted the fact that France has been permitted, with the consent of England, to extend her conquests in Africa and in Cochin-China, and to take quiet possession of Egypt and the Suez canal, and was associated with England in the Crimean and Chinese wars, can hesitate to believe that France and England were in accord, and that the occupation of Mexico and the colonization of the Isthmus and South America, were parts of a deliberate system of measures intended to arrest the progress and prevent the maritime and commercial supremacy of the United States? If there be any so incredulous as to doubt this, they are referred to the following

EXTRACT FROM LIST'S POLITICAL ECONOMY,

A work which has become a standard authority in France. He says:

"In all ages there have been cities or countries surpassing others in manufactures, trade, and navigation; but the world has never witnessed a supremacy to be compared with that existing in our time. In all ages states have aspired to domination, but no edifice of power has ever been constructed upon so broad a base. How miserable appears the ambition of those who attempted to establish universal domination upon the power of arms, in comparison with the great attempt of England to transform her whole territory into an immense manufacturing and commercial city, into an immense port, and to become to other nations what a vast city is to the country, the centre of arts and knowledge, of an immense commerce, of opulence, of navigation, of naval and military power; a cosmopolitic country supplying all nations with manufactured products, and asking in return from each country its raw materials and commodities; the arsenal of extensive capital, the universal banker, regulating, if not controlling, the circulating money of the whole world, and making all nations tributary to her by loans and the payment of interest. . . . . The maxims of state, by aid of which England has become what she is at present, may be reduced to the following formulas:

"To prefer constantly the importation of productive power to that of commodities.

"To maintain and carefully protect the development of productive power.

"To import only raw materials and agricultural products, and to export only manufactured articles.

"To employ, in founding colonies and reducing to her rule barbarous tribes, only the surplus of her productive power.

"To reserve exclusively for the mother-country the supplying of the colonies and conquered territories with manufactured articles; in compensation for which receiving in preference their raw materials, and particularly their tropical commodities.

"To reserve also the coasting trade and the navigation between the mother-country and the colonies; to encourage maritime fisheries by aid of premiums; to obtain the greatest possible share of international navigation.

"To become thus the chief naval power, and by means of that supremacy to extend her external commerce and enlarge constantly her colonial establishments.

"To grant commercial facilities, whether colonial or relating to navigation, only to such extent and in that way which most favored her own interest, not yielding any reciprocity in matters of duties upon shipping, except when the advantage was on the side of England, or as a means of preventing foreign powers from imposing maritime restrictions for their own benefit.

"Not to make concessions to independent nations, except touching the importation of agricultural products, and only upon condition of analogous concessions relatively to the exportations of manufactured products.

"When such concessions could not be obtained by way of treaties to attain the same end by smuggling.

"To declare war, or to conclude alliances, with an exclusive view to the interests of manufactures, commerce, shipping, and colonies; to extract, in this way, profit from friends and foes; from the latter by interrupting their trade; from the former by running their manufactures through subsidies and loans, paid in the products of her manufactures."

. . . .

"If we compare the total amount of the manufacturing product and capital of England with that of its agricultural products and capital, we find that the chief part of the wealth of the country consists in the value of the real estate. McQueen furnishes the following table of wealth and annual income of England:

1. NATIONAL CAPITAL.

Capital invested in agriculture, land, mines and fisheries........	£2,604,000,000	
Circulating capital, in cattle, implements, provisions, and money......	655,000,000	
Total of agriculturists.............	52,000,000	
		£3,311,000,000
Capital invested in manufactures and commerce, manufactures and internal trade in manufactured goods...........	178,500,000	
Commerce in colonial goods.......	11,000,000	
Commerce in manufactured goods, with foreign countries..	16,500,000	
To which may be added for increase since 1836, when this estimate was made........ ...	12,000,000	
		218,000,000
Town buildings of every kind, and buildings for manufactures........	605,000,000	
Ships.............	33,500,000	
Bridges, canals, railroads...........	118,000,000	
Horses, other than those for agriculture......	20,000,000	
		776,500,000
Total of the national capital, deducting what is invested in the colonies, foreign loans, and the public debt of England		£4,305,500,000

2. GROSS NATIONAL INCOME.

Agriculture, mines, and fisheries...	£539,000,000
Manufacturing industry..........	259,500,000
Total	£798,500,000

"From this table it results—

"1st. That the value of the soil devoted to agriculture, comprehends twenty-six forty-thirds of the total wealth of England, and is nearly twelve times greater than that of the whole capital invested in manufactures and commerce.

"2d. That the sum employed in agriculture comprehends more than three fourths of the capital of England.

"3d. That the whole value of fixed property in England, viz., lands, etc., is........ ....£2,604,000,000

Towns, buildings, and manufactories...............	605,000,000
Canals and railroads......	118,000,000
Total.............	£3,327,000,000

composing more than three quarters of that capital.

"4th. That the manufacturing and commercial capital, including ships, does not exceed £241,500,000, and constitutes, therefore, about one eighteenth of the national wealth.

"5th. That the agricultural capital of England, which is £3,311,000,000, produces a gross income of £539,000,000, that is, about thirteen per cent., while the manufacturing and trading capital, which is but £218,000,000, yields a yearly gross product of £259,500,000, or one hundred and twenty per cent. It must not be overlooked here above all, that £218,000,000 of manufacturing capital, yielding a yearly income of £259,500,000, is the main cause which swells the agricultural capital to the enormous sum of £3,311,000,000, with its yearly product of £539,000,000. By far the greater portion of agricultural capital consists in the value of the land and cattle.

"By doubling and tripling the population of the country, by sustaining an immense external commerce, by furnishing a vast quantity of shipping, by acquiring and employing a multitude of colonies, manufacturers have increased in the same proportion the demand for food and raw material; they have created in cultivators the desire, and furnished the means of indulging to that increased extent; they have raised the exchangeable value of agricultural products, and thus determined a proportional increase in quantity and exchangeable value of the rent of land, and of the value of the soil. Destroy that manufacturing and commercial capital of £218,000,000, and not only the income of £259,000,000 would disappear, but also far the greater part of the £3,311,000,000 of agricultural capital, and, consequently, of the income of £539,000,000 derived from that capital. The income of England will be diminished not merely £259,500,000, the value of the manufacturing production, but the exchangeable value of the soil will fall to the rate it bears in Poland, that is, to the tenth or to the twentieth of its present value.

" Hence, it follows that the capital usefully employed in manufactures by an agricultural nation increases in time the value of the soil ten fold. . . . . . .

" By his continental system, Napoleon wished to organize a coalition against the maritime and commercial preponderance of England. To succeed in this, he ought to have first secured the continental nations against the fear of being conquered by France. He failed, because among those nations the fear of his continental preponderance far exceeded the disadvantages of English maritime supremacy. With the fall of the empire the great alliance ceased to have an object. . . . . Since that time the continental powers have neither been threatened by revolutionary tendencies nor by the conquests of France. On the other hand, the superiority of England in manufactures, shipping trade, colonies, and naval power, increased immensely during the struggle against revolution and conquest. *From that time it became the interest of the continental powers to unite with France against that commercial and maritime supremacy.* . . . . The commodities of the torrid zone being chiefly purchased with the products of temperate climes, *the consumption of the former depend-*

ing on the market for the latter, and every *manufacturing* nation being interested, consequently, to open and prosecute its own trade with tropical countries, if the manufacturing nations of the second rank should ascertain their own interests and prosecute them earnestly, the monopoly of the colonial or tropical trade will cease to exist."

After speaking of the British monopoly in India, he proceeds :

" Wherever the decaying civilization of Asia begins to be touched by the fresh winds of Europe, it falls into dust ; and Europe will, soon or late, be under the necessity of taking all Asia under guardianship, as England has already done with the East Indies. In all this poll-mell of territories and populations there is not a single nationality worthy of being regenerated or capable of any prolonged duration. The complete dissolution of Asiatic nations seems, therefore, unavoidable, and the regeneration of Asia seems possible only *by means of an infusion of European life by the gradual introduction of Christianity, of our manners, and our culture, by European emigration and the guardianship of European governments.*

" Reflecting on the course which this regeneration may take, we are favorably struck at once by the fact that the greatest part of the East is abundantly supplied with natural wealth ; that it is capable of producing for the *manufacturing nations of Europe* large quantities of the raw material and food, especially commodities of the torrid zone ; thus opening an immense market for the products of their manufactories. . . . . European nations should, therefore, begin by admitting the principle, that no one of them should retain any exclusive commercial privileges in any part of Asia —that no one should be favored to the exclusion of others.

" All the continental powers have a common and powerful motive to prevent the two routes, the Mediterranean by the Red sea, and that by the Persian gulf, from becoming the exclusive possession of England ; or their remaining inaccessible in the hands of Asiatic barbarism. *It is ob-*

rious that the solution offering the safest guarantee to Europe would be in making Austria the guardian of these important points.

"The idea of a continental system will never be given up. The necessity of the realization will be the more felt by the continental nations as England's industry, wealth, and power, increase. This is evident in our day, and will become more so as time progresses. But it is not less certain that no continental alliance can be successful until France shall be willing to avoid Napoleon's errors. It may undoubtedly be painful to the English, greedy of supremacy, to see the continental nations developing, by mutual commercial facilities, their manufacturing industry, strengthening their merchant marine and their naval power, seeking participation everywhere, in the culture and colonization of barbarism and uncultivated countries; enjoying full commerce with the torrid zone, and thus reaping their rightful portion of the advantages which nature has bestowed on them, but a glance at the future may console them for their supposed losses, and the good fortune of their rivals—*the very same causes indeed to which England owes her present elevation will raise America, probably in the course of the next century, to a degree of industry, wealth, and power, which will place her as far above England as England is now above Holland.* By the force of events the United States will in the meanwhile have attained to a population of a hundred millions. They will extend their population, their constitution, their culture, and their spirit, over all Central and South America, as they have already extended them over the border provinces of Mexico. The federal bond will unite all those immense countries; a population of several hundred millions of souls will develop the power and resources of a continent, the extent and the natural wealth of which will vastly exceed those of Europe; and the maritime power of the western world will then exceed that of Great Britain in the same proportion as its seacoast and its rivers surpass the seacoast and the rivers in size and grandeur."

"At no very distant period, then, the same necessity which now urges the French and the Germans to establish a continental alliance against British supremacy, will make it necessary for the English to organize a European coalition against the supremacy of America. Great Britain will then seek and find in the control of the united European powers, her security against the preponderance of America, and an indemnity for her lost supremacy. England will act wisely if she accustoms herself in good time to the idea of resigning her supremacy; and if she secures by timely concessions the friendship of the European powers, among whom she must soon be content to hold the place of first among equals."

NAPOLEON AND MEXICO.

With these extracts before us, and in explanation of the occupation of Mexico by France, the letter of the Emperor Napoleon to General Forey is given. The date is important.

"FONTAINEBLEAU, *July* 3, 1862.

"MY DEAR GENERAL: At the moment when you are on the point of setting out for Mexico, charged with the political and military powers, I think it useful to let you know my ideas. This is the line of conduct you will have to follow:

"1. To issue, on your arrival, a proclamation, the principal points of which will be indicated to you.

"2. To welcome with the utmost cordiality all Mexicans who offer themselves to you.

"3. To side with the quarrels of no party, to declare that everything is provisional so long as the Mexican nation has not pronounced itself, and to show great deference for religion, but to reassure at the same time the holders of national property.

"4. To feed, pay, and arm, according to your means, the auxiliary Mexican troops, and to make them play a principal part in the battles.

"5. To maintain among your troops, and among the auxiliaries, the severest discipline; to vigorously repress any act or word insulting to the Mexicans, for you must not forget their proud nature; and to secure the success of the undertaking, the disposition of the people must be conciliated above all things.

"When you shall have reached the city of Mexico, it would be desirable for the principal persons of all parties who have embraced our cause, to come to an understanding with you, with the view of organizing a provisional government. That government will submit to the Mexican people the question of the political system to be definitively established. An assembly will be afterwards elected in accordance with Mexican law. You will assist the new powers in introducing into the administration, and especially into the finances, that regularity of which France affords the best example. With this view persons capable of assisting its new organization will be sent out.

"The object to be attained is not to impose upon the Mexicans a form of government which they dislike, but to aid them in their endeavors to establish according to their inclinations, a government which may have some chance of stability, and which can secure to France the redress of the grievances of which she has had to complain. It is obvious, that if they prefer a monarchy it is to the interest of France to support them in that view.

"*There will not be wanting people who will ask you why we go to lavish men and money to found a regular government for Mexico.*

"*In the present state of the civilization of the world the prosperity of America is not a matter of indifference to Europe, for it is she who feeds our manufactories and gives life to our commerce. We have an interest in the republic of the United States being powerful and prosperous, but not that she should take possession of the whole Gulf of Mexico, and be the sole disburser of the products of the New World. We now see by sad experience, how precarious is the fate of an industry, which is reduced to seeking its chief raw material in a single market, to all the vicissitudes to which it has to submit.*

"If, on the other hand, Mexico maintains her independence and the integrity of her territory; if a stable government be there

constituted with the assistance of France, we shall have restored the Latin race, on the other side of the Atlantic in all its strength and prestige; we shall have guaranteed security to our West India colonies, and to those of Spain; we shall have established our beneficent influence in the centre of America; and that influence by presenting immense openings for our commerce, *will produce us the raw materials indispensable to our industry.* Mexico, thus regenerated, will always be well disposed towards us, not only from gratitude, but also because her interests will be in harmony with ours; and because she will find a powerful support in her friendly relations with the European powers.

"At present, therefore, our military honor engaged, *the necessities of our policy, the interests of our industry and commerce, all combine to make it our duty to march upon Mexico, to boldly plant our flag there, and to establish either a monarchy, if not incompatible with the national feeling, or at all events a government which may promise some stability.*

"NAPOLEON."

RESISTANCE TO THE EUROPEAN COALITION.

These extracts prove that the same "unsatiable rapacity of monopoly," which induced the British Parliament to compel the colonists to sell their surplus products in the British market, and also to buy whatever they might purchase of foreign articles "exclusively from the merchants and manufacturers of England," constitutes now as it did in the days of Lord Chatham and Lord Sheffield, the ruling policy, not only of the "merchants and politicians" of England, but of Germany, as indicated by the extracts from List, and of France as indicated by the letter from Napoleon to General Forey; and the latter, with the contemporaneous history of events, proves that the purpose of organizing "a European coalition against the supremacy of America," as recommended by List, under the guardianship of France and Germany combined, had become a leading feature of European policy. That this "*coalition*" had been precipitated by the late unhappy conflict between the North and the South, no intelligent observer of passing events can question. Our ability to resist that "coalition" depends upon our UNION—upon bringing the united resources and the united energies of the whole united American people to the support of American principles and of American interests, whenever any one or all of those interests are or may be assailed by any one, or all of the several combinations which it is the declared purpose of the "European coalition" to array against us; whether that combination be made under the leadership of England, of France, or of Germany; or whether it be the creature of the power and influence of all combined.

Before proceeding to speak more fully of the necessity and of the manner of preparing to resist the European combination against the supremacy of the United States, a few short

EXTRACTS FROM FRAZIER'S MAGAZINE,

For 1841, will show the animus which stimulated the zeal of the British abolitionists. In an article headed "WAR WITH AMERICA A BLESSING TO MANKIND," Frazier said:

"The United States are England's only rival on the seas. . . . . France is burning for an opportunity of striking a blow at her ancient enemy. . . . . . Russia is fomenting mischief in the East; and the very moment that sees England fully occupied in other directions will see a Russian force on its way to Northern India. . . . . . On all these points, then, and on others which might be added, we should look on our entanglement with America, as the too probable commencement of our national humili-ation, dismemberment, and ruin. . . . . . But America has three millions of slaves, and these slaves are America's foemen; this is the sin and the weakness of America. What possible doubt can exist as to the propriety, the expediency, nay the absolute duty of making a war subservient to the great and permanent object of freeing these three millions of cruelly oppressed human beings? *Policy*, too, not less than philanthropy, prescribes such a course of warfare. By this mode, and this only, a war with America may be brought to a speedy and inevitably a triumphant close. As we have already observed, a struggle between the people of England and their descendants in America must be a fearful, a protracted, and a lamentable one. But if assailed in this quarter, a vital part is instantly and surely reached. *The Union is dissolved and the war is at an end.* . . . . In one morning, a force of ten thousand men could be raised in Jamaica for the enfranchisement of their brethren in America. Such a force, supported by two battalions of Englishmen and twenty thousand muskets, would establish themselves in Carolina, never to be removed. In three weeks from their appearance, the entire South will be in one conflagration. The chains of a million of men would be broken, and by what power could they ever again be riveted. We say that this course is dictated alike by *self-preservation* and by *philanthropy*."

COMMENT.

Blackwood's Magazine, for 1842, says that Bishop Butler, on one occasion, remarked, "I was considering whether, as individuals go mad, whole nations may not also go mad," and adds: "It will be seen that men may act *en masse* as much in contradiction to common sense, to common interest and experience, as if they were mistaking crowns of straw for crowns of jewels, and that millions of men may be as easily duped, chicaned, and plundered, as the simplest dreamer of waking dreams who takes counters for guineas and canvas for cloth of gold." Now why did Frazier say that the emancipation of American slaves, by means of a servile war on America, was, to England, dictated "*alike by self-preservation and* by philanthropy?" He himself gave the answer. He said: "*The United States are England's only* RIVAL *on the seas.*" And hence a servile war and the emancipation of American slaves was dictated to England as a measure of "*self-preservation,*" as well as of "*philanthropy.*" But why of philanthropy? Why incite a servile war to emancipate American slaves, when England herself held many millions more in India in a more abject and oppressive slavery? The answer is, the maintenance of English slavery in India was indispensable to the "future prosperity," and to the maritime and commercial supremacy of England, and the emancipation of American slaves, was a part of the system of measures, indispensable to prevent "the successful rivalry of America," from placing England "second in the rank of nations."

HOW DID ENGLAND BECOME THE FIRST IN THE RANK OF NATIONS?

How did she acquire her maritime, commercial, and financial supremacy? How is she enabled to produce so great a surplus of manufactured goods? It is by the use of her improved machinery. And how did she obtain her machinery? It was by converting her public debt into capital, and using it to pay the wages of labor and purchase machinery. Of the fifty-six millions eight hundred thousand spindles in use, in Europe and America, in 1864, it is estimated that Great Britain had thirty-four millions. And in 1842, it was estimated that she had in her machinery a creative power equal to the labor of six hundred millions of men; and Ure says that one little girl can tend four hundred and eighty of these spindles, revolving at the rate of four thousand times per minute ! ! It was, therefore, with the product of her machinery, protected by her insular position and her command of the ocean, that she subsidized her allies and conquered and imprisoned the elder Napoleon. And it is the same "insatiable rapacity of monopoly" which induced her to unite with his nephew in the wars on Russia and China, to divide with him the commerce of Africa and Asia, and to unite with France and Germany in the organization of a "*European coalition against the supremacy of America.*"

That such a coalition was formed we have proof in the letter from Napoleon to the commander of his army in Mexico, in which he declares his purpose to be to establish a government in Mexico, which, being in "*harmony*" with France, and supported by the "European powers," will circumscribe our power and influence in the "New World."

WE MUST USE OUR CREDIT AS CURRENCY.

How are we to counteract this coalition? How are we to compete with this powerful combination? and what is the prize for which we are to contend? With the facts before us, the answer to these important questions are on the surface—we must *unite* our people, economize our expenditures, and increase our resources, by giving the greatest possible activity to our productive industry. England has made her public debt the basis of her currency, the support of her credit, and the source of her manufactures and her commerce. What is the Bank of England? Debt, nothing but British debt—(fourteen millions of pounds of three per cents.). And yet the notes of that bank are a legal tender in England. They purchase property and pay debts. They build railroads, create machinery, pay wages, construct ships, and sustain the commerce of England. They are *now* convertible, it is true, into gold, and a class of political economists argue that their value consists in the fact that they are so convertible. The bank suspended specie payments in 1797, and did not resume until 1825, and yet bank notes were at par with gold in 1800, and the subsequent depreciation was caused, it is well known, by the demand for specie to pay the expenditures of the war and the subsidies remitted to the continent—and yet during no period of her existence as a nation has the progress of the material prosperity of England been greater than it was during the suspension of the bank. And we may refer to a parallel fact in the great development of the industrial prosperity of Scotland, whose system of banks, resting chiefly on the national credit and the products of the industry created by the use of bank credits, dispenses almost entirely with the use of specie.

CHAPTER XII.

FINANCIAL.

IT is proper that at this point we should pause and inquire, what have been the motives which have regulated the measures and policy of the bank of England? And what has been the effect of the financial management of that bank? It originated in a loan, at eight per cent., of six millions of dollars to the government, and became the agent for the collection and disbursement of the public revenue. Besides the eight per cent. as interest on the sum advanced, the bank received twenty thousand dollars per annum as the expense of management.

The capital is now seventy-two millions seven hundred and sixty-five thousand dollars, all of which is lent to the government at a rate of about three per cent. per annum, and yet it pays a dividend of seven per cent.! Its notes are a legal tender, except at its own counter, and it is the only company which can issue notes or accept bills of exchange in London, or within sixty-five miles of it. It receives the public revenues, and holds the deposits of the various public offices—being not less than twenty millions of dollars. For discharging these duties and registering transfers, and paying the dividends on the public debt, it now receives six hundred and forty thousand dollars. It is a close corporation, managed by twenty-four directors, *who furnish no accounts* to the proprietors. Eight go out every year and eight come in. When the period of election draws near, the directors make out what is termed a house list, giving the names of those whom they wish to have as colleagues, and this list is uniformly elected. *This body is absolute in the extreme, and perfectly free to act as it sees fit under all circumstances. It is led by no authority and restrained by no responsibility.*

The following table, carefully prepared from official data, shows the amount of exchequer bills and public deposits, the bank notes in circulation, the commercial bills discounted, and the actual taxation, from 1808 to 1831 inclusive:

	Exchequer Bills.	Public Deposits.	Circulation.	Bills Discounted.	Actual Taxation.
1808..	$74,781,970	$53,807,240	$85,556,450	$64,750,500	$310,733,605
1809..	76,538,865	55,468,240	97,870,900	77,377,500	319,399,410
1810..	85,983,385	59,750,233	123,969,950	100,353,000	339,126,985
1811..	109,421,240	50,959,270	116,534,250	71,777,000	326,355,560
1812..	105,825,950	51,950,650	115,134,400	71,458,000	323,769,625
1813..	127,956,800	51,967,020	124,140,600	61,651,000	341,514,360
1814..	174,912,425	60,791,135	141,141,450	66,429,000	351,201,765
1815..	130,970,430	58,637,180	136,243,350	74,735,500	355,015,710
1816..	130,487,155	54,038,300	133,793,600	57,082,000	313,203,355
1817..	135,491,190	43,495,655	147,718,900	19,803,000	260,678,745
1818..	136,285,060	35,334,435	131,010,750	21,826,000	269,836,090
1819..	127,095,740	22,684,865	126,263,420	32,575,000	256,455,510

	Exchequer Bills.	Public Deposits.	Circulation.	Bills Discounted.	Actual Taxation.
1820..	95,869,985	18,567,210	121,496,700	19,418,000	275,319,465
1821..	78,864,765	19,600,785	111,476,500	13,383,500	277,650,365
1822..	68,344,795	20,539,265	87,323,950	16,833,500	226,278,072
1823..	59,313,385	27,633,175	96,156,200	15,619,000	272,234,845
1824..	73,245,935	36,110,835	100,660,600	19,849,000	277,282,375
1825..	87,672,830	20,786,570	96,994,200	24,607,500	268,857,500
1826..	87,569,405	21,071,355	107,817,800	24,541,500	156,574,650
1827..	99,048,975	21,119,335	213,788,000	6,222,000	256,558,585
1828..	103,413,880	19,108,485	106,787,550	5,317,000	263,715,950
1829..	100,362,200	19,313,280	97,786,900	11,253,500	251,188,915
1830..	104,558,080	23,809,760	107,223,500	4,599,500	253,541,925
1831..	92,282,760	19,700,510	92,633,150	7,668,000	233,097,870
	$2,451,493,265	$877,252,000	$2,720,183,100	$881,449,500	$7,330,022,260

COMMENT.

The first thing deserving notice in this table, is the fluctuation in the amount of bills discounted—varying from $100,353,000 to $4,599,500, and to the fact, that at the time of this severe contraction of the loans and discounts, the bank held $104,558,080 in exchequer bills, and $23,809,760 in public deposits! The bank is the agent for the collection, and is the depository of the public revenue. It will be seen that the exchequer bills and public deposits are more than the whole amount of notes in circulation, and nearly four times the sum of the commercial bills discounted. It is obvious, therefore, that a large, a very large, part of the circulation had been used in advances on exchequer bills, and that the advances thus made were repaid through the revenue! It is also apparent that the chief value of the bank note consisted in the fact that it was receivable as a legal tender in payment of taxes. Now why should the government pay interest on the $2,451,493,265 of exchequer bills, at the same time that the bank was owing the government $7,330,022,260 on its notes received in payment of taxes? It is obvious that the $2,720,183,100 in bank notes were used as the basis on which $881,449,500 of commercial bills were discounted, and that the $7,330,022,260 of taxes were levied and collected in bank notes. Why should the merchants and people of England pay interest, to the bank, on this $2,720,183,100 of bank notes, when the government, by the issue of a like sum in "greenbacks," receivable in payment of the $7,330,022,260 of taxes, could have given to the people of England a better currency—more stable in value, because, not being money elsewhere, it would not, like gold, be subject to the foreign demand? Is it not apparent, that if, instead of borrowing the credit of the bank, the government of England had issued its certificates, receivable in the payment of taxes, and fundable at a proper rate of interest, the value of the public credit would have been equal to the value of the notes of the bank of England? The table shows that the annual average of

THE EXCHEQUER BILLS HELD BY THE BANK,
Upon which government paid interest,
was...................$102,145,552
and the average public deposits, was......... 35,552,166
and the average sum of taxes, was........... 305,446,758
making a fund of........$444,144,476

placed by the government with the bank as its agent, and which sum was used by the bank as the basis of its issues. If the government had applied these resources to sustain its own credit, and that credit had been made a legal tender, instead of making the notes of the bank a tender, inasmuch as the public credit of England would not have been subject to the laws which regulate the export and import of specie, the quantity of public credit, in circulation, could have been regulated by Parliament, and the value of the currency would have been much more uniform and stable than it has been under the regulations of the bank. Is it not also apparent that, in that case, there would have been no such fluctuations in the quantity and values of money and of credit ; no such suspension of banks ; no such depreciation in the values of property and of labor ; and no such individual distress and bankruptcies as the management of that bank has caused, not only in England, but throughout the commercial world ?

WHY DID THE GOVERNMENT PAY INTEREST ON THE EXCHEQUER BILLS ?

Was it not because these bills, instead of being a tender, represented the unfunded debt, and the payment of interest was necessary to make them of equal value as bank notes, which were a tender ? If so, by making the public credit, issued as certificates, receivable in payment of taxes, a tender (that is, converting them into money), the payment of interest would no longer be requisite to maintain the value of so much as was requisite for use as money ? Is it not further apparent that such a use of the public credit would save the people and the government the whole of the interest on the sum used as currency ?

If we assume that the sum thus used would be no more than the annual taxes, as this average, as given in the table, was $305,446,758, the interest upon that sum, at three per cent. only, would be an annuity of $9,163,402 74, which, if compounded at three per cent., would create a sinking fund which would soon absorb the whole public debt of England ! This, however, is apart from the ruinous effect which the management of the bank has had, and will have, upon individual credit and upon the progress of individual industry and the general prosperity of the kingdom.

That England herself is not satisfied with that system appears in the fact stated by Hardcastle, in his treatise upon banks and bankers, that the bare titles of the acts of Parliament, passed upon the subject of the affairs of the bank, " occupy more than two hundred pages of the index of the statutes at large." Surely there must be some defect in a system which requires so much tinkering—and I, for one, am unwilling that the tinkers who have so botched their own system shall be permitted to regulate ours. And that is the very danger which threatens us.

Let me be distinctly understood. I do not complain of or censure the bank as a bank. It is not the bank, but the system as regulated by Parliament, and those who manage the bank under that system, which I believe rests upon

THREE FUNDAMENTAL ERRORS.

1st. That the paper circulation should at no time exceed the value of the gold and silver of which it supplies the place.

2d. That the paper circulation should depend upon the quantity of the bullion in the bank, and be regulated by the foreign exchange.

3d. That whenever there is a foreign demand for gold, the bank, by refusing to discount commercial paper, and the sale of exchequer bills, shall diminish the quantity of bank paper in circulation, and so increase the demand for gold, as a means of payment, as to render gold of more value in England than it may be in the country to which it may have gone, and thus coerce its reflux to the bank.

These, we believe, are fundamental principles in the management of the bank, and we believe them to be fundamental errors, as the history of the bank and of the world, so far as the world has been under the influence of the bank, demonstrates. This error is the more striking, when we take into consideration the causes which induce the export of gold. In case of wars, gold may be in greater demand elsewhere, and being at a premium, will be sent abroad. In case of foreign loans, a premium will be given which will cause it to be exported. In case of bad harvests, foreign wheat must be paid for in gold. In all such cases the bank refuses to renew discounts. If this does not produce a sufficient pressure, then she goes into the market, sells exchequer bills in exchange for bank notes, and thus renders the demand for gold so severe as to compel the reflux. That some idea may be formed of

THE EFFECT OF THIS TURNING OF THE BANK
SCREW,

I quote from Hardcastle. He says: "Our banking system is bad in the extreme; it has been everything by turns, but what it ought to be, and nothing long. It is not only bad itself, but it communicates evil to everything around it. It is an epidemic that arrests and affects all classes; a plague that corrupts and kills high and low, poor and affluent, without distinction—

a thousand incidents have taken place in this city, within a year [London in 1842] which exhibit our monetary affairs in a most deplorable condition. . . . . I have seen, last spring, a bill broker go from house to house of an afternoon, with the bills of a country bank, accepted by first-rate firms in Lombard street, and cash could not be got for them at five per cent. interest and one and a half per cent. commission. I have known, about the same time, a man with ten thousand pounds in exchequer bills, unable to raise four thousand pounds upon them at his banker's, and that bank one of the best in Lombard street. I have known a city banker, at the beginning of last year, confess, in a mixed company, that he would be glad to allow ten per cent. for money for six months to come. At the same time, I have known another banker in Lombard street pay eight per cent. for an advance of money on exchequer bills; and ten per cent. to be charged on the discount of a bill of exchange, the acceptor of which was then and still is, a bank director. These are facts that tell the true story of our banking system—these are realities that prove our distress. . . . . While they last, credit is prostrate, labor fails of its market, and property almost ceases to be wealth. . . . . Our currency has resembled the shifting sands that impede the navigation of some of our most capacious harbors, and defy the skill of the most experienced mariners. We have been dealing with a series of experiments, and each succeeding writer has distinguished himself by showing where and how it was that the last experiment had proved a particular failure . . . . . . The bank of England had the complete control and absolute management of the finances of the whole country, and the losses which the country has now for fifty years or so, sustained by repeated abuses of that currency in the hands of the bank, have been incalculable; so wild and extravagant have been the alternate expansions and contractions; so suddenly and capriciously, have the value of money and prices been jerked up and tossed down, that it is not unreasonable to compare the bank directors to a set of awkward showmen at a fair, with the trading interests of the nation in a great ill-conceived swing-swong, which at one moment they fling up high in the sky, and at another bring down so low as to drag the ground and rake the gutters with it. . . . . The habit of tampering with the currency was contracted by these gentlemen at an early period. We can trace it distinctly as far back as 1782, and find it persevered in up to 1839, invariably with the same pernicious results. . . . . . A heavy panic, fraught with great commercial distress, ran through the years 1783 and 1784, which has been brought home to the bank by more than one conclusive witness.

. . . . . In 1814, the Dutch ports were opened, the harvest was deficient; and that most searching of the calamities, to which our artificial condition is exposed no sooner visited the land, than the importation of foreign corn occasioned a great decline in the price of this principal article of agricultural produce, which gradually extended to the prices of commodities generally. Unprecedented suffering now took place; the storm swept the country through, and raged with increasing violence until 1819, by which time the agricultural and banking interests, generally were reduced to the lowest pitch of distress. Farmers were insolvent everywhere; mercantile firms became bankrupt by thousands and levelled their connections indiscriminately in the dust; while as to the bankers, between those who either partially suspended business or wholly broke, in the year 1815 or 1816, there was a diminution of no less than two hundred and forty firms. . . . . . In noticing the moving causes of the calamities of 1816, we should bear in mind that the cessation of hostilities on the continent was an established condition of the long-promised resumption of cash payments. Much of the panic then existing is referable to a proposal for carrying that measure into effect, in 1818."

The bank made some preparations for the change by a partial contraction of its issues. But the depression of all the leading interests of the country was too intense, and the notion was quickly abandoned.

He quotes Mr. Atwood, in 1818, as saying:

"In the midst of this fall of prices, what operation in business could proceed without loss or ruin? There has been no form in which the capital of the merchant, none in which the capital of the manufacturer, could be invested without the half of it being sacrificed during this calamitous period. We have been thrown back upon a condition of events in which all industry and enterprise have been rendered pernicious or ruinous, and where no property has been safe, unless hoarded in the shape of money, or lent to others on double security."

He quotes further from Mr. Atwood's evidence before a committee:

"The reward of labor being destroyed, the laborers, who can each produce four times as much of the comforts of life as they and their families could possibly consume, are starving while superabundance reigns around them. They find no employment, because the organ of industry, which is money, does not exist in sufficient quantities to give the productive classes a reward for their exertions. The peasant idly wanders about, and looks over the hedge of the uncultivated farm, where the land is suffering for want of his labor, but at the same time the farmer has neither the profit nor the labor to bring the land into cultivation."

Speaking of the crisis in 1836, Hardcastle says:

"Of the bankruptcies that then took place, and of the extreme depression of our manufactures and commerce, it would be impossible to give any exact account. Prices fell forty per cent. In the manufacturing districts there was no employment for the workmen; merchants stopped payment in numbers, not because they were insolvent, and had no property, but because no market was to be had for their goods, no discount for their bills, no advance upon their stocks. It was a rare and melancholy sight to behold English merchants going through the Gazette in numbers, while their warehouses were full of commodities.

and their characters unimpeached for knowledge of business, integrity, and exemplary conduct; yet such were the incidents that characterized the panic of 1836.

. . . . "There was another panic in 1839, which may be said to have extended itself by a series of fits and convulsions all through the years 1840 and 1841, at which date our commercial system was reduced to the lowest ebb of distress. The number of banks which stopped or disappeared during this interval was unusually great, the difficulty of getting money as rigid as ever, and the stagnation of our commerce, the scarcity of good mercantile paper, extreme. . . . . Late in 1840 began the storm which continuing to rage all through 1841, and not even as yet [in 1842] blown over, has swept away, during its protracted and ruinous course, an unusual number of banking establishments. A history of these misfortunes, in their various details, is here out of the question; to trace the separate cases to their source, and detail at length their consequences, would fill a volume, and then, in all probability, leave the subject unexhausted. I had prepared a summary of the losses occasioned by the different failures among the private and joint-stock banks during the last two years, but the amount appears so formidably large on the one side and so small on the other, that it would be invidious to publish it."

The cause of these disasters is explained by the eminent banker, Jones Loyd, who, speaking of the crisis of 1840, said:

"Against the actual exhaustion of its treasure by a drain through the foreign exchanges, the bank, under almost any circumstances, has the power of protecting herself; but to do this she must produce upon the money market a pressure ruinous from its suddenness and severity; she must save herself by the destruction of all around her."

FOREIGN LOANS.

I have said that, among other causes, the creation of foreign loans in England will cause a demand for bullion for export, and, consequently, cause fluctuations in the quantity and value of money, and, in proof of this, I refer to the Edinburgh Review, of 1826, which gives a table showing in detail the sums advanced by England on loans to Prussia, Spain, Naples, Denmark, Colombia, Chili, Poyais, Peru, Portugal, Austria, Greece, Buenos Ayres, Brazil, Mexico, Guatemala, Guadalaxara, which, with other advances on French, Russian, and American securities, made the sum $522,692,500 advanced by England, on foreign account, during the eight years, from 1818 to 1825 inclusive. It is apparent that the advances made upon these loans must have created an extraordinary demand for specie in England, and it is obvious that, as the loss of five and a half millions of dollars, in 1857, by the banks of New York, created results so disastrous, as described by Gibbon, the export of so large an amount to pay off the foreign loans, produced the overwhelming losses, bankruptcies and distress, so forcibly referred to by Hardcastle and the Edinburgh and London Quarterly Reviews, and that that monetary crisis was caused by the fact that the currency of England was convertible into specie, and that the demand for specie thus produced, compelled the bank, to use the words of Jones Loyd, quoted above, to "save herself by the destruction of all around her."

CHAPTER XIII.

FINANCIAL.

I GIVE the following from the London Quarterly, of September, 1832, illustrating the effect of

CHANGING A PAPER INTO A METALLIC CURRENCY.

" As a single specimen of the condition of our internal trade, we give the memorial of the iron and coal masters of Shropshire, Staffordshire, and Wales, presented to Earl Grey by a deputation in October last, after being signed by more than three fourths of the trade in those great manufacturing districts :

" ' We, the undersigned, iron masters and coal masters of the Staffordshire iron and coal districts, think it our duty respectfully to represent to His Majesty's government the following facts :

" ' 1. That, for the last five years, ever since what is called the panic of 1825, we have found, with very slight intermissions, a continually increasing depression in the prices of the products of industry, and more particularly in those of pig and bar iron, which have fallen respectively from upward of eight pounds per ton to under three pounds per ton, and from fifteen pounds per ton to under five pounds per ton.

" ' 2. Against this alarming and long-continued depression, we have used every possible effort in our power to make bread. We have practised all manner of economy, and have had recourse to every possible improvement in the working of our mines and manufactories. Our workmen's wages have in many instances been reduced, and such reduction has been attended with, and effected by, very great distress ; but the royalties, rents, contracts, and other engagements, under which we hold our respective works and mines, have scarcely been reduced at all, nor can we get them effectually reduced, because the law enforces the payment in full.

" ' 3. The prices of the products of our industry having thus fallen within the range of the fixed charges and expenses which the law compels us to discharge, the just and necessary profits of our respective trades have ceased to exist, and in many cases a positive loss attends them.

" ' 4. Under these circumstances, we have long hesitated in determining what line of conduct our interest and our duties require us to adopt. If we should abandon our respective trades, our large and expensive outlays in machinery and erections must be sacrificed at an enormous loss to ourselves, and our honest and meritorious workmen must be thrown, in thousands, upon parishes already too much impoverished by their present burdens to support them ; and, if we should continue our present trades, we see nothing but the prospect of increasing distress and certain ruin all around us.

" ' 5. In our humble opinion, the great cause which has been mainly instrumental in producing this depression and distress in our respective trades, and among the productive classes of the country generally, is the attempt to render the rents, *taxes*, royalties, and other various engagements and obligations of the country, convertible, by law, into gold, at three pounds thirteen shillings and ten and a half pence per ounce. This low and antiquated price of the metallic standard of value is no longer capable of effecting a just and equitable distribution of our products between the producer and the consumer ; it renders incompatible the permanent existence of remunerating prices, without such a reduction of taxation as we cannot hope to see effected in time to afford us any relief—and it thus tends, ultimately and surely, to destroy the industry, and the peace and happiness of the country.

"'6. That, until the establishment of a circulating medium of a character better suited to the various and complicated demands of society, and to the increased transactions and population of the country, and more competent to effect an interchange, and preserve a remunerating level of prices in the products of industry generally, we can see no prospect of any permanent restoration of the prosperity of our trades, or of the country being able to escape the most frightful sufferings and convulsions.

"' We, therefore, most respectfully, but very earnestly, request the early attention of His Majesty's government to these great facts and considerations, and we insist that they will recommend to Parliament the speedy establishment of some *just, adequate* and *efficient currency,* which may properly support the trade and commerce of the country, and preserve such a remunerating level of prices as may insure to the employers of labor the fair and reasonable profits of their capital and industry, as well as the means of paying the just and necessary wages to their workmen.' "

Such are the views of practical working men in England of the operation of contracting a debt in paper money at the rate of one hundred and fifty dollars for one hundred, and paying the interest of three per cent. on it in specie. If such was the effect there, what will be the effect here of paying the interest, in specie, on so large a debt as we have contracted, at the rate of two for one?

THE LONDON QUARTERLY SAYS:

"Our country gentlemen must learn to penetrate the arcana of the *exchanges,* and fathom the depths of the banking system, if they mean to preserve their broad acres from the grasp of the mortgagee, and their title deeds and mansions from the blaze of revolutionary fires. Difficult and obscure, indeed! Yes, the subject is difficult, just as difficult to the public comprehension as is a juggler's trick, by which, with a 'heigh, presto!' he conjures the half-crown we thought we had safe in our pocket into his own. How the money vanished it is not so easy to say; but it is nevertheless certain that we had it, and ought still to have it, but he has got it. So it was exactly with the currency juggle. Few of the sufferers can explain or understand how it happened, but the fact is very plain to them that they have somehow lost a great deal of money, and other persons have got hold of it. A little consideration, however, may, we think, render the nature of the trick intelligible to the simplest. It is very clear that those who are in business *pay nearly the same sum in taxes,* at present, as when the goods they deal in sold for double their present prices; so that they really pay two hundred weight of wool, or of cheese, or of sugar, or two pieces of cloth, linen, or calico, or two tons of iron or hardware, to the tax-gatherer, for one that they formerly paid; and the taxes, *reckoned in goods,* the only sure way of knowing their cost to the producers of goods, by whom they are paid, are clearly twice as high at the end of sixteen years of peace, as they were at the close of a long war! Is it wonderful, then, that the productive classes are laboring under severe distress? That Peace, who usually brings plenty, has thrown away her emblematic horn, and selected hunger for her motto? And can there be any doubt that the fall in prices, which has wrought this fearful evil, is the necessary result, foretold by ourselves and many others at the time, of the legislation of 1819 and 1826, which, by crippling the banking system of England and attempting a currency of *dear metal* for one of *cheap paper,* has caused a continually increasing scarcity of money and contraction of credit? . . . . . .

"If we succeed in showing that the unjust restrictions, kept up by the present laws, on the circulating medium of exchange, have had the effect, within a few years past, of silently but forcibly transferring a vast amount of property from the possession of one class to that of another, who had no just right or title to it—of covertly despoiling, in short, one portion of the community, namely: the persons engaged in industry, for the benefit of another portion, the owners of fixed money obligations, payable out of the labor and capital of the former—it will be acknowledged that, until the laws which have perpetuated and continue to sanction this wholesale swindling are repealed, there is is no safety for property; nor can there be any reliance on the stability of those institutions, of which a confidence in the security of property is the indispensable foundation."

Remarking upon the Staffordshire memorial, the Review says :

"The sufferers here most correctly attribute their losses to the late increase in the value of money, but they seem to look for relief in a deterioration of the standard. In this view we do not concur with them, only because we think so desperate a remedy is not necessary, for that other and unexceptional plans may be resorted to for the relief of industry. . . . . Next to a direct increase of the supply of the precious metals, the most obvious resource seems to be to augment the efficiency of that which we possess, by a degradation of the standard—in other words, by diminishing the intrinsic value of the coinage ; cutting, for instance, our sovereigns, shillings, and other pieces of money, into two or more parts, which should each, by law, retain the nominal value of the whole. This is, in substance, the proposal which seems to find most favor with the persons who have spoken or written on the subject of the currency for some years past. It is this, as we have seen, that is advocated by the iron trade, and by their powerful champions, the Messrs. Atwood. It is this to which Mr. Weston, and a large body of agriculturists, have been long pointing as the only practicable mode of permitting them to come to an equitable adjustment with their creditors *public* and private. . . . . We acknowledge, indeed, the force of the retorts levelled by the advocates of this alteration against their opponents, when the

necessity of preserving the national faith inviolate is thrown in their teeth. They ask, with bitterness, and with justice too:

"'Is faith to be kept only with the moneyed interests ? Was no good faith to be kept with the landholder, the merchant, the manufacturer, the vast laboring population who bore the weight of the national struggle, who cheerfully made great and numerous sacrifices during the war, and who continue the real strength and greatness of the kingdom ? *No faith whatever was kept with them.* They, through their representatives, engaged themselves to a debt of so many pound *notes*—but not to the same number of sovereigns—to a debt consisting of money, *at its then value,* but they protest against being held responsible for the same annual sum now that its value has been artificially *doubled.* Does not good faith require that the scale should be held fairly between debtor and creditor ? Was it consistent with the national faith, upon the plea of arresting the progress of depreciation in 1819, to turn the tables wholly the other way, and, by reviving an obsolete standard, to give to moneyed obligations a value *that is a command over the produce and property of others,* which the persons originally forming those contracts could never have contemplated, and which consigned at once to overwhelming and unmerited ruin, the commerce, the manufactures, and agriculture of the empire ?'

"We freely admit the weight of these remonstrances. We acknowledge that, through an overstrained anxiety for observing the letter of the national faith, the spirit of the obligation was disregarded, and a gross injustice committed on the great body of producers throughout the kingdom, as well as on all debtors. It is true—

"'Nothing could be more honorable than the feeling which induced our statesmen to return to the ancient standard ; but, to our sorrow, their estimate of its effects was much below the mark. They did not see what a revolution of property would ensue. They consulted our honor, our reputed solvency, but not our real means. Mr. Ricardo told them the change would be five per cent. Events have proved it fifty. . . . . . There remains another course for consideration; one which we have urged for some time past upon the public, as the true mode of relief from our monetary difficulties. . . . . . We mean the removal of the mischievous restrictions which now fetter the circulation of credit through this country, and the concession of the free right of commerce to provide itself with whatever instruments it may require for effecting its exchanges uninterfered with by those officious legislative intermeddlings which experience has sufficiently proved to be fatal to almost everything they touch, but to nothing so much so as to the currency. It is physically impossible to carry on the commerce of the civilized world by the aid of a purely metallic currency—no, not though our gold and silver coins were every tenth year debased to a tenth! Why, in London alone, five millions sterling ($25,000,000) are daily exchanged at the clearing-house in the course of a few hours. We should like to see the attempt made to bring this infinity of transactions to a settlement in coined money. Credit money, i.1 some shape or other, always has, and must have, performed the part of a circulating medium to a very considerable extent. And (by one of those wonderful compensatory processes which so frequently claim the admiration of every investigation of civil as well as of physical economy) there is in the nature of credit an elasticity which causes it, when left unshackled by law, to adapt itself to the necessities of commerce and the legitimate demands of the market. . . . . . The only measures which appear to us to be needed upon the expiration of the bank charter, are: 1st. That all banks be required to deposit security in government stock to the full amount of the notes they issue. 2d. That the law be repealed which forbids the issue of notes under five pounds. 3d. We would make the notes of *metropolitan banks only* convertible into bars of bullion, on the plan of Mr. Ricardo, and allow the notes of country banks to be paid in those of the metropolitan banks.' "

CHAPTER XIV.

FINANCIAL.

THE following table, compiled from data, given by John Taylor, Jr., and Ayres' *Financial Register*, gives the amount of debt bonded, the equivalent in three per cent. consols, the stock created for one hundred pounds in money, the highest and the lowest prices for consols, and the market value of paper currency per cent., from 1800 to 1824 inclusive:

Years.	Amount of Debt Bonded.	Equivalent in 3 per cent. Bonds.	Stock created for £100 in Money.	The Highest Price.	The Lowest Price.	Market Value of Paper Currency per cent.
1800....	£20,500,000	£32,185,000	£158 50*d.*	67½	60	£100 00*s.* 2*d.*
1801....	36,910,000	63,578,100	174 54	70	54¼	91 12 6
1802....	25,000,000	32,990,630	132 17	79	66	91 14 2
1803....	12,000,000	20,483,330	173 55	75	50¼	97 6 10
1804....	14,500,000	26,390,000	185 00	56⅞	53¾	97 6 10
1805...	22,500,000	41,800,000	177 20	62	57	97 6 10
1806....	20,000,000	33,200,000	167 70	64⅝	58⅛	97 6 10
1807....	15,700,000	24,798,290	159 20	64⅜	57⅝	97 6 10
1808 .	14,500,000	23,530,622	102 67	69⅛	22⅝	97 6 10
1809.. .	22,532,100	35,218,740	161 39	70⅜	63⅜	97 6 10
1810....	21,711,000	33,112,106	152 67	71	63¼	97 6 10
1811..	24,000,000	39,724,620	166 53	66¾	61¾	86 10 6
1812	34,721,325	57,198,380	180 00	63	55⅛	93 3 2
1813..	64,755,700	118,736,690	184 87	67½	54½	79 5 8
1814...	24,007,400	36,839,930	154 17	72¼	61½	77 2 0
1815. .	54,135,589	102,787,340	191 52	65¾	57⅞	74 16 6
1816..	....	....	......	64⅝	59½	83 5 8
1817.. .	....	....	......	62	62	70 6 10
1818....	....	....	......	72	73	95 11 0
1819....	....	....	......	79	64⅞	97 8 0
1820....	....	....	......	70¼	65¾	106 0 0
1821....	....	....	......	78¾	68¾	100 0 0
1822....	....	....	......	83	75⅜	100 0 0
1823....	....	....	......	85¾	72	100 0 0
1824....	....	....	......	96⅞	83¾	100 0 0
Total...	£427,473,114	£723,570,672	......	....	....	....
Average.	....	....	£167 60	73	63	£93 15*s.* 1*d.*

It will be seen that, although the bank of England suspended payment in 1797, the notes were at par with gold in 1800, and again in 1820, and continued at par until it resumed payment in 1825, the average depreciation during the suspension being less than seven per cent. It is a striking fact that the greater part of this depreciation was during the years from 1810 to 1815 inclusive, when the loans and subsidies given to her allies,, and the expenditures of the French war, created an extraordinary demand for specie to be disbursed on the continent (these loans and subsidies amounting to the enormous sum of $301,047,813 !)

McCulloch, in a note, (p. 78), says :

"So early as December, 1794, the Court of Directors (of the bank) represented to government their uneasiness on account of the debt due by the government to the bank, and anxiously requested a repayment of at least a considerable part of what had been advanced. In January, 1795, they resolved to limit their advances upon treasury bills five hundred thousand pounds; and, at the same time, they informed Mr. Pitt that it was their wish that he would adjust his measures for the year, *in such a manner, as not to depend on any assistance from them.* On the 11th of February, 1796, they resolved, '*that it is the opinion of this court, founded upon the experience of the late Imperial loan, that if any further loan or advance of money to the Emperor, or to any of the foreign states, should, in the present state of affairs, take place, it will, in all probability, prove fatal to the Bank of England.*'"

COMPARATIVE VALUE OF MONEY.

If we recur to the value of money, as compared with the value of the mass of circulating commodities, it will be seen that this difference between the value of bank notes (paper money) and specie indicates an increased value of the precious metals rather than a decreased value of paper money.

By reference to the table given above, it will be seen that, in 1814, the public credit was depreciated nearly eighty-four per cent., and that the value of paper, as compared with gold, fluctuated between seventy-two and a half and sixty-one and a half per cent., and yet, the Edinburgh Review, speaking of the effect of the causes then operating on prices in England, says :

"The bank failures that then occurred were the more distressing, as they chiefly affected the industrious classes, and frequently swallowed up in an instant the fruits of a long life of unremitting and laborious exertion. Thousands upon thousands, who had, in 1813, considered themselves as affluent, found they were destitute of all real property, and sunk, as if by enchantment, and without any fault of their own, into the abyss of poverty! The late Mr. Horner, the accuracy and extent of whose information on such subjects will not be disputed, stated in his place in the House of Commons, that the destruction of the country bank paper, in 1815 and 1816, had given rise to a universality of wretchedness and misery, which had never been equalled, except, perhaps, by the breaking up of the Mississippi scheme in France."

BRITISH SUBSIDIES.

Engaged, as England was, in a struggle upon which, as she believed, depended her maritime and commercial supremacy, she was compelled to advance loans and subsidies to her allies, and hence we find that the bank was allowed to suspend specie payment in 1797, and that in the years 1814 and 1815, England advanced, in loans and subsidies, to Spain, Portugal, Sicily, Sweden, Russia, Prussia, Austria, *France*, Hanover, Denmark, and other minor powers of the continent, £19,366,307 15s. 9d. (or $96,-831,539), and it is, therefore, apparent, that inasmuch as the current expenditures of the British army on the continent, as well as these large loans and subsidies, were paid in specie, the demand for specie to meet these payments caused the relative depreciation of bank notes, the fall of prices, the destruction of the country banks, and the consequent failures, bankruptcies, and distress. Had England used her credit, as I propose, instead of using the bank credit, there would have been no such failures of her banks, and no such fall of prices or depreciation of the values of property. Is it not obvious that, inasmuch as the whole capital of the bank consisted of the public credit, the government, having the power of taxing and funding, could have purchased gold at the same price, or less, than that which the bank paid for it? Why, then, did the government give her credit bearing interest in exchange for bank notes bearing no interest?

As bank notes were not current on the continent the government could not pay the loans and subsidies to their allies in bank notes, and were, therefore, compelled to give a premium for gold; and hence the depreciation of bank notes as compared with gold.

PAPER MONEY.

McCulloch, in his article upon the general principles of banking, says:

" Every country has a certain number of exchanges to make; and whether these are effected by the employment of a given number of coins of a particular denomination, or by the employment of the same number of notes of the same denomination, is, in this respect, of no importance whatever. Notes which have been made a legal tender, and are not payable on demand, do not circulate because they are of the same real value as the commodities for which they are exchanged, but they circulate because having been selected to perform the functions of money, they are as such received by all individuals in payment of their debts. Notes of this description may be regarded as a sort of tickets or counters to be used in computing the value of property, and in transferring it from one individual to another. And as they are nowise affected by fluctuations of credit, their value, it is obvious, must depend entirely on the quantity of them in circulation as compared with the payments to be made through their instrumentality, or the business they have to per-

form. By reducing the supply of notes below the supply of coins that would circulate in their place were they withdrawn, *their value is raised above the value of gold;* while by increasing them to a greater extent it is proportionally lowered.

" Hence, supposing it were possible to obtain any security other than convertibility into the precious metals, that *notes declared to be a legal tender* would not be issued in excess, but that their number afloat would be so adjusted as to preserve their value as compared with gold nearly uniform, the obligation to pay them on demand might be done away. But it is needless to say that no such security can be obtained. Whenever the power to issue paper, not immediately convertible, has been conceded to *any set of persons* it has been abused, or, which is the same thing, such paper has been uniformly over issued or its value depreciated by excess."

EXCESS OF PAPER MONEY.

It will be seen that McCulloch's objection to an unconvertible paper is limited to the fact that whenever the power to issue such paper has been conceded *to any set of persons* they have uniformly issued it in excess. It is apparent that he refers to an issue of such paper by banks and bankers, and not to an issue by government under such a system of taxation and funding as would limit the sum in circulation to the sum wanted as money. I agree that an over-issue will depreciate the value of such a paper, and therefore I propose not that it shall be issued by the banks but by the government, and that the excess be funded, and that the funding shall be coerced by a judicious system of taxing. He adds:

" In 1793, 1814, 1815, 1816, and in 1825, a very large proportion of the country banks were destroyed, and produced by their fall an extent of ruin that has hardly been equalled in any other country. And when such disasters have already happened it is surely the bounden duty of government to hinder by every means in its power their recurrence."

BARS OF GOLD.

McCulloch was the partisan of the bank of England, and his remedy for the evils of which he complains was to strengthen that bank by making large bars of gold instead of the current coins a tender, and to prevent an issue of small notes by the country banks. He believed that the large dealers would not run upon the bank for specie, and that the holders of small notes were liable to become alarmed and demand payment. His remedy was suspension on small sums and masses of bullion for large. I would recur to the large sums remitted by the government to the continent, for the support of the armies and in the payment of subsidies, as the cause of the demand for gold in 1814, 1815, and in 1816, and I would explain the monetary crisis of 1825, by the fact that the foreign loans contracted, and the vast speculations entered into in England after the war, and before the resumption of specie payments created so great a demand for specie, to comply with the engagements then entered into, that the pressure upon the bank, and the contraction of the currency below the *specie level* produced, then the ruinous depreciation of the values of property as compared with gold. For, as before remarked, it is obvious that it was the increased value of gold, and not the decreased value of bank notes, which caused the disasters so forcibly described. If, instead of placing in the bank an annual average of exchequer bills of.......$102,145,552 and of deposits......... 36,552,166 and of public revenue... 305,446,344
———————
making of public resources $444,044,062

the government had issued its own credit, in a shape suitable for currency, *which was a legal tender*, and receivable in payment of the public dues, and fundable at a proper rate of interest and reconvertible into currency, and had required each bank to place in the treasury an amount of the reconvertible funded debt as a security for the payment of their notes, there would have been no such speculations in foreign loans ; no such depreciation of the value of credit or of property would have then occurred ; and consequently there would have been no such bankruptcies and distress.

PAPER MONEY PREFERABLE TO AN INCREASED ALLOY.

The power to coin money and regulate its value is vested in the British and French governments as in ours, and as the French *livre* of 1789 contains only the seventy-eighth part of the original *livre* of the year 800, and the English *pound unit* contains but a small fraction more than a fourth part of the original pound sterling, and the individual obligations, as well as the *public debt* of England, had been contracted when the currency was abundant and cheap, instead of urging the issue of the public credit as money regulated as proposed, an effort was made to reduce the value of the coinage by increasing the alloy or diminishing its weight, and the issue before the British public was the use of bank notes, or of a metallic coin thus depreciated, they preferred a bank note convertible into specie ; I would restore the value of our currency by making it convertible, not into specie, but into a four per cent. reconvertible bond : instead of depreciating the value of metallic coins by increasing the alloy or reducing the weight.

Few, I presume, will deny the power of Congress thus to depreciate the coins of gold or silver; and as in that case the depreciated dollar would still be a dollar, it is clearly in the power of Congress to reduce the value of metallic coins much below what would be the value of the currency under the system which I propose. If the alloy in the metallic coins was so increased, or the weight was so reduced, as that its exchangeable value would be no more than the value of the paper dollar issued by government, the dollar would be a dollar still, and as much a legal tender as it now is. If Congress can so reduce the value of gold, as a tender, the argument that Congress cannot make paper a tender, because to do so would impair the obligation of contracts, by authorizing payment in a less valuable medium, is untenable.

CHAPTER XV.

FINANCIAL.

I HAVE devoted the energies of a long and eventful life in a continued effort to reform the system of credit, finance, and currency, of the United States. One of the first acts of my public life, as chairman of a committee of the legislature of Missouri, was to examine into and report upon the causes of the

SUSPENSION OF THE BANK OF MISSOURI.

One of the measures adopted in 1812 by "the English party in the United States," to enable England "to carry into effect her own projects in Europe," was the organization, *in Boston*, of a combination to depreciate the credit of the government of the United States, and it was found necessary to permit the banks in the Middle, Southern and Western states to suspend specie payments, that they might lend their notes to the government, in exchange for treasury notes. It was with the notes of these suspended banks that the government fed, clothed, and paid our armies, and gave protection to the "beauty and booty" of New Orleans, and to our women and children, who were exposed to the tomahawk and scalping-knife of the merciless allies of Great Britain. The war of 1812, carried many volunteers into the Indian territory, the Indian title to much of which was extinguished by the treaties of peace. The revival of our foreign trade, and the sales of public land, placed a large amount of the notes of the suspended banks in the public

treasury, and the bank of the United States was chartered to aid in the process of resumption. Under the pressure thus produced, the Southern and Western banks did resume, but the bank of the United States being the depository, and required to convert into specie the notes received for customs and for the public lands, the pressure for specie became so severe, that Mr. Cheves, who had been elected president of the bank, made an arrangement with Mr. Crawford, then Secretary of the Treasury, under which it was agreed that large sums, nearly equal to the whole amount of their own circulation, should be left as deposites, with certain selected state banks, upon condition that they would convert the notes of other banks, received in payment for public lands, and remit the specie to the branches of the bank of the United States. And thus we found that the bank of Missouri, in St. Louis, and the bank of Edwardsville, in Illinois, both being deposit banks situated on opposite sides of the river, were required to convert the notes of each other into specie, to be sent, by the same steamer, to the branch of the bank of the United States in Louisville. The committee ascertained this fact. We saw that the arrangement was intended to relieve the bank of the United States from the odium, by making the local deposit banks war upon each other for the benefit, as we then supposed, of the bank of the United

States. We did not then realize, nor did I do so until long thereafter, that the bank of the United States—and, indeed, the whole banking system of the United States—was but a part, and the weaker part, of the financial system which, as then organized, enabled England, at will, " to carry into effect her own projects in Europe." The specie which the bank of the United States then took from the Southern and Western banks, was remitted, through the agency of our commerce, to London, to aid the bank of England to resume specie payments. The effect was to reduce the exchangeable value of land and other western property more than one half—the government of the United States compelling the purchasers of public land, from whom unpaid instalments were due under the then existing system of land sales, to relinquish their purchases, for which they were unable to make payment, at a loss of more than fifty per cent. on the sums previously paid.

THE POWER OF THE BANK OF ENGLAND.

With the knowledge which I then had, I attributed the monetary pressure upon the South and West, and the fluctuations in the values of property, to the controlling influence of the bank of the United States ; and believed that the power of that bank consisted chiefly in her control of the public deposits. I was, therefore, no less opposed to the system of pet banks, organized, upon the removal of the deposits in 1833, as a party measure, intended to promote the election of Mr. Van Buren. It was not until I visited London in 1841, and conversed with Mr. Wiggin, that I came to understand the power and influence which the bank of England had exerted and could at any time exert, over our monetary system, by the export of our specie. I then saw that the crisis of 1837 and 1840 was the result of a deliberate combination to revolutionize the machinery of the American trade.

THE BANK OF THE UNITED STATES—THE CAUSE OF ITS FAILURE.

The failure to renew the charter by Congress compelled the bank of the United States to accept a charter from the state of Pennsylvania, which made it necessary for that bank to sell out its branches. The funds thus obtained were chiefly in the notes of the pet banks, the payment of which in specie would have created a monetary crisis. The directors, therefore, invested the greater part in state bonds, and in advances upon cotton and American exports, relying upon the sale of these in Europe to reinstate the capital of the bank. With this view, the produce was consigned to a house established in Liverpool for that purpose, and Mr. Jaudon, the cashier of the bank, was sent to London with the state bonds. Relying upon the sales of cotton and state securities for funds to make the payment, the bank drew bills on their correspondents in London and Paris to enable the merchants, who had lost by the great fire in New York, to pay their European creditors. Fully aware of the arrangements made by the bank of the United States, and that the produce held by Biddle and Humphries, apart from the much larger amount of state securities held by Mr. Jaudon, was more than ample to meet the bills drawn by the bank of the United States, the bank of England passed an order that no bill predicated on the purchase of any American produce should be discounted. The consequence was that Biddle and Humphries could not sell cotton, nor could Mr. Jaudon sell state bonds, and on the last hour of the last day he had to go forty miles into the country to get Morrison & Co. to lend him the funds, on an hypothecation of state bonds, to save the bank from protest. The process of hypothecation and renewal, at ruinous rates, was continued until the balance was paid by a surrender of securities, at rates so much below their par that the increased value was estimated in 1843, by the American correspondent of Messrs. Morrison & Co., at two and a half millions of dollars.

We have seen the effect of that combination upon the interests of the people of the South, as illustrated in the depreciation of the market value of cotton caused by the utter destruction of American credit. But no estimate has been or can be made of the aggregate losses of the American people, by the surrender, to the bank of England and the money changers of Europe, of the entire control of our currency and of credit, including, as that surrender does, the control of the value of our industry and our commerce and of their products.

THE MONETARY CRISIS OF 1857.—BARON ROTHSCHILD.

That we may form some imperfect estimate of the effect of that "control," we refer to the monetary crisis of 1857, and of the causes which produced it. As we have said the traditionary policy of Russia has been to seize upon Constantinople and the Dardanelles, as the gate to the commerce of India. It so happened that I was in Paris in the winter of 1841-2. England, wishing to so adjust the boundary of Maine as to obtain a more direct communication between Halifax and Quebec, had just announced the appointment of Lord Ashburton as a special envoy to Washington ; having made a treaty with other powers, the purpose of which was to so modify the law of nations as to enable her to seize American ships suspected of being engaged in the slave trade, to be condemned by a British court, and thus enable her to monopolize the trade of Africa, the ratification of which was then pending before the French Chamber of Deputies. A few days after I reached Paris, I was invited to a diplomatic dinner, by Gen. Cass, who introduced me to Baron Rothschild, saying that I was just from the United States, and could give more information about American securities than any person then in Europe. "Ah," said Rothschild, rising from his seat, "what can you say about your country ?" I replied, "What about my country ?" He said, "About paying your debts—paying your debts, sir. My London correspondent writes to me to-day asking whether you can borrow any money on the continent, and my reply is not a dollar, sir, not a dollar." "Ah," said I, "if you suppose that we are like the kings of Europe, compelled to come to you to ask permission to go to war, you are under a great mistake, sir : a very great mistake." "How so ?" said he. I replied : "No one knows better than you do, the value of credit ; you know that we have paid our national debt. You know that we have all the elements of war within our own control, and that having the power of taxation, we can command the requisite resources, with our treasury notes. We have no wish to go to war, and do not intend to make war, but we have more than three millions of freemen, whose privilege it is to fight in defence of their country, in case we are invaded ; and more than that, sir, we can, in a very short time, create a fleet of steamships which would drive back the whole piratical fleets of Europe, if you dare send them with your money, to invade us. You greatly mistake, if you suppose that we want your money to enable us to defend our country." "Ah," said he, " will you come and see me? I would like to talk with you."

SIR HENRY ELLIS.

At dinner, I was seated between an American on my left and an Englishman on my right, and repeated to the American the substance of what had been said, and added, that it seemed that the purpose of England was war, as a means of emancipating our slaves, but that, in case of war, we would form a European alliance which would emancipate her East India subjects, and open the trade of India to the world. I noticed that the attention of the Englishman was excited. On the next day, General Cass said : " Do you know the gentleman who sat next you, on the right, at dinner yesterday ? I inquired who he was. General Cass said : " Sir Henry Ellis, the brother-in-law of Mr. Robinson, the president of the board of trade. He was one of the governors of India, and British embassador to Persia. He is a chosen diplomat of England, and is now attached to the British embassy in Paris, because Paris is the centre of European diplomacy." " Then," said I, " he heard that at dinner which interested him." " Yes," said General Cass, " he asked me who you were ; and you lost nothing by passing through my hands."

A few days afterwards, Sir Henry called on me, and we had a full and frank conversation, in which I told him that our desire was to maintain peaceful relations with England, but that instead of uniting with England to emancipate our slaves, it was manifestly the interest of the other powers of Europe to unite with us in abolishing her monopoly of the trade with India. He urged me to write out the substance of my remarks, saying that he wished to communicate what I had said to Lord Aberdeen. I hesitated, saying, that I was but a private citizen, and doubted the propriety of making such a communication. He insisted, saying that I was not aware how important it might be. Thus urged, I assented, and began to write, but before I had finished, reflecting upon the remarks of Baron Rothschild, and the conversation with Sir Henry, and the tone of the London press, I became so much excited that I could not write in terms sufficiently respectful, and called upon

COUNT MEYENDORF,

Who was then in Paris, as a special confidential agent of the Emperor of Russia, who explained to me, that Russia was building a railroad from St. Petersburg, through Moscow to Odessa, and had then commenced building a fleet at Sevastopol with a view to the command of the Black Sea, and the occupation of the Dardanelles, and gave me letters to the present Emperor and others at St. Petersburg, with the understanding that in case of a rupture with England, I would go to St. Petersburg to aid in the organization of a European and American coalition against the maritime supremacy of England. Upon communicating what I had done and heard to the President, Mr. Tyler, he forwarded to me, in Paris, an autograph letter, instructing Mr. Todd, then our minister in Russia, to introduce me to the Emperor.

CHAPTER XVI.

ENGLAND AND TEXAS.

THE progress of the negotiations at Washington, promising a peaceable adjustment of pending issues, I returned to London, and having been furnished by the State Department with an abstract of the statistics of the census of 1840, and having been invited by Mr. Delane to write for the London Times, my letters led to an intimate acquaint-with Mr. Cobden, Joseph Hume, Mr. McGregor, and other influential persons, and brought me into direct communication with Sir Robert Peel, Lord Aberdeen, Lord Palmerston, and Lord John Russell. I was told that the Queen had said to Lord Melbourne, that, when he would say to her that the whigs could maintain themselves in power, she would authorize him to organize a government of which Lord John Russell should be the chief. I was told who were to form his cabinet, and saw and conversed with them as to the means of maintaining friendly relations between the United States and England. I conversed upon this subject with Lord John Russell himself; and, at the request of one of his intimate and confidential friends, who now holds a high, confidential trust, spent two weeks at his residence, that we might the more fully discuss the relations between the two countries.

ENGLAND AND TEXAS.

I had ascertained that a negotiation was pending for a loan of five millions of dollars to the Texan govern-ment, on a pledge of land in **Texas,** and on the condition that, if Great Britain would guarantee the payment of the interest, Texas would stipulate that she would emancipate her slaves, and give a pledge that she would not be annexed to the United States. I remonstrated against such an interference in our relations with Texas, and complained that the purpose of England seemed to be to place a barrier between us and the Pacific, and asked why did not Lord Ashburton adjust the Oregon as well as the northeastern boundary. To this the reply was, that if I would look upon the map of the world I would see that Oregon is the most remote part of the habitable globe to England, and that, therefore, England did not want Oregon; because "the policy of our government [meaning Lord John Russell's government] *will be rich customers rather than poor colonies*, we, therefore, don't want Oregon, but, as no British government can sacrifice any British interest, if you want Oregon you must pay us a sum sufficient to satisfy the Northwest Fur Company." A sum then not estimated at more than five hundred thousand dollars, or, at most, one million of dollars. In a subsequent conversation with Lord John Russell, he said : "Tell Mr. Tyler, that I cannot take power now, because I wish Sir Robert Peel to adjust the Irish question, but that the first act of my government, when I do take power, will be to place the relations between the United States and England on the most friendly basis. If you want Texas, take it. If you want Mexico, take it. *Our policy will be rich customers rather than poor colonies*, and we know that both Texas and Mexico will be worth much more to us if you have them than if we have them ourselves."

MR. CALHOUN, TEXAS AND MEXICO.

These facts and conversations were communicated from London to Mr. Tyler and Mr. Calhoun, in letters urging upon the President the appointment of Mr. Calhoun as Secretary of State, and upon the latter, that it was his duty to accept, that he might conduct the negotiation for the annexation of Texas, the purchase of California, and the adjustment of our northwestern boundary.

The following is an extract from a letter to Mr. Calhoun, dated London 29th September, 1843 :

"If you go into Mr. Tyler's cabinet you can control events. It will not do for you to say that you cannot consent to take a subordinate station. That is placing yourself above the public interests. As a citizen of the republic you owe your services wherever they can be available. The crisis in which the relations between the United States and England are placed, is such as to demand of you any sacrifice. I do not believe that there is any man who can render as much service to the country, especially to the cause in which you have so long labored, as you can do by coming into the State Department, and it is manifest that being there you can do much if you cannot accomplish all that we desire in relation to England. If you are in the State Department, and invite that government to send a commission, and they fail to send them, or sending them fail satisfactorily to adjust all the points of difficulty between us, it will, I am sure, cause the

overthrow of the present ministers, and bring in men prepared and pledged to grant us all that we ask, both in relation to trade and to boundary."

Mr. Calhoun was tendered and accepted the appointment as Secretary of State, and reference to his negotiation will show that his purpose was to maintain our right in Oregon up to 49°, intending, that being conceded, to extinguish the British claims on the Pacific coast by purchase. At his request I went to Mexico to aid in conducting the negotiation for the acquisition of Texas, New Mexico, and California, and upon handing me his letter of instructions, he remarked : "If you succeed in this negotiation our commerce in the Pacific will, in a few years, be greatly more valuable than that in the Atlantic."

INTERFERENCE OF THE BRITISH CHARGE.

Upon reaching Mexico I found Santa Anna at the head of an army opposed to Herera, who was at the head of Congress, and as nothing could be done without the concurrence of the President and Congress, an arrangement was made for a movement in Texas which would enable the United States to interpose, and thus obtain the concessions wanted. I came to Texas, explained to the President of Texas and to the Congress, the measures which had been agreed on, and which would have been approved and adopted but for the interference of Mr. Elliot, the British *Chargé* to Texas, who induced the President, Mr. Jones, to believe that he could and would induce the Mexican government to recognize the independence of Texas ; and having, by that assurance, defeated the pending measures, did go to Mexico and obtained a proposition of the Mexican government to treat with

Texas, for the recognition of her independence, *upon the condition that Texas should not be annexed to the United States.* (See Appendix.)

THE PURPOSE OF THIS REFERENCE

To the past history of this country, as connected with the measures and policy of England, is to connect that past history with subsequent events. The war in the Crimea, and the destruction of the Russian fleet by the combined armies and navies of England and France, and the closing of the Black sea and the Dardanelles, compelled Russia to look to the navigation of the Amoor river (the Mississippi of Northern Asia), and a railroad connecting that navigation with Moscow and St. Petersburgh, as the only means of participating in the trade with India and China ; and therefore the ink, upon the treaty of Paris, was scarcely dry before the agents of Russia were found in Japan and China, and proposals were issued for a loan of two hundred and fifty millions of dollars to construct a railroad connecting St. Petersburg and Moscow with the Amoor and the Russian territory newly acquired from China. It will be remembered that during the Crimean war the British fleet were repulsed in their attack on the Russian fleet at the mouth of the Amoor, and with this knowledge of the purposes of Russia, and of England and France, we are at no loss to account for the wars in India and China. Who so blind as not to see

THE INCREASED VALUE OF VANCOUVER'S ISLAND AND PUGET'S SOUND ?

Oregon is no longer the most remote part of the habitable globe to England. Its value is no longer estimated by the fur trade. It has become the depot whence the British navy, which is to enforce and protect British maritime and commercial supremacy in the Pacific, is to communicate with and receive the orders of the admiralty in London ; and hence, Sir Morton Peto and his associates expended more than seventy millions of dollars in the construction of the Grand Trunk Railroad of Canada. Hence, the elder son of the Queen of England crossed the ocean and laid the capstone of the Victoria bridge ; and hence, again, Sir Morton and his associate capitalists have appropriated their hundreds of millions to build railways connecting their Grand Trunk Railway with the Pacific ; and hence, they promise to give any sum that may be required to facilitate their communications with *their* navy and *their* commerce on the Pacific. Does any one ask what connection there is between the Grand Trunk Railroad of Canada, Sir Morton Peto and the Pacific road, the British naval depot in Puget's Sound, the French movement in Mexico, and the anti-slavery conspiracy ? In reply we refer to the fact, that France united with England in the wars in the Crimea and in China—that while England arrests the progress of Russia by a bloody and expensive war, she not only tolerates the acquisitions of France, including the Suez canal, and her conquests in Cochin-China, but she recognises and approves the occupation and appropriation of Mexico, as part of the measures, which are intended to prevent the maritime and commercial supremacy of the United States, who are admitted to be her only rival on the seas.

TRIBUTE TO FOREIGN CREDITORS.

Let us pause for a moment and survey our position. We have seen that the annual contributions levied upon us by our foreign creditors, in the shape of interest and dividends on federal and state bonds, and railroad bonds and shares, are at least one hundred millions of dollars, which sum, compounded at six per cent. per annum for thirty-two years, will give nine thousand and eighty-eight millions dollars. Suppose that by the use of foreign capital to build our roads, we treble this annual tribute, we will pay three hundred millions of dollars per annum for the privilege of riding on American railroads owned by British capitalists, and paying British rates for the transportation of American produce, purchased by British agents at British prices ! ! Will not such a system convert us into hewers of wood and drawers of water for the benefit of British capitalists ? We have seen that the time once was when our ancestors were compelled to sell and to buy from our British task-masters and from them only. When " it was the decided opinion of almost all the merchants and politicians of England," that "*the only use of American colonies or West India islands is the monopoly of their consumption and the carriage of their produce.*" Then our ancestors were compelled to send their "sugar, molasses, ginger, fustic, tobacco, cotton, indigo, coffee, hides, skins, iron, corn, lumber," &c., &c., "in British-built ships, *to be laid upon the British shore*, before they could be forwarded to their final destination." The plan of restoring the control of the bank of England and of the "money merchants" of England, over our credit and our currency, and surrendering to them the construction and control of our railroads, will enable them to levy and collect a tribute upon our travel and transportation by land, like unto the tribute they levied and collected from our ancestors upon their travel and transportation by sea. Why should we go to England and pay her a tribute for the privilege of using her public debt to build our railroads ? Why should we not use our public debt as she has used hers ?

CHAPTER XVII.

CONGRESS TO REGULATE THE VALUE OF MONEY

THE Constitution gives to Congress power to coin money and to regulate its value, and of foreign coins. It also provides that no state shall coin money, emit bills of credit, or make anything else than gold and silver coin a legal tender in payment of debts, and it is obvious that, in the construction of these provisions, we should refer to the contemporaneous history of the times, as explanatory of their purpose. In doing this, we find that each of the states had issued paper money, which under the Constitution they were forbidden to do. We also find that the confederate congress had issued paper money, which, by the federal constitution, the federal Congress were not forbidden to do. It is, therefore, obvious that as the unrestricted power to coin money and regulate its value, whether metallic or paper, was given to Congress, and that although the states were forbidden to issue paper money, no such restriction was placed on the power of Congress, therefore Congress may issue paper money. And why were the states forbidden to issue paper money? It was because, if each of the states were permitted to issue "bills of credit," neither Congress nor the states could regulate their value. The purpose was to create a common money of like value in all the states, and the sole power of coinage and of regulating its value was, therefore, given to Congress, leaving with Congress the sole power to determine whether our money shall be metallic or paper.

OF WEIGHTS AND MEASURES.

As a further elucidation of the purpose of the Constitution, the same clause which gives the power to coin money and to regulate its value, gives to Congress power to fix a standard of weights and measures. It is manifest that the purpose was to give to Congress the control over the standard of values and of quantities so as to enable contracting parties to know precisely what the one is bound to deliver and the other is entitled to receive—for money bears the same relation to the values of property that the yard-stick does to the quantity of cloth, and that weights and measures do to commodities.

CAN CONGRESS REGULATE THE VALUE OF GOLD AND SILVER COIN,

So long as the Bank of England, by refusing to renew the discount of commercial paper, and raising the rate of interest, can so increase the value of gold in London as to cause large shipments of gold from New York to London? Would it be a proper discharge of their duty if Congress were to permit the Bank of England to reduce the length of the yard stick one half when we buy English cloths, and double the weights when we sell them American cotton? If Congress permits the Bank of England to quadruple the value of money, and to thus cause a corresponding depreciation in the exchangeable value of property, would that be a proper exercise of the power to regulate the value of money?

In view of the obligations devolved upon Congress by the Constitution, and the exigencies of the political, financial, commercial, and industrial crisis in which we are placed, I prepared and submitted to the Secretary of the Treasury the following

PLAN FOR NATIONAL BANKS AND NATIONAL CURRENCY.

1st. All payments by the United States to be made in gold or silver, or else in exchequer bills or four-per-cent. coupon bonds.

2d. The exchequer bills to be receivable in payment of all dues to the United States; to be of denominations suited for currency; to be a legal tender in payment of debts, unless otherwise stipulated by special contract; and at all times convertible, at the will of the holder, into four-per-cent. coupon bonds of the United States.

3d. The bonds to be of denominations not less than five hundred dollars, payable at the pleasure of the government, bearing interest, at the rate of four per cent., payable semi-annually, in exchequer bills, and at all times convertible, at the will of the holder, into exchequer bills.

4th. Any person, or association of persons, who may have deposited fifty thousand dollars or more with the Treasurer of the United States, in the four-per-cent. coupon bonds of the United States, as a collateral security for the redemption of their bank notes, to be authorized to become bankers and to receive from the Comptroller of the Currency bank notes, payable in gold or silver or in exchequer bills, for an amount equal to the sum of the four-per-cent. bonds deposited for their redemption.

5th. No one to be authorized to issue bank notes who shall not have deposited the requisite four-per-cent. coupon bonds as a security for their redemption in exchequer bills.

6th. The bonds deposited as a security for the redemption of bank notes, the exchequer bills held by a bank, the capital stock and the profits of banks, to be exempt from taxation by authority of the federal or state government.

7th. The rate of interest charged by banks on loans and on advances of money, never to be more than five per cent. per annum.

8th. Any person to be permitted to deposite gold or silver in the Treasury of the United States, and, with the assent of the Secretary, receive certificates payable in specie, which certificates shall always be receivable at par in payment of customs duties.

9th. Customs duties to be payable with the assent of the Secretary of the Treasury, in exchequer bills, at their current market value in gold.

COMMENT

A bank note is worth as much as gold if it be convertible into gold, and it is worth as much as gold because it is so convertible. The convertibility into gold, is therefore the principle which regulates its value; and therefore the value depends upon the value of the gold into which it may be convertible. We know that Mr. Cobb, while Secretary of the Treasury, paid off part of the national debt, at twenty per cent. premium; and therefore if our bank notes had then been convertible into our six per cents., then our bank notes would have been worth twenty per cent. more than gold. The PLAN proposes to make our bank notes convertible at all times into exchequer bills, which are convertible into four per cent. coupon bonds—which bonds being the only basis of the issue of bank notes, will give four per cent. on their coupons, and five per cent. on their bank notes, making nine per cent. And hence, I assume, that as before the war our six per cents. were worth, in the European market, twenty per cent. more than gold, an arrangement which will give the holders nine per cent. on our four per cents. will make them worth as much as gold. If so, then, as our exchequer bills would be convertible into four per cents., and as the bank notes would represent four per cents., and be payable in exchequer bills, our bank notes would be worth as much as gold. And I argue that although the fact, that gold and exchequer bills would each be a legal tender, will equalize their value as money, yet, inasmuch as neither our four per cents., our bank notes, nor our exchequer bills, will be a legal tender in England, and our bank notes will represent four per cents., which are convertible into exchequer bills which are a legal tender here, and no pressure of the bank screw in London can export our bank notes or our exchequer bills, and the amount of our public debt is such as to enable us at all times to command the amount of four per cent. which may be required as the basis for bank issues ; therefore, our four per cents. will be a better basis for a national currency than gold and silver. It will be more abundant and therefore cheaper—and yet as it will represent our four per cents., which under the plan will yield nine per cent., and cannot be exported as gold would be, it will be more stable in value, and therefore a better money than gold.

Gold and the treasury note are both a legal tender, and the value of both as money consists in that fact. Gold has a speculative commercial value, because it is a legal tender in London, which the treasury note is not. If Congress were to make the treasury note the only legal tender in the United States, and gold should cease to be a tender elsewhere, then gold would cease to be money, and as our treasury note would be money here although it would not be money in London, yet then the treasury note would be more valuable than gold, because it is money, and only so because it is money. The value, therefore, of gold as money as well as of paper, depends upon the fact that it is a legal tender, and is therefore money ; and the value of both gold and paper depends upon the uses to which they are applied and the relative demand for them.

THE PURPOSE OF THE PLAN.

1st. To divorce the government from the banks, except that as inasmuch as bank notes will be used as money, and it is the duty of Congress to regulate the value of money, by requiring the bank notes to be redeemed with the national currency, and requiring the banks to deposit with the Comptroller of the Currency, a sufficient amount of four per cent. convertible, to redeem the bank notes put into circulation, Congress will regulate the value of bank notes, by providing the fund for their redemption.

2d By refusing to receive bank notes in payment of public dues, Congress will increase the demand for, and will consequently increase the value of the national currency.

3d. By receiving the national currency, and that currency or gold and silver only, in payment of public dues and in payments from the Treasury, the interest on the sum thus used will be saved to the government, and to that extent lessen the burden of the public debt.

4th. By authorizing the organization of national banks upon a deposit of four per cent. convertible federal bonds, and upon such deposit only, there would be a reduction of two per cent. upon the whole of the bonds thus deposited, which would be an additional diminution of the public debt, and to that extent diminish the taxes.

5th. As by this process the whole sum of the four per cents. thus used, would be converted into capital, and be more valuable, as a basis of banking, than so much gold, the fund thus deposited should be made payable at the pleasure of the government, and inasmuch as the demand for it as the basis for banking would be permanent, there would be no inducement to pay it, and thus the people would be relieved from so much taxation, which the advocates of a specie basis would impose upon them.

6th. It would convert so much of the public debt into capital, and through its agency create a currency so abundant and consequently so cheap, as to stimulate the industry and enterprise of the whole country, by enabling every one who has sufficient intelligence and can give the requisite guarantees for integrity, to obtain, for any required term, sufficient funds to enable him to undertake and prosecute any proper enterprise.

7th. To create a currency stable in value, and therefore, as the public debt is ample to create all the four per

cents. that may be wanted as a basis of banking, the inducement to invest in the four per cents. should be such as to command all the capital required for that use ; and hence, as the rate of interest paid upon the bonds is to be but four per cent., and the interest charged by the banks five per cent., the reduction of the rate of interest upon the bonds and upon bank loans will be so much saved by the people, and should therefore exempt the banks from taxation, because that exemption will tend to increase the capital engaged in the business of banking, and thus render it more available for the development of the resources of the country.

8th. By organizing a system of free banking, on a deposit of four per cent. bonds, and making their notes payable in exchequer bills, it will give a common currency, and create a community of interests, identified with the public credit, and blending our sectional feeling in support of our common country.

9th. It will create an American money, resting upon and sustaining American credit, which will be more valuable than gold, because it will be American, and therefore not liable to be exported as gold would be. Say that the current annual expenditure be reduced to four hundred millions of dollars, the revenue should be the same. Say that, of the four hundred millions, paid out in the current expenditure, two hundred millions be converted into four per cents., as a basis of banking, and that fifty millions more be held in reserve by the banks to redeem their bank notes ; there would remain but one hundred and fifty millions of exchequer bills to pay four hundred millions of taxes. The deficiency of exchequer bills would soon bring them on a par with gold. Hence the necessity of authorizing the six per cents. to be converted into four per cents., and permitting the four per cents., and the four per cents only, to be used as the basis of banking, and convertible into exchequer bills. The purpose is to create a currency more stable in value than gold, and yet to regulate its exchangeable value by the *proper* value, not the fluctuating *commercial* value, of gold. Hence the bank note should be convertible into an exchequer bill, which should be convertible into a bond, which should be worth as much, but not more than the *proper* value of gold. And the merit of the plan consists in the fact, that while the privilege of banking which is a bonus given by the government, but which costs the public nothing, reduces the interest on the six per cents. which may be converted into four per cents. as a basis of banking, that privilege, so to use them, enables the holders to make at least three per cent. per annum, profit, by converting the six per cents. into four per cents., and thus secures a supply of bank notes, equal to the demand; and regulates the demand by the value of the public credit, and the benefits derived from a proper use of private credit.

THE CHIEF VALUE OF THE REFORM,

For reform it will be, is, that it will give an abundant and cheap currency, uniform and stable in value, which will cultivate our fields, open and work our mines, construct our machinery, erect and operate our factories, build and navigate our ships, dig our canals, improve our rivers and make our railroads. Ay, it will make us one people, by making the public credit the basis of the industry and prosperity of the whole country regulating and sustaining the values of our property.

By enabling us to build our own railroads, and stimulating domestic industry it will enable us to create a large surplus for export, and thus pay our foreign debt, and relieve us from the tribute which we now pay to foreigners in the shape of interest and dividends. It is believed that the interest and dividends paid to foreigners on federal and state bonds and on railroad bonds and shares, now amount to at least one hundred millions of dollars per annum. This is an annuity, and as an annuity of one dollar compounded at six per cent., will, in thirty-two years give ninety dollars and eighty-eight cents, it will be seen that the tribute thus to be paid, will, in thirty-two years be nine thousand and eighty-eight millions, being more than twice the sum of our national debt! And what has Europe given us that we should pay her such a tribute? She has not given us gold. We are the producers and we send our gold to them—they do not send theirs to us. What, then, have they given us? A small percentage of the profits which they have charged on the goods which they have made, by using the machinery, purchased by the use of their credit, to convert our cotton into cloth, and a much less part of the profits which they have made by the use of their credit in the purchase and sale of our cotton and other exports.

CHAPTER XVIII.

OF THE USE OF BRITISH AND AMERICAN CREDIT.

HERE again, facts become important. Before 1835, the date when England found that she must look to Africa, to India, and China, for her "future prosperity," any American merchant who could get an acceptance of Wilde, Wiggins, or Wilsons, three American houses established in London, in connection with the American trade, could purchase British goods on a credit of six and twelve months, and, under our revenue system as it then was, he could, upon custom-house bonds, get time to sell the goods for funds to pay the duties ; but contemporaneous with the emancipation of her West India slaves and the opening of the trade of India to British enterprise, the Bank of England, uniting with the "*money merchants*," made a systematic warfare on American credit—the three W.'s became bankrupts, and the American merchants could no longer buy British goods on credit. The American planters had been accustomed to anticipate the sale of their cotton by bills drawn on their factors, which being endorsed, were discounted by the Southern banks and the funds used to purchase slaves. The intelligent financiers who had combined to emancipate the West India slaves, and open the trade of India as the source of future prosperity to England, and as part of their system of finance had made war on American credit, knew full well the value of the American trade, and hence they established agencies in New York and in the Southern ports, who, finding the Southern cotton in the hands of factors who had endorsed the notes of the Southern planters, and who were compelled to sell the cotton to meet the payment of their notes and protect their own credit, were, therefore, enabled to fix the price. They purchased and paid for it, not in money, but in bills upon New York, which bills were discounted by the Southern banks because the Southern merchants, no longer able to purchase goods in Manchester, bought in New York, and money in New York was, therefore, worth more than money in Mobile. When the bills upon New York became due they were paid, not with money, but by bills upon London, and as the New York merchants dealt in Manchester, money in London was worth more than money in New York, and therefore the New York banks discounted the second bills. In the meantime the cotton had been shipped to Liverpool, and sold at ninety days' credit, and as the first and second bills were each at sixty days, the British banker was enabled, by this change, in the machinery of the American trade, to convert his credit at seven months into capital in the shape of American cotton. A small part of the profits thus realized has been invested in American securities and in American railroads, but at what cost to the American planter ?

It appears, from the published statistics, that the average price of American cotton from 1790 to 1835 was twenty-five cents per pound, and that the product from 1836 to 1860, inclusive, was 25,703,464,900 pounds, which if sold at twenty-five cents per pound, would have produced $6,425,-866,225. The market value at the prices for which it was sold was $1,770,790,000, making a loss by the depreciation of $4,955,076,225, giving an annual loss of $198,202,249, which as an annuity, at compound interest of eight per cent., would in twenty-five years be $15,846,169,807 55, and compounded at seven per cent. would give in twenty-five years $12,334,310,225 76, and compounded at six per cent. would give in twenty-five years $10,635,375,-215 56. Who does not see that the producers of cotton in the Southern states are deeply interested in preventing the recurrence of a system of trade which so much reduced the value of their labor? This, it is sincerely believed, the proposed system of currency and credit will do.

REDUCTION OF TAXES.

We have debt enough of our own and to spare. We can greatly economize on the British system of using the capital invested in the public credit. Instead of borrowing and using bank notes in the payment of our current expenditures, we can use our own treasury notes receivable in payment of public dues—and, by making these notes the legal money of the United States, and making all bank notes payable in this money or in specie, the treasury notes will soon approximate the value of gold. By the substitution of these legal tender notes for bank notes and specie in payments to and from the Treasury of the United States, we may safely estimate that

the amount outstanding will at least be twice the sum of the current revenue, but say that it is six hundred millions of dollars only, this will be a saving of thirty-six millions of dollars per annum. If the principle of making a deposit of four per cent. convertible bonds, and four per cent. only, the basis of the issue of bank notes be adopted, and we assume that the amount of bank capital is but fifty per cent. more than in 1860, we have $632,835,096 of bank capital, and the reduction of the rate of interest on the bonds deposited will be $12,656,-701 92, which added to the $36,000,000 (the interest saved by the issue of legal tender certificates), and we have a saving of $48,656,701 92—this sum as an annuity compound, at six per cent., would give in thirty-two years $4,421,921,070 48, a sum sufficient to build and equip one hundred and forty-seven thousand three hundred and seventy-seven miles of railroad; estimating the cost at thirty thousand dollars per mile! being nearly five times as many miles of roads as there are now in the United States. But the plan proposed does not rest its chief claims for approval on the reduction of the interest on the public debt. I affirm and believe that its

CHIEF MERIT CONSISTS IN REDUCING THE RATE OF INTEREST CHARGEABLE ON LOANS AND DISCOUNTS,

In giving an abundant and cheap currency, and the stimulus which it will give to our productive industry, by enabling every man, whose habits of sobriety and industry are such as to command the confidence of capitalists, to obtain the means of profitable employment. Does any one own land? He could obtain the means to pay the wages of labor to make it productive.

Does he own a mine? He could obtain the funds to open and work it. Does he own a water power? He could obtain the funds to erect a factory, to purchase machinery, and to pay the wages of labor. Does he wish to build a railroad? All that will be required will be an exhibit showing that such a road will benefit the public, and pay more than five per cent. dividends. Does he wish to build ships to compete with European combinations for the trade of the Pacific? All that will be required will be to show that the productive industry of America has so far progressed in the manufacture of articles suited to the trade of China, Northern Asia, and the South Pacific Islands, as to require American ships to carry our surplus manufactures to an appropriate market; and the six per cents. will become four per cent. convertible bonds, and furnish the funds to build the ships, and, if necessary, to furnish and maintain the navy that may be required to protect them in every sea against every combination, whether English, French, or German, or all combined.

AN ABUNDANT AND CHEAP CURRENCY.

That some estimate may be formed of the saving which will result from the reduction of the rates of interest on loans and discounts to five per cent. per annum, I refer to the fact, stated by Colwell in his able work on the ways and means of payment. He estimates the payments made through the banks, in 1857, at ninety thousand millions of dollars. If we divide this sum by six, estimating the several discounts at sixty days, it will give the sum of fifteen thousand millions of dollars under discount; the saving upon which, at the rate of *two* per cent. per annum, will be three hundred millions of dollars per annum; and this sum, as an annuity compounded at six per cent., will give twenty-seven thousand two hundred and sixty-four millions of dollars, a sum sufficient to build nine hundred and eight thousand eight hundred miles of railroad, estimating the cost at thirty-thousand dollars per mile, as the saving in thirty-two years on the discount on bank loans, without taking into account the immense amount of interest paid on transactions which do not go into the bank accounts. These are sums which may well startle persons accustomed to estimate the transactions of the whole people of the United States by the standard of their own private dealings. But the data are within the comprehension of the simplest intelligence, and the conclusions are deduced by the plainest rules of arithmetic.

CHAPTER XIX.

SPECIE PAYMENTS.

WITH such data and these conclusions before us, the question of the currency resolves itself into the inquiry of whether we should resume specie payments before, by fostering our home industry, we have created a foreign export trade, creating a balance in our favor, which will prevent the export of specie in payment of the large tribute which we would otherwise pay to foreign creditors.

Jacobs says :

" The gold and silver in a country, contrary to the opinions of the vulgar, are the the least part of its wealth. They can scarcely, under any of the changes of metallic value which they may cause in other commodities, amount to a hundredth part of the wealth of the country ; and in a prosperous state, they will bear a much less proportion. The possession of them is real wealth only in a small degree, though every addition to them produces real wealth by the stimulus which the apparent advance of prices gives to every kind of industrious exertion."

Adam Smith says :

" The gold and silver which circulates in any country, and by means of which the produce of its land and labor is annually circulated and distributed to the proper consumers, is, in the same manner as the ready money of the dealer, all dead stock ; it is a very valuable part of the capital of the country which produces nothing to the country. The judicious operations of banking by substituting paper in the room of a great part of this gold and silver, enables the country to convert a great part of this dead stock into active and productive stock, which produces something to the country."

Mr. Calhoun, in his speech on the recharter of the bank in March, 1834, said :

" If we take the aggregate property of a community, that which forms the currency constitutes in value a very small proportion of the whole. What this proportion is in our country and other commercial and trading communities is somewhat uncertain. I speak conjecturally in fixing it as one to twenty-five or thirty, though I presume this is not far from the truth."

Adam Smith tells us that :

" A paper money consisting in bank notes, issued by a people of undoubted credit, payable on demand without any condition, and in fact always readily paid as soon as presented, is, in every respect, equal in value to gold and silver money."

Ricardo says :

" If there was perfect security that the power of issuing paper money would not be abused ; that is, if there was perfect security for its being used in such quantities as to preserve its value relatively to the mass of circulating commodities nearly uniform, the precious metals might be entirely discarded from circulation."

This we assume to be the real and

PROPER TEST OF THE VALUE OF PAPER MONEY.

Is the quantity such as to maintain its value relatively to the mass of circulating commodities ? If the quantity in circulation, be so restricted by making it convertible into specie, or into four per cent. convertible bonds, as to preserve the same relative value to the mass of circulating commodities, then the fact that the same quantity of paper will purchase the same quantity of these commodities, is proof that the quantity is not in excess, and *vice versa*. By making the bank note convertible into currency, we prevent an over-issue of bank notes ; and by making the currency convertible into four per cent. convertible bonds, we prevent an over-issue of currency ; and by making the bonds convertible into currency, we prevent a ruinous contraction of the currency ; and, by maintaining the proper quantity in circulation, we prevent the depreciation of the exchangeable values of property ; which was the purpose of the Constitution when the power of regulating the value of money was given to Congress. And as the value of money depends on the quantity, the question is, can Congress so regulate the action of the bank of England, and of the " money merchants" of Europe, as to prevent an undue export of specie, under a system of specie payments? I believe that Congress cannot do this otherwise than by giving us a legal tender, which will not be a legal tender in London. We need not go beyond the crisis of 1857 to demonstrate this.

THE CRISIS OF 1857.

The money unit of England is gold. In France it was silver, until the discovery of gold in California and Australia. The average annual coinage of silver in France, for a series of years preceding 1848, was $16,200,000. During the eight years ending December, 1857, it was but $8,091,400 per annum, and from January, 1852, to January, 1858, the export of silver was $225,400,000 more than the import ;

and although the coinage of gold for the year 1857 was $114,512,245, the bank of France was compelled, between the 1st of July, 1855, and the 1st of January, 1858, to purchase $212,000,000 in gold. Whence did France get her supply of gold, and why did she export her silver? The custom-house returns show that during the seven years ending July, 1857, the export of gold from the United States was $320,000,000 ; and the official statements show that, during the years 1856 and 1857, England sent to India, by one steamboat company, chiefly in silver, $154,591,885. England took the French silver to pay the expense of her war in India, and she took our gold to pay for it.

WHAT WAS THE EFFECT OF THIS LARGE EXPORT OF OUR GOLD ?

Gibbon, in his account of the crisis of 1857, says :

" The regular discount of bills by the banks had mostly been suspended, and the street rates for money, even on unquestionable securities, rose to three, four, and five per cent. a month. On the ordinary securities of merchants, such as promissory notes and bills of exchange, money was not to be had at any rate. House after house, of high commercial repute, succumbed to the panic, and several heavy banking firms were added to the list of failures."

The New York Commercial Agency tells us that they had on their books statements showing the commercial transactions and condition of 204,031 firms ; and that the loss by 337 fraudulent firms was $5,222,500 ; by 543 firms unable to pay, was $20,300,000 ; by 5,123 failures, $143,780,000 ; that the commercial debt of the country merchants was $2,282,000,000 ; and that the business transactions during the year was $4,564,000,000. Now what was the cause of these ruinous losses? Gibbon tells us that "the banks suffered depletion in coin to the amount of $5,483,864; and that they could not withstand such an on-slaught!" The cause of the crisis is manifest. The loans, on August 8, 1857, were $122,077,252; on November 28, they were reduced to $94,963,-130. The loans were predicated, not on the ability of the borrowers to pay their indebtedness in specie, but upon the exchangeable values of the mass of commodities under their control, and upon the sale of which they relied for the means of payment. The pressure for money in London caused by the

EXPENDITURES OF THE ARMY IN INDIA,

Caused so great a demand for specie to be remitted to London, as to so reduce the exchangeable value of the commodities which were the means of payment, as to destroy that private credit upon which the $4,564,000,000 of the business transactions of that year were predicated. If we assume that the depreciation of the price of the products of the soil, and of labor given in payment by the consumers of the $4,564,000,000 worth of commodities was but twenty-five per cent., it will be seen that the loss of less than six millions of dollars in specie by the banks of New York, caused a depreciation in the exchangeable values of American property of more than one thousand millions of dollars.

RELATIVE SUM OF CASH AND OTHER PROPERTY.

That the sum in cash required to pay wages and develop the agricultural, mineral, and manufacturing resources of the country is much less than many believe, will appear by a careful analysis of the uses of money and of credit

in the several industrial employments of a prosperous community.

Thus we find that, by the census of 1860, the population of the state of Virginia was 1,593,199—

That they had sixty-five banks, with a capital of	$16,205,156
That their loans and discounts were	24,975,792
That their specie fund was but	2,943,652
And that their circulation was but	9,812,197
The value of her real estate	417,952,228
The value of her personal property was	239,069,108
The value of farms was	371,696,211
The value of farming implements and machinery	7,021,772
The value of live stock	47,794,256
That her product of wheat was (in bushels)	11,212,616
That her product of rye was (in bushels)	794,024
That her product of Indian corn was (in bushels)	38,360,704
That her product of oats was (in bushels)	10,184,865
That her product of tobacco was (in pounds)	123,967,757
That the value of animals slaughtered was	$11,133,441

WHY THE GOVERNMENT SHOULD PROTECT VALUE OF CREDIT.

If to this vast aggregate of capital be added $51,309,000, given as the product, in 1860, of 33,050 males and 3,549 females, employed in manufactures in the state, and we compare the transactions connected with the capital thus invested in this mass of property, with the sum of the specie held by, and the circulation of the banks, we will see how small is the sum of money as compared with the credit used in these transactions; proving conclusively that the business and credit of the country is not predicated on the specie held by the banks, nor upon the bank notes, but upon the property, the product of the soil and of labor, in *transitu* from the producer to the consumer. It should be the especial duty of the government to protect and sustain the *value* of this *credit* while engaged in the production of the mass of commodities which constitute the elements of commerce, and to maintain the values of those commodities while they are being placed upon the market. For it is upon the maintenance of the value of the credit thus used, and not upon the small sum of specie held by the banks, that the stability of the values of property, and, consequently, the prosperity of the community, depends. Their credit rests upon the mass of their property—the credit of the banks is made to rest on the pitiful sum of specie held by the banks! I again ask the reader to contrast the value of the specie held by the banks with the value of the few articles as given in the above extract from the census; and I ask—emphatically ask—whether that is a wise system of finance which attempts to regulate the value, not only of the mass of property indicated by the extract, but of all our property, by the small sum of specie held by the banks, and leaves that small sum of specie subject to a foreign moneyed corporation, managed and controlled by an association of foreign capitalists, jealous of our progress, our rivals in power, in manufactures and commerce? Such I assert and maintain would be the inevitable consequence of compulsory specie payments.

WHAT WAS THE CAUSE OF THE CRISIS OF 1857?

The city banks of New York reduced their loans in a few days from one hundred and twenty millions of dollars to ninety-four millions of dollars. Why did these banks so reduce their loans? They feared that their eight millions of specie would be taken and sent to London, under the pressure created by the bank of England.

It is estimated that each ventricle of the heart contains one ounce of blood. The heart contracts four thousand times every hour, consequently there passes through it two hundred and fifty pounds of blood every hour. The blood is the vital principle of animal life, and, therefore, as the heart, by the force of its contraction, drives the whole of the blood of the human system, ten times every hour, through all the thousand ramifications of veins and arteries, so does a proper use of the money of the country, acting through the avenues of trade, maintain the vitality of credit, as the medium of commercial exchanges, giving a healthful stability to the values of property; and, therefore, as the sudden loss of blood will prevent the action of the heart and cause the system to sink until, by air and food, the requisite quantity is restored, so an undue export of the money of any country will so depress the prices of commodities as to destroy the credit which is the indispensable agent in the transfer of the products of the soil and of labor from the producer to the consumer.

JACOBI TELLS US THAT THE QUANTITY

Of money, as compared with the values of the property of a prosperous community, is not more than one per cent., and hence, although the average quantity of specie in the bank of England, requisite to maintain its value at the proper level, is not more than ten millions of pounds sterling, there were at one time in 1857 in circulation, as appears by the official statement of the stamp-office, nine hundred millions of dollars of bills of exchange; and by reference to Gibbon's account of the banks of New York, we find that the average specie in the banks of New York, from January 1, 1853, to January 1, 1858, was about eleven millions of dollars, the loans were as much as one hundred and twenty millions of dollars, and the settlements between the banks, at the clearing-house, were thirty millions of dollars daily, or nearly *nine hundred millions* of dollars per month, or ten thousand millions of dollars per annum; and Colwell tells us that an analysis of the payments through the banks in the United States, in 1857, shows that the sum thus paid was ninety thousand millions of dollars. Is it necessary to illustrate further the necessity of protecting this mass of credit, so as to prevent its depreciation?

The means of preventing the recurrence of such a crisis is not the vain and costly process of piling up useless millions of unproductive gold in the vaults of our banks, to await the recurring demand for specie caused by the "money merchants" of London, operating through the bank of England, but it is to convert the capital, of which we have an abundance in the shape of the public debt, into a fund to be always held in reserve and always convertible into money, with which the consumer may purchase and pay for the "mass of circulating commodities" which constitute the available basis of credit. If we had had such a currency in 1857, the export to London of all our gold, as well as of so large a part of the silver of France, would not have caused a panic in New York.

ROTHSCHILD.

While I write, the European mails bring me a statement of the examination of Baron James de Rothschild

before an Imperial Commission at Paris. I make a few extracts:

"President: So you think there has been a little excess, either because the resources of the country, created by the labor and economy, have not been in proportion with the expenditure, or because the circulation of money has been such in Europe that the long time it takes to return has been out of proportion to the issue of paper, that there have been issues remaining unpaid owing to a delay in the return of specie? *Is there not a loss of specie almost absolute for Europe with regard to the extreme East—a loss which has been compensated by the discovery of gold in America?*

"Baron Rothschild: It is precisely those discoveries which came to our relief. But for them we should not have been able to do what we have done. *There has been a substitution of Australian gold, new or old, in place of the specie which we have sent to China or to India*, and which will be long before it returns, if it ever does return.

"President: A time may come, perhaps, when those countries will have a monetary circulation, and be able to effect exchanges with us. At present we pay them in specie; it is to be hoped that some day we shall pay them in merchandise.

"Baron Rothschild: Indeed that is to be hoped; for there was a moment when I trembled for a crisis in Germany, because silver had disappeared. So much had been bought to send to China and India; it had become so scarce at Hamburg, Frankfort, and in many other towns in Germany where silver is the only circulating medium, as in China and India, that we knew not what to do. Silver was at one time at from thirty francs to forty francs premium per mille." (See an account of Baron Rothschild's examination given in the New York Herald.)

By reference to the report of that examination, it will be seen that Baron Rothschild urged that it was necessary to authorize the bank of France to raise the rate of interest, and curtail her discounts, and thus make money scarce and dear in France, as a means of preventing the export of specie to India and China. On the 4th of April, 1860, I submitted

A MEMORIAL TO CONGRESS

(Senate Mis. Doc. 48), in which I referred to the fact, that, instead of relying upon Australia and America for a supply of the precious metals to replace the specie sent to India and China, it was then necessary to adopt measures to counteract the disastrous consequences of permitting the bank of England to regulate the quantity of our currency and of our credit, and, consequently, to regulate the value of our property. We have seen that the loss of less than six millions of specie in 1857, by the banks of the city of New York, caused so great a reduction of the exchangeable values of property, that the loss by five thousand one hundred and thirty-three commercial failures was $143,780,000. This was apart from the general effect upon the industry and the values of the other property of the country.

The purpose of the Constitution, in giving to Congress power to coin money and to regulate its value, was to give

STABILITY TO THE VALUES OF PROPERTY ;

And the preference was given to a metallic over a paper currency, because it was then supposed that it would be less difficult to regulate the *quantity* of specie than of paper, and that, therefore, the precious metals would be more stable in value than paper money. The question is not whether Congress will forbid the use of *paper* money—(for in the present state of the progress and civilization of the world, no one would forbid the use of paper money). The question is, in what shape, and under what restrictions shall our paper money be issued? If it shall appear that in the great struggle in which the more civilized nations of the earth are now engaged, it is impossible for our Congress, to so regulate a metallic currency as to maintain its value relatively to the value of the mass of circulating commodities, and that Congress can so regulate the issue of paper money, as to give it a fixed and uniform value, relatively to the exchangeable value of those commodities ; then, the relative value of paper money being much more stable, than the fluctuating value of gold, it is the duty of Congress, under the power " to coin money, and to regulate the value thereof," to pass such laws as are necessary to regulate the value of paper money.

WHY PAPER MONEY IS BETTER THAN GOLD.

It is admitted by all that the value of a metallic as well as a paper currency is regulated by the quantity. It is admitted that whenever the tendency of the foreign exchange is to diminish the specie in the vaults of the bank of England, that bank raises the rate of interest and curtails her discounts—that is, the bank so regulates her discounts as to create a greater demand for money, at the same time that they increase the rate of interest, and thus coerce an export of our specie to London. Congress cannot prevent this. Therefore the regulation of the value of our metallic currency is vested in the bank of England and not in our Congress. To illustrate this fact, I submit a diagram, prepared after a careful examination of the official returns of the bank of England, showing the fluctuations in the quantity of bullion in the bank from January, 1852, to September, 1859, and the rates of interest charged

Diagram showing the Fluctuation of the Amount of Bullion in the Bank of England, and Rate of Interest charged by the Bank.

The figures on the margin indicate the amount of Bullion, in Millions of Dollars, held by the Bank at the dates indicated by the intersection of the irregular and horizontal lines, and the figures on the irregular line indicate the rate of Interest, per cent, charged by the Bank at the dates then indicated.

by the bank. The marginal figures from thirty-five to one hundred, indicate the bullion, in millions of dollars, which was in the bank at the dates, when the irregular line, which shows the fluctuation of the amount of bullion in the bank intersects the corresponding horizontal lines—thus, on the 1st of January, 1852, the bullion in the bank was eighty-five millions of dollars. It rose, in July, to nearly one hundred and five millions, and fell, on the 10th December, 1857, to thirty-five millions—and rose again, in October, 1858, to ninety-five millions. The figures on the irregular line indicate the rate of interest charged. Thus, in September, 1852, interest was two per cent., and on the 10th of December, 1857, it was ten per cent. And why? Because, in September, 1852, the bank had more than a hundred millions, and on the 10th December, 1857, it had but thirty-five millions of dollars. Does any one pretend that, after resuming specie payments, our Congress can prevent this fluctuation in the quantity of specie in the bank of England? Or that failing to do this, they can prevent the fluctuations in the quantity of specie or in the relative values of property in London or in New York?

WHY CANNOT CONGRESS REGULATE THE QUANTITY OR THE VALUE OF SPECIE

Or of property in London or in New York? It is because specie is *money* in New York as well as in London, and because being money in London as well as in New York, our specie will go from New York to London, whenever the bank of England, by refusing to renew her discounts and increasing her rates of interest, makes the demand for specie in London so great, that the "*money merchants*" can make a profit by sending specie from New York to London. Our national currency is money in New York, but it is not money in London, and, therefore, no pressure of the bank screw can export our paper money to London. Congress, therefore, can regulate the quantity, and, consequently, the value of our national currency—not by making it convertible into specie, but by a proper system of funding—into convertible bonds bearing not more than four per cent. interest, and making that interest payable in currency, instead of making it payable in gold.

For it should be borne in mind that the purpose is not to make our currency convertible into specie, which must fluctuate in value as the quantity of specie fluctuates in the bank of England, but to regulate its value so that it shall at all times bear a uniform value, as compared with the value of the mass of circulating commodities. Thus, if Congress shall make the currency convertible, at will, into a four per cent. convertible bond, then the bond will regulate the value of the currency, and the currency will regulate the value of the bond.

The importance of

REDUCING THE RATE OF INTEREST

So as to prevent our bonds from going abroad, is illustrated by the fact that England, by issuing her stock at a low rate of interest, kept her public debt at home, and hence, what she pays as interest she receives as dividends. She pays little or no tribute to foreigners in the shape of interest on her debt—no combination of foreign "money merchants," by sending home a large amount of her public stocks, can export her specie and prostrate her credit—private or public. What would be the effect upon our currency, if we resume specie payments, and a combination, formed to depreciate our credit, were to send to New York one hundred millions of the fourteen hundred millions of dollars of our securities, now held abroad, to be sold for the purpose of exporting our specie? Will it not be unwise in us to provoke the attempt before, by the use of our national currency, we have so increased our industry as to give us sufficient surplus exports to create a balance in our favor, and thus prevent the export of our specie? The public debt was created by an issue of paper money. The effect of an early resumption of specie payment will be to

INCREASE THE BURDEN OF TAXATION,

while it will diminish the means of payment! The amount of taxation will be the same whether it be paid in specie or in paper—while all must see that the wages of labor and the price of commodities must be reduced in the ratio of the difference between the price of gold and of paper. Why should Congress pass laws to reduce the market value of the poor man's labor and the farmer's corn? Is it to increase the price of United States bonds held by the rich speculators in the public credit? Why should Congress make the rich richer, by making the poor poorer? Who does not know that when the foreign demand for gold has compelled our banks to suspend specie payment, the whole country, with one accord, has used paper money as a substitute for gold? And why? Is it not because every one knows that—"If there was perfect security that the power of issuing paper money would not be abused, that is, if there was perfect security for its being issued in such quantities as to preserve its value relatively to the mass of circulating commodities nearly uniform, the precious metals may be

entirely discarded from circulation?" Can Congress so regulate the issue of paper as to "preserve its value relatively to the mass of circulating commodities nearly uniform"? If so, then there is no sufficient reason why they should again give to the bank of England the power to regulate the value of our money and of our property—a power which has been so often used to our injury—and which will be greatly increased by the large sum in our public securities now held abroad, and which, under the pressure of the bank screw, will be sent to New York and sold, and the proceeds remitted to London in specie.

THE EFFECT OF AN ATTEMPT TO MAINTAIN SPECIE PAYMENTS,

Under such circumstances, is illustrated by a diagram, copied from Gibbon's book on the banks and banking in New York, showing that the loss of less than six millions of dollars by the banks in New York, in 1857, caused a reduction in bank loans from one hundred and twenty to ninety-four millions of dollars, which, as we have explained, caused the loss by commercial failures alone of one hundred and forty-three millions, seven hundred and eighty thousand dollars !!! Surely it cannot be necessary to do more than refer to the fact, that the dates given in the diagrams showing the fluctuations in the quantity of bullion in the bank of England, and of bank loans in the city of New York, prove conclusively that so long as that bank can export our specie at will, and our banks are compelled to pay specie, the regulation of the value of our money, of our credit, and of our property, will be placed in the discretion of the bank of England and not, as the Constitution has said it should be, in the power of our Congress.

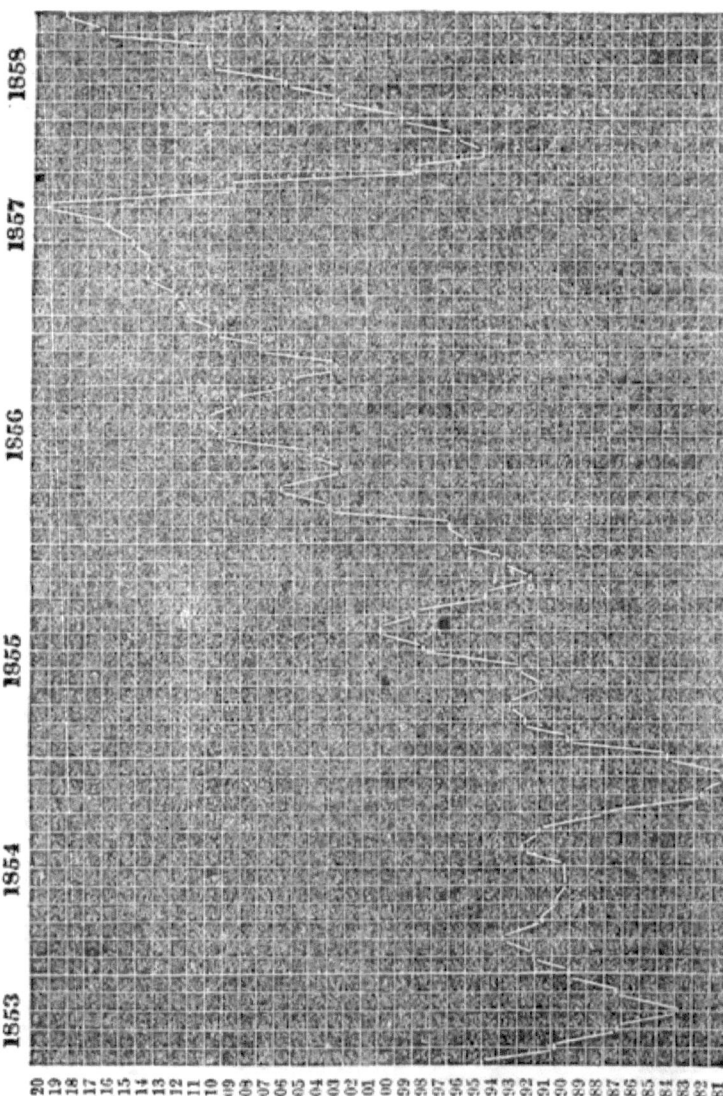

Diagram showing the Fluctuation of Discounts in the Banks of the City of New York.

By comparing the diagram, showing the fluctuation in the quantity of bullion in the bank of England with the diagram, illustrating the diminution of the bank loans in New York, it will be seen that the loss of specie and the increased rate of interest charged by the bank of England, caused a corresponding reduction in the loans and discounts in the banks of New York, and that the fearful depreciation in the values of property and the overwhelming commercial losses, which then occurred, were produced by the pressure of the bank screw in London, and the fruitless effort to continue specie payments by the banks in New York.

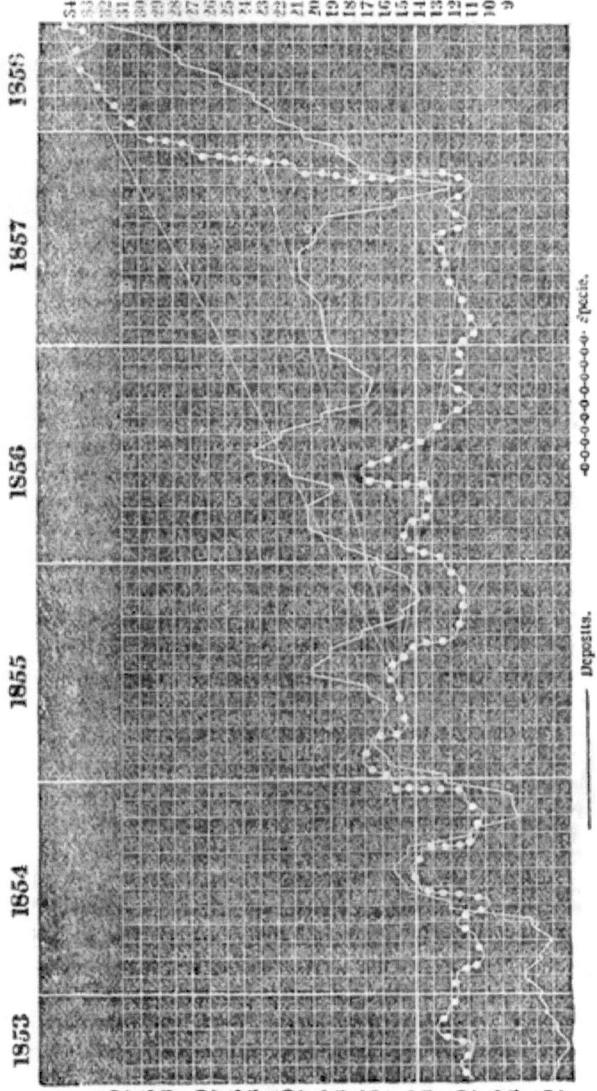

Diagram showing the fluctuations in the deposits and the specie in the banks of the city of New York, the marginal figures, from 37 to 91, showing the sum of deposits, and the figures from 9 to 34 showing the sums in specie, in millions of dollars, at corresponding dates, as indicated by the diagram ; also showing that the reduction of discounts, as indicated in the diagram on page 105, from one hundred and twenty millions to ninety-four millions of dollars, caused a loss of deposits which, acting on the internal commerce, compelled the payment of balances in specie ; so that, although the average required to maintain the value of specie at a proper level was not more than thirteen millions, the sum in the banks increased, in six months, to thirty-five millions. This surplus accumulated by depleting the banks of the interior and producing a corresponding reduction of the values of property.

CHAPTER XX.

THE "MONEY MERCHANTS" OF EUROPE.

WE have spoken of the proposals issued by Russia for a loan of two hundred and fifty millions of dollars for the purpose of building a railroad from Moscow to the Amoor river. I quote from the London Spectator of the 11th April, 1857, the following notice of that loan :

THE NEW POWER IN EUROPE.

" The present state of affairs on the Continent suggests the existence of some influence which is not generally recognized, *though its power must be overruling and its operation universal.* It is not seen, yet it reverses the councils of governments which appear to be supreme; it disregards equally public opinion and the interests of the states in which it has its agents. The monetary condition of France and of Northern Europe draws attention once more to the irregular and dangerous speculation which the most powerful man in Europe tries in vain to curb; it would seem that there is some greater power than he, irresponsible, and absolute; and when we turn to ascertain the fact, we are not long in discovering at least to create uneasiness and to demand scrutiny. We perceive some corroborative proof that such an influence does exist, *that its power is becoming supreme, that it is now doing mischief, and that it may become dangerous alike to the material condition, the political independence, and the domestic order of states.* Nor are we speaking of any imaginary or mere 'moral' influence; we speak of a powerful combination more than political, more personal than a congress of diplomatists or princes.

" The Emperor Napoleon has long been engaged in the endeavor to draw out the enterprise of his subjects, and the effect throughout France is great. Any traveller in the most outlying provinces perceives a remarkable change in the aspect, action, and condition of the people. The trading class, as well as the industrious classes, are animated by a spirit of energy hitherto unknown to the Celtic population. They have learned not only to employ their time with more vigor, but employ their savings—to venture that which they once hoarded. In that economical sense France was almost a virgin soil, and the effect is described by the traveller as marvellous. Thus far a blessed change. But look beyond. The very capitalists who fostered if they did not implant the idea in the Imperial mind, have seized the same opportunity to project movements for the further development of capital, its power and productivity. The great speculator in this sense differs in some degree from the ordinary trader. *The money merchant obtains his profit entirely from the simple act of exchange, and he does so equally whether the original holders are profiting in the transaction or not. He may be the broker between two communities who are ruining each other ; and build his fortune upon their downfall. And the individual trader in this merchandise will be instigated by the desire principally to grasp large and prompt profits.* He is not a safe councillor for those who have in charge the permanent interests of states. For the welfare of a community, immensely accumulated wealth, hoards of gold, are not so essential as well-diffused supplies of the necessaries of life and its enjoyments. But the same movement which gave an impulse to the commercial spirit in France made the largest opening that the world has ever seen for a forward

8

movement of great capitalists; and they have snatched it. Alarmed at the vast proportions which these joint-stock combinations have attained in France, the Emperor and his political ministers have issued their protest against excesses in that direction; they have followed up protests with restrictive imposts; but still the movement goes on.

"The commercial activity directed to the development of real trade would with as much steadiness as rapidity increase the available means of the French people; would make them more independent of the casualties of the seasons—would make them more comfortable, more orderly, more capable of supporting their ruler, more obedient to his decrees. It is easily to be understood why the Emperor Napoleon desires to add that element of English order to the military capabilities and energy of the French. He has in great part succeeded. But the excess of speculation involved by those who have stood ready to take advantage of the impulse, has, again in the present moment, as it did in the autumn of last year, threatened to defeat the improvement by overdoing it; and we in England are under the same commercial pressure which visited us in the autumn. At the same time there appears to be no suspense in developing, extending, and multiplying the immense joint stock combinations which the French Emperor has endeavored to restrain; though at such a time such operations ought to be entirely suspended. We see on the stocks the new International Society of Commercial Credit, whose founders are connected with the great money corporations in every capital of Europe—the banks of France, England, Amsterdam, &c. The list of the Council of Administration of the great company lies before us. Of the great Russian Railway Company half of the members short of one are Russians, and the greater number in that half are Councillors of State and officers in the service of the Emperor Alexander. In that Russian half, however, we see the name of "Thomas Baring, banker, in London." The other half consists of men whose names are well known

in every capital: S. Gwyer, member of the Council of Commerce, Earnest Sillem, a partner in the house of Pope & Co., at Amsterdam; Guillaume Borski, banker in Amsterdam; Francis Baring, banker in London; Henri Hottinguer, banker in Paris; Isaac Pereire, administrator of the Paris and Lyons Railway; Baron Seillere, banker in Paris; M. Auguste Thurneyssen, administrator of the West of France Railway; and M. Louis Fould, brother of the well-known state financier. *Some of those are the names we so constantly encounter in that comparatively small list of men who are administering the greatest financial operations in Paris, Vienna, St. Petersburg, Amsterdam, and London.* The object of this company is to take forty-five millions of capital—a sum which could easily be raised for reproductive purposes, but which they intend to sink in railways through the Russian deserts; while the actual state of the whole world—of Europe, England, America, and the far East—proves that we cannot spare that forty-five millions, nor even the first instalment of it. Yet these few gentlemen, who rule the world at present, have determined that it shall be taken, despite the Emperor of the French, the bank of England, or the commercial public of this country.

"It is said that the position of M. de Morny is not satisfactory either to the Emperor of all the Russias or to the Emperor of the French; but M. de Morny is fulfilling a corner which has become independent of Emperors. He has attached himself to the Grand Council of the International Finance, and it is that Grand Council at present which arranges the affairs of the world by the power of the purse, let potentates and parliaments think what they may. The Emperor of the French is at present engaged in attempting to restrain the use of fictitious titles—counties, vis-counties, and baronies—baubles at which the aristocracy of wealth may laugh. *The power of that order, which is the more powerful, because its members are comparatively limited, proceeds in its action independently of those ordinary political movements, and shows itself pursuing its course uninterrupted, undiverted, whatever may be the state of the commercial world, whatever may be the mood of the Imperial mind, whatever may be the action of ordinary statesmen.*

"We are not considering the diversion of capital, the dangers that may arise from over-speculation, the ruin that may visit shareholders in these huge joint stock companies, from which the directors always withdraw before the crash. We are not considering the commercial disturbance created by the necessity which is forced upon Europe just at present, of undergoing a high rate of interest for ordinary commercial accommodation, while millions are lavished upon the fancies or the schemes of those millionnaire statesmen. *We are simply considering the magnitude and the independence of that power of combined millions. It is a new order, a new administration in the world. The names most conspicuous in it are remarkable for certain characteristics. Read them again—Rothschild, Baring, Steiglitz, Pereire, Hottinguer, and Fould; with a second order, comprising the Weguelins, the Hopes, and the Sillieres. They form a grand council of small numbers, that could all be assembled in a dining-room. They are remarkable for being closely connected with the governments of all the principal states in the world, while at the same time they are not closely connected with the states under those governments.* You would not accept a Baring as being peculiarly representative of England; you must choose many other names before it—the Russels, the Stanleys, the Salts, the Crawshays, Cobdens, and Tyrells. France would certainly not be represented by Pereire, no country by a Rothschild; a Steiglitz is by no means exclusively Russian, any more than Fould is French. *The class is alien to any particular country, and yet is deeply rooted in the administration of each country. It can command not only a mass of capital enough to determine the financial operations of a government, the success or failure of a state loan, but it can influence, beneficially or fatally, the course of trade, by turning upon any one branch the combined mass of capitals from states elsewhere, just as the five potentates of Europe can muster* an army which would crush the people of any one empire mutinying against any one of the five. But this grand council of millionaires has proved that it is superior to the political administration of the separate countries. It is at once alien to the aristocracy of any country, and yet becoming more powerful, and therefore more respected, than any one aristocracy. Unlike any order which we have yet seen, it has its home equally in Paris, Berlin, Vienna, Amsterdam, St. Petersburg, or London. It is republican, but of the aristocratic republic, more close than the Grand Council of Venice, infinitely more arbitrary. Like that commercial republic, kings bow down to it; but the kings that now bend are the giant emperors of our day, not the brawling leaders of the middle ages. The debates of this council are not reported; its constitution is as yet unascertained and undetermined. We feel its power before we can define it. It is independent of political councils, higher than political responsibilities, ignorant of constitutional checks.* It stands confessed in the actual events of the present week; and in its independence, perhaps disregard of the interests which it overrides, it extorts from us the question whether any account has yet been taken of the immense institution that has sprung up while emperors and common politicians were thinking to settle the world with armies and treaties."

I have marked parts of this article in italics, and quote it thus at length, because it is conclusive proof not only of the existence of that

COMBINATION OF "MONEY BROKERS,"

To which I have referred, but is a graphic description of that combination, and of their purpose and mode of action; and proves, not only that France and England are in accord as to the measures and policy by which they seek to promote their own manufactures, as the source of their "futue prosperity," but that this "NEW POWER" is in accord with them, and is one of the most potent agents through which they act, for the advancement of their "projects in Europe ;" and upon which they rely, to arrest and control the progress of "rival" nations. We know that the combined influence of England and France defeated the loan to Russia, and fearing that Russia, although defeated in that means of participating in the trade of India, Japan, and China, would nevertheless obtain a preponderating influence in Japan and China. France and England united in the

WAR IN CHINA.

No one can doubt the motive or the purpose of that war, nor with the facts I have stated, and the authorities I have quoted before him, can any intelligent American doubt that there is a purpose to "organize a European coalition against the supremacy of America ;" nor can he doubt that this "new power in Europe," which it was said "*is becoming supreme*," and "*may become dangerous alike to the material condition, the political independence and the domestic order of states*," will be enlisted on the side of the "European powers" in the struggle which is to prevent our "taking possession of the whole gulf of Mexico," and becoming "the sole disburser of the products of the New World ?"

Is it necessary that I should remind the intelligent reader, that "the money merchant obtains his profit entirely from the simple act of exchange, and he does so equally whether the original holders are profiting in the transaction or not. He may be the broker between two communities who are ruining each other ; and build his fortunes upon their downfall. And the individual trader in this merchandise will be instigated principally by the desire to grasp large and prompt

profit," and that there has been no period in the history of speculation when stronger inducements were offered to the "money merchant" than he can now find in the Southern states, and that, therefore, the proposition to

ORGANIZE THE LAND OWNERS IN AN ASSOCIATION,

which will identify their homes, their industry, their credit, their property with the public credit of the United States, and make that public credit the basis of their "future prosperity," merits and should receive the approbation of the people of the United States. For while I refer to the fact, that the purpose of European governments, as indicated in the extracts I have quoted, is "to organize a European coalition against the supremacy of America," I do not make that reference in any feeling of hostility to the people or the governments of Europe, nor do I refer to the "money merchants," " the new power in Europe," in any feeling of hostility to them. It is the duty of the governments of Europe to protect and foster the interests and welfare of their respective peoples, and in the exhibition I have given, of the measures and policy of the European governments, and in the fact that they believe that it is necessary for them "to organize a European coalition against the supremacy of America," I would argue the necessity, and, consequently, the imperative duty of our own government to foster and protect the interests and welfare of the American people, and hence, I urge the necessity of so organizing our system of currency and finance as to deprive the bank of England, aided as it has been and will be by the "money merchants" of Europe, of the power to regulate the quantity of our money, and, consequently, of the power to regulate the value of our credit and of our property; and I argue that that it is impossible to do this otherwise than by using the public credit as our money of account, and making it the basis of our private credit, of our industry and of our progress, of our power, of our wealth, our union and prosperity.

The use of public credit is of comparatively recent origin. The extent to which it may be used by an enlightened people, is illustrated by the progress of the public debt of England. We are indebted to Ayres' Financial Register, of 1857, for a series of tables derived from official sources. The following shows the aggregate amount of the public debt of the United Kingdom, at different periods, with the amount of the public revenue:

Periods.	Debt.	Interest.	Pub. Revenue.
Public Debt at the Revolution in 1686..........	$3,321,315	$199,325	$10,009,425
Debt contracted during the reign of William III.	78,652,195	6,355,430	
" at the accession of Queen Anne, in 1702....	81,973,510	6,554,760	19,476,000
" contracted during this reign	188,753,305	10,202,080	
" at the accession of George I., in 1714. ..	270,726,815	16,756,840	29,459,000
" reduced during this reign...............	10,265,640	669,035	
" at the accession of George II., in 1727....	260,461,175	16,087,805	33,810,000
" reduced during 12 years peace, ending 1739	25,688,060	1,267,630	
" at commencement of Spanish war in 1739..	234,773,115	14,820,175	34,370,000
" increased during seven years' war........	156,693,445	5,484,895	
" at the end of the Spanish war, in 1748....	391,466,560	20,305,070	34,615,000
" reduced during eight years of peace.......	18,607,360	3,321,385	
" at commencement of war in 1756.........	372,859,200	16,983,685	35,635,000
" increased during seven years of war.......	360,555,020	12,220,520	
" at the end of the war in 1763.............	733,414,220	29,204,205	42,617,220
" reduced during thirteen years of peace....	53,698,965	1,820,000	
" at opening of the American war, in 1775...	679,715,255	27,384,205	51,325,000
" increased during eight years of war. . ..	512,709,095	19,215,420	
" at the end of the American war...........	1,192,424,350	46,599,625	59,820,000
" reduced during ten years of peace.........	23,756,305	717,945	
" at commencement of French war, in 1793	1,168,668,045	45,881,680	83,294,070
" contracted during French war, ending 1815	3,655,444,160	115,244,740	
" of the United Kingdom at the consolidation of the English and Irish Exchequer, in 1817...............................	4,824,112,205	161,126,420	370,000,000

The entire amount of the public debt of the United Kingdom is made up of several distinct items, under the heads of funded debt, in the shape of loans contracted, or by funding securities, of terminable and life annuities, and of the unfunded debt, consisting of exchequer bonds and exchequer bills. The following table, compiled from parliamentary documents, shows the total amount of debt funded and unfunded, and the total annual charge from 1820 to 1855, inclusive:

Years.	Total Amount of Debt Funded and Unfunded.	Total Annual Charge.
1820....	$4,162,656,050	$158,198,885
1821....	4,134,396,585	159,334,500
1822....	4,164,056,475	148,596,190
1823....	4,132,216,820	148,020,035
1824....	4,067,608,360	145,784,065
1825....	4,030,612,335	144,099,895
1826. ..	4,041,837,950	145,437,170
1827....	4,025,118,710	144,857,700
1828....	3,999,897,700	144,587,025
1829....	3,983,712,410	144,009,615
1830....	3,915,483,230	138,720,245
1831....	3,905,476,170	139,930,930
1832....	3,898,982,745	139,859,140

Years.	Total Amount of Debt Funded and Unfunded.	Total Annual Charge.
1833....	$3,807,828,915	$140,767,835
1834....	3,860,984,245	139,683,435
1835....	3,937,632,330	144,837,450
1836....	3,941,992,850	144,525,565
1837....	3,931,598,690	146,665,740
1838....	3,926,868,700	145,248,075
1839....	3,923,562,670	146,791,005
1840....	3,937,240,375	145,856,905
1841....	3,954,373,040	147,077,355
1842....	3,956,252,200	146,281,860
1843....	3,952,881,960	145,221,435
1844..	3,937,990,725	141,947,495
1845....	3,925,265,110	140,246,525
1846....	3,914,594,920	139,592,235
1847....	3,931,741,755	140,780,090
1848....	3,059,046,690	142,238,300
1849....	3,954,635,985	140,842,255
1850....	3,935,145,812	139,301,650
1851....	3,914,346,910	138,910,810
1852 ...	3,896,826,020	138,578,970
1853....	3,854,115,005	137,302,015
1854...	3,873,986,000	135,466,700
1855....	4,017,476,975	140,929,790

We know that many persons, speculating on the immense weight of the public debt of England, have anticipated her national bankruptcy; but it is an important fact that the people of England are themselves the creditors, as well as the debtors, and that they are enabled to bear this immense burden, great as it is, because the immense sums paid by themselves as taxes, are received by themselves as dividends. This fact is so important as illustrating the capacity of an industrious and intelligent people to absorb a *domestic* public debt, that we give a table, showing the number of persons entitled to receive dividends on the public debt of the United Kingdom, which proves that, large as that debt is, it has been absorbed and is held by the masses—by the persons of small incomes—by the people, who have placed their surplus earnings in that fund, as a safe and permanent investment, and who have thus become interested in the stability of the government. There were, in 1856 :

DISTRIBUTION OF THE DEBT.

185,181 persons entitled to dividends of..................					$25 and under.		
86,401	"	"	"	"	50 and exceeding		$25
179,884	"	"	"	"	250	"	50
46,596	"	"	"	"	500	"	250
26,204	"	"	"	"	1,000	"	500
7,400	"	"	"	"	1,500	"	1,000
4,981	"	"	"	"	2,500	"	1,500
2,201	"	"	"	"	5,000	"	2,500
780	"	"	"	"	10,000	"	5,000
448	"	"	"	"		exceeding	10,000

Giving 540,166 as the number of all classes entitled to dividends.

As a further illustration of the capacity of a people to place large sums in the shape of a funded debt, bearing a low rate of interest, we refer to the savings banks of Great Britain and Ireland.

THE FIRST SAVINGS BANK

In England originated in 1804, with a woman, Mrs. Priscilla Wakefield, who, in charity, agreed to receive pennies from the laboring poor during the summer, to be repaid at Christmas, with five per cent. interest. The sums deposited in savings banks had so increased that Parliament required the amount to be placed under the control of commissioners, by whom it was invested in the public debt; and the following statement shows the number of depositors with the amount of deposits in November, 1855. There were :

185,310	persons depositing	$5,	and sums not exceeding	$5,	making	$283,550
249,876	"	"	5,	"	"	25,	"	3,179,700
169,638	"	"	25,	"	"	50,	"	5,895,255
122,787	"	"	50,	"	"	75,	"	7,345,605
75,501	"	"	75,	"	"	100,	"	6,474,285
130,154	"	"	100,	"	"	150,	"	15,590,030
105,614	"	"	150,	"	"	200,	"	17,671,815
51,459	"	"	200,	"	"	250,	"	11,416,850
86,229	"	"	250,	"	"	350,	"	26,187,529
41,285	"	"	350,	"	"	500,	"	17,889,015
27,036	"	"	500,	"	"	575,	"	15,013,340
16,508	"	"	575,	"	"	750,	"	11,247,225
25,200	"	"	750,	"	"	1,000,	"	21,422,480
1,480	"	"	more than	1,000,	"	1,655,410

1,288,077 individuals who deposited $161,243,220
14,148 charitable institutions which deposited.......................... 3,386,190
8,758 friendly societies   "   "   6,686,265

1,300,983 total number of depositors who deposited......................$171,315,675

These depositors received but 2.94 per cent. per annum as interest—the difference between 2.94 and 3 per cent. being charged for management. Surely if the working classes of England can absorb so large a part of the public debt of England, and the depositors in the savings banks can place to the use of the government more than one hundred and seventy millions of their surplus earnings, the people of the United States need not ask the "money merchants" of Europe to buy any part of their public debt.

SUBSIDIES.

A more significant feature of the financial strength of the people of England is, that during the war with France, they advanced as loans and subsidies to Hanover, Hesse Cassel, Sardinia, Prussia, Hesse Darmstadt, Baden, Germany, Brunswick, Portugal, Prince of Orange, Bavaria, Russia, Sweden, Spain, Sicily, Austria, Morocco, Denmark, Holland, and to *France!* the sum of $301,047,813.

The imagination may well be start-led at the magnitude of these sums, and accustomed, as we have been, to consider the Bank of England as the regulator of the monetary system and credit of the world, we naturally assume that it is to the financial strength and great resources of that bank that the people of England are indebted for the ability to sustain the weight of such a burden of taxation. We are the more inclined to do this because it is known that the bank is the financial agent of the government, and that Parliament, in 1797, passed an act requiring the bank to suspend specie payment as a means of enabling the bank to aid in sustaining the public credit.

In this connection, the following table, showing the equivalent of three per cent. stock for the amount of debt funded, the stock created for one hundred pounds in money, the market value of the paper pound in gold, and the value per cent. of the paper currency, with the average circulation of Bank of England notes, is given :

Years.	Amount of Debt funded.	Equivalent in three per cent. Stock.	Stock created for £100 in Money.	Market Value of Paper £ in Gold.		Market Value per cent. of Paper Currency.			Average Circulation of Bank of Eng. Notes.
	£	£	£	s.	d.	£	s.	d	£
1800....	20,500,000	32,185,000	158.50	20	0.0	100	0	0	15,160,000
1801....	36,910,450	63,578,100	174.54	18	3.8	91	12	4	15,800,000
1802....	25,000,000	32,990,630	132.17	18	6.5	92	14	2	16,427,000
1803....	12,000,000	25,483,330	173.55	19	5.6	97	6	10	16,500,000
1804....	14,500,000	26,390,000	185.00	19	5.6	97	6	10	17,408,000
1805....	22,500,100	41,800,000	177.20	19	5.6	97	6	10	16,876,000
1806....	20,000,000	33,200,000	167.70	19	5.6	97	6	10	16,791,000
1807....	15,700,000	24,798,290	159.20	19	5.6	97	6	10	16,705,000
1808....	14,500,000	23,530,622	162.67	19	5.6	97	6	10	17,128,000
1809....	22,532,100	36,218,740	161.39	19	5.6	97	6	10	18,917,000
1810....	21,711,000	33,112,100	152.67	17	6.3	86	10	6	22,541,000
1811....	24,006,000	39,724,520	166.53	18	5.1	92	3	2	23,282,000
1812....	34,721,325	57,198,380	180.60	16	3.7	79	5	3	23,437,000
1813....	64,755,700	118,736,690	184.87	15	5.4	77	2	0	24,529,000
1814....	24,007,400	36,839,990	154.17	14	11.7	74	17	6	26,901,000
1815....	54,135,589	102,787,340	191.52	16	7.8	83	5	9	26,887,000
1816....	....	....	......	16	7.8	83	5	9	26,574,000
1817....	....	....	......	19	5.6	97	6	10	28,274,000
1818....	....	....	......	19	5.6	97	6	10	27,221,000
1819....	....	....	......	19	1.3	95	11	0	25,227,000
1820....	....	....	......	19	5.8	97	8	0	23,569,000
1821....	....	....	......	20	0.0	100	0	0	22,471,000

These tables show that in 1800, three years after the bank of England had suspended specie payments, the bank note was at par, although the public credit was fifty-eight and a half per cent. below par; and that although the value of the paper pound was in 1814 reduced to 14 shillings 11.7 pence, it was again at par with gold in 1821, although the bank did not resume specie payment until 1825. And another striking fact is, that while the average depreciation of the bank of England notes, as compared with gold, was less than two per cent. the depreciation of the public credit as compared with the bank notes, was 67.60 per cent. Yet in 1806 the whole capital of the bank was but $58,212,000, which was then increased to $72,765,000, of which $70,000,000 was invested in the very securities which were thus depreciated. Can any one doubt that

THE CAUSE OF THIS DIFFERENCE BETWEEN THE VALUE OF THE BANK NOTES AND THE PUBLIC CREDIT

Was, that the bank notes were money, while the public credit was a commodity to be purchased and paid for with money. The use of money is to purchase property and pay debts—and hence he who held the bank notes could purchase property or pay debts with the notes, while he who held the public credit was compelled to exchange it for bank notes, because he could not buy property or pay debts without money? By making the United States four per cents. convertible into money, in the shape of currency, the value of the bond is equal to currency, because it will be convertible into money at the will of the holder. As the bank note convertible into gold is worth as much as gold because it is so convertible; and the fact that the four per cent. interest will be payable in currency instead of specie, will act as a further reduction of interest, being at the present price of gold, less than three per cent. instead of six per cent., and this will further tend to prevent the export of United States bonds as an investment of foreign capital. The effect of this reduction of interest to be paid in currency will be to lessen the burden of the public debt and increase the means of payment, while the early resumption of specie payment will be to more than double the burden of the public debt, and to reduce the means of payment more than fifty per cent. In this connection, I would quote the following appropriate extract from the late

LETTER OF THE SECRETARY OF THE TREASURY

to the committee of ways and means :

"In regard to the other important feature of the bill—the authority to withdraw United States notes—I have merely to remark, that I conceive it to be of great importance to the business of the country, the welfare of the people, and the credit of the nation, that such a financial policy should be adopted by this Congress as will prepare the way for a return to specie payment. When this can be brought about will depend on the condition of national industry and the trade relations between the United States and foreign nations. It is not desirable that species payments shall be restored until that restoration can be made permanent by increased industry and a proper adjustment of the trade with Europe. The tendencies now are all in the right direction, and if they shall be adjusted by judicious legislation, I shall be hopeful that the currency of the country may be brought up to the specie standard without a large reduction of it. The apprehension which exists, that if power is given to the Secretary to retire United States notes, the circulation of the country will be ruinously contracted, is

without any substantial foundation. If no reliance can be placed upon the discretion and carefulness of the Secretary, the very condition of finances of the country will prevent such a reduction of the currency as will make either a tight money market or depress business. Authority to reduce the currency will go very far to prevent the necessity for a reduction. The battle will be more than half fought when the government shall adopt a healthy financial policy."

The purpose of the Secretary is here declared to be to prepare for a return to specie payments, "by increased industry and a proper adjustment of our trade with Europe." Can we increase our industry without the means of paying the wages of labor ? And can we properly adjust our trade with Europe so long as the bank of England can, at will, compel us to pay, in gold, the large balances due and to become due to European creditors ?

The following extract from the London News of December 27, 1856, shows

THE EFFECT OF THE EXPORT OF SILVER TO INDIA AND CHINA

Upon the money market of Europe, and its bearing on the values of money and of property in the United States. He is blind to the purpose and tendency of the war in Europe who does not see that extraordinary efforts will be made to consummate the measures recommended by List, as quoted in a previous chapter, and that Prussia intends to participate in, if she does not monopolize a large part of, the trade of Asia, and that the inevitable tendency of that trade will be to increase the demand for the precious metals—placing the quantity of our specie more under the control of the "money merchants," and, consequently, rendering it more necessary for us to adhere to our system of paper money.

(Extract.)

"IMMENSE DRAIN OF BULLION TO THE EAST.

"The constant flow of silver to the East forms one of the most remarkable commercial movements of the day. Its importance consists in the fact that it is not a mere temporary feature, exercising a momentary influence upon the money market. On the contrary, the efflux has been steadily increasing for some years, and has now assumed such proportions as to challenge general attention. Its effect upon our money market is direct and important, for it causes the instant diffusion over the continent of the gold which is imported in such enormous quantities from Australia and the United States, and which would, in all probability, be retained here to a considerable extent if it were not used to pay for the silver which we import from the continent in order to be transported to the East. Nor is the interest felt in the question confined to this country, for a serious monetary derangement has been created nearly throughout Europe by this silver movement. We see it estimated, that in some instances upward of a hundred thousand pounds worth of silver has been conveyed to this country in a single steamer from Antwerp. Very recently it was mentioned in the Belgian Chambers that three millions of francs, or about £120,000, in silver, had left Antwerp by one vessel for London. Of the £488,085, in silver, taken out by the Indus on the 20th inst., about £450,000 is estimated to have been drawn direct from the continent, chiefly in coin. Of course, when we, as purveyors of silver to the East, obtain the metal from the continent, we make payment for it in some shape, either in gold or in other commodities. As the commerce of Europe is undeniably increasing year by year, it is reasonable to assume that for all the silver coin withdrawn from circulation a proportionate quantity of gold is coined. Nevertheless, it is quite evident that *this process of the displacement of silver by gold in many European countries cannot go on at the present rate without seriously disturbing the money market, and, in many cases, deranging the balance of commercial transactions.* The constant movement of gold and silver in large masses from place to place of itself involves a considerable demand for money. Besides, the exchange of gold for silver in the continental cities is not effected by means of one single transaction. For instance, we will suppose a circumstance which happened lately, namely, the receipt in London of news of a rise in the exchanges in India. Large buyers of silver for the East immediately come forward, and our market being very scantily supplied with the metal, there is no resource but to transmit orders for the collection of the requisite quantity upon the continent. Among the markets thus applied to will be, probably, Hamburg. In that city the English demand, coming in addition to the demands of other markets, has in several instances of late caused a sudden, though perhaps temporary rise in the value of money. The pressure at Hamburg reacts in a still more violent manner upon other contiguous but more limited markets. For example, within the last fortnight, the rates of discount for good bills rose at Copenhagen to eight and ten per cent., owing chiefly to the extensive withdrawals of silver. Doubtless the equivalent of the commodity withdrawn will be eventually restored in due course of trade, but this consideration does not tend to diminish the pressure for the time. The inconvenience sometimes occasioned being thus severe, it is not surprising that the silver movement is watched almost as narrowly on the continent as in London. The great current of silver flowing constantly to the East is mainly fed, so to speak, by rivulets from every country in Europe; and there is reason to believe that within a few years the monetary system of many continental states will be subjected to important modifications arising out of this one potent case.

"We have remarked that the drain of silver eastward is increasing in severity. Means for proving the assertion are afforded by some remarkable tables compiled by Mr. James Low, the details of which are given in our city article. *During the year now about to close the direct shipments of silver alone from England to the various Eastern ports have amounted to more than twelve millions sterling ;* the exact sum is £12,118,985. It would be an important point to ascertain how much of this immense mass of silver has been drawn from the metallic circulation of the continent, but no reliable statistics upon this subject are obtainable. There is ground to believe, however, that the larger proportion of these twelve millions has consisted of continental silver coins, chiefly of French and Belgium five-frank pieces. During the first six months of the year the total shipments of silver were £4,898,908. During the last six months they have increased to £7,220,077. In the former period the monthly remittances varied from £481,516 to £944,319, and in May reached £1,152,013. In the latter half of the year the minimum monthly amount has been £1,104,882; and the largest amount £1,286,716, has been shipped in the current month of December. While the aggregate shipments of 1856, as already stated, were £12,118,985, the sum in 1855 was £6,409,889; in 1854, £3,132,003; in 1853, £4,710,665; in 1852, £2,630,238; and in 1851, £1,716,100. *During the last six years the English bullion dealers have thus supplied the East with £30,717,880 in silver.* It is well known that this branch of business pays well; and the profits realized by the collectors, exporters, carriers, and consignees of this vast mass of treasure must represent a very important sum. England will probably always remain the greatest market in the world for the precious metals; but the French dealers show also an increased disposition to embark in the Eastern bullion trade. In addition to the sums already recorded, £5,813,532 in silver has been remitted during the last four years direct to the East from the Mediterranean. In 1856, the sum has been £1,989,916, of which £1,842,016 was despatched from Marseilles alone.

"It will be noticed that of the £12,118,985 in silver sent direct from England to the East in the year now about to close, the proportion despatched to China was £3,167,014, the rest being absorbed by India and the Straits settlements. At certain periods of the year the demand for China has been extremely animated, while that for India has slackened. At other periods—and this seems to be the case now—the Indian demand has proved active, and the Chinese moderate. From one source or another, however, there has been a continual demand throughout the year; and the probability is that the drain both to China and to India will continue heavy for a considerable time to come. The great houses engaged in the tea and silk trade seem unanimous in thinking that, in the present state of China, cash must be remitted to a great extent in payment for the supplies of these articles of produce. That populous country is still internally distracted; and the native dealers want silver, not goods, in exchange for their commodities. *The failure of the French silk crop, and the extraordinarily high price which that article commands, must render considerable shipments of bullion to China a matter of certainty for many months to come.* Within the last few weeks, moreover, there has been a sensible rise in the price of tea; and this circumstance will also exercise some influence in the same direction, though to a minor extent.

"But it is to India that the bulk of the silver flows; and to the social and commercial progress of India we must look for the explanation. Statistics previously quoted have proved that a great proportion of the silver introduced into that country is at once converted into its most useful form—that of coin—and conveyed into the interior. All the commercial details transmitted from India tend to show that the absorption of silver is a necessary consequence of the steady development of trade. The last annual report on the trade of Calcutta, extending to May last, showed an increase of some eight millions sterling in the aggregate movement of the commerce of that port, as compared with the previous year. All the staple articles of export, especially indigo, rice, silk, both raw and manufactured), jute, &c., present largely increased totals. Increased exports of produce involve, of course, increased payments to the producer; and the Indian producer must be paid in silver. Turning our attention to another portion of our Indian empire—the lately acquired province of Pegu—we find that the exports of rice last season amounted to two thirds of the average annual exports of Bengal, exclusive only of the year 1855-56. Considering how recently Pegu has been brought under British rule, this result is very remarkable. For a large portion of these supplies of rice settlement must have been made in silver. At the opposite extremity of our Indian possessions—the Punjaub and contiguous provinces—the field awaiting development is still more important. In that quarter the Scinde Railway is being rapidly pushed forward, and, in conjunction with contemplated extensions, and with a well-devised system of steam river transit, will soon, in all likelihood, give an immense stimulus to trade. When we find that in the year 1853-54 the price of wheat in the Punjaub averaged about 16s. per quarter, in the following year 14s., and in the year 1855-56 twelve shillings per quarter, delay in the providing of means of transport in that region would indeed be reprehensible. The capacity of some of these districts is described as almost unlimited. While commercial developments upon this immense scale are in progress almost throughout India, is it not perfectly natural that increased quantities of coin should be required. Each mail from India brings accounts of progress in the construction of roads, railways, bridges, and other means of communication, all involving large local disbursements. Nor must we overlook another consequence of the improvement which is gradually taking place in the condition of the native population. *The passion of many classes—especially of the artisans, shopkeepers, &c., for personal ornament, is surprising;* and this deeply-rooted tendency would of itself account for the absorption of a large quantity of the precious metals annually. But we have said enough to prove that the efflux of silver to the East must be regarded as an ordinary and necessary feature of commerce."—*See London News, December 27th, 1856.*

I quote this article thus at large because it forcibly illustrates the effect of an increased trade with India, China, and other parts of Asia, which is the chief inducement to the readjustment of the map of Europe, contemplated as the result of the war between Prussia and Austria. It will be seen that instead of absorbing the specie of Europe, as the trade of India will do, we, as the producers of gold and silver, can, by a proper use of paper money, furnish gold to supply the deficiency of specie caused by the drain to India. Europe will be dependent upon us for the life-blood of her credit and her commerce.

CHAPTER XXI.

BRITISH POLICY—THE QUINTUPLE TREATY.

HAVING referred to the Quintuple treaty as one of the measures intended to increase and perpetuate the maritime and commercial supremacy of England for the better understanding of that measure and the comments in relation to it, I give the text as submitted to the French chambers and published in Galignani's Messenger of March 1, 1842:

SUPPRESSION OF THE SLAVE TRADE.

The following is the text of the Quintuple treaty for the suppression of the African slave trade, signed in London, Dec. 20, 1841:

ART. I.—Their Majesties the Emperor of Austria, King of Hungary and Bohemia, the King of Prussia, and the Emperor of all the Russias, engage to prohibit all trade in slaves, either by their respective subjects, or under their respective flags, or by means of capital belonging to their respective subjects; and to declare such traffic piracy. Their Majesties further declare that any vessel which may attempt to carry on the slave trade shall, by that fact alone, lose all right to the protection of their flag.

ART. II.—In order more completely to accomplish the object of the present treaty, the high contracting parties agree by common consent that those of their ships-of-war which shall be provided with special warrants and orders, prepared according to the forms of the annex A of the present treaty, may search every merchant-vessel belonging to any one of the high contracting parties which shall, on reasonable grounds, be suspected of being engaged in the traffic in slaves, or of having been fitted out for that purpose, or of having been engaged in the traffic during the voyage in which she shall have been met with by the said cruisers; and that such cruisers may detain, and send, or carry away such vessels in order that they may be brought to trial in the manner hereafter agreed upon.

Nevertheless, the above-mentioned right of searching the merchant-vessels of any one or other of the high contracting parties shall be exercised only by ships-of-war whose commanders shall have the rank of captain or that of lieutenant in the royal or imperial navy, unless the command shall, by reason of death or otherwise, have devolved upon an officer of inferior rank. The commander of such ship-of-war shall be furnished with warrants according to the form annexed to the present treaty, under letter A.

The said mutual right of search shall not be exercised within the Mediterranean sea. Moreover, the space within which the exercise of the said right shall be confined shall be bounded, on the north, by the 32d parallel of north latitude; on the west, by the eastern coast of America, from the point where the 32d parallel of north latitude strikes that coast, down to the 45th parallel of south latitude; on the south, by the 45th parallel of south latitude, from the point where that parallel strikes the eastern coast of America, to the 80th degree of longitude east from the meridian of Greenwich; and on the east, by the same degree of longitude, from the point where it is intersected by the 45th parallel of south latitude up to the coast of India.

ART. III.—Each of the high contracting parties which may choose to employ cruisers for the suppression of the slave trade, and to exercise the mutual right of search, reserves to itself to fix, according to its own convenience, the number of the ships-of-war which shall be employed on the service stipulated in the second article of the present treaty, as well as the stations on which the said ships shall cruise.

The names of the ships appointed for this purpose, and those of their commanders, shall be communicated by each of the high contracting parties to the others; and they shall reciprocally apprize each other every time that a cruiser shall be placed on a station, or shall be called thence, in order that the necessary warrants may be delivered by the governments authorizing the search, and returned to those governments by the government which has received them, when those warrants shall no longer be necessary for the execution of the present treaty.

ART. IV.—Immediately after the government which employs the cruisers shall have notified to the government which is to authorize the search the number and the names of the cruisers which it intends to employ, the warrants authorizing the search shall be made out according to the form annexed to the present treaty, under letter A, and shall be delivered by the government which authorizes the search to the government which employs the cruiser.

In no case shall the mutual right of search be exercised upon the ships-of-war of the high contracting parties.

The high contracting parties shall agree upon a particular signal, to be used exclusively by those cruisers which shall be invested with the right of search.

ART. V.—The cruisers of the high contracting parties authorized to exercise the right of search and detention in execution of the present treaty shall conform themselves strictly to the instructions annexed to the said treaty, under letter B, in all that relates to the formalities of the search and of the detention, as well as to the measures to be taken, in order that the vessels suspected of having been employed in the traffic may be delivered over to the competent tribunals.

The high contracting parties reserve to themselves the right of making in these instructions, by common consent, such alterations as circumstances may render necessary.

The cruisers of the high contracting parties shall mutually afford to each other assistance in all cases where it may be useful that they should act in concert.

ART. VI.—Whenever a merchant-vessel, sailing under the flag of one of the high contracting parties, shall have been detained by a cruiser of the other, duly authorized to that effect, conformably to the provisions of the present treaty, such merchant-vessel, as well as the master, the crew, the cargo, and the slaves who may be on board, shall be brought into such place as the high contracting parties shall have respectfully designated for that purpose, and they shall be delivered over to the authorities appointed with that view by the government within whose possessions such place is situated, in order that proceedings may be had with respect to them before the competent tribunals in the manner hereafter specified. When the commander of the cruiser shall not think fit to undertake himself the bringing in and the delivery up of the detained vessel, he shall intrust that duty to an officer of the rank of lieutenant in the royal or imperial navy, or at least to the officer who shall at the time be the third in authority on board the detaining ship.

ART. VII. If the commander of a cruiser of one of the high contracting parties should have reason to suspect that a merchant-vessel sailing under the convoy of, or in company with, a ship-of-war of one of the other contracting parties, has been engaged in the slave-trade, or has been fitted out for that trade, he shall make known his suspicions to the commander of the ship of war, who shall proceed alone to search the suspected vessel; and in case the last-mentioned commander should ascertain that the suspicion is well founded, he shall cause the vessel, as well as the master, the crew, the cargo, and the slaves who may be on board, to be taken into a port belonging to the nation of the detained vessel, to be there proceeded against before the competent tribunals, in the manner hereafter directed.

ART. VIII.—As soon as a merchant-vessel,

detained, and sent in for adjudication, shall arrive at the port to which she is to be carried in conformity with annex B to the present treaty, the commander of the cruiser which shall have detained her, or the officer appointed to bring her in, shall deliver to the authorities appointed for that purpose a copy, signed by himself, of all the lists, declarations, and other documents specified in the instructions annexed to the present treaty, under letter B; and the said authorities shall proceed, in consequence, to the search of the detained vessel, and of her cargo, as also to an inspection of her crew, and of the slaves who may be on board, after having previously given notice of the time of such search and inspection to the commander of the cruiser, or to the officer who shall have brought in the vessel, in order that he, or some person whom he may appoint to represent him, may be present thereat.

A minute of these proceedings shall be drawn up in duplicate, which shall be signed by the persons who shall have taken part in, or who shall have been present at, the same; and one of those documents shall be delivered to the commander of the cruiser, or to the officer appointed by him to bring in the detained vessel.

Art. IX.—Every merchant vessel of any one or other of the five nations, which shall be searched and detained in virtue of the provisions of the present treaty, shall, unless proof be given to the contrary, be deemed to have been engaged in the slave-trade, or to have been fitted out for that traffic, if in the fitting, in the equipment, or on board the said vessel during the voyage in which she was detained, there shall be found to have been one of the articles hereafter specified, that is to say—

1. Hatches with open gratings, instead of the close hatches which are used in merchant-vessels.

2. Division or bulk-heads, in the hold or on deck, in greater number than are necessary for vessels engaged in lawful trade.

3. Spare plank fitted for being laid down as a second or slave deck.

4. Shackles, bolts, or handcuffs.

5. A larger quantity of water, in casks or in tanks, than is requisite for the consumption of the crew of such merchant-vessel.

6. An extraordinary number of water-casks, or of other receptacles for holding liquid, unless the master shall produce a certificate from the custom-house at the place from which he cleared outward, stating that sufficient security had been given by the owners of such vessel that such extra number of casks or of other receptacles should only be used to hold palm oil, or for other purposes of lawful commerce.

7. A greater quantity of mess tubs or kids than are requisite for the use of the crew of such merchant-vessel.

8. A boiler, or other cooking apparatus, of an unusual size, and larger, or capable of being made larger, than requisite for the use of the crew of such merchant-vessel; or more than one boiler, or other cooking apparatus, of the ordinary size.

9. An extraordinary quantity of rice, of the flour of Brazil manioc, or cassada, commonly called farina, or of maize, or of Indian corn, or of any other article of food whatever, beyond the probable wants of the crew; unless such quantity of rice, farina, maize, Indian corn, or any other article of food, should be entered on the manifest, as forming part of the trading cargo of the vessel.

10. A quantity of mats or matting greater than is necessary for the use of such merchant-vessel, unless such mats or matting be entered on the manifest as forming part of the cargo.

If it is established that one or more of the articles above specified are on board, or have been on board during the voyage in which the vessel was captured, that fact shall be considered as *prima facie* evidence that the vessel was employed in the traffic; she shall in consequence be condemned, and declared lawful prize, unless the master or the owners shall furnish clear and incontrovertible evidence, proving to the satisfaction of the tribunal that at the time of her detention or capture the vessel was employed in a lawful undertaking, and that such of the different articles above specified as were found on board at the time of detention, or which might have been embarked during the voyage on which she was engaged when she was captured, were indispensable for the accomplishment of the lawful object of her voyage.

Art. X.—Proceedings shall be immediately taken against the vessel detained, as above stated, her master, her crew, and her cargo, before the competent tribunal of the country to which she belongs; and they shall be tried and adjudged according to the established forms and laws in force in that country; and if it results from the proceedings that the said vessel was employed in the slave-trade, or fitted out for that traffic, the vessel, her fittings, and her cargo of merchandise, shall be confiscated, and the master, the crew, and their accomplices, shall be dealt with conformably to the laws by which they shall have been tried.

In case of confiscation, the proceeds of the sale of the aforesaid vessel shall, within the space of six months, reckoning from the date of the sale, be placed at the disposal of the government of the country to which the ship which made the capture belongs, in order to be employed in conformity with the laws of that country.

Art. XI.—If any one of the articles specified in Article IX. of the present treaty is found on board a merchant-vessel, or if it is proved to have been on board of her during the voyage in which she was captured, no compensation for losses, damages, or expenses, consequent upon the detention of such vessel, shall in any case be granted, either to the master, or to the owner, or to any other person interested in the equipment or in the lading, even though a sentence of condemnation should not have been pronounced against the vessel, as a consequence of her detention.

Art. XII.—In all cases in which a vessel shall have been detained in conformity with the present treaty, as having been employed in the slave-trade, or fitted out for that traffic, and shall, in consequence, have been tried and confiscated, the government of the cruiser which shall have made the capture, or the government whose tribunal shall have condemned the vessel, may purchase the condemned vessel for the service of its royal navy, at the price fixed by a competent person, selected for that purpose by the said tribunal. The government whose cruiser shall have made the capture shall have a right of preference in the purchase of the vessel. But if the condemned vessel should not be purchased in the manner above pointed out, she shall be wholly broken up immediately after the sentence of confiscation, and sold in separate portions after having been broken up.

Art. XIII.—When, by the sentence of the competent tribunal, it shall have been ascertained that a merchant-vessel detained in virtue of the present treaty was not engaged in the slave-trade, and was not fitted out for that traffic, she shall be restored to the lawful owner or owners. And if, in the course of the proceedings, it shall have been proved that the vessel was searched and detained illegally, or without sufficient cause of suspicion; or that the search and detention were attended with abuse or vexation, the commander of the cruiser or the officer who shall have boarded the said vessel, or the officer who shall have been intrusted with bringing her in, and under whose authority, according to the nature of the case, the abuse or vexation shall have occurred, shall be liable in costs and damages to the masters and the owners of the vessel and of the cargo.

These costs and damages may be awarded by the tribunal before which the proceedings against the detained vessel, her master, crew, and cargo, shall have been instituted; and the government of the country to which the officer who shall have given occasion for such award shall belong shall pay the amount of the said costs and damages within the period of six months from the date of the sentence, when the sentence shall have been pronounced by a tribunal sitting in Europe; and within the period of one year when the trial shall have taken place out of Europe.

Art. XIV.—When in the search or detention of a merchant-vessel effected in virtue of the present treaty any abuse or vexation shall have been committed, and when the vessel shall not have been delivered over to the jurisdiction of her own nation, the master shall make a declaration upon oath of the abuses or vexations of which he shall have to complain, as well as of the costs and damages to which he shall lay claim ; and such declaration shall be made by him before the competent authorities of the first port of his own country at which he shall arrive, or before the consular agent of his own nation at a foreign port, if the vessel shall in the first instance touch at a foreign port where there is such an agent.

This declaration shall be verified by means of an examination upon oath of the principal persons amongst the crew or the passengers who shall have witnessed the search or detention ; and a formal statement of the whole shall be drawn up, two copies whereof shall be delivered to the master, who shall forward one of them to his government, in support of his claim for costs and damages.

It is understood, that, if any circumstance beyond control shall prevent the master from making his declaration, it may be made by the owner of the vessel, or by any other person interested in the equipment or in the lading of the vessel.

On a copy of the formal statement above-mentioned being officially transmitted to it, the government of the country to which the officer to whom the abuses or vexations shall be imputed shall belong, shall forthwith institute an inquiry ; and if the validity of the complaint shall be ascertained, that government shall cause to be paid to the master or the owner, or to any other person interested in the equipment or lading of the molested vessel, the amount of costs and damages which shall be due to him.

ART. XV.—The high contracting parties engage reciprocally to communicate to each other, when asked to do so, and without expense, copies of the proceedings instituted, and of the judgment given, relative to vessels searched or detained in execution of the provisions of this treaty.

ART. XVI.—The high contracting parties agree to insure the immediate freedom of all the slaves who shall be found on board vessels detained and condemned in virtue of the stipulations of the present treaty.

ART. XVII.—The high contracting parties

agree to invite the maritime powers of Europe which have not yet concluded treaties for the abolition of the slave-trade to accede to the present treaty.

ART. XVIII.—The acts or instruments annexed to the present treaty, and which it is mutually agreed to consider as forming an integral part thereof, are the following :

A. Forms of warrants of authorization, and of orders for the guidance of the cruisers of each nation, in the searches and detentions to be made in virtue of the present treaty.

B. Instructions for the cruisers of the naval forces employed in virtue of the present treaty, for the suppression of the slave-trade.

ART. XIX.—The present treaty, consisting of 19 articles, shall be ratified, and the ratifications thereof shall be exchanged at London at the expiration of two months from this date, or sooner, if possible.

In witness whereof, the respective plenipotentiaries have signed the present treaty, in English and French, and have thereunto affixed the seal of their arms.

Done at London, the 20th day of December, in the year of our Lord 1841.

ABERDEEN ; KOLLER ; SAINT
AULAIRE ; SCHLEINITZ ; BRUNOW.

ANNEX.—INSTRUCTIONS TO CRUISERS.

1. Whenever a merchant-vessel belonging to, or bearing the flag of, any of the high contracting parties, shall be visited by a cruiser of any one of the other high contracting parties, the officer commanding the cruiser shall, before he proceeds to the visit, exhibit to the master of such vessel the special orders which confer upon him by exception the right to visit her ; and he shall deliver to such master a certificate, signed by himself, specifying his rank in the navy of his country, and the name of the ship which he commands, and declaring that the only object of his visit is to ascertain whether the vessel is engaged in the slave-trade, or is fitted out for the purpose of such traffic, or has been engaged in that traffic during the voyage in which she has been met with by the said cruiser. When the visit is made by an officer of the cruiser

other than her commander, such officer shall not be under the rank of lieutenant in the navy; unless he be the officer who at the time is second in command of the ship by which the visit is made; and in this case, such officer shall exhibit to the master of the merchant-vessel a copy of the special orders above mentioned, signed by the commander of the cruiser; and shall likewise deliver to such master a certificate, signed by himself, specifying the rank which he holds in the navy of his country, the name of the commander under whose orders he is acting, the name of the cruiser to which he belongs, and the object of his visit, as heretofore recited.

If it shall be ascertained by the visit that the ship's papers are regular, and her proceedings lawful, the officer shall certify upon the log-book of the vessel that the visit took place in virtue of the special orders above mentioned; and when these formalities shall have been completed the vessel shall be permitted to continue her course.

2. If, in consequence of the visit, the officer commanding the cruiser shall be of opinion that there are sufficient grounds for believing that the vessel is engaged in the slave-trade, or has been fitted out for that traffic, or has been engaged in that traffic during the voyage in which she is met with by the cruiser; and if he shall in consequence determine to detain her, and to have her given up to the jurisdiction of the competent authorities, he shall forthwith cause a list to be made out, in duplicate, of all the papers found on board, and he shall sign this list and the duplicate, adding, after his own name, his rank in the navy, and the name of the vessel under his command.

He shall, in like manner, make out and sign, in duplicate, a declaration, stating the place and time of the detention, the name of the vessel, and that of her master, the names of the persons composing her crew, and the number and condition of the slaves found on board.

This declaration shall further contain an exact description of the state of the vessel and her cargo.

3. The commander of the cruiser shall, without delay, carry or send the detained vessel, with her master, crew, passengers, cargo, and the slaves found on board, to one of the ports hereinafter specified, in order that proceedings may be instituted in regard to them, conformably to the laws of the country under whose flag the vessel is sailing, and he shall deliver the same to the competent authorities, or to the persons who shall have been specially appointed for that purpose by the government to whom such port shall belong.

4. No person whatever shall be taken out of the detained vessel; nor shall any part of her cargo, nor any of the slaves found on board, be removed from her, until after such vessel shall have been delivered over to the authorities of her own nation; unless the removal of the whole or part of the crew, or the slaves found on board, shall be deemed necessary, either for the preservation of their lives, or from any other consideration of humanity, or for the safety of the persons who shall be charged with the navigation of the vessel after her detention. In any such case, the commander of the cruiser, or the officer appointed to bring in the detained vessel, shall make a declaration of such removal, in which he shall specify the reasons for the same; and the masters, sailors, passengers, or slaves so removed, shall be carried to the same port as the vessel and her cargo, and they shall be received in the same manner as the vessel, agreeably to the regulations hereinafter set forth.

Provided always, that nothing in this paragraph shall be understood as applying to slaves found on board of Austrian, Prussian, or Russian vessels; but such slaves shall be disposed of as is specified in the following paragraphs:

5. All Austrian vessels which shall be detained on the stations of America, or Africa, by the cruisers of the other contracting parties, shall be carried and delivered up to the Austrian jurisdiction at Trieste.

But if slaves shall be found on board any such Austrian vessel at the time of her detention, the vessel shall, in the first instance, be sent to deposit the slaves at that port to which she would have been taken for adjudication if she had been sailing under the English or French flag. The vessel shall afterwards be sent on, and shall be delivered up to the Austrian jurisdiction at Trieste, as above stipulated.

All French vessels which shall be detained on the western coast of Africa by cruisers of the other contracting parties shall be carried and delivered up to the French jurisdiction at Goree.

All French vessels which shall be detained on the eastern coast of Africa by the cruisers of the other contracting parties shall be carried and delivered up to the French jurisdiction at the Isle of Bourbon.

All French vessels which shall be detained on the coast of America to the southward of the 10th degree of north latitude, by the cruisers of the other contracting parties, shall be carried and delivered up to the French jurisdiction at Cayenne.

All French vessels which shall be detained in the West Indies, or on the coast of America to the northward of the 10th degree of north latitude, by the cruisers of the other contracting parties, shall be carried and delivered up to the French jurisdiction at Martinique.

All British vessels which shall be detained on the western coast of Africa by the cruisers of the other contracting parties shall be carried and delivered up to the British jurisdiction at Bathurst, on the river Gambia.

All British vessels which shall be detained on the eastern coast of Africa by the cruisers of the other contracting parties shall be carried and delivered up to the British jurisdiction at the Cape of Good Hope.

All British vessels which shall be detained on the coast of America by the cruisers of the other contracting parties shall be carried and delivered up to the British jurisdiction at the colony of Demerara, or at Port Royal, in Jamaica, according as the commander of the cruiser may think most convenient.

All British vessels which shall be detained in the West Indies by the cruisers of the other contracting parties shall be carried and delivered up to the British jurisdiction at Port Royal, in Jamaica.

All Prussian vessels which shall be detained on the stations of America or Africa by the cruisers of the other contracting parties, shall be carried and delivered up to the Prussian jurisdiction at Stettin.

But if slaves shall be found on board any such Prussian vessel at the time of her detention, the vessel shall, in the first instance, be sent to deposit the slaves at that port to which she would have been taken for adjudication if she had been sailing under the English or French flag. The vessel shall afterwards be sent on, and shall be delivered up to the Prussian jurisdiction at Stettin as above stipulated.

All Russian vessels which shall be detained on the stations of America or Africa by the cruisers of the other contracting parties shall be carried and delivered up to the Russian jurisdiction at Cronstadt, or at Revel, according as the season of the year may allow the one or the other of those ports to be reached.

But if slaves shall be found on board any such Russian vessel at the time of her detention, the vessel shall, in the first instance, be sent to deposit the slaves at that port to which she would have been taken for adjudication if she had been sailing under the English or French flag. The vessel shall afterwards be sent on, and shall be delivered up to the Russian jurisdiction at Cronstadt, or at Revel, as above stipulated.

6. As soon as a merchant-vessel, which shall have been detained as aforesaid shall arrive at one of the ports or places above mentioned, the commander of the cruiser, or the officer appointed to bring in such detained vessel, shall forthwith deliver to the authorities, duly appointed for that purpose by the government within whose territory such port or place shall be, the vessel and her cargo, together with the master, crew, passengers, and slaves found on board, and also the papers which shall have been seized on board the vessel, and one of the duplicate lists of the said papers, retaining the other in his own possession. Such officer shall at the same time deliver to the said authorities one of the original

declarations, as hereinbefore specified, adding thereto a statement of any changes which may have taken place from the time of the detention of the vessel to that of the delivery, as well as a copy of the statement of any removals which may have taken place, as above provided for.

In delivering over these several documents the officer shall make, in writing and on oath, an attestation of the truth.

7. If the commander of a cruiser of one of the high contracting parties, who shall be duly furnished with the aforesaid special instructions, shall have reason to suspect that a merchant-vessel sailing under convoy of, of in company with, a ship-of war of any of the other contracting parties, is engaged in the slave-trade, or has been fitted out for the purpose of that traffic, or has been engaged in the traffic in slaves during the voyage in which she is met with by the said cruiser, he shall confine himself to communicating his suspicions to the commander of the ship-of-war; and he shall leave it to the latter to proceed alone to visit the suspected vessel, and to deliver her up to the jurisdiction of her own country, if there should be cause for doing so.

8. By Article IV. of the treaty it is stipulated, that in no case shall the mutual right of visit be exercised upon ships-of-war of the high contracting parties.

It is agreed that this exemption shall apply equally to vessels of the Russian-American Company, which, being commanded by officers of the imperial navy, are authorized by the imperial government to carry a flag which distinguishes them from the merchant navy, and are armed and equipped similarly to transports-of-war.

It is further understood that the said vessels shall be furnished with a Russian patent, which shall prove their origin and destination. The form of this patent shall be drawn up by common consent. It is agreed that this patent, when issued by the competent authority in Russia, shall be countersigned at St. Petersburgh by the consulates of Great Britain and France.

9. In the 3d clause of Article IX. of the treaty it is stipulated that, failing proof to the contrary, a vessel shall be presumed to be engaged in the slave-trade, if there be found on board spare plank fitted for being laid down as a second or slave-deck.

In order to prevent any abuse which might arise from an arbitrary interpretation of this clause, it is especially recommended to the cruisers not to apply it to Austrian, Prussian, or Russian vessels employed in the timber trade, whose manifests shall prove that the planks and joists which they have, or have had, on board are, or were, a part of their cargo for trade.

Therefore, in order not to harass lawful commerce, cruisers are expressly enjoined only to act upon the stipulations contained in the 3d clause of Article IX., when there shall be on board the vessel visited spare plank evidently destined to form a slave-deck.

The undersigned plenipotentiaries have agreed, in conformity with the 18th article of the treaty signed by them this day, that these instructions shall be annexed to the treaty signed this day between Great Britain, Austria, France, Prussia, and Russia, for the suppression of the African slave-trade, and shall be considered as an integral part of that treaty.

In witness whereof, the plenipotentiaries of the high contracting parties have signed this annex, and have thereunto affixed the seal of their arms.

Done at London, the 20th day of December, in the year of our Lord 1841.

ABERDEEN; KOLLER; ST. AULAIRE; SCHLEINITZ; BRUNOW.

GENERAL CASS AND THE TREATY.

In explanation of this, and as part of the history of that eventful period, I give a brief statement. The acknowledged, controlling wish of the king of the French (Louis Philippe) was to perpetuate his dynasty, and England, availing herself of the influence, which the question of the succession was known to have on the measures of his government, had negotiated the treaty. Knowing that there was yet a considerable slaveholding interest in the

French West Indies, and that the measures proposed by England were adverse to the manufacturing and commercial interests of Germany and of France, I went from London to Paris and urged General Cass to protest against the ratification of the treaty. I wrote a series of articles which were published in the Paris Journal of Commerce, then the organ of the Bonapartists. I wrote an essay which was published in the Revue Des Mondes, which was translated and extensively circulated in Germany. In these publications I illustrated the fact, that the purpose of England in her warfare on African slavery and the slave-trade, was to monopolize and give greater value to her trade with Africa and India. My arguments were reproduced in the French Chamber of Deputies, and Mr. Guizot, under the pressure of public opinion, assented that General Cass should send in his protest, which was then urged as an argument against the treaty. Such was the force of the public opinion thus created, that Gallignani, in his issue of 1st March, 1842, said :

"The treaty of 1842 for the suppression of the slave-trade, and the affair of M. Isambert, again form the burden of the original columns of our Paris contemporaries. On the first of these subjects, which furnishes an opportunity to some of the journals to attack the prerogative of the crown, under cover of the responsibility of the ministry, there is the same violence displayed against M. Guizot as was evinced immediately after the discussion on the subject in the Chamber of Deputies, and the evident, indeed avowed, object of the writers, is to keep up such an excitement in the country as shall compel M. Guizot either to retire from office or declare in the Chamber that he will not, under any circumstances, ratify the treaty; for either of these results would be a signal triumph for the opposition."

The question, then, of absorbing interest in England being the extension of her commerce and the increased consumption of her manufactures, Sir Robert Peel and the tories urged that the emancipation of the slaves in Cuba, Brazil, and the United States, was the measure which would best promote the "future prosperity" of England, while Mr. Cobden and the anti-corn-law league urged that the repeal of the corn laws would give laborers cheap bread, and that with cheap bread England could command the markets of the world. I saw that the nature of the conflict would predispose

MR. COBDEN AND THE POWERFUL PARTY,

Of whom he was the representative, to receive favorably the arguments which I was prepared to suggest against the measures urged with so much pertinacity by Sir Robert Peel, and I wrote and published in London a series of letters which it is my purpose hereafter to republish. The application of the following is so appropriate that they are inserted here :

ENGLAND AND THE UNITED STATES—SLAVERY AND THE RIGHT OF SEARCH.

To Editor of Morning Chronicle

When, in a former letter, I gave my thanks to her Majesty's government for the special mission of Lord Ashburton, and to the Times for its moderation in relation to American affairs, I did so under a hope that these events indicated a sincere desire to adjust the matter in dispute. I had not then read the declaration of Lord Palmerston that :

"Her Majesty's government *have decided* that the flag of the United States *shall exempt no vessel* (whether American or not) from search by her Majesty's cruisers in the African seas, unless such vessel shall be found provided with papers entitling her to the protection of the flag she wears, and proving her to be United States property, *and navigating the ocean according to law.*"

Nor had I read Lord Aberdeen's declaration reaffirming and asserting the same right ; nor had I then read the declaration of the Times of the 7th of January, that the question concerns the enforcement of a *necessary* right, which the British Government "*are determined not to yield.*"

The Times proceeds to say :

"Our [the British] government, after *great* and praiseworthy *exertions*, has *managed* to conclude treaties with almost every maritime power, by which the slave-trade, among the subjects of these powers, is punishable as piracy, and a right of search is mutually conceded to secure the firm execution of the law."

It then argues that the United States having refused to become a party to the treaty, or to concede the right of search, other vessels are navigated by subjects of the contracting parties, who, if arrested, would be punishable as pirates, may escape by hoisting the American flag, and hence insists on enforcing the right to search American vessels.

There has been no period of the civilized world when the interests of nations were so much blended, and at no former time was their responsibility to public opinion so great. Hence these declarations of Lords Palmerston and Aberdeen, and of the Times in its peculiar relation to the mission of Lord Ashburton, are doubly important.

I can readily see that the mission is important, whether the purpose of her Majesty's government be peace or war—and the more so if war has been firmly resolved upon—for such are the relations between the two countries—so varied and direct are the interests

to be sacrificed, that no British minister will venture on a war with the United States without first preparing public opinion at home to sustain it. Hence, it is wise in Sir Robert Peel to send a special mission ; and wiser still, perhaps, to have selected as the minister one whose relations to the United States have been such as to justify him in asserting that all has been done that could be done to preserve peace. All must foresee that, should Lord Ashburton return without adjusting pending difficulties, it will be charged that the fault is ours, and that Great Britain is compelled to go to war, or be dishonored.

If the Times be right, and war has been resolved upon—if the great exertions to *manage* other powers into conceding a right of search, in which they had comparatively no interest, was to pave the way for enforcing it on us, knowing that, with us, speaking as we do the same language, it involves the right of impressment, and that, consequently, it would be resisted—then this mission of Lord Ashburton, so far as we are concerned, is a most insulting mockery. The purpose is not peace, but war ; it is not to negotiate, for the British government, we are told, have "*determined not to yield.*" If this be so, the mission is not to us, but to you ; it is not to preserve peace, but to prepare for war ; it is part of the management deemed necessary in carrying out a foregone conclusion, and is but a means to arouse *British* pride and British patriotism, that you may yourselves be united and rally around your own government.

Hence, although I cannot permit myself to believe that the Times truly represents the British government, although the character of Sir Robert Peel forbids a suspicion that he is capable of acting such a part, yet, as I before remarked, the declarations of Lords Palmerston and Aberdeen in their official correspondence, and the relation which the Times is supposed to bear to the administration, to Lord Ashburton and to his mission, will give a kind of official sanction to its declarations, and will arouse in the United States one common sentiment of resistance ; and my apprehension is, that war may become inevitable unless the good sense of the British people shall intervene and turn aside so great a calamity.

Let us pause for a moment and examine the question as presented by the Times. I quote its own words :

" It is no question in which English interests alone are concerned, it concerns the enforcement of a necessary right which we claim as inherent in all nations equally, and which we are as ready to submit *to as we are determined not to yield.* It has arisen, however, upon the slave trade treaties, in the following shape :

" Our government, after great and praiseworthy exertions, has *managed* to conclude treaties with almost every maritime power, by which the slave trade, among the subjects of these powers, is punishable as piracy, and a right of search is mutually conceded to secure the firm execution of this law. To a treaty of this kind it was, of course, hoped that America would become a party. Such, however, has not been the case," &c.

Now, here is the question as made and presented by the *Times* for your government and their minister. Let us put it into plain English. It will then read thus :

Great Britain is the first maritime power in the world. It is her pride, and she arrogates to be the " MISTRESS OF THE OCEAN." Claiming the right of impressment, she insisted upon the right of search. It was resisted by the United States, and led to the last war between the two countries. Peace was concluded without a concession of that right, and Great Britain herself has since admitted it to be a violation of the law of nations. The United States are progressing in wealth and population, and it is manifest that such is the extent of her territory, and so ample are her resources, that she will soon exceed Great Britain herself in commerce and manufactures. This is the more palpable because your productive industry, the real source of wealth and greatness, no longer able to find profitable employment at home, are migrating to the United States, thus detracting from your power and adding to ours as a people. Under these circumstances, your sole reliance is your mines and manufactories ; without these you cannot give employment to your surplus population. They must migrate or starve. It is equally apparent that you cannot employ them in your mines or your manufactories unless you find markets for the sale of their products. Upon this subject you are divided among yourselves—some, looking to us as consumers, advocate free trade and a mutual interchange of the products of labor ; others, considering us to be rivals, look to the East Indies and to China. It was found that, to enable the East Indies to consume your manufactures, you must take their agricultural products—that they could not purchase your calicoes but by an exchange of cotton, rice, and sugar ; and then, for the first time, were the sympathies of your government enlisted in behalf of the persecuted African. It was in vain that Virginia, as a colony, protested against the slave trade. You compelled her to receive the slaves whom you carried to her. In vain did Wilberforce clank their chains. The voice of philanthropy could not be heard until avarice contrasted the *hundreds of millions* of Asiatic subjects with the eight hundred thousand of West India slaves, and demonstrated that it was your interest, as a question of dollars and cents, to become abolitionists. Then, and not until then, those who, even yet, are so blind that they cannot see the wretchedness, and so deaf that they cannot hear the cries of misery even at their own doors, were enlisted in the crusade against the slave-trade. Slavery in the West Indies was abolished—the commerce of the East, as well as of the West Indies, was placed under new regulations—tons of American cotton seed, and experienced American cotton planters, were transported to India under an openly-avowed purpose of substituting the cotton and rice, and the pauper labor of India for the cotton, and rice, and slave labor of America. But all this did not increase your territory, nor did it retard the onward progress of America. Wherever the necessities of British commerce may force a British ship, there, too, has Yankee enterprise carried the Yankee cruiser; and what is more germain to *this* question, that same cruiser, wherever it goes, bears with it conclusive proof that the *cheap bread, low taxes,* and *superior intelligence* of the American are gradually enabling him to supersede the British laborer in the markets of the world. Again, these facts could not be concealed from your own people. The example and the influence and condition of America were becoming subjects of comment in the lowest as well as in the highest classes of your society. Your suffering poor, especially the aged, the sick, the widow and the orphan, were made to envy the lot of our slaves,[*] and many of your manufacturers look to us as the consumers of their manufactures; many of your merchants look to us as their best customers; many of your retired officers, your widows and orphans, persons of small means wanting large returns, look to our stocks as the surest and safest investment; many of your laboring and starving poor look to our granaries for bread; many of your liberal statesmen look to ours as the freest and best of governments, and urge our prosperity as an argument in favor of those improvements which they would engraft on your own constitution; Ireland, suffering Ireland, looks to us for sympathy, and as a refuge when driven houseless and destitute, to earn that subsistence, which neither industry nor economy, nor both combined, can wring from their heartless oppressors;[†] many of your divines look to us as

[*] See report of the poor-law commissioners on the destitute condition of the poor of Ireland.

[†] *Extract from the Report of the Poor Law Commissioners.*—Robert Darcy, Esq., a man of landed property, says: "His servant counted one hundred and twenty beggars that called at his door in the day." "Vagrants are ejected tenants from the absentee estates."

"They pay high rents for holdings which, if they had them for nothing, would not support them.

"When you ask them why they beg, they will answer, *we were turned out* into bogs and swamps, and when we had reclaimed our little spots, we were sent in further, till we were beggared at last, else we would be now comfortable.

"They all attribute their misfortunes to high rents, and low prices for produce, and the consequent want of employment.

"The small farmers have no motive for industry; they are afraid to improve either their land or houses; *the moment they do so the rent will be raised.*"

Protestants, they sympathize with us as living in the same faith, and protecting all those who are persecuted for opinion's sake ; and, in addition to all this, the spirit of the age is for peace ; we are your descendants ; your brothers, your sisters, your sons, and your daughters, have gone out from among you, they have entered into our doors which were open to receive them, and they and we have become one and the same people. A war on us, therefore, will be a war on your own interests, on your own sympathies, on your own opinions, and upon your own children. Yet, if the Times is to be believed, that war is determined upon, and has been long and long ago the settled purpose of your government !! If the quotation before us means anything, it means that the question has not been war or peace, but upon what pretence that war should be commenced !! It is true that the question of boundary is open, but a war for the possession of part of Maine, or even of the mouth of the Columbia river, might not be so popular at home or with the civilized world, as a war for the suppression of the slave-trade. The first would be charged to a spirit of conquest, a thirst for dominion, and might excite the jealousy, certainly it would not enlist the sympathy, of other powers—and hence we are told that by *great exertions* your government has *managed* to make most of the other maritime powers, parties to the treaty interpolating the right of search into the law of nations, and that having done so, they are now *determined* to *compel* us to submit to it, although they well knew from the first, that we would not do so, and that it must end in war ! ! !

Take this question as presented by the Times, examine it in any and in all its aspects, and does it not amount to this and to this only — that Great Britain, having resolved on war, has made "*great exertions*" to create an issue, upon which the other powers of Europe and her own people could be united against us ; that for this purpose she "*has managed*" to make other maritime powers, having comparatively no interest in the question, parties to the treaties on the slave-trade, and that having done this she now sends Lord Ashburton, as part of the same system of management, not to accomplish peace, but, by a show of conciliation, to enlist against us the public opinion and the sympathies of those powers, and of the British people ?

I repeat that my respect for Sir Robert Peel and for the British people will not permit me to attribute to them such purposes, but it is time that he and that they should know that such is the construction that will be put on the language of the Times in America, and that recent events render it impossible to preserve the peace of the two countries, unless you be sincerely desirous of peace, and recede from the pretension which, it is admitted, is now, for the first time, made. It is proper that you should know that no question could be presented upon which the people of the United States are more resolved or united. If one drop of blood be shed in this cause, one thrill of indignant animosity will pass through every American bosom. War once begun will not end but with the deepest disgrace and lasting humiliation of one of the parties. Are you sure that, after all your management, you have secured either the sympathy or the co-operation of the other powers of Europe. If you go to war with us, it is because you fear our rivalry. Are you sure that France, or Austria, or Russia, wish to see your power increased at our expense? Are you sure that these other powers will not avail themselves of their neutral rights to increase their commerce and their navies? Are you sure that they, too, will not look to the east, and unite with us in emancipating your colonies, that they may be permitted to purchase of them free from the conditions you now impose? Do you not know that a war, and especially one giving a common sentiment to our people, will give new life to our manufactures, and that it may end in your ruin? I am well aware that the tone and language of this letter are not such as are usually addressed to the British public. But seeing as I do that the danger is imminent, I fear that the only means of preserving peace is to expose the consequences, and by holding up, in its deformity, the pretence on which, if the Times is to be believed, it has been *determined* to wage war, give a new direction to the benevolent sympathies of your own people, by whose influence it is to be hoped your government may be induced to provide for the necessities of their own subjects before they enter upon this crusade, the end of which is a fruitless effort to excite a servile war among our slaves.

I say fruitless, because, when you engrafted domestic slavery, as a part of our social system—when against our remonstrances you compelled us to purchase the slaves whom your avarice forced upon your then dependent colonies, we did all that we could do to alleviate their condition. We enacted laws for their comfort and protection, *and as soon as your power to enforce it ceased, WE abolished the slave-trade.* We made the interest of the master and of his slave identical, until under the influence of religion, benevolence, affection, and law, the condition of the black man in the United States is better than it could be under any other regulation of society—it is incomparably better than that of your own laboring poor, if one half of your official statements be true.

And is it possible that under such an aspect of the case you can be so blinded by prejudice, misguided by fanaticism, or warped by a false conception of your interests, as not to know that a war upon us, under a pretence of ameliorating the condition of Africa, so far from enlisting the sympathy of other nations, will expose your treatment of free white men to the most humiliating comparison with our treatment of the black slave? Indeed it was but the other day that the Times boldly asserted that Mr. O'Connell and the repeal association must be put down by law, and that if the law be not strong enough it must be made stronger for that purpose. The purpose of O'Connell is to feed and clothe his starving and naked countrymen. No one denies that they are naked and starving, yet there is no plan of relief mingled with the proscription of O'Connell!!

Now hear what your poor law commissioners say of these Irishmen. They say:

"As to animal food except once a year (at Christmas), even those that are by comparison called comfortable people, not only never eat it, but never think of eating it."

Mr. Cotter, rector of Templeton, says that he has seen women gather the cabbage-stumps thrown out of his kitchen, and that, after the fowls and pigs had first picked them bare. He says:

" I saw myself, six or seven poor women turn their faces to the wall and eat the stumps the pigs had picked."

The Rev. Peter Ward states that in his parish—

" In the year 1831 six persons died of actual want. Since that period I take upon myself to say that of every five persons who have died three always die of starvation, brought on by bad food, bad clothing, and bad or no bedding!"

One witness says :

" I have not had a new coat or small clothes for the last *six years*; this hat I found cast behind a ditch four or five years ago and I have worn it ever since."

Yes, such is the condition of the suffering poor in Ireland whose hopes of deliverance are to be extinguished by law, and which law, if it is not strong enough to bind them in their SLAVERY must be made strong enough, not only to rivet their chains, but to hush every whisper of complaint —they must not only suffer, but they must suffer in silence, and the leading organ of the administration, which speaks thus of suffering Ireland, tells us that that administration have *determined* to enforce the right of search, even at the expense of a war, under a pretence of suppressing the slave-trade!!! Manacles, starvation, and death, for Ireland, but millions and sympathy for Africa!!

Is it possible that any one can be so blinded as to suppose that, under such circumstances, such a war can be justified in the face of the civilized world? Or, can any one believe the real motive to be benevolence?

I will tell you what we in the United States will think of it : We have 56,000 of our people on the ocean. Comparatively all of these are from New England, many of them are in the Pacific. The question involves, necessarily, the right of impressment, as well as the right of search ; and there is not a man, women, or child, among us who will not believe that your real purpose is the dominion of the seas—that your wish is to monopolize the Pacific ocean, and there will be but one sentiment from Maine to Louisiana. The devoted wife, whose husband rides upon the stormy wave— the affrighted mother who starts, and in every noise hears the yell of the ruthless savage, and the timid virgin who dreams of brutal outrage, will unite in one voice of execration. They will call down Heaven's vengeance, and unite, by the highest motives that can actuate a people, a love for our country, a love for woman and our tender offspring ; a common sentiment of unmitigated hatred will pervade our whole community. Such a war can end but by the deepest humiliation of one of the parties. We fear not the issue. But to return to the slave-trade :

A friend has just placed in my hands a pamphlet, addressed to Lord Stanley. It says :

" To your Lordship, as colonial minister of this great country, fell the pleasing task of proposing the extinction of slavery throughout the Queen's dominions. To your Lordship the colonists now look for the ultimate success of this eventful measure. Finish, then, the work which it is the most distinguished honor of your political career to have begun; extend to the benighted African the blessings which have been procured for his brethren in the West; prove to the world that justice and sound policy are one, and let posterity applaud as well the wisdom as the magnanimity of this great experiment."

The great experiment thus spoken of is the abolition of slavery in the West Indies, of which the writer says :

"As a great national sacrifice to interest it stands alone, a triumph in the cause of humanity, of which the people of this country [England] have more reason to be proud than all their victories by land and sea."

Yet it will be seen that the work is not *finished*; there is more yet to be done. Let this same writer tell what that is. He says:

"*The startling fact that the exports of these colonies have diminished nearly one half since the change intrudes itself upon us.*"

The statistics are then given, and after verifying this statement, he proceeds:

"The *high wages* which, in most of the islands, the negro peasantry have received, have enabled them, in a remarkably propitious climate, to obtain in abundance all the requisites of life. But the same wages, encroaching, as they have done, upon the capital of the planter, have compelled him to limit the cultivation proportionately; *nor would anything but the late high prices of sugar have preserved a majority of them from ruin.*"

This is plain enough. The planter, having his capital invested, is compelled to surrender it to the negro; that is, he is compelled to give such wages that all the capital remaining to the West India planter is in the gradual process of being absorbed by the high wages paid for labor. In Ireland the peasantry is in the power of the landlord, because land is scarce and labor abundant, and the poor laborer is compelled to work for dry potatoes and clothe himself; if he gets sick or aged he must beg or starve. In the West Indies land is plenty and labor scarce, and the negro preys upon the land owner. Now, this same writer proceeds to point out the remedy, which is, "*to import* FREE NEGROES *from Africa until free labor shall be cheaper than slave labor,*" and then the work which is the most distinguished honor

of Lord Stanley's career, of which you have more reason to be proud than of all your victories by land and by sea, will be complete!! That is: you must reduce the black peasantry of the West Indies to the condition of the white peasantry of Ireland!!!—you must substitute the lash of hunger and nakedness for the lash of the taskmaster, and then you can do what? Under-sell the slave labor, because your free labor will be cheaper!!!

And this is British philanthropy!!! Is it for this and for the honors to be gained in such a cause, that the Times would enforce the right of search, at the expense of millions of treasure and oceans of blood? Is it for this that the slave is to be armed and bribed, with the promise of *such* freedom, to murder the master who clothes and feeds him, and nurses and comforts him in sickness and old age?

Indeed, we are told that this new system of slavery has already commenced, and that ten thousand Africans have been or are being transferred from Sierra Leone to your colonies by the order of your government!!

Is it possible that a government thus countenancing the worst possible form of slavery and of the slave-trade will make war on us under the pretence of suppressing the slave-trade? I repeat, that whatever may be the purpose of your government there is no hope of peace but in the immediate and satisfactory adjustment of the points in issue.

Much will be done towards doing so if the American people can be satisfied that the Times does not represent the British government or the British people. I am fully convinced, that whatever your ministers may have *determined* to do, the feeling of your people is for peace, and that they will be the first to be stricken with horror at the true question presented in its naked deformity. I have some striking facts and forcible illustrations which I must reserve for another letter.

AN AMERICAN IN LONDON.

ENGLAND AND THE UNITED STATES.

Will there be war between England and the United States, and what will be the effect of a war on the interests of the two countries?

These are grave questions, the answers to which depend upon the British government.

Such is the nature of the conflict now waged between classes in England, that there is great cause to fear that the attempt to reconcile local interests may bring on collision with the United States.

On the other hand, such is the peculiar relation of society in America, and such the nature of the questions between the two countries, that it is to be feared a war once begun will not be terminated short of the dismemberment and ruin of the British Empire.

In the late debate in the House of Lords on the corn-laws, it was admitted that the prosperity of England depends upon the *extension* of her commerce, and that this depends upon an increased consumption of her manufactures. One party insists upon a repeal of the corn-laws and free trade; on the other hand, the Duke of Wellington declared his belief that, *a repeal of the corn-laws would not enable you to sell a yard of cloth or a pound of iron in Europe, or any part of the world over which England does not exercise a control.*

Let us see the bearing which these opinions have on the questions pending between the United States and England?

It is admitted that your population has out-grown your means of subsistence, that Great Britain cannot grow bread for the people of Great Britain, and the question is, how are you to employ your surplus population? The Marquis of Lansdowne says: "Repeal your corn-laws and get bread by exchanging your manufactures with the people of the United States." The Duke of Wellington says: "No; if you repeal your corn-laws you cannot sell a yard of cloth or a pound of iron more in Europe, or in any part of the world over which you do not exercise a control; because," he adds, "other nations profiting by your example now manufacture for themselves."

Is it not therefore apparent that the real question is, by what means can England increase the consumption of her manufactures?

The Duke of Wellington tells us, and he is the organ of the tory administration, "that you must rely on the consumption in those countries over which you exercise a control; that is, that your sole reliance is upon your colonies, and upon these only, because you exercise a control over them.

Reduced to a dependence upon your colonies, the next questions are, why cannot India, with her one hundred and forty millions of population, consume more of your manufactures, and why are you now dependent on the United States for raw cotton to be manufactured in England and sold in India, when, thirty years ago, you imported the cotton produced and manufactured in India to be sold in the United States?

The Duke of Wellington answers: he tells us that the introduction of machinery has produced the revolution;

that labor cannot compete with machinery, and it follows, that as the eighteen millions of people in England control the one hundred and forty millions in India, and prevent the use of machinery in India, India has ceased to manufacture.

But it may well be asked why, if India has ceased to manufacture, she does not produce the raw material. The answer to this is that slave labor in the United States, in Cuba and Brazil, is more productive than the slave labor of India, and that India, cheap as labor is in India, cannot compete with the slave labor of Cuba, Brazil and the United States. The consequence is that other manufacturing states receive their supplies of these staples from Cuba, Brazil and the United States, whereas, could India sell at a lower rate, then those states would purchase India cotton, rice, sugar and coffee from the British merchants who would receive them in exchange for British manufactures.

It is apparent that measures which would destroy the culture of these staples in Cuba, Brazil and the United States, or which would increase the cost of production above what would be a remunerating price in India, would enable England, by her control of India, to monopolize the supply of cotton, rice, sugar, and coffee. Is it necessary to ask what would be the effect on the condition of England, if she could accomplish this? Would it not enable her to destroy all rival manufacturers by enabling her to compel all other nations to pay her own prices for these articles of first necessity?

Now it is the deliberate opinion of well-informed statesmen in the United States that such is the purpose of England, and that she seeks to accom-plish it by the abolition of slavery in the United States, Cuba, and Brazil.

We admit that there are many pious and benevolent persons in England who sincerely believe that, inasmuch as the mother-country compelled the colonies against their remonstrance, to receive slaves, it is now the duty of England to do all that she can do to abolish slavery; but if, in the face of admitted facts, with a perfect knowledge that the experiment in the West Indies has failed, and that the effect has been, as declared by the London Courier and the Times, to compel the planter to hand over his entire property to the emancipated slaves, and to convert these fertile islands into black colonies, while the demoralization of the black progresses; we repeat, if, in the face of these admitted facts, England perseveres in her attempt to emancipate the slaves in Cuba, Brazil, and the United States—if, under the pretence of benevolence, she adheres to a system the inevitable effect of which would be to hand over Cuba, Brazil, and the Southern States of the American Union, to the black race, degenerating as they must, and certainly would do, becoming more and more demoralized as the emancipated blacks in Jamaica and Demarara have done, it would be impossible to persuade the enlightened people of the United States that the real motive was not the aggrandizement of England at the expense of all the rest of the world.

Your aristocracy, rolling in wealth and steeped in luxury, may well be enamored with a *system of benevolence* which magnifies their power and increases their rent rolls, but it is presented in a very different aspect to the American planter, who, inheriting the institution of slavery from *your* ancestors, sees in it no alternative but poverty, coupled with exile, from the home of his fathers.

What is there in the institution of slavery, as it now exists in the United States, to warrant your attempt to abolish it? Or by what right does England obtrude her sympathies between the master and his slave? By what right have you established orders and classes in society? Why is it that the elder son inherits and takes the position as well as the estates of his ancestors? Why is it that the tenant labors for his landlord, and that the poor man upholds the government that oppresses him? By what right does England control her colonies, and by what right does her eighteen millions compel the one hundred and forty millions in India to consume her manufactures?

These questions are dictated by no feeling of impertinence. They are intended to show that the constituent elements of all society are such as of necessity to create distinctions. The question before us is not whether the relation between the master and slave is the best that could be organized—is it such that England would be justified in an attempt to dissolve it?

Whatever may be the mask assumed by her diplomacy, such, in the belief of the people of the United States, is the only motive that could induce England to go to war with them; and whatever may be the opinion in England, the manner in which the question of *slavery in India* has been treated will confirm that belief; for a clause abolishing slavery having been inserted in the charter of the East India Company, the Duke of Wellington is reported to have urged the House of Lords to reconcile themselves to the existence of slavery if they wished to continue their control over India, and the clause was stricken out with an understanding that that company would take effectual measures for carrying *silently* into effect the wishes of the government; and accordingly the Governor-General, in his despatch dated 6th of May, says that, as "the object is the earliest possible extinction, *first practically*, and in the end *even avowedly*, of slavery," with a view to avoid all "claims of consideration and compensation," he recommends "prohibiting every kind of coercion by the master over the person, and all summary interference of authority for the return of a person claimed as a slave to his assuming owner," and his lordship adds, "We shall, in truth, do away with all such practices, for no one will be found to purchase that of the continued possession of which he can have no assurance."

The measures adopted for the abolition of slavery in the United States, Cuba, and Brazil, are, under existing circumstances, precisely in character with those recommended for India. It is to do "*silently*" *first*, "*practically*" that which may be "*afterward*" "*avowed*," when property in the slave shall become valueless. The mode in India is to withhold from the master the protection of the law. It is to stimulate the slave to abandon the service due to the master, and to deny to the master the means of coercion. And why does the benevolence of England assume this shape? Why is this *silent* mode adopted of doing "*practically*" that which it is not deemed prudent now to avow? Is it not to avoid "claims of consideration and compensation?"

We cannot close our eyes to the fact that this is the act of the British government, and that it is admitted that an increased consumption of her manufactures is indispensable to her prosperity, and that the Duke of Wellington admits that her sole dependence is on those countries under her control.

Am I asked to reconcile the abolition of slavery in India with the effect of abolition in the United States, and the purposes attributed to England? That purpose is to monopolize the product of raw cotton, &c., &c., by abolishing slavery in the United States, Cuba and Brazil. How can that be done by the abolition of slavery in India?

The purpose of England is to monopolize the product of cotton, abolition is but an incident.

When, after the peace, she found that other nations, profiting by her example, were manufacturing for themselves, she saw the necessity of opening new markets; she turned her attention to her East India possessions, but she soon found that the ability of India to purchase was limited to the products of India which she could receive in exchange. Her West India planters had a monopoly, a repeal of which became indispensable, and the one hundred millions paid, under pretence of abolishing slavery, was, in fact, an indemnity for abolishing the West India monopoly.

You must well recollect that it was said that free labor is cheaper than slave labor, and that the philanthropists of that day argued that the emancipated slave would do more labor, and on better terms, as a freeman than as a slave. Time has demonstrated the inferiority of the African race. The soil of Africa is as rich, yet the African in Africa cannot compete with the Indian in India. It is only when the labor of the black man is guided by the skill and energy of the white that it is more productive than that of the East Indian. It follows, therefore, that all that is required to enable England to produce cotton in India cheaper than it will be produced in the United States, is to emancipate the negro and separate him from the white man. When England can purchase in India cheaper than other nations can purchase in the United States, she will have achieved a monopoly at a higher price it is true, but it is a question of monopoly and not of price.

By what mode can England emancipate the slaves in the United States?

If her public writers are to be believed, her mode of operations is, first, as in India, practically to destroy the value of the slave by bringing the public sentiment of the world to bear against it; and next, *avowedly*, by sending her black regiments to invade our Southern States, and thus create a servile insurrection.

The real question is not whether such is the purpose of England. It is what would be the effect of a sincere belief in the United States, and on the continent of Europe, that it is. Would it not give color to the war, and would it not lead to combinations formed to disrobe England of the power to accomplish that purpose?

This brings us to speak of the elements that would combine for the dismemberment of the British Empire, and first of the United States. The United States desire peace, but they do not fear a war. With a population of three millions—without resources—without means of creating a navy, or of clothing an army, they achieved their independence. They have now near twenty millions of population; they have all the elements of war within themselves, and will grow in strength and resources in war or in peace. They have room to grow, and a war will bind them more closely together, while the other European states will, of necessity, become parties. They will declare the colonies independent, and stripped of her dependencies, England will be left with the burden of her enormous debt, greatly increased, to depend on her own individual resources. If her manufacturers are now transferring their capital and skill to the continent and to the United States, to avoid her ruinous system of taxation, what will they do when the power to compel India and her present colonies to consume her products shall have ceased? If the repeal of the corn-laws would not enable England to sell a yard of cloth or a pound of iron more, because other countries, over which England does not exercise a control, manufacture for themselves and at a cheaper rate, how can England subsist her population when she no longer has the power to compel India and her colonies to purchase her manufactures?

It is manifest that England can have no motive for a war with the United States but that which is here explained—the alternative of that war will be the desolation of the South, and the ruin of the manufactures of the North, *or else the entire overthrow of the dominion of England.* If England is wise we will have peace.

THE NOMINATION OF HARRISON AND TYLER.

In 1836 I received a letter from my friends, J. V. L. McMahon, and James W. McCulloch, of Baltimore, informing me that they had participated in the nomination of General Harrison for President, and Willie P. Mangum, of North Carolina, for Vice-President, and asking my co-operation.

I wrote to them, in reply, that I was opposed to the election of Van Buren, and would unite in support of General Harrison, if they would place upon the ticket as Vice-President, a proper representative of our state rights, and suggested that Mr. Tyler, of Virginia, had remained in the Senate, and given the single vote against General Jackson's force bill. They acted on my suggestion, and substituted Tyler for Mangum. Mr. Van Buren was elected in 1836, and Harrison and Tyler were renominated and elected in 1840. The death of General Harrison made Mr. Tyler President. When he came to Washington he sent for me, and said that Mr. Tazewell had advised him to make an address, in which he would declare that he would not be a candidate in 1844, and asked my advice. He said that he was anxious to adjust the currency question, and had a plan of a bank, which he believed he could carry through Congress, if he could prevent the opposition of the rival aspirants for the Presidency. I replied that the declaration that he would not be a candidate, would be taken as an evidence of weakness; that no one had asked him to be a candidate, and that, if asked, he could then decline, or not, as he might then deem expedient.

It became necessary to convene Congress in an extra session. I received a letter from my brother which made it necessary for me to go to Kentucky. I called on the President, who said, "Congratulate me." "Upon what?" said I. He replied, "We have agreed upon the plan of a bank. The Cabinet have, after consultation, agreed, and the Secretary of the Treasury is preparing the bill." I asked, "What is your plan?" He said, "We have agreed to charter a national bank for the District of Columbia, with the privilege of establishing branches in the states, *with the consent of the states.*" I asked, "Have you consulted Mr. Clay?" He said, "No, why should we consult him?" I said, "Mr. Clay and Mr. Van Buren are rival candidates for the Presidency. The bank is Mr. Clay's capital, upon which he most relies to secure his election. Anti-bank is Mr. Van Buren's capital, upon which he and Benton most rely. Mr. Clay has asserted the power of Congress to charter a bank, with power to establish branches in the states, without the consent of the states. Neither Mr. Clay nor Benton will consent to an adjustment of the currency question by you, and unless you will consent to become the active partisan of Mr. Clay, and devote the patronage of the government to promote his election, he will make an issue with you on the right to establish branches." He replied, "You never did like Clay, and you shall not abuse him to me." "Very well," said I, "time will very soon show whether you or I have the best appreciation of his character and action."

I left the next morning for Kentucky. I was detained there but a few days, and, on my way back, called on my friend, Charles A. Wickliffe, where I read, in the paper of the day, a notice of Mr. Clay's bank bill, in which, as I had anticipated, he had made an issue on the power to establish branches. At breakfast I asked Miss Wickliffe, now Mrs. Merrick, of Maryland, if she would like to live in Washington, and upon her reply in the affirmative, I told her that I believed that the President would veto Mr. Clay's bank bill, and that some of the Cabinet would, as I believed, resign, in which case her father, as a friend of the President, would be probably tendered a seat in the Cabinet.

I hastened to Washington, and, on my arrival, was told that, before reporting his bill to the Senate, Mr. Clay had submitted it to a caucus of his friends, at which all the members of Mr. Tyler's Cabinet were present, and each of the Cabinet had said that if Mr. Tyler vetoed the bill, he would resign. Having assured myself of the truth of this statement, I called on the President the next morning, and told him what I had heard. He said that he could not believe that gentlemen, members of his Cabinet, who had been consulted, and who, knowing that he did not believe that Congress had power to establish branches in the states, without first obtaining their consent, and had, after full discussion, agreed with him on the details of his bill, could so far forget what was, under the circumstances, due to him and themselves, as to give such a pledge to Mr. Clay. I became satisfied that he would veto the bill, and went from him directly to the State Department.

I SAID TO MR. WEBSTER,

"You may think what I am about to say to you is not appropriate to the relations heretofore existing between us. I am, as you know, the personal friend of the President. You are Secretary of State, and as such a member of his cabinet. I do not call on you as Mr. Webster, but as the Secretary of State; and my purpose is to discuss with you, what it will be proper for you, as Secretary of State, to do in a given contingency. I do not wish you to say to me whether what I have heard be true or not. It is not of the past, but of the future that I wish to confer with you. I am told that you and all the other members of the cabinet were consulted by Mr. Clay before he reported his bank bill to the Senate, and that you all pledged yourselves to him, that you would resign in case Mr. Tyler vetoed the bill. I come to tell you that Mr. Tyler will veto it." He sprang from his seat, and after walking the room in great excitement, he came to me, and said, "General Green, Mr. Tyler must not veto that bill." I replied—"The question is not whether Mr. Tyler shall veto the bill, but it is what should Daniel Webster, his Secretary of State, do when he does veto it?" He took his seat and listened while I endeavored to present to him a brief review of the condition of the country and of parties, and his duty as the representative of the interests of New England. Mr. Tyler did veto the bill. The other members of the cabinet resigned. Mr. Webster did not.

MR. TYLER SENT FOR ME,

And said, "I know your value, and want you near me; say what office in my gift you will accept, and you shall have it." I replied, thanking him for his confidence, and the favor he tendered me, but said that my own private affairs were such as to make it impossible for me to accept any office, adding, that I had negotiations pending which would take me to London, and that as he would be sending despatches, I would accept the appointment of messenger of the State Department, and that if he would furnish the abstract of the census of 1840, which had not then been published, I would, while in London, prepare a series of letters for the London press explanatory of our resources, and tending to restore American credit. To this he assented. It will be seen that, although I was in Europe as a private citizen, my relations to the government and to public men, and to the great issues then pending, were such, as to make it no less my duty than my privilege to take the part which I did in the discussion of, and comment upon, the questions, affecting the interests and credit of the United States.

It is my purpose hereafter to publish more in detail my correspondence with the press and prominent persons in England and in the United States, bearing on the great questions which have led to the late calamitous conflict between the North and the South, and I regret that the want of time prevents my doing so now. My present purpose is to present a few facts and suggestions illustrating the tendency and effect of the issues in question, omitting as far as practicable the mention of the names and conduct of individuals, who are greatly responsible for the war and its consequences, but who, or at least some of whom, under the pressure of present circumstances, may be induced, either by a desire to atone for past errors, or from a hope of profiting by taking part in the restoration of the Constitution, to exert their influence in behalf of peace. Yet it is deemed necessary to explain the issues involved, and that

THE ORGANIZATION OF THE RADICAL PARTY

And their past and present measures and policy, are subordinate to the measures and policy of England, in direct violation of the letter and spirit of our Constitution, and subversive of the interests and prosperity of the United States. The intelligent reader will not fail to see that the letters and publications now reproduced tend to demonstrate these truths.

CHAPTER XXII.

LORD ASHBURTON'S MISSION.

MR. WEBSTER had given me a letter to Mr. Bates, and, a few days after my arrival in London, I was invited to dine with him. The party consisted of Messrs. Bates, Baring, and myself. During the dinner, they indicated a very earnest desire to ascertain the probable result of the border difficulties between Canada and the United States, and, among other questions, Mr. Bates asked, "What about our friend, Mr. Webster?" I replied— "To tell you the truth, some of us in the United States think that the time has come when we should be better friends or open enemies. We desire peace, but are tired of your continued warfare on our interests and our credit, and we are, therefore, anxious to know what your purpose is, and whether the pending issues can be peaceably adjusted, and I should not be surprised if the next arrival informs us that Mr. Webster will come here as a special minister. I saw that Messrs. Bates and Baring telegraphed each other, and considered the information sufficiently important to be immediately communicated to others. They hurriedly arose from the table. I said to Mr. Bates, that one purpose of my coming to London was to write, for publication, a series of letters, which, I hoped, would tend to promote a better feeling, and allay the irritation then existing between the two countries ; and that, with this view, I had obtained an abstract of the statistics of the census,

in advance of its publication, which, I hoped, would be interesting to the British public, and tend to restore confidence and good will ; and that, as I wished to avail myself of the Times for that purpose, he would oblige me by giving me a letter to the editor. He replied, "If you can get into the Times it will be more than I could ever do," and thus declined giving me the letter. I replied, "If I cannot get into the Times, you will see that I can get at it, or I greatly mistake." They manifested so much impatience that I left immediately after rising from the table. The next day, or the next but one,

LORD ASHBURTON'S APPOINTMENT

on a special mission was announced. Mr. Everett called on me, and expressed his surprise that the appointment had been made without any intimation of such a purpose having been given to him. I told him what had been said at the dinner, and we both believed that the appointment was intended to anticipate the probable announcement of the purpose of the government of the United States, to send Mr. Webster to London, and that the sending Lord Ashburton to Washington indicated a consciousness on the part of ministers that the anti-corn law league and the opposition were opposed to war, and that the sending a special envoy to the United States was intended as an assurance, on the part of ministers, of their desire to preserve peace, and to charge any failure of the negotiations, if failure there should be, as the fault of the United States.

The conversations with Baron Rothschild and Sir Henry Ellis, and the tone of the British press, especially of the London Times, led me to apprehend that the best, if not the only, means of preserving peace, was to show that England had much more than the United States to apprehend from was; and acting on this impression, I wrote the letters to Mr. Everett, to the President, and to Mr. Calhoun, which are given below. More: I saw that, as the purpose of England was to enlist the principal European powers in support of her measures, so prejudicial to the United States, it was of the first importance to defeat the proposed combination by unmasking the

SELFISH POLICY OF ENGLAND,

And demonstrating that it was the interest of the continental powers, and especially of France and Germany, to take part with the United States upon the issues pending between them and England; and, believing that I could make this so apparent, not only to France and Germany, but to England herself, in these letters, and in the publications through the French and English papers, I appealed directly to and contrasted these interests. More: After consulting General Cass, I prepared a letter to Admiral Duperre, the French minister of marine (which I also give), intended to awaken France to the value of our trade and the necessity of a system of railways which would give great facilities to our intercourse with northern and western Europe. The result of this communication was a proposition on the part of the French

government, for a treaty for a co-operation in the establishment of a direct trade, and maintaining a line of steamers. This was then defeated because Congress would not make the appropriation. With this explanation, the intelligent reader will be at no loss to appreciate the following

LETTERS TO MR. EVERETT.

PARIS, *January* 20, 1842.

DEAR SIR: I send you a letter which is written, that you may, if you think proper, show it to Lord Ashburton, as indicating the opinion of one who is well informed on the state of parties and of opinions at home. I have done so because the more I reflect on the subject, the more I am satisfied that the only means of avoiding a war is for the British government to recede, and because I fear that no one in England rightly appreciates the question as it is now made.

You must remember Mr. Pickens' report. That report indicates the feeling of a much more powerful mind than of the reputed author.

I have seen the letter of the American correspondent of the Chronicle. The man does not understand the a b c. He tells us that we cannot go to war because forty-four of the one hundred and two millions of exports of last year came to England. Does he not know that these same exports will go to the continent, and that a war now, before England has matured her East India policy, will build up for us customers who have no colonies, and that continental Europe will unite with us in dissolving her colonial system, and thereby open markets for our manufactures? But enough. I will write to you more at large on this subject.

Yours,   DUFF GREEN.

To Hon. EDWARD EVERETT,
American Minister at London.

PARIS, *January* 18, 1842.

DEAR SIR: When I last saw you I promised to write to Mr. Calhoun and other members of Congress, urging them to contribute, as far as they could, toward an early adjustment of the matters in dispute between the United States and Great Britain, and I gave you an assurance that Mr. Calhoun would do so.

I had not then read the correspondence between Mr. Stephenson and her majesty's government, nor had I read the report of the Secretaries of the Treasury, of the War and Navy Departments. It is now apparent to my mind that that correspondence has created a feeling in the United States which renders it impossible to avoid a war, unless the British government *immediately*, and in the most unequivocal manner recedes from the ground assumed in relation to the right of search.

The President's message is explained by the reports from the heads of the departments, and, knowing as I do, the sentiment of leading men in the South, and believing that they, many of them, desire a war, I fear that they will seize the occasion to blend the case of the Creole with the question of the right of search and the boundary, and thus embarrass the negotiation.

It may be proper to point out to you some facts in relation to our local politics, which will have a most important bearing on this question.

You know that there has been for many years a sectional jealousy between the North and the South, and that there has been much excitement upon the subject of slavery. You know that the organization of the present cabinet has recognized that sectional prejudice. Mr. Webster and Mr. Spencer being from the North, there is no sectional discontent. The question of the right of search involves the right of impressment, and is a question with New England, and hence the pretension put up by Great Britain will be resisted by Mr. Webster and Mr. Spencer with a zeal equal to that of any Southern man. But there is this in the question in the present aspect which cannot be fully appreciated in England. There are many intelligent men in the South who believe that the true secret of the abolition of West India slavery was jealousy of our manufactures and of our commerce; that the war on our credit was an effort to divert British capital to the East Indies, and that the late treaties in relation to the slave-trade were intended to pave the way for a monopoly of the ocean, and especially of the Pacific.

Do you not see, therefore, that a war on the pretence that the right of search is necessary to suppress the slave-trade, will be understood in the United States to be a war on our manufactures, on our fisheries (especially in the Pacific), and upon our commerce as well as upon slavery—that it is indeed but following up the same system of which the shipment of cotton-seed and experienced cotton-planters to India was part, and that the belief in the United States will be universal, that finding herself unable to compete with us on equal terms, in the cultivation of cotton, and fearing the competition of our manufactures, Great Britain has resolved upon a war, under a belief that she can thereby retard our progress; and that having resolved on war, she has selected the slave-trade as the pretence, under a belief that we are divided on the question of slavery, and that she can cover her real designs under a pretence of benevolence.

Some of us in the United States have, for years past, had our eyes on this abolition movement, and no one has noted its progress with a more intense interest than Mr. Calhoun. I have had many conversations with him in relation to it, and I know that although he sincerely desires peace, he is prepared for war, and believe that he, and all his friends of the South, will greatly prefer that it should come now, and on the present issue, to a postponement without a full and satisfactory arrangement of all questions, and especially of the slave question. By this I mean the case of the Creole, and other vessels in like circumstances.

If I have made myself understood, you will see that Mr. Calhoun and his friends will believe that a war upon the present issue will be a war in defence of the commerce and manufactures of the North, and of the slavery of the South, and that while New England and the North are defending *their* commerce and *their* manufactures, they will be defending *our* slavery, the consequence will be that the whole country will defend in argument what they defend in arms—slavery will cease to be the slavery of the South—it will be an institution of the Union, and we will become one people on this, as other questions. With analogous views some of us some eight years ago resolved to force the defence of slavery into our general politics. Before I began to discuss the subject in relation to federal politics, our Southern planters were unwilling to speak of slavery in the hearing of their slaves. I took the ground that unless it could be de-

fended on principle, and enforced as a system *permanent* in its duration, the sooner it was abandoned the better.

It was carried into the late Presidential election, and no candidate can be found to array himself as an abolitionist even in the North. Much was done by our anti-abolition movement during the late Presidential canvass. A war with England would put an end to abolition in the United States for many, many years. It would prepare the mind of all our people for all that could be said in contrasting our treatment of our slaves with their treatment of the poor, especially the poor in Ireland and in India, and so far from enlisting the sympathy of Europe in behalf of the unfortunate African, all nations will charge the war to a thirst for empire, and a determination to crush us, their most formidable rival, in commerce and manufactures.

I have said that the correspondence between Mr. Stephenson and her majesty's ministers has changed the tone of our government. I argue this from the President's message, and the reports from the heads of departments. When I left the United States the President was confident of the preservation of peace. The message and these reports are preparations for war.

I look upon the report of the Secretary of the Treasury on the exchequer as conclusive. I have had repeated conversations with Mr. Calhoun in relation to such an issue as it contemplates. It is his opinion, that during a term of peace, while the banks are paying specie, the government, by refusing to receive anything but its own paper or specie, could maintain eighty millions at par, with specie, on a revenue of thirty millions. If we have war there will be a suspension by the banks, and the exchequer bills, fundable at the option of the holder, will become our circulation. The expenditure of the government will be many millions, the taxes will be paid in these bills, and as all that we want is the means of developing our industry, and as the war will call out a large issue of exchequer bills, it will create many millions of capital, and *the states* will spring forward with an impulse equalled only by the energies of steam, the great agent of modern improvement. The government may spend some three or four hundred millions, but it will pay no interest to British capitalists. Our privateers and public steamships will cover every sea. France must become a party to the war, or she must lend us her ports, *and her sailors, too.* Ireland will become independent. England will be driven from the continent of America. The tory administration will be driven from power, and their successors will attain a peace by the most humiliating concessions.

When I saw you I did not think it possible that her majesty's government could think of going to war on the plea of the slave-trade. I hope that the calamity may be averted, but I now believe that there is no other means of averting it, but for the British government to recede, and do what is right as well in relation to the Creole as the boundary, for you may rest assured, that, whether the views I have presented be correct or not, they are the views which will control events at home, and you should entertain no hopes inconsistent with them. The war if made on this issue will be popular with all parties. Another fact you should bear in mind. Mr Fox is the last man to see the real state of things at Washington. He sees nothing and he knows nothing of what is going on in the United States. His habits and opinions disqualify him to judge of the progress of public opinion among us, and we should make some allowance for the effect of his opinions on Lord Ashburton and on his own government. You may rest assured, that unless Lord Ashburton goes out fully authorized to yield all that our government requires, and fully impressed with the importance of preserving peace, all that remains is to prepare for war. One means of doing this is to put the European powers right in relation to the true question in issue, and you will be gratified to learn that that is now in progress by one fully competent to the task.

I am deeply anxious to hear from you. Will the British government recede, or will she have the folly to force us into a war?

Yours, &c.

DUFF GREEN.

To Hon. EDWARD EVERETT,
American Minister at London.

FROM THE SAME TO THE SAME.

PARIS, *January* 20, 1842.

DEAR SIR: Since my letter of the 18th was written, I have read the letter of the Philadelphia correspondent of the London Morning Chronicle, and see that Mr. Clay has resolved to oppose the bill proposed by the Secretary of the Treasury, and that it is said to be probable that Mr. Calhoun and the democratic party will also oppose it.

That Mr. Clay will oppose any measure that does not look to his own advancement I am prepared to believe. He is, and has ever been, essentially selfish. He is the centre around which all his purposes revolve, and I am not surprised to learn that he is opposed to this measure, nor am I surprised to learn that a majority of the whig members of Congress are acting with him.

It may be well to examine what bearing this opposition of Mr. Clay and of Mr. Calhoun will have on the question of peace.

In 1837, Mr. Calhoun proposed to issue twenty millions of treasury notes receivable in payment of the public dues, and he told me repeatedly that the great financial error of the late war was the receiving of bank notes in payment of taxes.* He condemned the late administration for issuing interest-bearing treasury notes, because he said that such notes, not bearing interest receivable in payment of public dues to the exclusion of bank notes, would be at par with specie. He and the whole democratic party in Congress opposed the $12,000,000 loan, on the ground that they preferred an issue of treasury notes. It is true that the discount is a new feature, but the report of the Secretary is, with this exception so much the same as Mr. Calhoun's own suggestion, that I do not believe he will refuse to unite with the administration on some measure founded on this report. But say that Mr. Calhoun, and Mr. Clay, and their friends unite against the Secretary's scheme. What, then? What bearing will that have on the question of war with England?

Let us see what would be the effect of a war without this scheme. The credit of the states is prostrate. Illinois bonds seventeen cents on the dollar. Indiana no better, and government six per cents. under par. We must come to Europe and depend upon the Barings, and the Rothschilds, and the bank of England, for money to defend our cities and to protect our firesides!! Do you believe that we will do this?

Now, look at the state of the country with this bill in operation? The bill, as it now is, proposes to make the exchequer bills convertible into specie. If we have a war, all that the government will be required to do is to make them convertible into government six per cent. stocks, and it will command all that we require?

See how it will act on the states. We have some six hundred steamboats on the Mississippi. Illinois has commenced her canal, and requires some five or six millions of dollars to complete it. In case of a war, the federal government will issue six millions of exchequer bills, and the canal will be completed in a single season. Let there be war, and Virginia, Georgia, Louisiana, Alabama, Tennessee, Ohio, Indiana, and Illinois, will receive the aid of the federal government to complete their railroads as part of the military defence of the country, by an issue of exchequer bills fundable in six per cent. stocks. These exchequer bills will purchase provisions and labor, and give a certain income to all who have surplus to invest in interest-bearing stocks. They will be paid away to our own people as the price of our labor, and if they remain, as they probably will do, under par in the European market, so much the better—they will be so much added to the wealth of our country—they will in the first place have created our railroads, and in the next place they will remain as interest bearing capital in the hands of our people. What I have said of our railroads will be equally true of our navy. England herself is but a nation of smugglers. She will import our cotton in neutral

* See Appendix.

bottoms, or she will drive her manufactures to the continent.

Now, as I read the message and the reports of the heads of the departments—the President understands these things well. He sees that a war with England is popular, and if Mr. Clay is so much blinded by his ambition as to oppose a measure so essential to the independence of the country in case of war, I do not believe that Mr. Calhoun will do so, and if they do they will both find that the days of their power are departed. I presume to know something of public opinion in the United States, and venture to assert that no combination of politicians can resist the financial scheme presented by the President, whether we have peace or war. I do not say that it will prevail precisely as presented—the discount is, in my opinion, wrong, but such is the deep interest which the Western, and even the Southern States will have in calling in the aid which the scheme will give them in case of a war, and so palpable are the benefits to them, in case of war, that it will be almost impossible to prevent them from urging a war on that account. Another view of this case is that the President and the men by whom he is surrounded are but men. I admit that the President and his personal adherents are a small minority, but they are so because the country had divided between Mr. Clay and those opposed to Mr. Clay. The question of war and the system of finance as a war measure, are measures of the administration, and the moment that the question is presented in that shape neither Mr. Clay, Mr. Calhoun, nor any other public man can resist the overwhelming impulse of public sentiment. President Tyler will be hailed from one end of the country to the other as the representative of his country's honor, and no President has ever been so popular as he will be. He cannot fail to see this, and, charged as he is with the issues of war or peace, it will require on his part the rarest virtue to resist the temptation to force the country into war. If Mr. Clay and Mr. Calhoun unite to keep the currency question open, that will force the President before the country on the issue he has made. He need fear no competition. If the bill fails in this Congress, it will not fail in the next; but do you not see that the tendency of things will be to induce the President and his advisers to strengthen themselves still more on the issue they have made by calling in the war feeling.

I repeat, that so far from dreading a war, the leading statesmen in the South, many of them, believe that a war with England on the issue now before us, would be the most fortunate thing for them.

Let us pause for a moment and consider the bearing on them and on England. It is admitted that Great Britain has reached a point where her population trenches upon the means of subsistence. Her political economists may be said to divide into three schools—one for free trade and the independence of the colonies—one for free trade with all the rest of the world, and a modification of the colonial regulations, so as to enable them to consume more, but to secure a preference for British goods in the colonies, and both of these parties agree on an abolition of the corn laws, or such a modification of them as will let in foreign corn. These two parties constitute the present opposition; they argue that the British commercial system must undergo an essential and radical modification, or it must sink under the competition organized on the continent and in the United States. On the other hand, the landed interest and a controlling influence in the clergy and nobility are opposed to any change. They are now in power, and are pushing their conquest in China ; and if they are in favor of a war with us, it can only be under a belief that by a war they will break up our commerce and destroy our manufactures.

This party do not realize our condition. They do not know that they cannot injure us by an invasion—that all our magazines of war, our breadstuffs, our arms and our men, are in the interior which they cannot reach—that in such a war we can put any required number of troops at any required position in a few days—that we are out of debt and do not depend upon any foreign country for a single article, or a single means of defence—that for all the purposes of creating or supporting an army, or a navy, the credit of our government—I mean Mr. Tyler's exchequer bills, convertible into six per cent. stocks—will suffice. The operation of these bills may be imagined from the fact that the Baltimore and Ohio Railroad Company made an issue of one and a half millions predicated on Baltimore city stock, at fifteen per cent. below par, and yet the notes were at par, or one per cent. below par, with bank paper, and because they were received at par by the company, on a revenue of some four hundred thousand dollars. Imagine, then, what the United States could do with these exchequer bills ? They could become the currency of the whole country, and gradually absorb the idle capital.

How would it be with England ? It would be a war of interests. The European powers would not only become the carriers, but they would unite with us in emancipating all her colonies. They would become the rivals of England in manufactures, and would themselves see their interst in compelling England to permit free trade with the colonies. In the mean time the British funds would receive a shock which would greatly embarrass the operations of the government. Capitalists would transfer a part of their means to the continent, or even to the United States ; and if she finds it difficult to meet her present expenditures, what would she do when one half of her commerce shall be diverted to the continent ? If the deficiencies of a few quarters of corn produce so much distress, what will be the consequences of a war superadded to one or two bad crops ? It must end in revolutionizing political power, and a change of administration under such circumstances must cost the tories and the aristocracy many humiliating concessions, if it does not trench upon some of the present prerogatives of royalty. There is a feeling in England which will be brought into action by a war with us, that when once aroused may not be easily arrested. But England has much to fear from the feeling on the continent, and especially in France. I give you an incident. Last week, in a crowded party, an American gentleman came in contact with a young French officer, some words passed, and the Frenchman gave his card. It was accepted. The American gave his name and residence. As soon as the Frenchman ascertained that the other was an American, and not an Englishman, he apologized, asked the return of his card, and the matter was arranged. Add to this the fact that some of the leading friends of the king of the French are taking ground against the slave-trade treaties, and that Mr. Guizot has upon more than one occasion said that it is not yet ratified, and you will see that the sympathies of Europe will be enlisted with their interests on the side of America.

I assure you that these things are well understood in the United States, and that I fear that the present ministers do not rightly appreciate their own position in relation to their own people, or to the continent—nor do they understand the people of the United States—nor the relation which the President and parties in the United States bear to the question of war or peace. I repeat that Mr. Fox is the last man to understand the people or parties in the United States. It is not possible for one of his habits and associations to do so, and I fear that he has misled his own government, and that he will mislead Lord Ashburton. I am sincerely desirous for peace. I would avert if possible the calamity of war, but it becomes the friends of peace who have any influence to exert it with the British government, and I hope that as far as you can do so with propriety you will prepare Lord Ashburton for this new state of things.

I feel the greater responsibility, because in my letters by the last steamer, I gave assurances of a desire on the part of the British government to preserve peace, which I fear is not entertained.

Do write to me and let me know what are your opinions on these points.

Yours, sincerely,

DUFF GREEN.

To Hon. EDWARD EVERETT,
 American Minister at London.

DUFF GREEN TO DANIEL WEBSTER.

PARIS, *January* 24, 1842.

DEAR SIR : I take the liberty to refer you to letters which I send by the same packet to the President, for my views in relation to the present aspect of our affairs with England. Before I read the correspondence with Mr. Stevenson, and before I came here and examined the subject with the light cast upon it by European diplomacy, I was of opinion that England was sincerely desirous of peace. But although I believe that she sincerely desires to accomplish her purpose by peace if she can, I as sincerely believe that she has made up her mind to accomplish it by war, if it cannot be done without war.

I take the liberty also to refer you to copies of letters which I enclose to Mr. Wickliffe, that you may see what I have done toward preparing the way for forcing England to recede, because she cannot go forward unless she is sustained by the public opinion of her own people, and will hesitate to do so unless she is sustained by the public opinion of continental Europe.

Through the influence of Gen. Cass much has already been done to arrest the current which the British press had put in motion against us, but I hope to be able to do something more through the French and German press, and, at the suggestion of Dr. Niles, I will prepare an article for the " Revue des Deux Mondes," in which I will demonstrate, as I can, that the purpose of England is to render continental Europe dependent on her for the supply of the raw material for the manufacture of cotton, and that her war upon slavery is a war on our commerce and manufactures, through our domestic institutions.

No one is more sincerely desirous of preserving peace than I am, and it is because I would preserve peace that I would urge on you, and every friend of America, to prepare for war. We can gain nothing by concession. If you are firm, England must yield, or if she goes to war she must forfeit her greatness. We will fight the battles of Europe. Almost every European state will sympathize with us ; they will all see that we are fighting their battles, and that our trade and resources will increase, while England must lose her colonies.

If I am correct, and I am confident I am not mistaken, the war will be on New England. This must be understood in New England, and this fact will unite our people. I have read the Secretary's report on the issue of exchequer bills. I look on it as the ablest paper to which the discussion on the currency has given rise.

I do not see how Mr. Clay or Mr. Calhoun can sustain themselves in opposing it. But the strongest argument in its favor is the strength it will give the government in time of war. We have all the elements of war within ourselves, and the exchequer bills will command them. The bank of England rests upon the public credit. The exchequer bills may be made convertible into six per cents., or five per cents., and we need not go abroad for a dollar.

I repeat that no opposition can resist this bill if the public can be made to realize the views of England. The purposes are so palpable, and the intelligence of our people is such, that they cannot fail to see them. Much— very much depends upon you, and I confidently hope that babes, yet unborn, are to lisp your praise for the ability and firmness with which I am sure you will assert and maintain the interests of our common country.

Prepare for war. This is our only hope. I repeat, if you desire peace, prepare for war.

The British government have one of two modes of maintaining their ascendency. One is by a repeal of their corn laws, and a general reduction of taxes, to diminish the cost of production, so as to enable her manufacturers to compete with us and other rival manufacturing states ; the other is by destroying slavery—to render it impossible for other manufacturing states to obtain the raw material as cheaply as through her. She prefers the last mode, and if she can accomplish it by negotiation, she would much prefer to do so. She does not wish war for the sake of war, but she is prepared to accomplish it by war. If she finds that we are prepared for war, and that there is cause to apprehend that, instead of rendering the European continental states dependent on her, through her colonies, there is great danger that her colonies will become independent of her, she will hesitate, and may be compelled to fall back on the principles of free trade. She will, in that event, open her ports to our corn, and, having abandoned her warfare on our manufactures, will cease to annoy our domestic institutions.

Rest assured that these suggestions are not fancy sketches. I give them to you, relying on your ability to make plain what I can clearly understand myself, but cannot so forcibly impart to others.

By all means let our friends urge the fiscal agent, as a war measure, and let every friend of the administration speak out boldly and decidedly on the pressing necessity of preparing for war, as the only means of preserving peace.

Your obdt. servt.,
DUFF GREEN.

To Hon. DANIEL WEBSTER,
Secretary of State.

DUFF GREEN TO JOHN TYLER.

PARIS, January 24, 1842.

DEAR SIR: I enclose you the paper containing the report of the remarks of Mr. Guizot in reply to Mr. Theirs. I also send a copy of Gen. Cass's pamphlet, and you will find that Mr. Guizot has taken the ground prepared for him by Gen. Cass.

France as well as England and the United States has her parties, and the most important consideration with the King and his party is to secure the succession to his family. Connected with this is the possession of Algiers, because France will not consent that her present King shall surrender what Charles X. had won. England has annoyed the French, by subsidizing the Arabs, under the avowed purpose of keeping open the overland communication with India. It is now apparent that France has been induced to sign the slave-trade treaty under an assurance that England will cease to annoy her in Africa, and that England will favor the succession in the line of the present King. It is not a matter of surprise that under such circumstances France should be overreached, and that to secure what she considers a permanent good, she yields what would seem to be a barren right of search. But examine the subject and you will find in this arrangement with France, proof that England has an interest far beyond the mere suppression of the slave-trade, in her late slave-trade treaties. What is that interest? Why should she agree to quiet France in her possessions in Africa? Why should she give assurance of support to the King of the French? Do you suppose that the suppression of the slave trade "per se" is an equivalent for the risk she encounters by permitting France to quiet her African possessions? Rest assured that benevolence has nothing to do with the matter—that her purpose is to make the labor of her East India subjects available, and to render the whole world dependent upon her, through them for the supply of the raw material, so that by rendering them thus dependent, she may, through the supply of the raw material, control the manufacturers of other nations, and thus compel all nations to pay her tribute. You will thus see that our quarrel is the quarrel of continental Europe, and it is due to Gen. Cass, that I should say, that he is contributing greatly to open the eyes of Europe on this subject. In the first place, by the able pamphlet which I send you, and in the next, by his activity in resisting British influence, through the representatives of other European nations here.

Paris may be said to be the heart of continental Europe, and the ablest diplomats are located here. This, then, is the point at which Europe is to be acted on, and aware of this, Gen. Cass has by his deportment and conciliatory manner won upon the King and ministers as well as the opposition in France, that he has more power than any other American has had for many years—this enables him again to act on the other states—especially on the smaller states who are beginning to feel the importance of their relation with us.   Yours, &c.

DUFF GREEN.

To JOHN TYLER,
President of the United States.

PARIS, *January* 24, 1842.

MY DEAR SIR: When I last wrote to you, I had not seen Mr. Stevenson's correspondence with the British government, nor the reports from the heads of the departments at Washington. I have, since I came here, satisfied myself that under the pressure of the public debt, England finds it impossible to maintain her commercial and manufacturing superiority, because she cannot raise cotton, sugar, &c., as cheap in India as it can be raised in the United States, Cuba, and Brazil, and that her war on slavery and the slave-trade is intended to increase the cost of producing the raw material in the United States, Brazil, and Cuba, that she can sell to other rival manufacturing, continental powers, the product of her East India possessions cheaper than they can purchase from us. If she can do this, having the power to compel her East India subjects to purchase her manufactures, and hers alone, she can, through her manufactures, command the supply of raw material, and thus compel rival manufacturing nations to pay her tribute, while she, in a great measure, controls the manufacture itself. This is part of her policy. Do we not see one fourth of her iron manufactories now idle? and why? because she says the supply exceeds the demand; and, do you not believe that, if it comes to a question of whether her spinning jennies, or those of continental Europe, or of the United States, shall stand idle, she will hesitate as to which is to be employed? or that, having the command of the raw material, she will fail as to means to accomplish her purpose.

Under the aspects of the case, you will find that England has much more than a work of benevolence in the suppression of the slave-trade.

She has the alternative of repealing her own corn laws, and abolishing her protective duties, or of enforcing her present colonial policy by stratagem or war.

If she goes to war there will be great danger that it will end in the emancipation of her colonies, and that this will be followed by the abolition of her national debt, and protective duties, if it does not end in the reorganization of society, the entire prostration of the present aristocracy, and a modification of the present prerogatives of the crown.

Under these aspects of the case, I am satisfied that our only hope of peace rests in being well prepared for war, and that the first measure is such an organization of the financial condition of the treasury, as that we can use the credit of the government at home. We have nothing to expect from Europe, at least for some time to come. I was introduced to Baron Rothschild by General Cass, at a diplomatic dinner, and speaking of the question which now absorbs all circles, the probability of war between England and America, he said to me, "But how can you go to war? you can get no money. I received a letter, to-day, from my correspondent in London, inquiring to know whether the United States would borrow money on the continent, and my reply was, not a dollar." He proceeded to say to me, "You may tell your government that you have seen the man who is at the head of the finances of Europe, and that he has told you that they cannot borrow a dollar, not a dollar."

I then explained that there had been a systematic effort, on the part of England, to depreciate the credit of the

United States; that her purpose was to compel those continental powers of Europe, as well as the United States, who are engaged in rival manufactures, to depend on her East India colonies for the raw material; and, therefore, the war with us would be a war on the manufacturing states of Europe; that we had within ourselves all the elements of war, that we had six hundred steamboats on a single river, and that, so far from having anything to fear from England, we did not fear to go to war with England, with Europe at her back; but that Europe would have a common interest with us, that by the use of exchequer bills, convertible into six per cents., we could command men, ships, and munitions. He said, "Yes, you may get men and ships, but such is the character of your state debts, that the United States cannot borrow a single dollar in Europe." This was before dinner. After the dinner was over, he came to me, and urged me to come and see him, and converse with him on this subject. He said, "You may be able to go to war, but you must get the means at home."

After he went away, General Cass remarked, that he had had a long conversation with me, and was impressed with its importance. I have not yet gone to see him, but I purpose to prepare for the "Revue des Deux Mondes," the leading European review, an article in which I will demonstrate the purposes of England so plain, that I am confident there will be a powerful re-action in our favor.

Do you not see that this is a war upon the commerce and manufactures of New England, through our domestic institutions, and that this is the time to unite all parties and all sections in their support? If England be defeated in the present movement, she has no alternative but to fall back on free trade—there is a strong party in England who are in favor of free trade—and thus the manufacturing continental states will unite with the South in a common support of your long-cherished measure of free trade. But permit me to urge on you, that although I believe this can be accomplished without war, the only means of doing it is to be prepared for war; and that, under this aspect of the case, I feel a deep anxiety to learn that you are acting in concert with the administration on the measure of finance.

I consider this the most important crisis of your active and eventful life. When I remember the many times you again and again explained to me that the great end of your labors was to establish for the United States a free trade; and reflect that it is, as I verily believe it is, now in your power, by uniting with the President and those of your own personal friends who are in his cabinet and united with him, in perfecting the exchequer bill, to accomplish not only free trade for the United States, but for the greater part of the civilized world, I cannot permit myself to believe that you will not render your advice and co-operation, and believing that, by your advice and co-operation, the measure can be made efficient, I cannot permit myself to fear its failure.

I have been requested by persons here, interested in American securities, to prepare a small manual, historical and geographical, of the United States, with the statistical resources of the United States and the several states. It is to be published in England, and will be translated into French and and German. I wish to make it a manual for the politician as well as the banker, merchant, and emigrant. It will, of course, embrace a very short review of the discussion on free trade, and the question of nullification. The time has come when the eyes of the whole world are fixed on us, and my desire is to make the vindication of our principles as efficient as it can be done. Will you do me the favor to embody, in as brief a manner as you can, a review of the tariff question, and the points agitated and adjusted by the nullification question. Do justice to the little state. Prepare it at your earliest convenience. It is a matter in which your own character, and that of your state, and our principles, are so deeply involved, that I am sure I may rely on you for this aid. It will be important, too, in its bearing on the question of free trade, as now discussed in England, and upon which the question of war with us depends.

I beg you to bear in mind that there is a powerful free-trade party sprung up on the continent of Europe, and that England is now divided ; and the real question is war with us, or free trade.

Let me have any suggestions you can give, growing out of the question.

Your friend,

DUFF GREEN.

P. S.—General Cass has been very kind to me, and I am not without hopes that I will be able, through him, to bring my negotiations to a fortunate conclusion. General Cass requests to be remembered to you, and says that he has never ceased to be your personal friend.

To Hon. JOHN C. CALHOUN,

Washington, D. C.

DUFF GREEN TO ADMIRAL DUPERRE.

HOTEL DE HOLLANDE,

RUE DE LA PAIX, 4 *Mars,* 1842.

MONSIEUR LE MINISTRE : During the last summer, in a conversation with Mr. Barcourt at Washington, I made some suggestions which he requested me to communicate to his government through General Cass, who advises me to address them to you.

I am the proprietor of extensive mines in the United States, from which, owing to the price, it can be delivered at, and the superior quality of the coal, the supplies of fuel for steamships crossing the Atlantic should be furnished, and, indeed, I am not without hopes, that arrangements may be made advantageously with your government to introduce this coal for consumption in France, and especially on your railroads.

I submit these remarks, that what I am about to say may not be considered impertinent interference on the part of a stranger in questions relating to the domestic affairs of France.

The establishment of a line of steamships, necessarily connects itself with the proposition now pending before the Chamber of Deputies for the construction of a system of railroads, because the success of a line of packets will depend upon whether it will have such advantages as to command a fair proportion of the passengers and freight between Europe and America. It is this which I propose to examine.

Steam has produced a revolution in commerce. The effect and capabilities of railroads must be seen to be realized.

Greater progress has been made in the United States, and the system has been more developed there than elsewhere. I shall, therefore, be excused

11

for referring to the system in operation there.

The apprehension that railroads were not suited to the transportation of merchandise has vanished before experience, and so has the belief that they are suited only to short distances. It is found that long routes pay the best dividends on the capital invested, because they are worked at less cost, and command more business. The only exception to this rule is, roads between large cities or to mines.

Experience in the United States has demonstrated, that merchandise and passengers can afford to pay much higher prices for expeditious transportation on railroads, and that where railroads come in competition with water transportation, much the greater part of freight and passengers prefer the railroads, because they are found to be more punctual, as well as more expeditious.

These facts have an important bearing on the system which France is about to execute.

If it were possible for France to turn the course of the great rivers of Russia, of Prussia, of Germany, Holland, and Belgium, and to compel their mingled waters to pass through Paris to Brest, what would be its influence on the commerce and the political relations of the continent? The conception is so vast, that the mind is lost in contemplating its results.

France cannot turn the course of these great rivers; but by creating railroads, which will pay a fair dividend on the capital invested, and would be preferred as a medium of transportation, she will do more than if she could accomplish it.

The railroads of France must compete with the navigation of the British channel, the Northern, German, and Baltic seas, and the rivers of Russia, Prussia, Germany, Holland, and Belgium. One important duty of your railroads will be to furnish freight and passenger for your steamships and packets, and the first inquiry is, has France a seaport which has advantages over the ports of England? Most of the passengers and much of the merchandise passing between the north of Europe and America, go by way of Liverpool. Can France induce them to prefer her steamships and packets to those of England?

Such is the importance of time that a proposition to construct a railroad from Dublin to the southwest point of Ireland, as the starting point of the steamers for America, has been seriously agitated in England. This route would have to encounter the dangers and delays of crossing the Irish channel; whereas, if we look upon the map of Europe, we shall see that that part of the continent which projects farthest westward on the route to America is Brest. We here find a capacious and fortified harbor, capable of protecting any fleet. It is easy of access and egress, and in time of war would command the British channel. If we place the map before us and draw a straight line from Brest to Vienna, it will pass nearly through Paris and Strasbourg. If we draw a line from Paris to Moscow it will pass near Frankfort, Dresden, and Warsaw. I am told that railroads have already been projected, and either completed, or are now in the progress of execution from Raab and Brun, by way of Vienna to Augsburg, and also from Bamburg and Nuremburg to Augsburg; also, from Frankfurth and Stettin on the Oder, by way of Berlin, Halle, Cassell, Dusseldorf, Aix, Liege, and Brussels, to Lille.

When we take into consideration the dangers, difficulties, and delays of the navigation of the British channel, and contrast them with the punctuality and despatch of a railroad from Brest to Vienna, or from Brest to Moscow, we cannot doubt that all the travel from the north of Europe to America, and most of the merchandise, would prefer the railroad, which would bring Paris as near to New York as Liverpool now is.

A passenger coming from New York to Brussels would save one day, and the expense, delays, and inconvenience of passing through England and crossing the channel. For other points on the continent the saving would be greater. A merchant wishing to send merchandise to America, would avoid the delays and risks of the channel, and would consequently prefer the railroad. In confirmation of this, we give the following statements and tables relative to railroads in the United States and England.

At the beginning of 1841, the number of miles of railroads, constructed in the United States and England, were :

```
"In England, completed lines........................1,100
      "       In progress.........................1,000—2,100 miles.

"In the United States, complete......................3,332
      "          In progress ...................1,707—5,039    "

"In England the capital invested was...................... $288,000,000,
    and the average per mile $100,000, principally of double
    track.
"In the United States the capital invested was.......  .....   98,000,000,
    and the average cost per mile $18,000—single track, graded
    for two."
```

The following shows the dividend and value of stocks on some of these roads :

Camden and Amboy.....................	6 to 7	p' ct. dividend per annum.
Baltimore and Ohio....................	4	" " "
Boston and Worcester.................	6 " 7	" " "
Boston and Providence................	7 " 8	" " "
Georgia Central	8 " 9	" " "
Schenectady and Utica...............12 " 13	" " "
Champlain and St. Lawrence...........10 "	" " "
Baltimore and Philadelphia.............	6 " 7	" " "
Baltimore and Washington.............	7	" " "
Charleston and Augusta................	7 " 8	" " "
Boston and Lowell.....................	8 " 9	" " "
Mohawk and Hudson...................	6 " 7	" " "
Mine Hill (Coal).....................11 " 12	" " "
Utica and Syracuse...................	9 " 10	" " "

The following is a statement of the value of some of the railroad stocks in Great Britain :

Stockton and Darlington (coal mine) at.........	£75	for £100 paid.
Grand Junction	215	" 100 "
Liverpool and Manchester............................	175	" 100 "
London and Birmingham..............................	179	" 100 "
Great Western.......................................	92	" 100 "
York and Midland....................................	67	" 57 "
North Union..	83	" 75 "
London and Southampton.............................	58	" 30 "

The following tables show the operation of several railroads in different parts of the United States in 1839 :

Railroads.	Miles	Gross Receipts per Annum.	Expense per Annum.	Passengers through per Annum.	Per Cent. of Expense on Gross Receipts.	Dividends in 1839.
Schenectady and Utica..	78	$400,700	$113,700	130,000	28	11 per cent.
Utica and Syracuse......	53	251,200	69,300	122,000	27½	11 "
Mohawk and Hudson.....	16	150,500	68,000	188,000	45½	7 "
Camden and Amboy...	92	685,300	258,000	182,000	39	7 "
		$1,487,700	$509,000	....	Av. 34½ per cent.	

The above table shows the Northern roads are used for passengers almost exclusively.

EASTERN ROADS.—ABOUT HALF OF THE RECEIPTS BEING FOR FREIGHT.

Railroads.	Miles.	Gross Receipts.	Expense per Annum.	Per Cent. on Gross Receipts.	Dividends.
Boston and Lowell...........	26	$241,200	$92,100	38	8 per cent.
Boston and Providence.......	41	312,900	93,600	30	8 "
Boston and Worcester........	44½	231,800	126,400	54½	6 "
Taunton branch..............	11	58,000	40,700	72	6 "
Eastern Railroad	25	125,600	53,200	42¾	4¾ "
Nashau and Lowell..........	14½	55,000	29,900	54	6 "
	....	$1,024,500	$435,900	Av. 42½ per cent.	

SOUTHERN ROADS.—RECEIPTS MAINLY FROM FREIGHT, EXCEPT THE FIRST AND LAST.

Railroads.	Miles.	Gross Receipts.	Expense per Annum.	Per Cent. on Gross Receipts.	Dividends.
Baltimore and Washington....	40	$202,700	$85,200	42	7 per cent.
Baltimore and Ohio..........	88	433,000	280,200	65	4½ "
Georgia Central	110	113,800	34,400	30	8 "
Georgia Railroad	87½	184,600	70,300	38	9 "
Baltimore and Philadelphia...	93	490,500	164,100	33½	7 "
	....	$1,424,600	$634,200	Av. 44½ per cent.	

The following table shows the increase of business on some of these roads :

Boston and Lowell—net revenue, 1836..... $89,800
           "   1839..... 149,100

                          $59,300 increase in 3 years.

Boston and Worcester—gross revenue, 1835... $119,100
            "   1839... 281,800

                          $112,700 increase in 4 years.

Baltimore and Ohio—gross revenue, 1833..... $195,700
            "   1840. . 432,900

                          $237,200 increase in 7 years.

Camden and Amboy—net revenue, 1833..... $181,000
            "   1839..... 427,000

                          $246,000 increase in 6 years.

Liverpool and Manchester—net revenue, 1832, $303,000
            "   1839, 556,000

                          $253,000 increase in 7 years.

Columbia and Philadelphia—net revenue, 1835, $229,351
            "   1840, 449,267

                        $219,916 increase in 5 years.

A Brussels paper gives an abstract of the report of the minister of public works, from which it appears that the receipts on the Belgian railroads, from the year 1835 to 1840 inclusive, exceed the expenditures, and show that the increase was progressive, as follows :

Date.	Francs.	c.
1835................	100,224	77
1836................	393,997	18
1837................	226,994	12
1838................	342,777	00
1839................	1,165,414	76
1840................	2,338,053	06
Total,........	4,567,461	49

The following extracts have an important bearing on the system in France, because they demonstrate the value of railroads for the transportation of merchandise :

" On the Central Railroad—Georgia.

"The opinion has generally prevailed that a road to be profitable must have a large amount of travel, and that the only source of profit is the transportation of passengers, and that, as a general rule, the freight of heavy commodities yields little or no profit. The experience so far, on our road, demonstrates, in the most satisfactory manner, the *error* of this opinion. Our freighting business is more than *double* that of passengers and the mail, and this has been done under the disadvantage of having but one train for both purposes, and, consequently, keeping up *a speed* altogether too great for the most advantageous transportation of freight.

" I have no doubt that freight trains, with full loads, and a velocity not exceeding ten miles per hour, would yield as much profit per trip as passenger trains carrying fifty passengers each way. I am confident the merchants will find it to their advantage to abandon altogether the steamboat business on the Oconee and Ocmulgee rivers."

(Signed)   "L. O. REYNOLDS,
      "*Civil Engineer*."

"On the Georgia Railroad.

"I can now state, with confidence, that wherever the transportation is of a mixed character, such as agricultural products, general merchandise, and passengers, and sufficiently large to justify the construction of a good railway, that railways will be found to be, not only the most expeditious, but the *cheapest* artificial means of conveyance at present known."

"It should be taken into consideration that the down freight is principally cotton, bulky and expensive to handle, yet we find it leaves the rivers and seeks the railway. Facts of this kind are worth more than theory."

(Signed)   "J. EDGAR THOMPSON,
      "*Civil Engineer*."

The following, it is believed, will give the business load of a single locomotive of eleven tons weight at an average speed of ten miles per hour over roads of different grades, and the relative expense:

"Level,	83 cars,	3 tons each,	net freight	250 tons,	at a cost of 53c.	per ton,	per 200 miles.
10ft, grade,	60 "	"	"	180 "	"	62 "	"	"
20ft. "	50 "	"	"	150 "	"	67 "	"	"
30ft. "	40 "	"	"	120 "	"	75 "	"	"
40ft. "	30 "	"	"	90 "	"	90 "	"	"
50ft. "	25 "	"	"	75 "	"	100 "	"	"

Late experiments in the United States show, that a single locomotive of eleven tons weight, on a level road, travelling at the rate of ten miles per hour, is equal to a load of five hundred tons gross, or three hundred tons net, and that a ten-ton engine is equal to a load of two hundred and thirty tons gross, or one hundred and fifty-two tons net, over a grade of nineteen feet to the mile, travelling at the same rate.

The table given above states the cost of transportation after the road is made. It does not take into the account the interest of the capital invested in the road, or the expense of keeping it in repair. The cost of construction it will be seen has been much less in the United States than in England. The following extract from the last report of the Baltimore and Ohio railroad shows the cost of keeping that road in repair for one year:

"The repairs of the nineteen miles of the heavy H rails, not having as yet required any new material, have cost $180 per mile; while for the ninety-two miles of old plate rail, the cost for material is $325 46, and for labor and superintendence $399 per mile."

If constructed on piles, as the New York and Erie Railway, and the Utica and Syracuse roads are, the cost of repairs, as well as of construction, will be less.

That some idea may be formed of what railroads may do, we give a statement of the operations of the Utica and Schenectady Railroads. It is a great thoroughfare, but although it is the most successful road in the United States, it has to labor under many disadvantages. The statement shows its business for the first four and a half years. We have seen that the business on railroads increases from year to year.

100 miles graded for two tracks.

"Capital, $2,000,000, paid in $100 shares............................ $1,500,000
Right of way paid from dividends.......................$322,500
Purchase of Mohawk turnpike, dividends.............. 62,500
Sundries 17,000
                                                    ——————— 402,000
                                                             $1,902,000
"Total cost, equal for road to $18,500 per mile; right of way, etc.,
   $5,000, together $23,500.
It has been in operation four years five months up to the 1st January,
   1841, during which time it has received from passengers, mail,
   etc., etc... $1,618,500
The total expenses for the same period average per annum 29½ per
   cent., were.. 532,000

Net earning 50 per cent. for four and a half years on $1,800,000
   capital...$11,065,500"

This road is restricted from carrying freight, because it comes in competition with the canal.

The following is given as the cost of travel on some of the roads, being those on which travel is cheapest:

"Utica and Syracuse, 53 miles, 122,000 passengers carried for $69,400, or 57 cents each.

"Mohawk and Hudson, 16 miles, 188,000 passengers carried for $68,100, or 37 cents each.

"Utica and Schenectady, 78 miles, 135,000 passengers carried for $87,400, or 67 cents each.

"These charges include all expenses of repairs to road, etc."

There are no people in the world, more practical in the application of labor than those of Massachusetts. They have just now completed a railroad from Boston to Albany on the Hudson river in the state of New York. That some idea may be formed of what railroads are doing in the United States, I insert an extract from an American paper just received. The distance from Rochester to Albany is two hundred and nineteen miles, the distance from Albany to Boston is two hundred miles, from Albany to New Bedford two hundred and fifty-five miles; making a continuous route from Rochester to Boston of four hundred and nineteen miles.

Extract from the Baltimore American, January 4, 1842:

"BOSTON AND ALBANY.—The incident which we mentioned a few days ago, that sperm candles, made in New Bedford on the morning of the 27th ult., were burning in Albany on the evening of that day, having, in the interim, been conveyed 255 miles over the railroads connecting the two places, has been answered by another, of a similar character, in Western New York. Gentlemen who left Rochester on Monday, brought with them to the festival at Albany, that evening, a barrel of flour, ground on Monday from wheat taken from the sheaf, and thrashed, that morning. The barrel was also made from staves, taken from a tree, which was growing in the forest, near Rochester, on Monday morning. The flour was conveyed to Boston in the train which carried the guests to that city on Wednesday, and was used at the dinner which was given in Boston on Thursday.

"At the festival in Albany, Governor Seward read a letter, written in 1762, by the then governor of New York, to the authorities of Massachusetts, proposing to establish a *monthly* mail between Boston and Albany."

Flour is transported on this road from Albany to Boston for twenty-five cents per barrel of 212 pounds, or 100 kilogrammes.

The people of Massachusetts, in a publication on the subject of railroads, say :

"A railroad, by economy of time, saves three quarters of the labor and expense of transporting burdens and persons. At a low estimate for Massachusetts, this expense is calculated at $16,000,000, of which $12,000,000 per annum could be saved."

The state has, therefore, advanced its credit to borrow the money for the construction of the principal railways, the purpose being to create a sinking fund to pay the cost, when the rates of fare will be reduced, so as to collect no more than is sufficient to pay expenses, and keep the road in repair. I have not the material to make an estimate of the cost of travel and transportation in France ; but, if the saving is so great in Massachusetts, with a population of 937,699, what must it be in France, with a population of thirty-four millions ?

The capacity of railroads are not limited to the transportation of merchandise, or of passengers. Their bearing on the military and political relations of France. are equally important as upon its commerce ; and it is characteristic of railroads, that while they constitute the most efficient means of defence against invasion in time of war, or of rebellion, they furnish a profitable investment of capital, and contribute to increase the wealth and productive energies of the country in time of peace.

But the value of the system to France, whether it be considered in a military, political or commercial view, depends upon whether it conforms to the exterior, as well as the interior, relations of France. If it be limited to the interior, then all that is required is to determine how the several sections can best be united to Paris as a common centre ; and the interests of each district should be carefully and impartially considered. But, if it conforms to the exterior, as well as the interior relations of France, then that system which is best calculated to secure to France all the advantages of her position under the application of steam, should be adopted. Can the system conform to the exterior relations of France without prejudice to the interior ? And can a system be adopted under the influence of local, sectional interests, which will sacrifice all the natural and political advantages of France, as it relates to her exterior policy ?

As a stranger, looking on the map of Europe, it would seem that there could be no difference of opinion as to a proper location of the main stem, or stems. But experience in the United States proves that private interests often so far misleads the judgment as to defeat its own ends.

The characteristic of Frenchmen is a jealousy (I will not call it enmity) of England. And yet, Frenchmen are not envious, or jealous, or malignant. Why are they jealous of England ? Is it not because England thrusts herself into the affairs of the continent, and is constantly fomenting jealousies of France ? Why is England able to do this ? Is it not because, so far as it relates to the northern powers, she commands the British channel, and thus commands their commerce passing through it? Is it not obvious, therefore, that the most efficient countercheck to the European policy of England is for France to furnish to all European nations a better, a safer, and more expeditious medium of travel and of commerce than the British channel? If this question be answered in the affirmative, then the question is, can this be done? It can only be done by a railroad. The next inquiry is where should the western terminus of that road be? If at Havre, it is in the British channel, and subject to the risks, dangers, and delays of that channel, and if it were equally safe, it will not be nearer to America than Liverpool. If, at Nantes, it will be subject to the delays and dangers of the Bay of Biscay, and yet no nearer to America. But if at Brest, it could be connected with Havre and Nantes, Orleans, Lyons, and even with Bordeaux and Marseilles, as well as with Paris, Strasburg and Lille, by dependent lines.

Brest is one day nearer to New York than Liverpool. It is easy of access. It is the "land's-end," and commands the commerce of England, as the British channel commands that of the north of Europe. It would, therefore, seem that Brest should be the western terminus, because no other terminus will contribute so much to render the North of Europe independent of England.

When France can do this, their natural relation to France will induce the continental powers to prefer the alliance of France to an alliance with England.

These roads (the main stems at least) should belong to the government which could indemnify itself by a moderate charge for transport, and could allow a free transit to all mer-

chandise. And if semi-annual fairs were established, at which the manufactures and works of art of the civilized world could be exhibited, and manufactures and merchandise sold by pattern cards or samples, the effect would be to make Paris the commercial emporium, and Brest the greatest seaport town of Europe. It would enable France greatly to increase her tonnage, and by concentrating their commerce at Brest, would induce the northern powers of Europe to sympathize with France in case of war with England.

If its position indicates Brest as the natural depot for the commerce of the European continent in time of peace, and for the navies of France and America, in case of a war with England, it is an indispensable part of the system, that it should be connected with the principal towns of France by railroads. This would not only create a large local population to supply any immediate resistance ; but would enable the government to concentrate a force to repel any invasion. The route from Paris to Brest would pass near many other towns, which could, at small expense, connect themselves with the main stem.

Permit me again to repeat, as an apology for this letter, that believing a line of steam packets to ply between Brest and the United States, is an essential feature of the railroad system of France, and believing that the construction of a road from Brest to Paris, and thence connecting with and intercepting the routes now in progress in Austria, Prussia, Holland, and Belgium, to be indispensable to its success, I have ventured to submit these remarks, hoping that the importance of the subject of which they treat, and the obvious relation which they bear to my own private interests, will constitute an apology for trespassing so much on your valuable time.

I will be greatly obliged, if you will inform me whether your government desire a supply of coal, and if so, the price they are willing to give, the time and place of delivery, and the quantity wanted.

Respectfully, yours, &c.,

DUFF GREEN.

Monsieur l'ADMIRAL DUPERRE,
Ministre Secretaire d'Etat,
de la Marine, &c., &c.

CHAPTER XXIII

FINANCIAL.

THE value of money, as compared with the value of other commodities, depends upon the quantity, as compared with the uses to which it is applied. Thus Jacobs tells us that in Wilkins' leger (Saxon), as quoted by Doctor Henry, we have the prices of various articles in England, in the reign of Ethelred, about the year 997, which the learned doctor has estimated with great correctness in the money of the present time—giving the price of a man or slave at £2 6s. 3d.; of a horse, £1 15s. 2d.; of a mare or colt, £1 3s. 5d.; of an ass or mule, 14s. 1d.; of an ox, 7s. ½d.; of a cow, 6s. 2d.; of a swine, 1s. 10½d.; of a sheep, 1s. 2d.; of a goat 4½d. We are told upon the same authority, that at the end of the tenth century a bushel of wheat was sold in Alsace, in Saxony, for a penny farthing, and that two hundred and sixty years later the same measure of wheat sold for three and a quarter pence. Jacobs tells us that the

WAGES OF LABOR,

And the rates allowed for subsistence of persons may both be usefully employed to estimate the value of the precious metals. In 1351, *workmen* took their wages in wheat at sixteen pence per bushel; and weeders and haymakers were paid at the rate of two and a half pence per day; reapers, four to six pence per day; masons and tillers six and a half pence per day, and other laborers one penny farthing per day!

Jacobs estimates that in 1492, before the discovery of
America, the sum which formed the stock of money
current in Europe was $170,000,000
The increased product in 112 years..................... 690,000,000

Making... $860,000,000
Deduct export to Asia and applied to other uses.......... 210,000,000

Leaving.. $650,000,000
Deduct for loss by abrasion............................ 215,000,000

Leaving.. $435,000,000
Produce of mines in one hundred years......... .. .. $1,687,500,000
Sent to India and China........ 166,025,000

Leaves 1,521,250,000
Deduct for sums otherwise used....................... 301,250,000

Leaves..................................... $1,220,000,000
Deduct for loss by wear............................... 170,000,000
                                                            $1,050,000,000

Leaving in Europe in 1600.. .... $1,485,000,000
Jacobs further estimates the coin in 1809, at............................. 1,900,000,000
Deducting for abrasin and loss in twenty years........................... 90,476,100

Leaves... $1,809,523,900
To this he adds the product of twenty years....................... 518,680,000

Making... $2,328,203,900
Deduct the sum sent to Asia and used otherwise...................... 761,261,100

Leaving in Europe in 1829, but................................. $1,566,942,800

It will be seen that the sum of the coin in 1829 was $761,261,100 less than in 1809, owing to the revolutionary condition of Spanish America.

There was, consequently, a corresponding appreciation of the precious metals and of fixed incomes.

THE DISCOVERY OF GOLD IN CALIFORNIA, AUSTRALIA, AND SIBERIA,

As estimated by Chevalier, increased the annual supply of gold at the rate of $175,000,000 per annum, giving in ten years		$1,750,000,000
He estimated in 1857 that there would be used for currency, in states then short of gold	$250,000,000	
To meet increase of population and commerce	154,000,000	
For increased currency of the world	154,000,000	
For wear and tear during ten years	24,500,000	
For hoarding and losses in ten years	105,000,000	
For use of jewelers and manufacturers	345,000,000	
Giving an aggregate increase in ten years of		$892,500,000
Leaving to act on prices		$857,500,000

He argues that the effect of this increase of specie will diminish the value of fixed incomes, and adds : " Capital invested in public securities, railway bonds, bank shares, and similar establishments, will diminish by a self-acting process, and waste away, so to speak, by a species of consumption."

MR. PEABODY.

I was sitting in Mr. Peabody's office in London, in 1842, when one of his clerks brought in a large bundle of Illinois bonds. Mr. Peabody asked, "What have you done with them?" The clerk replied, "I have sold them." Said Mr. Peabody, "What did you get for them?" The clerk replied, "Seventeen." "There," said Peabody, "I gave eighty for those bonds, and you see I am compelled to sell them for seventeen. Repudiation has ruined us—we can never get along in the United States until we have an established church and privileged orders."

Said I, "It is strange that you should speak to me in this manner. If I did not know that you are a rich man, if any one, having a transaction with you, were to consult me, I would say, 'Take care of Peabody he is about to fail.'" "Why would you say that?" said he. I replied, "You know that these bonds will be paid, every dollar of them. You tell me that you gave eighty for them, and yet you now say that you are *compelled* to sell them for seventeen. You must be hard pressed for money." "Oh," said he, "I can buy on the other side of the water at *fifteen*."

Thus it will be seen, that even Mr. Peabody, who now is enabled to make such donations to the poor of London, as to command a letter of thanks from the Queen of England, was, in 1842,

DEPRECIATING THE CREDIT OF THE UNITED STATES,

Because he was enabled to make a profit of two dollars, and the exchange on fifteen invested on state bonds, whereas if they had been at par he could have realized no more than the exchange. I reasoned upon this fact, and I saw that Mr. Peabody was but part of a system which had been organized in London with branches in the United States, which, if permitted to prevail, would impoverish us. I saw that the sectional warfare waged by the North upon the rights and interests of the Southern states, was a struggle for power, an effort, by a combination of political aspirants, seeking office, as a means of imposing illegal and unconstitutional burdens upon the people, that they might enrich themselves and their dependent associates by jobs, contracts, and speculations, and from that day until this I have devoted my talents, my energies, my resources, and my influence, to counteract their measures and policy.

I had been furnished by the State Department with an abstract of the census of 1840, which enabled me to publish a series of letters, giving statistics, showing the resources of the several states, the distribution of capital and labor, the unity of interests, and the assurance of increased prosperity, demonstrating the value of our commerce, appealing to the manufacturing and commercial interests, illustrating the advantages of an early

RESTORATION OF AMERICAN CREDIT.

Mr. Chapman, of the firm of Overend, Guerney & Co., called upon me and said that he had read my letters with much interest—that their house were largely interested in the American trade, and anxious to revive American credit—that they had been requested to contribute to a fund to be used in the United States in aid of the election of members of Congress, pledged to assume the states' debts, and asked my advice as to their doing so. I replied that Congress had no power to assume the state debts, and advised that the creditors should unite and restore the credit of the states of Illinois and Indiana, by advancing the funds to finish the

ILLINOIS AND INDIANA STATE CANALS AND RAILROADS,

Assuring him that the land fund was an ample security, independently of the canals. They acted on my advice, the canals were finished, and, in a few years, Illinois state bonds, which Mr. Peabody and his associates had purchased at fifteen cents on the dollar, were worth more than one hundred ; and a glance at a railroad map of the Northwestern states will show what the use of credit has done towards the development of that section.

Aware that the same combination who had made war upon American credit, on seeing that the effect of the increased quantity of gold would be to diminish the relative value of the bonded debt of our railway companies, would endeavor to convert that debt into shares, I endeavored, by a series of letters addressed to persons interested in railroads, and especially to the governor of Virginia, to the Postmaster-General of the United States, and to the Congress, to demonstrate the necessity of enabling the railway companies to pay their bonded debt by modifying their contracts for mail service, capitalizing the payment by an issue of five per cent. government bonds, the interest upon which, at six per cent., would be equal to the sums paid under existing contracts. My purpose was to enable the railway companies to pay their bonded debt by substituting the government bonds for their own ; and, by the change of system, the saving of one per cent. per annum would create a sinking fund which would pay the debt and ultimately give to the United States the use of the railroads free of charge for mail service.

I forbear, for the present, the explanation of the manner and of the names and the motives of the combination which defeated this arrangement, contenting myself with giving the following letters and explanations of what was then done :

DUFF GREEN TO THE POSTMASTER-GENERAL.

WASHINGTON, *Nov.* 5, 1851

SIR : My circular of the 15th August, proposing that a convention of persons interested in railroads, and in the manufacture of iron, be held in this city on the first Monday in January next, for the purpose of consulting with you and the proper committees of Congress, and arranging, in concert with your department, the details of a plan for capitalizing the payments for carrying the mails, has been favorably received, and I am encouraged to believe that many of the railroad companies will be represented; but it has been suggested that a preliminary meeting should be held on the first of December, and that the attendance would be greater if an assurance can be given, that, if a plan can be suggested, alike advantageous to the government and the railroad companies, you will aid in maturing its details and recommend its adoption by Congress. By permitting me to give that assurance you will greatly oblige

Yours truly,   DUFF GREEN.
Hon. A. V. BROWN,
        Postmaster-General.

REPLY.

WASHINGTON, *Nov.* 9, 1851.

DEAR SIR : In reply to your note of the 5th inst., I have the honor to state that I will very cheerfully consult with you and any others in devising any plan, and maturing its details, by which the railroad and iron interests of this country may be promoted, advantageously to the government and the people, and which may be thought calculated to prevent the recurrence of those dreadful pecuniary revulsions which have so often overtaken the country.

With very great respect,

Your obd't servt.,
        AARON V. BROWN.
Gen. DUFF GREEN.

CIRCULAR TO THE PRESIDENTS OF RAILROAD COMPANIES.

WASHINGTON CITY, *Dec.* 10, 1851.

SIR : By the enclosed proceedings of a meeting held in this city on the 3d instant, it was made the duty of the undersigned as a committee to correspond with the several railroad companies in the United States, and to report to an adjourned meeting, to be held in this city on the first Tuesday in March next, to consider a proposition to petition Congress for a change in the law regulating mail contracts, so as to enable the Post-office Department to deliver to railroad companies United States five per cent. coupon bonds, upon permanent contracts for carrying the mail, to an amount the interest of which, at five per cent., would be equal to the payments to be made under existing laws ; and they therefore respectfully call the attention of your company to the subject, and invite your co-operation. They greatly prefer that you should send delegates to the adjourned meeting ; for the opinions expressed by a convention of practical men, representing so much wealth, enterprise, and intelligence, will command, as they will deserve, the confidence and respect of Congress, and thus promote the adoption of such details as may be agreed upon in convention ; but if it should not be convenient to send delegates, we would ask your company to submit, through us, your wishes and opinions upon the main proposition, and upon the details connected therewith.

It is well known that many persons are opposed to internal improvements by the general government—some denying the power of Congress to make appropriations for that object ; others fearing that the exercise of such power will lead to combinations resulting in partial and unjust legislation. It will be seen that the proposition under consideration is free from these objections. It asks no appropriation of money in aid of the construction of railroads. The contracts will be restricted to the service which the several railroad companies are in condition to execute when the payments are made.

It is true that the proposed modification of the laws regulating mail contracts will give similar payments *pro rata*, as new roads are made and as old ones are extended, and will so far increase the credit and resources of railroad companies. The same effect, although to a less extent, results from existing laws, and surely it cannot be urged as a valid objection to the proposed change that it will aid in the extension of the railroad system. We claim as a merit, that the proposed modification will aid in extending the system by giving greater value to railroad investments. Under existing laws contracts are made for four years, and the payments are continued, if not increased, *ad infinitum*. Under the proposed modification, the contracts will be made, giving the United States perpetual use of railroads ; and the rate of compensation is so reduced that at the end of thirty-three years the payments will cease, and the department will forever thereafter have the use of such railroad free of all charge.

It is objected that old routes may be superseded by new ones, and the present service so diminished as to render it inexpedient to make the permanent that the contracts will be made by a board appointed for that purpose, and that no contracts will be given unless that board be fully satisfied that mail service adequate to the payments will be amply secured to the United States.

We desire to obtain the views of your company upon these and all other matters of detail, and respectfully ask of you to furnish us such statistics as will enable us to submit to the convention and to Congress, a statement showing the comparative increase or diminution, as the case may be, of the mail service performed by your company—the past and probable future increase of the weight of mails carried over the route of your road. And in this connection we wish to learn what, in your opinion, will be the probable increased weight of the mails, if newspapers and periodicals are sent free of postage.

We wish you to state what is the present current price of your shares, what rate of dividend does your company now pay, and what dividend could you pay under a contract such as we propose.

The committee venture to invite the co-operation of the railroad convention to be held in New Orleans on the first Monday of January, and that newspapers in the South and West will urge upon all those who are interested in railroads, or in the extension of the system, a favorable consideration of the measure proposed, and the necessity of prompt and efficient co-operation.

In behalf of the committee.

DUFF GREEN, *Chairman.*

consider a project for modifying the existing laws regulating the letting of mails to railroad corporations—

Gen. Morton, of Florida, was chosen president, and Albert Smith, of Maine, secretary.

The meeting was addressed by Gen. Green in explanation of his proposition; after which a desultory conversation was held by all the gentlemen present, and the following resolution was adopted:

Resolved, That a committee of five be appointed, with authority to correspond with the several railroad companies in the United States, upon the subject of an application to Congress for a change in the mode of compensation for transporting the mails on railroads, and to digest a plan, to be submitted to a meeting to be hereafter convened by the said committee.

Gen. Duff Green, Mr. Blunt, of Florida, Albert Smith, of Maine, Robert H. Gallaher, and Col. Fontaine, of Virginia, were chosen said committee.

Voted, that the meeting be adjourned.
ALBERT SMITH, *Secretary*.

LETTERS FROM DUFF GREEN TO GOV. FLOYD, OF VIRGINIA.

To His Excellency GOV. FLOYD, *President of the Board of Public Works, in Virginia:*

DEAR SIR: Other engagements have prevented an earlier compliance with my promise to submit, in writing, an examination of the causes which produce the periodical expansions and contractions of the currency, and of the combinations formed in England and the United States to depress the price of American produce—especially of cotton. As the subject deeply interests the whole people of the United States, I avail myself of the press as the medium of communication.

It is urged that commerce is a reciprocal exchange of the products of labor, and that, therefore, high duties on British manufactures necessarily diminish the value of American produce in the British market, for it is said that England cannot buy from us unless we buy from her.

It is also said that, inasmuch as the price must be controlled by the universal law of supply and demand, the value of our cotton in the British market must depend on the quantity produced.

I admit that commerce should be a reciprocal exchange of the products of labor, for then the law of supply and demand would regulate the price; but our merchants, acting on the theory that England will buy from us as much as we buy from England, are, from year to year, compelled to remit large sums in specie to make up for the depreciation in the price of American produce, and this occurs so often, and operates so much to our injury, that it becomes our duty to ascertain why it is so, and whether it be possible to prevent it—whether this is the legitimate operation of commerce, or the effect of a powerful combination organized for that purpose.

Agents of British bankers are located in most of our seaports—not to buy and pay for our cotton—but to make advances upon bills of lading for cotton sent to their houses in Liverpool, to be sold there on account of the American shipper. The funds to make these advances are obtained by the sale of bills of exchange, which are so drawn that before they become due the cotton will have reached Liverpool, and if sold there for the sum advanced (which seldom, if ever, exceeds seventy-five per cent. of the American price), the banker receives the fund to make the payment, and gets his interest, his profit on the exchange, and his two-and-a-half per cent. commission, without advancing one dollar in money. In other words, the American producer advances the cotton and pockets the loss—the British banker advances his credit and secures the profits.

This is not all—the deficiency must be paid in specie. Thus, if we assume that the value of the cotton crop is one hundred millions, and that American merchants, relying on the sale of that crop in Liverpool, purchase one hundred millions of dollars of British manufactures, it follows that if, from any cause, the cotton crop sells for ninety millions only, there will be a deficiency of ten millions to be paid in specie ; and who does not know that the export of specie to pay that balance will so act upon the money market as to reduce the value of all the other property of the country ?

Now, let us see how this balance is produced, and how it affects the interests of these foreign bankers. Their agents have drawn bills, payable in Liverpool, after the cotton has reached that market, for seventy-five per cent. only of the American price. Do we not see that, if the cotton be sold for ninety millions, these bills will be paid from the proceeds of the cotton sold ; that the bankers will realize their interest on the sum advanced, the profit on the exchange, and two-and-a-half per cent. commission on the ninety millions of dollars, while the shipper has lost ten millions of dollars ? and do we not see that the importation of one hundred millions of merchandise will have created a balance of ten millions to be paid in specie ? It is a well-known law that the value of the property of a commercial country bears a relation to its currency of thirty to one ; the effect, therefore, of this export of specie would be to diminish the value of the property of this country, not ten millions only, but

thirty times ten, or three hundred millions, were it not that the extraordinary demand thus created will cause the importation of specie, and that, therefore, the effect is limited to the derangement of commerce, the fluctuations in the currency, and the extra cost of importing specie.

Now, these bankers deal in exchange, and it is their business to make profits by these derangements. They desire to make London the centre of the financial world, and to compel all the world to pay tribute to them through their financial agency. They regulate the exchange of continental Europe chiefly through the dividend arising from the public funds, and their purpose is to regulate the exchange between the United States and London through their control of the American staples, which they have obtained in the manner above explained—not by an advance of money —not by any use of capital—but by the use of their credit. It will thus be seen that commerce, as now organized, enables the British banker to depreciate the price of American produce in the British market, and that he is interested in creating a balance to be paid by us in specie, because it gives greater value to bills of exchange, and because the British consumer obtains our cotton at reduced prices, and is thus enabled to sell his goods to the British merchant at a lower rate. A brief review of the past will cast a flood of light on the subject. In 1835 the bank of England increased its discounts more than thirty-five millions of dollars. The effect was to stimulate the circulation in England and greatly increase the price of cotton in the British market. Congress having refused to renew its charter, the bank of the United States applied,

12

to the state of Pennsylvania, and thus became a state institution, which made it necessary to sell out its branches located in other states. These were paid for in the notes of local banks. If the bank of the United States had required these notes to be paid in specie, it would have destroyed the greater part of the local banks, and greatly injured the bank of the United States. It was, therefore, wise in that bank to invest these funds in state bonds and in advances made upon cotton and other American produce, sent to a commercial house in Liverpool, created for that purpose, and having the confidence of the bank. The great fire in New York had destroyed a large amount of merchandise. To enable the New York merchants to meet their payments to British manufacturers, the bank of the United States made large advances in bills upon England, relying upon the sale of American produce, and of American securities in that market, to provide the means of payment.

The Barings, the Rothschilds, Hottinguer & Co., and Hope & Co., had been the agents of the bank of the United States. Failing to make a satisfactory arrangement with them, Mr. Jaudon was sent to London to protect the credit of the bank. When he reached there, Pennsylvania and Maryland sixes were selling at sixteen per cent. premium ; but a combination was immediately formed, which, aided by the bank of England, so depreciated the price of American produce and of American securities, that Mr. Jaudon was unable to realize funds, by the sale of cotton or of American securities, to pay the bills advanced to the New York merchants, and it was announced, by one if not more of the interested parties, that the bank would be dishonored. When driven to the last extremity, and at the last moment, Mr. Jaudon borrowed money, by a hypothecation of his state bonds, at a rate far below their value ; but as the bank of England had issued a notice that no bill drawn on account of American produce would be discounted, and the combination was such as to prevent the sale of his state bonds, Mr. Jaudon was unable to pay the money borrowed when it became due, and he could not renew the loan unless he paid an instalment of fifteen per cent. To enable him to do this, the bank of the United States was compelled to issue its post-notes, which were sold in the market at a depreciation of twenty per cent. This and other causes, growing out of the combination referred to, compelled a suspension of specie payments. Mr. Jaudon was yet unable to sell his state bonds, and could not renew the loan but upon the condition of a resumption of specie payment by the bank. All who are familiar with the proceedings of that day will remember that certain brokers, whose relation to this combination of foreign bankers cannot be doubted, came down upon the bank, and, by absorbing all their specie, compelled another suspension. This was followed by a refusal to renew the loan, a sale of the hypothecated bonds at nominal prices, and a demand for the balance due, which was paid in other assets of the bank at such reduced rates, that a person interested in the operation told me in London, in the year 1842, that one of the parties who had thus obtained the funds of the bank had, during that year, realized near three millions of dollars by the increased value of the securities thus taken from the bank.

I have said that the failure of the bank of the United States was caused by a combination of certain bankers, aided by the bank of England, and this was done by depreciating the price of American produce and of American credit in the European market. I am aware of the responsibility which I incur in making such a declaration, and that I must array additional facts to sustain it. I will be told by these bankers and their agents in this country that there could be no motive for such a combination. Let us see.

When in London, in 1842, I had the following fact from the best authority. After the revulsion of 1819, the trade between the United States and England was carried on chiefly through the agency of three commercial houses in London. One of these, who had realized near three millions of capital, wrote to his correspondents in the United States and in Canada that he would not accept bills drawn on account of American produce, or for the purchase of British goods. This came to the knowledge of the bank of England; the governor called upon the writer, and urged him to countermand his letters, saying that the English warehouses were filled with merchandise, and that the directors were apprehensive that his letters would greatly diminish the trade with America, which it was their desire to increase. The writer replied that he feared a revulsion in the money market, and that he could not sustain himself unless the bank would carry him through. To this the governor said that he was not authorized to give a pledge binding on the board of directors, but added, "You know that the bank has always aided you, and, as governor, I pledge myself to do all that I can for you." Thus assured,

he did countermand his letters, and when the bank issued its notice discrediting all bills drawn on account of American produce, he was under acceptance for more than fifteen millions of dollars, and was ruined. Yea, . more. An elder brother, who had retired with a much larger fortune, sacrificed much the greater part of it in the vain attempt to sustain him.

This is not all. When a short time before that, the bank of England sent an agent to the United States, Mr. Biddle gave him a room in the bank in Philadelphia, and aided him in the transaction of business by all the facilities which the numerous agents and correspondents of the bank of the United States could give. Yet when Mr. Jaudon reached London, the bank of England refused the privilege of opening an account with them, and the reason of this will presently appear. So much as to the bank. A word as to the bankers. It will be remembered that Mr. Jaudon took with him certain Indiana, Illinois, and Mississippi bonds, which were hypothecated with certain bankers, and that after those states failed to pay the interest, it was paid by the bank of the United States. It will also be remembered that some time after the hypothecation, those bankers made a trust, by which these bonds were transferred to certain widows and orphans, and persons of small income, who, relying on their reputation and character, had deposited large sums with them to be invested at discretion. It will also be remembered that, at the time of this distribution, certain newspaper paragraphs praised the generous liberality of these eminent bankers, who had thus permitted their customers to participate in the speculation; and that no one—no, not even the degenerate

Americans who made merchandise of the character and credit of their country—were so clamorous in denouncing the United States, or so profuse in sympathy for the poor widows and orphans, as these bankers and their agents. And who can believe that they were not previously notified that the bank of the United States would cease to pay the interest on the hypothecated bonds, and that the trust was created, and the newspaper paragraphs written, to cover the transfer of these Indiana, Illinois, and Mississippi bonds to those widows, orphans, and confiding customers, who had placed funds in their hands for investment? And who cannot see that the subsequent denunciation of American dishonesty, and pretended sympathy for widows and orphans, was intended to conceal or mystify the agency by which the losses were transferred from these wealthy bankers to the widows and orphans in question?

One other fact. I was in London in 1842. A friend who wished to come to the United States, had one hundred and forty thousand dollars in American securities, upon which he wished to borrow three thousand dollars. I myself took those securities to the principal man of business of the house which, as I before said, had during that year realized near three millions of dollars as a profit on the securities which they had taken from the bank of the United States, and proposed that he should take any amount of the securities in question which he might require, and forward them to their agent in New York, advancing thereon three thousand dollars, to be refunded immediately on our reaching the United States. His reply was: "If it were known upon 'change that we had advanced you one hundred dollars on any American security whatever, our house would immediately be put in coventry."

One other fact. When the agent sent by President Tyler to London, to negotiate the loan of five millions of dollars, had been dissuaded from offering the loan in that market by the Messrs. Baring & Co. and Mr. Peabody, acting in concert, he went to Ireland and left the negotiation with me. I negotiated the loan, and the agent would have received the money (five hundred thousand dollars in hand, and the rest in instalments as wanted) but for the interference of persons connected with and interested in the combination in question. (I may, hereafter, make this the subject of a special letter, with some other striking facts bearing on the issue in question.)

Do these remarks challenge your belief, because you cannot see an adequate motive for such a combination? I now proceed to illustrate the motive and policy. The public debt of nine of the principal European states, in 1842, is given, as nearly as I could then ascertain it, in the following table:

THE POPULATION, PUBLIC DEBT, AND AREA OF THE EUROPEAN STATES.

Country	Population.	Area in Acres.	Debt.	Interest.	Total Debt.	Total Interest.
Belgium ..	1,230,000	8,044,165	$6,000,000 4 per ct.		$26,000,000	$1,240,000
			20,000,000 5 "			
Denmark..	2,097,400	3,247,680	65,000,000 3 "		65,000,000	1,950,000
Holland...	2,820,000	8,889,600	82,900,000 5 "		407,900,000	12,170,000
			325,000,000 2½ "			
			588,500,000 5 "			
France ...	33,000,000	129,340,000	47,500,000 4½ "		884,500,000	38,539,444
			238,500,000 3 "			
			10,000,000 4 "			
Portugal...	3,400,000	22,080,000	28,755,500 5 "		58,755,500	2,627,775
			30,000,000 4 "			
Prussia...	13,800,000	67,942,000	97,500,000 4 "		97,500,000	7,800,000
Russia ...	51,100,000	1,306,757,700	368,000,000 5 "		47,259,375	2,362,968
Spain.....	11,963,000	112,947,200	32,500,000 4 "		400,500,000	19,600,000
Great Britain, }	26,861,000	74,688,000	2,418,100,650 3 "		3,430,478,980	111,476,260
			1,112,378,330 3½ "			

Grand aggregate............ ... ...$5,407,893,855 $197,666,647
To these should be addded the unfunded debt of England   237,269,510
In annuities............................   306,867,085

You will see that, by computing interest on the last two items, the dividend arising from this source is more than two hundred and twenty-five millions of dollars. A large part of this interest is payable in London, and passes through a few bankers, who are agents to receive and reinvest it. Those who know the value of our cotton crop as a medium of exchange between this country and England, must see the power which the control over the interest on the European debt gives to these bankers in the regulation of European exchange, and how much these bankers are interested in maintaining the value of the funds from which that interest is derived. It will also be seen that the greater part of this European debt bears an interest of not more than four per cent.; and it follows that these bankers, who were the agents of these European governments for the sale of their bonds, and of the fundholders for receiving and, reinvesting their dividends, knew that, if Mr. Jaudon was permitted to establish in London a market for the sale of American bonds, bearing an interest of six or seven per cent., the holders of European three and four per cents. would sell out and invest in American six and seven per cents., and they saw that Mr. Biddle could, through the agency of Mr. Jaudon, furnish American bonds sufficient to absorb the whole value of the European debt, and they knew that the existence of those European governments, whose agents they were, depended upon the maintenance of their credit, and therefore, as the question presented by Mr. Jaudon's appearance in London involved at the same time the credit and the duration of the monarchies of Europe, and the business and profit of the bankers, who were their agents, they combined to destroy the bank of the United States, as the best and only means of defeating the measures adopted by that bank for the sale of American securities in the European market.

Had Mr. Biddle placed his state bonds with these bankers, they could have regulated the quantity sold, and the price, and as they could have controlled the market and fostered British commerce, without destroying the bank or annihilating American credit, it will doubtless be said by their partisans in this country, as well as in Europe, that their combination was the necessary consequence of Mr. Biddle's refusal to allow them one half on one per cent. commission, and of his attempt to build up a rival American agency in the European market.

In reply, I submit that my purpose is so show that the failure of the bank was caused by a combination of European bankers who are the agents of the monarchies of Europe, and that that combination originated in the necessity of protecting the credit of these European monarchies, when brought in competition with the credit of the United States, and of the individual states of America ; and to show that, as these bankers then combined to destroy the Bank of the United States, so will they again combine, whenever it may be convenient or necessary for them to do so, for the advancement of their own private gain, or to protect the credit or to promote the purpose of the monarchies whom they represent.

More : My purpose is to show that the system of European credit constitutes the chief strength of the existing European governments—that the debt of these European nations represents the expenditure heretofore made in wars, and in the maintenance of armies and navies, and privileged persons, and would have no value if the people were to refuse to pay taxes. It is, therefore, the fundamental policy of these monarchical governments, and of the bankers who are their agents, to distribute these public securities in the hands of many persons, knowing that, as the value of these securities depends on the payment of taxes, the more they are distributed the greater will be the number of those interested in maintaining the existing forms of government. In other words, my purpose is to show that, if the toiling millions, who now pay the enormous sum of two hundred and twenty-five millions of dollars per annum, in taxes, on account of the previous expenditure in wars, armies, and navies, were to apply the sponge to that debt by a revolution, then these bankers, now so strong in the power of their combinations, would be weaker than poor Nicholas Biddle after they had crushed and destroyed his bank ; and to show that, as the resources of the United States are developed, and our strength and prosperity advance, will the power and resources of these European bankers be exerted to maintain their system of European credit and finance at our expense. That such is their purpose and policy is apparent to the most careless observer. In proof of this, I call your attention to the following table, furnished, while I write, by the New York Herald :

MOVEMENTS OF SPECIE AND BULLION TO NOVEMBER 1, 1851.

Months.	Receipts of California Gold.	Gold Coinage.	Specie Exported.
January	$4,940.000	$2,620,906	$1,266,281
February	2,860,000	5,082,987	1,207,689
March....................	2,634,500	6,285,735	2,363,361
April....................	2,785,500	3,176,058	3,482,182
May	3,205,600	3,201,262	4,506,135
June....................	3,570,000	3,653,243	6,462,367
July	3,053,000	3,240,495	6,004,170
August	4,048,800	4,078,329	2,653,444
September....................	3,960,500	4,087,423	3,493,142
October....................	4,670,000	5,231,019	1,779,707
Total..............	$35,727,900	$40,657,522	$33,026,978

Why is it that so much of our specie goes to England? Is it not because there is a balance against us? Is it not because our produce does not sell in the British market for as much as we have agreed to pay for British goods imported? And why does not our produce pay for the British goods imported? Is it not because we place our produce under the control of British bankers, who sympathize more with the British consumer than with the American producer, and because these British bankers are interested in creating a balance against us, to be paid in specie? If there be any who doubt this to be so, I bespeak a careful examination of what I have further to say in my next.

Your friend,
DUFF GREEN.

DUFF GREEN TO GOV. FLOYD.

To *His Excellency* Gov. FLOYD, *President of the Board of Public Works, in Virginia:*

DEAR SIR: In my former letter I gave a table, showing that the annual interest on the public debt of nine European states exceeds two hundred and twenty-five millions of dollars, with a statement of facts, proving that the bankers, who are their agents for the sale of their bonds, and of the fund-holders for the receipt and reinvestment of the accruing interest, aided by the bank of England, combined to break down the bank of the United States, because that bank attempted to create an agency in London for the sale of American securities, bearing an interest of six and seven per cent., in competition with their European three and four per cents. I explained that this was a matter of necessity on their part, because inasmuch as the public debt of these European monarchies bears interest at the rate of three and four per cent., and represents the sums expended in wars, and in maintaining armies and navies and privileged persons, it is the policy of those governments to distribute their debt into the hands of many persons, because they thereby increase the number of those who are directly interested in maintaining their credit, and upholding the present forms of government, which would be endangered if the European fund-holders were to sell out their three and four per cents, and invest in American six and seven per cents. Since that letter was written I have read Kossuth's London speech, from which the following is an extract. He said :

"*London is the regulator of the money market of the world.* These few words spoken to you suffice to state the importance of this principle. Well, if London is the regulator of the public credit of the world, and if a very considerable quantity of the loan shares of every government in the world are concentrated here in London, let me ask, where is the security of those loans? Where is the possibility to see paid the money under the governments of the world? Is the security in the victory of the absolutist principle, or is it the victory of the principle of freedom? Take despotic governments, what is their basis of existence? Is it the love of the nations? Oh, how could the principle of despotism be love? Love in such a case is a contradiction to our nature. Is the basis of the absolutist governments the contentment of nations? How can men be content without freedom? What is the connection of the principle of absolutism? It can be marked out in a few words: 'People pay, because I want soldiers and spies to be your illimitable master.' How could the principle of these nations be contentment? Therefore, what is the basis of their existence? Immensely costly armies, and not less costly diplomatic intrigues. The sweat of the people cannot suffice to provide for all those necessities—not for the happiness of nations, but to keep them in servitude. Therefore, the absolutist governments must come again and again to the money markets to get some loans. Every new loan, in whatever unproductive manner applied, diminishes the resources out of which it should be paid; and when the same goes on again and again, who could take the guarantee upon himself for the nations of the world with their eternal loans, employed not for their benefit but against their benefit and against their liberty? Who can take the guarantee upon him, that once these nations, groaning under their material sufferings, will not

say, '*Let him pay who made the debt, we made it not?*' Here is the prospect which absolutist principles point out in that respect. But there is a prospect, especially to the House of Austria—that prospect is inevitable bankruptcy."

I call your attention to these remarks of the great Hungarian, because they verify what I said in my former letter, and because our distinguished fellow-citizen, the late Secretary of the Treasury, is understood to have asserted the principle, that England and the United States are to act in concert for the subversion of the absolutists governments in question, and because such is the desire in certain quarters to obtain the vote of our naturalized citizens in the next Presidential election, that there is cause to fear that many will be enlisted in the effort to involve our government in a war with the continental powers of Europe, under the vain hope that England will be our ally, and that such a war will advance the cause of Republican liberty. Let me be understood. No one desires more than I to favor the cause of liberty on the continent of Europe; but I do not believe that we can rely upon the English government, or upon English bankers, who are the agents and creditors of absolute governments, to aid us. I do not believe that the cause of liberty, on the continent of Europe, will be advanced by a war in which we, as a nation, take part. Kossuth himself, in the speech from which we have quoted, says:

"When I spoke so, I intended not to ask England to take up arms for our liberties. No, gentlemen, that is the affair of Hungary; we will provide for our own freedom. All I wish is, that public opinion should establish, as the ruling principle in the politics of England, the acknowledgment of the right of nations to dispose of their own affairs—not to give a charter to the Czar to dispose of whole nations."

That the time is near at hand when the interests and policy of Russia and Great Britain may bring them in conflict, and the whole power and influence of British gold and British diplomacy will be exerted to make us a party to that war, I can readily believe. It is, therefore, important that we should carefully examine into the motives and policy of England, before we permit our sympathies to mislead our judgments so far as to make us again the victims of her avarice and ambition. Why has England been jealous of Russia? Why does the Christian Queen sustain the unbelieving Turk? Is it not because the conquest of Constantinople would enable the Emperor of Russia to seize upon the British possessions in India? And what interest have we in preventing that catastrophe? What matters it to us whether England or Russia rule in India? Would not the conquest of India by Russia, open the trade of India to all the world: Is it not rather the true policy of the United States to cultivate the arts of peace, and thus multiply our wealth and resources, and by a judicious organization of our credit, create, in the United States, a financial power strong enough to protect us against the money power of London, and to make New York and New Orleans, instead of London, the great centres of the financial world? Who doubts that this is the real issue of the present day, or that upon it, more than any other, depends the conflict now waging between despotism and liberty?

Kossuth is right in this :—The permanence of the absolute governments of Europe depends on their ability to obtain money. Their sole reliance is upon loans and taxation ; for whenever the people refuse to pay taxes, there will be an end of absolute governments.

Such is the foundation upon which rests the whole funded debt of Europe, which constitutes the basis of European credit, and is the vital principle of the money power of London—a power which, concentrated in the hands of a few individuals, enables them to regulate the policy of the kingdoms of Europe with more efficiency than the mandate of the Pope did in former ages, and especially in relation to the questions of war and peace. How far they may be able to arrest or delay the progress of Russia toward Constantinople and the British possessions in India, remains to be seen ; but we in the United States would be deaf to all the lessons of experience, if we presume, for a moment, that this concentrated money power will ever take part or sympathize with us in any effort to advance the cause of Republican liberty.

Kossuth is right :—The great question of *this* age is not *arms*, but *money*. We have seen that the chief element of the concentrated money power of London consists in the funded debt of monarchical governments ; and who does not know, that whenever a conflict between either of those governments and liberty may occur, the whole strength and energy of that concentrated money power will be exerted to crush the germs of liberty, wherever they may appear? Upon what, then, do the hopes of liberty rest? Upon what must the oppressed nations of the world rely? and whence must the means of their redemption come? Must they not look to us—and how can we help them so long as our credit and our resources are regulated by a combination of European monarchs, or the concentrated money power of their bankers and agents?

Have we the means of organizing a monetary system of sufficient strength to resist that combination, and to give efficient aid to European liberty in her conflict with despotism?

I beg you to bear in mind, that the combination which broke down the Bank of the United States, has given way before the energy, activity, and resources of this young and vigorous people—that American credit has revived, and that the greater security and increased dividends will induce many to sell out their European three and four per cents., and invest in American sixes—that this is the age of progress—that the words of that remarkable man, Kossuth, will be repeated, and make a deep impression on European fundholders—and that when once the process of transferring to the United States is begun, it will require no London agency to accomplish it. No one can foresee the effect of the panic thereby produced. Who, ten years ago, could have believed that so many wealthy European emigrants would have come to the United States? The transfer of capital by this process has but just commenced.

The following table shows the number of depositors in the savings banks of England, and the amount deposited on the 20th of November, 1840:

Class.	Number of Depositors.	Amount of Deposits including Interest.
Not exceeding £20	440,740	£2,904,207
" 50	209,463	6,437,846
" 100	85,118	5,847,811
" 150	28,449	3,408,037
" 200	15,538	2,639,648
Exceeding 200	3,066	742,248
Individual depositors	782,374	£21,979,797
Charitable institutions	7,988	485,908
Friendly societies	7,693	1,005,345
Total	798,505	£23,471,050

These deposits are by law invested in the public securities of the British government, and the effect of any panic which would induce the depositors to demand payment would be to compel these savings banks to force those securities upon a falling market, and thus depreciate their value.

The whole number of persons in Great Britain receiving dividends on the 5th of January, 1842, is given in the following table:

87,176	receiving incomes not exceeding	£10	per annum.
44,648	" "	20	"
93,305	" "	100	"
25,641	" "	200	"
14,701	" "	400	"
4,495	" "	600	"
2,827	" "	1,000	"
1,367	" "	2,000	"
266	" "	4,000	"

151 public companies and joint stock companies.......	£1,000 per annum.
35 " " "	6,000 "
40 persons with incomes not exceeding	6,000 "
15 " " "	8,000 "
24 public and joint stock companies.................	8,000 "
10 " " "	10,000 "
4 persons with incomes not exceeding...............	10,000 "
12 " " exceeding...................	10,000 "
34 public companies with incomes exceeding..........	10,000 "

When you examine these lists and see how many there are who have small incomes, and reflect upon the inducement which such persons have to emigrate to the United States, and to invest in American securities, we are justified in believing that American credit, resting upon a permanent and fixed basis, will be preferred by many persons in Europe, and that large sums will be remitted to the United States as a permanent investment.

It is estimated that there are near ten thousand miles of railroad now in operation in the United States, and that there soon will be at least twenty thousand miles, and the capital invested more than six hundred millions of dollars. The present disbursement for mail service on railroads is about one million of dollars. As this service is so rapidly increasing, for the sake of round numbers, we will assume that the proposed change of system will commence on a disbursement of twelve hundred thousand dollars, which will be the interest, *at six per cent.*, on twenty millions. We propose that the Postoffice Department shall make contracts with railroad companies for the perpetual use of their roads, and that instead of being paid, as now, on contracts for four years, the railroad companies shall receive an amount of five per cent. bonds, chargeable on the revenues of the Department; the interest of which, at six per cent., would be equal to the service rendered. Thus, we now pay

three hundred dollars per mile per annum for carrying the mail on first-class railroads, which is six per cent. on five thousand dollars, and which, at five per cent., would reduce the charge on the Department to two hundred and fifty dollars per mile per annum, leaving fifty dollars per mile per annum as a sinking fund to pay off the principal, which it would do in less than thirty-three years. The effect of this would be to give the use of the railroads for ever thereafter free of all charge, and consequently to save to the Department twenty millions of dollars in thirty-four years. As this would be so much money saved, whether it be applied to defray other expenditures of the Department, or availed of to reduce the rate of postage, the change of system is entitled to a credit for that sum; and as we are legislating not for to-day only, but for the future, the change of system is entitled to a credit, not for that sum only, but for the sum obtained by compounding the interest on that sum in perpetuity. As any sum compounded at six per cent. semi-annually duplicates itself in less than twelve years, the following table shows that the gain by the change of system—

Will be, in 33 years	.. .. $20,000,000
" 45 "	 40,000,000
" 57 "	 80,000,000
" 59 "	160,000,000
" 81 "	320,000,000
" 93 "	 640,000,000
" 100 "	967,674,470

But this will not be all; the effect would be greatly to enhance the value of the large fund invested in railroads. It would make railroad shares and railroad bonds available as capital, and thus furnish a basis for investments, and for the organization of a system of American credit, much more permanent and reliable than the system of European taxation. It should be identified with and controlled by the great body of our people. It should be essentially American in all its aspects, tendencies, and affinities. It should be identified with our soil, and so connected with our progress and welfare, that it may not, and never can, be any other than American in feeling or policy. It is strictly local, and yet connects itself beneficially with the most remote sections of this great country. It is an interest acting within prescribed limits, confined within its own sphere, but connected with, promoting, sustaining, and enlarging, other similar interests in each and every other part of this great republic; an interest self-sustaining, and rapidly increasing, whose power and strength consist not in taxes levied upon a down-trodden and oppressed people, but in the facilities, accommodation, wealth, prosperity, and blessings, which it gives, and whose beneficial power and influence may be so organized, increased, and concentrated, as to protect us from the powerful European combination to which I have referred, at the same time that each company preserves its individual powers, control, and influence.

We have seen that the change of system of mail contracts will save to the people of the United States, through the Postoffice Department, nine hundred and sixty-seven millions of dollars in one hundred years. It will do much more than this. The twenty millions of dollars which it purposes to issue, will not be a charge upon the treasury, for, inasmuch as the system provides a sinking fund out of the present disbursement, which pays the principal, it will be as much a creation as if it were California gold. It will not only be so much saved to the government, but it will furnish a basis of banking on the principle of the free banks of New York, which have now been in operation for many years, without the loss of a dollar to the bill-holder; and, it matters not whether it be so used by the railroad companies, or by others, the effect for good will be the same. It will create a capital which may be used to build up manufactories, stimulating and sustaining our domestic industry, and furnishing the means of enabling our agriculturists, our planters and farmers, to retain their cotton and their corn until the British consumers will be compelled to come here and purchase it at *American* prices, instead of buying it as they now do, in Liverpool, through British agents, at *British* prices.

Under the system proposed, the American banker who deposits these bonds, as the basis of a bank circulation, will receive the interest on his bonds and on his bank notes. These, together, will be at least twelve per cent. per annum; but, as the payment now made to railroad companies is six per cent., the change of system will be entitled to a credit for six per cent. compounded, and at this rate the saving will be—

On the first issue, say.........			$20,000,000
Which in 12 years will be..			40,000,000
" 24 "	"	. .	80,000,000
" 36 "	"	....	160,000,000
" 48 "	"	...	320,000,000
" 60 "	"	"	640,000,000
" 72 "	"	....	1,280,000,000
" 84 "	"	....	2,560,000,000
" 96 "	"	"	5,120,000,000
" 100 "	"	....	6,490,626,370

As the expenditure for transporting the mails will increase, as the system of railroads is extended, we must credit the system with the saving on the roads to be made, as well as on the roads now in operation. If we suppose that the system will be extended so as to increase the expenditure for carrying the mails on railroads at the rate of one hundred thousand dollars per annum, the saving will be at the rate of twenty millions of dollars for every period of twelve years, and the compound interest thereon. The amount will then stand thus: The saving will be to the United States, through the Postoffice Department, as before stated—

For the first 33 years				$20,000,000
For the next 12 years, or in 45 years				60,000,000
"	12	"	57 "	160,000,000
"	12	"	69 "	300,000,000
"	12	"	81 "	620,000,000
"	12	"	.93 "	1,260,000,000
"	7	"	100 "	1,903,206,000

Such would be the saving to the people, through the Postoffice Department, on the present system of expenditure for carrying the mails. If we apply the same rule for estimating the profit to the railroad companies, or to those who use the bonds as a basis of banking, it will be found that the accumulation of capital will be much more surprising. Thus, the first issue will be twenty millions, and a like sum in addition every twelve years. These sums, compounded at six per cent. per annum, semi-annually—

Will give, say			$20,000,000
Which in 12 years will be			60,000,000
"	24	"	140,000,000
"	36	"	300,000,000
"	48	"	620,000,000
"	60	"	1,260,000,000
"	72	"	2,540,000,000
"	84	"	5,100,000,000
"	96	"	10,220,000,000
"	100	"	12,942,264,000
Add saving through Post Office Department, as above			1,903,206,000

And we have the sum of (to the credit of the change of system proposed) $14,845,470,000

Let not these sums startle you. I beg you to run through the calculations, as I have done, and you will be satisfied that, enormous as this sum appears, it is, indeed, not a moiety of what would, in fact, be gained by the beneficial influences resulting from the plan proposed. It would create railroads, build up manufactories, create wealth and incalculable resources, by the stimulus it would give to the productive industry of the country. To the South and West it is indispensable as a means of exchanging their respective products, and this it would accomplish, not by one great mammoth bank, concentrating its power, and regulating the price of cotton by contracting the currency, but by so distributing and organizing the business of banking as to furnish a supply adequate to the wants of the country, of a currency deserving the public confidence, and not subject to the control of British intrigues or speculation, and, therefore, free from the pressure of the screws of the bank of England.

Yours, truly,
DUFF GREEN.

CHAPTER XXIV

THE TARIFF.

I HAD become satisfied that the use of machinery had so increased European manufactures, that the conflict of interest would cause an effort to readjust the commerce of the world, and that that adjustment must necessarily more and more identify the interest of the South, as the producers of cotton, with the interests of the North, as manufacturers, and of the Northwest, a large part of whose surplus provisions would find the best market in the manufacturing and cotton and sugar producing states, if the whole people could be made to realize that the North and the South, and the East and the West, are, or should be one people, united by one common bond of mutual interest, because the real conflict of interest was not between the North and the South, as slaveholding and non-slaveholding communities, but as between the North and the South, including the East and the West, as one political community, organized under a common government for the promotion and protection of their common interests, so far as those interests may or might be affected by their intercourse with each other, or with foreign nations. I saw that the effect of the sectional organization of the North was to cause a counter sectional feeling and political organization of the South, and therefore I did not content myself with appeals to the people of the North. I deemed it to be my duty to address the people of the South, and among numerous other letters, I addressed the following to the Hon. R. M. T. Hunter :

DUFF GREEN TO THE HON. R. M. T. HUNTER.

To the Hon. R. M. T. HUNTER :

In the Congress of the confederation, April 30, 1784, a report of a committee, of which the following is an extract, was agreed to :

"Unless the United States, in Congress assembled, shall be vested with powers competent to the *protection* of commerce, they can never command *reciprocal* advantages in trade ; and, without these, our foreign commerce must decline, and eventually be annihilated. Hence it is necessary that the states should be explicit, and fix on some effectual mode by which foreign commerce, not founded on principles of equity, may be restrained.

" That the United States may be enabled to secure such terms they have resolved," &c., &c.

The resolutions asked that the states should give to Congress " the power of *prohibiting* the subjects of any foreign state, kingdom, or empire, unless authorized by treaty, from importing into the United States any goods, wares, or merchandise, which are not the produce or manufacture of the dominions of the sovereign whose subjects they are."

Subsequently, on the 13th of July, 1785, the Congress, upon motion of Mr. Monroe, proposed an amendment to the ninth article of the confederation, providing, among other things, that

Congress should have the sole and exclusive right and power "of *regulating* the trade of the states, as well with foreign nations as with each other; and of laying such imposts and duties upon imports and exports as *may be necessary for this purpose*," and in a letter addressed to the several states, showing the principles on which the alteration was proposed, it was said:

"The common principle upon which a friendly commercial intercourse is conducted between independent nations, *is that of reciprocal advantages;* and if this be not obtained, it becomes the duty of the losing party to make *such further regulations,* consistently with the faith of treaties, as will remedy the evil, and secure its interests."

I make these quotations to prove that one of the chief objects of the adoption of the federal Constitution was to confer upon Congress the power to *protect* our interests in our commerce with foreign nations, and to adopt "such further regulations" as will secure to us "*reciprocal advantages.*"

By reference to the proceedings of the Virginia House of Delegates, Jan. 21, 1786, it will be seen that Edmond Randolph, James Madison, and others, were appointed to meet commissioners from the other states, "to take into consideration the trade of the United States; to examine the relative situation and trade of the said states; to consider how far a uniform system in their commercial relations may be necessary to their *common interest* and their *permanent harmony;* and to report to the several states such an act relative to this great object, as when unanimously ratified by them, will enable the United States in Congress assembled effectually to provide for the same."

These commissioners met others from some of the other states, at Annapolis, on the 11th of September, 1786, and their recommendation led to the adoption of the federal Constitution.

It will thus be seen that the chief purpose was to form a government with power to adopt such a system of commerce as may be necessary to our "*common interest*" and to the "*permanent harmony*" among the states—and by reference to these extracts we see that the purpose of giving to Congress "power to regulate commerce with foreign nations," was to enable Congress to make "such further regulations" as are "competent to the *protection* of commerce," and will "command *reciprocal* advantages in trade."

Such being the purpose of the federal Constitution, I ask whether the regulations made by Congress are such as to *protect* our commerce, and secure to us "reciprocal advantages," or whether they be such as to promote our "*common interest*" and "*permanent harmony*" among the states?

If it is true, as I allege it is, that the great issue now before the world is financial—that it is whether the monarchies of the Old World, and their system of taxation, represented by their funded debt, or the republicanism of the New World and our system of progress as represented by our railroads, is the best basis of credit, and that under our system of commerce, as now regulated by Congress, it is in the power of the Bank of England, at any time, to cause a ruinous contraction of our currency, by compelling the export of specie—and if a low rate of ad-valorem duties gives to the Bank of England increased facilities for exporting our specie, then it is the imperative duty of Congress to so regulate commerce with foreign nations as to "protect" our "common interest."

There are a few recognised and admitted principles of political economy about which there can be no difference of opinion ; and there are some facts, so well established, as to require no further proof or illustration. Thus it is admitted that the chief source of wealth and prosperity of a nation is its productive industry. Hence it follows, that it is the duty of Congress, charged as it is with the control of our foreign commerce, to so regulate that commerce as to bring into action and stimulate our home industry. By this I do not mean that Congress should enact a prohibitory tariff, and thus exclude competition with foreign labor, but I do insist that the chief end of the federal Constitution was to so regulate our intercourse with foreign nations as to protect our " common interests," in all questions connected with our foreign commerce, and that this power was given to Congress, with especial reference to our "*credit.*" If so, it follows that it is the duty of Congress to protect our " credit" against the contingencies arising from our intercourse with foreign nations. And hence I insist that, as the export of our specie necessarily produces a contraction of our currency, and as that contraction diminishes the value of property, it follows that it is the duty of Congress to protect our " common interests" by preventing as far as practicable, this export of specie ; and hence it follows, that if we can trace the export of specie to measures adopted by the Bank of England, then the measures of protection to be adopted by Congress should be such as to protect us against those by which the Bank of England causes the export of specie.

This brings us to the inquiry of how and by what means the Bank of England is enabled to cause the export of our specie.

The funding system is of comparatively recent origin, and its power and influence are imperfectly understood by the people of this country. The elder Peel said, "a public debt is a public blessing," and this saying has become a British proverb. His argument was—"The debt adds on one side to the existing capital an amount of £700,000,000 or £800,000,000, while, on no side, it ever diminishes the wealth or capital of individuals. . . . The debt, therefore, positively, increases the national wealth by its amount ; but if, in a statistical table, you deduct the amount of the wealth, or of the income of the country (a very doubtful application of the principal), still, as the *minus* and the *plus* are equal, it will follow that the debt is not a burden."

Such was the argument of the elder Peel. I do not admit its truth, for it will be seen that the case, as stated, assumes that the whole debt is owned in England, and that, inasmuch as the sum paid by the government is paid to the people of England, therefore it " is not a burden." It follows that, if any part of the debt be due to any one else, then, to that extent, it is a burden. It follows, also, that, as the debt is due from the government to those only who are the holders of it, it is necessarily a burden on those who pay more than they receive ; and that, if the payments are equal to the receipts, yet the sum invested in the debt is to that extent a dead loss of the sums thus invested ; for if A pays in taxes all that he receives as interest, then A receives nothing for the sum invested in the debt.

I had occasion to examine into this subject, and found that the whole number of persons receiving incomes in Great Britain, on the 1st of January, 1843, was as follows :

87,176 whose incomes did not exceed £10 per ann.
44,648   "   "   20   "
93,305   "   "   100   "
25,641   "   "   200   "
14,701   "   "   400   "
4,795   "   "   600   "
2,827   "   "   1,000   "
1,367   "   "   2,000   "
266   "   "   4,000   "
151 public companies,   "   4,000   "
85   "   "   6,000   "
40 persons' incomes not exceed'g 6,000   "
15   "   "   8,000   "
21 public companies   "   8,000   "
10   "   "   10,000   "
4 persons' incomes   "   10,000   "
12   "   "   10,000   "
34 public companies, exceeding 10,000   "

To this may be added the depositors in the savings banks, whose deposites are converted into the public funds, and upon fourteen days' notice may be withdrawn. The amount of these deposites on the 20th of November, 1840, was £23,471,050, on account of 798,055 depositors, as follows :

440,740 deposits not exceeding - - £20
209,463   "   "   - -   50
85,118   "   "   "   - - 100
28,448   "   "   "   - - 150
15,538   "   "   "   - - 200
3,066   "   "   "   - - 200

782,374 persons deposited - £21,979,797
7,988 charitable institutions dept'd   485,908
7,693 friendly societies deposited   1,005,345

798,055 depositors, and - - £23,471,050

If we compare the statement of persons receiving incomes, and add to the number of those whose incomes do not exceed £600, the number of depositors in the savings banks, it will be seen that the public debt of England, great as it is, is distributed among the masses. And this fact should admonish us that the funded debt of England, distributed, as it is, among the people, has become an essential part of the government of England ; for every one who is interested in the funds, is to that extent interested in upholding the government. The Emperor of France understood this well, when he distributed the war loans among the people of France, instead of placing it with the large bankers.

The interest upon the funded debt of *nine* principal European states, payable chiefly in London, is about two hundred and fifty millions of dollars per annum, and constitutes one of the means by which the exchange is ruled in favor of London. But this of itself, is not sufficient to regulate the exchanges. We have seen that the Duke of Wellington declared that England was indebted to her system of home manufactures and of commerce, for the power and strength which enabled her to subdue the elder Napoleon ; and it will be found, upon analysis, that England is enabled to sustain her public credit, not because the debtor and creditor sides balance each other, as assumed by the elder Peel, but because she has so regulated her commerce with foreign nations as to give employment to her home industry, and receive, in the shape of profits on her merchandise, *consumed by foreign nations*, more than sufficient to pay the interest upon her debt, the burden of which is thus transferred to those who consume her manufactures.

And it is therefore pertinent that we should inquire how it is that England is enabled to give profitable employment to her home labor, and at the same time undersell her competitors in the markets of the world ? The answer is : that she does this by the wisdom and forethought with which she "regulates commerce with foreign nations." so as to protect her public and private credit.

For example a merchant in San Francisco wishes to purchase British goods. Money in San Francisco is worth thirty per cent. per annum,

13

while in London it is worth but three per cent. ; yet he is compelled to pay a premium on funds which in San Francisco are worth thirty per cent., to obtain a like sum in London, where it will be worth but three per cent. Why is this so ? Is it not because the people of England have so regulated their commerce with San Francisco, that the merchant at San Francisco is compelled to transfer his funds from San Francisco to London, and therefore is compelled to pay the expense of the transfer ? Is it not because England has so regulated her commerce that she compels other nations to go to England to sell, and also to buy ? And how is she enabled to do this ? Is it not by the wisdom and foresight which "protects" her home industry, her commerce, and her *credit?* What constitutes her power and strength ? Is it the bullion in the Bank of England ? Or is it not rather the measures, by which she so regulates her commerce with other nations, as to enable the bank at all times to bring a supply of the precious metals to London as the centre of the financial world, and thus protect the public and private credit of England, so that they are available as capital, in giving employment to labor ? Is it not because she is enabled to use her *credit* as *capital*, that she is enabled to furnish the capital, at cheap rates, with which she employs her home labor, and creates the foreign commerce, the profits on which pays the interest on her public debt, and makes it available as capital ?

Let me be understood—gold and silver, are by common consent received at fixed rates, in all the operations of commerce ; gold and silver therefore are received in payment, and pass from man to man, at their standard value. A bank note is also received in payment, because, if the bank be in good credit, the note can be converted into specie. That is, the credit of the bank enables the holder of the note to use the note as gold or silver ; and, therefore the bank note is equal to gold and silver, so long as the credit of the bank is such as to give it currency as money. So with the public debt of England. So long as they are convertible into gold and silver, consols will be received as money, at the rates at which they are convertible, and therefore, although that public debt represents sums expended in wars, and in maintaining armies and navies, and other expenditures of the British nation—it represents also the actual sum in money which the holders have paid for it, if the sum thus paid be no more than the current market value

Yet we know that the value of the debt consists in the payment of interest, and that whatever may weaken the confidence of the public in the ability or stability of the government will diminish the value of the debt, and to that extent impair the power and resources of the British government. You will thus see that it is the imperative duty of the British government, and of all others who are interested in the prosperity of England to aid as far as they can in maintaining the public credit ; and hence it follows that the bank of England is compelled to adopt such measures, as will prevent such competition between our system of credit and the public credit of England, as will depreciate the value of British consols.

If we admit that it is the duty of the British government and of the bank of England to protect their credit, so as to prevent its depreciation, and it be true that the wise use made of their credit enables them to employ it as capital, giving profitable employment to their labor, and through its agency to make all other nations tributary to them, then it becomes us to inquire whether we may not organize a system of credit competent to give employment to our labor, and thus to render us independent of, and protecting us against the measures and policy of the bank of England? This inquiry however deserves a most careful consideration, and is reserved for another letter.

Very truly, your friend,
DUFF GREEN.

THE AMERICAN PARTY—A LETTER FROM DUFF GREEN.

(From the American Organ, Feb. 23, 1855.)

To Hon. R. M. T. HUNTER:

Before proceeding to speak of the measures which are indispensable to the proper regulation of our commerce with foreign nations, it may be well to submit some facts and propositions which I deem to be incontrovertible.

The purpose of Virginia and of the other states, in organizing the federal government, was "to enable the United States, in Congress assembled, to take into consideration the trade of the United States; to examine the relative situations and trade of the said states," and to adopt such "uniform system in their commercial regulations as may be necessary to their *common* interest and permanent harmony."

That the Constitution gave to Congress power "to regulate commerce with foreign nations," and "to coin money and regulate the value thereof."

That the purpose of granting these powers was to create a fixed and certain standard of values, and, as far as practicable, prevent uncertainty in the values of property.

That the value of the property of commercial nations is as thirty to one of the sum of their currency.

That if the commerce between two commercial nations be so regulated that one of them can, at will, contract the currency of the other, the effect will be to enable the nation having such control over the currency to regulate the value of money and of property in the country thus subject to that control, and by that means to regulate their commerce as well as the value of their money and of their property.

That the greater part of the debt of nine European governments bears an interest not exceeding three per cent., and that the annual accruing interest, payable, the greater part, in London, is more than two hundred and fifty millions of dollars per annum.

That the European governments, and especially the governments of England and France, have promoted, as far as they could, the distribution of this debt among the masses, because, to the extent that the masses are interested in the public debt, they are interested in preventing a revolution which may injure the public credit.

That, as the debt is a tax on their productive industry, the governments of Europe are interested in preventing an increase of the rates of interest; and that the governments and persons interested in maintaining the value of their public credit, are interested in preventing a competition between European three per cents. and American securities giving six and seven per cent.

That the bank of England can, by raising the rate of interest, create an extraordinary demand for bullion, and that the effect of such demand is explained by an intelligent English writer, who, commenting upon the exports of British manufactures, says :

"When a manufacturer is in immediate want of cash, he *dare* not make a forced sale in a *home* market. It would invariably pull down prices permanently. It would expose his necessities, and vitally injure his credit. He goes, therefore, quietly to a foreign agent. He consigns his goods to him for an advance of ready money, say fifty per cent. of what he expects to realize, with an understanding that as much of the remainder as the goods fetch in the foreign market shall be paid to him afterwards."

That, as under our system of commerce, as now regulated by Congress, such "*forced sales*" will give greater and more speedy returns if the goods are sent to New York, than if they are sent to any other market, it follows that, whenever the bank of England puts up the rate of interest so as to create "*an immediate want of cash*," manufacturers who are compelled to make these forced sales will send their goods to New York to be sold.

That the purpose of increasing the rate of interest is to create a money pressure in the London market, and to compel a shipment of specie from the United States, whence a supply is more cheaply and sooner obtained than from elsewhere.

That the necessary consequence of increasing the rate of interest by the bank, and the "*forced sales*" of merchandise will be an export of specie from New York to London, and a contraction of our currency, proportionate to the demand for specie thus created.

That the diminution in the value of our property will be in the proportion of thirty to one of the reduction of our currency ; that is, if the currency be reduced *thirty millions*, then the value of our property will be reduced nine hundred millions of dollars.

That such contraction of the currency must necessarily arrest our public improvements, by reducing the value of our public securities ; and that it will also greatly embarrass private as well as public enterprise, producing great distress among the laboring classes, by depriving individuals, as well as incorporated companies, of the funds requisite to pay for labor.

That the purpose of England in emancipating her West India slaves, was to repeal the West India monopoly of the supply of the British market with tropical products, and to enable the British manufacturers to exchange their goods for East India produce, under a belief that the cheap labor of India could successfully compete with slave labor in Cuba, Brazil, and the United States.

That the experiment has failed, inasmuch as Sir Robert Peel himself was compelled to say in the debate on the repeal of the sugar duties : "I must say that I have my doubts, if a colony in which slavery has been abolished by law, can at present enter into successful competition with a district in which the system continues to exist."

That the present war with Russia is an effort on the part of England to maintain her monopoly of the East India trade, because the continental European powers, having established home manufactures for themselves, England being unable to sell her manufactures to other European nations, now sends her manufactures to India, where they are exchanged for the tropical products of India, which are carried in British ships to the continent, and thus those European powers who have no tropical possessions are compelled to pay England tribute in the shape of profits on East India produce, purchased with British manufactures.

That a nation which sends her best blood and her noblest sons to perish before Sebastopol, that she may retain her present monopoly of the East India trade, will use whatever power she may have to cripple our resources, and prevent a competition with them for that trade.

That the most sure and efficient mode of arresting our progress, and preventing a competition for the East India trade, is the periodical contraction and expansion of our currency, which is now accomplished through the bank of England.

That it is apparent, upon the face of events, that the alliance between Lord Palmerston and Napoleon III., must embrace combinations hostile to our interests, and that a successful termination of the war with Russia, will be immediately followed by measures which may involve us in a war with England and France.

That, under these circumstances, the tendency of a movement which creates a strong American sentiment, and which commits the North to maintain the constitutional rights of the South, must be to promote that "common interest and permanent harmony" among the states, which was their purpose in adopting the federal Constitution ; and if so, it is the duty of the South to unite in the movement, and aid in the accomplishment of so desirable an end.

That the Wilmot Proviso originated in the sectional opposition to the "tariff of 1846," and that the anti-slavery agitation in the North is owing more to a sectional rivalry, created by a belief that the South have exerted an undue influence in the government, than to any well-defined public sentiment, religious or political, on the abstract question of slavery itself.

That so far as anti-slavery has become a religious or political sentiment of the North, it may be traced to British origin and sectional influence, and may be identified with the measures and policy of England, whereby she seeks to make all the world tributary to her as the consumers of the tropical products of her East India colonies.

It follows, that if the American party tenders to the South a "more perfect union," upon the basis that the legislation of Congress and the action of the federal government should be such as to promote the interests and protect the property of the *American* people, it will tend to allay the sectional feelings which have heretofore arrayed the North against the South, and prepare each section for those mutual concessions which are indispensable to a proper and permanent adjustment of sectional issues.

If, as I contend, the effect of the present tariff is to enable the bank of England to export our specie and thus contract our currency—and that the only means of depriving that bank of that power, is a proper exercise of the powers to regulate commerce, and the value of money, it follows that as the North and the South are alike interested in the proper exercise of those powers, and as the issue is not a question between the North and the South, but between the North and the South united, and the bank of England as the agent of the governments and financiers of Europe, it becomes the duty of the North and the South to cease their sectional bickering, and unite in the calm discussion of all questions connected with their relations with each other and with foreign nations, that they may be enabled to agree upon such a system as may be "*necessary to their common interests, and permanent harmony.*"—(*See Virginia resolutions.*)

The purpose of these regulations should be to "*protect* our commerce," and secure to us "*reciprocol* advantages." To do this, we must so strengthen our financial position as to prevent the contraction of our currency by the export of specie occasioned by the demand for bullion in the bank of England.

The strength of the financial position of England consists in the regulations which give a money value to her public debt, and enables the bank of England, through its control over British commerce with foreign nations, to increase its bullion by compelling those who consume British goods to pay therefor in specie.

As the periodical contractions of our currency are caused by the demand for bullion in the bank of England, and the power of the bank to compel payments in specie depends upon our indebtedness to England, it follows, that the only means of preventing these periodical contractions of the currency is to diminish our consumption of British goods, and to relieve ourselves from our dependence on British capital.

To do this, we must so organize our credit as to make it as available to us in giving employment to American labor as British credit is in giving employment to British labor.

It is now admitted that money properly expended on a well-located rail-road adds ten times the sum thus expended to the value of the property connected with the road ; and, as the funded debt of the monarchies of Europe represents sums expended in wars, and in maintaining armies and navies, and privileged persons. and will cease to have value if the people refuse to pay taxes, and yet, the financial arrangements by which their public credit is maintained gives to their funded debt a money value, it follows that, inasmuch as the money which is properly expended on our roads, so far from requiring a tax for the payment of interest, pays large profits on the investments thus made, and adds so much to the value of other property ; therefore, the money thus invested is a much better basis for public credit than the sums expended by European monarchies in wars and the maintenance of their existing governments, and, if so, then all that is required to render us financially independent of the bank of England is to so regulate our foreign commerce as to render the sums invested in railroads available as capital, for the purpose of giving profitable employment to American labor.

By a late statement of the iron trade, it appears that during the last two years there were imported into the United States, from England, 524,095 tons of iron, which, at forty dollars per ton only, cost us $20,963,800 ! Now, it is manifest that the greater part of this large sum was paid in the bonds of our railroad companies, at rates much below their nominal value. You will see that these bonds furnish to the London financiers the means of exporting our specie—for, in case of a demand for bullion in the bank, these bonds are remitted to New York, sold at a depreciation, and the proceeds remitted in specie. The effect is to recruit the bullion in the bank of England, and diminish the value of our property, and especially of railroad securities, by the contraction of our currency.

The effect of this export of specie being to depreciate the value of railroad shares and railroad credit, it consequently arrests railroad enterprise, and deprives our laborers of profitable employment ; whereas a financial system which would enable our railroad companies to purchase and use American iron, would not only diminish the power of the bank of England to act upon our currency, by forced sales of railroad bonds, but it would soon convert the productive labor of this country into a positive capital, competent and willing to maintain our credit by protecting our currency, and preventing the periodical contractions which it is the interest and policy of the bank of England now to produce.

We are now paying near two millions of dollars per annum for railroad mail service. This is the interest at six per cent. on *thirty-three* millions of dollars. Instead of paying this two million of dollars, as we now do on contracts for four years, I would make contracts for railroad mail service in perpetuity ; and deliver to railroad companies bonds, chargeable upon the revenues of the department, and redeemable at the pleasure of the government, and bearing an interest of *three* per cent. only, to an amount the interest upon which at six per cent., would be an equivalent for the service rendered, and to give current value to these bonds, and enable the railroad companies to purchase iron with them, I would provide that the surplus in the treasury, beyond the wants of the government, should be appropriated

to purchase, *at par*, such of these bonds as had been made the basis of bank issues, under the laws of the several states. The effect of this arrangement would be not only to reduce the present disbursement for railroad mail service one half, but to convert that disbursement into a positive capital, relieving our railroad companies from their dependence on English iron, and give a money value to the entire cost of our railroads. This conversion of the expenditures on our railroad mail service into a positive capital, would contribute to the daily augmentations of our wealth and resources, uniting and binding together all parts of the Union ; for the capital thus created, although distributed in each section of the country, would be deeply interested in the maintenance of our public credit, and in case of an emergency, could be made available for that purpose.

I am now an old man, having long since ceased to take an active part in party politics. I have, nevertheless, carefully noted the progress of events, and, being Southern in birth, education, feelings, sympathies, and principles, I have a strong preference for the men of the state rights party. Believing that the great body of the people of this country have a strong preference for our republican form of government, and that the American movement may be so directed as to promote a greater harmony between the North and the South, by creating an American sentiment stronger than the fanaticism which has so long misled many well-disposed Northern men, I would entreat you, and every other influential Southern statesman, to remember that the power of this government resides with the people, and that it is the duty of patriotism to act with, and give a right direction to, public opinion.

Let me entreat you, be not deceived by the false clamor. The American party are not Abolitionists, and, permit me to say, that a liberal, generous, and cordial confidence and cooperation in the American movement, adhering to what is right, and reforming what is wrong, is the best and surest means of arresting and counteracting the anti-slavery agitation. In a subsequent letter, I may take a brief review of parties, showing that the *people* can and will "*regulate*" the *politicians.*

     Very truly, your friend,

         DUFF GREEN.

(From the American Organ.)

GEN. DUFF GREEN ON THE TARIFF. NO. II.

To the Hon. R. M. T. HUNTER :

The "principle of the tariff of 1846" I understand to be an ad-valorem duty. I now proceed to prove it to be unwise, and inconsistent with the obligations imposed by the Constitution.

It will not be denied that one of the chief ends of the federal Constitution was to form a government to be charged with our intercourse with foreign nations ; nor can it be denied that many questions must arise which necessarily affect our prosperity, and upon which the action of our government should depend upon the relations which exist between foreign governments and ours. Thus Congress has power not only to "regulate commerce with foreign nations," so as to protect our interests and promote the common welfare, so far as it can be done by a proper exercise of that power, but Congress also has power to declare war, if it becomes necessary for that purpose. It must, therefore, be admitted that the power to "regulate commerce" is a much more comprehensive grant than the power to "levy and collect duties." The purpose of this latter power is to create a revenue, and it is therefore subordinate and auxiliary to the power to "regulate commerce with foreign nations." If the power to levy and collect duties be subordinate and auxiliary to the power to regulate commerce, then the power to "levy and collect duties" should be so administered as to aid the proper exercise of the power to "regulate commerce," with foreign nations. For as each power is a separate and distinct grant, and both are intended to promote the "general welfare," it is the duty of Congress to administer each in such manner as that each may aid the purpose for which the other was granted. Let us apply this principle to ad-valorem duties.

The Constitution gives to Congress power to "coin money and to regulate the value thereof," and to "fix a standard of weights and measures." The purpose was to give a certain and fixed standard of value regulating the exchanges and operations of commerce, so as to protect the property of individuals and determine the relation between debtor and creditor. Gold or silver are, by the common consent of nations, the standard of value, and hence all obligations for payment of money are held to be payable in gold and silver. Yet it is now admitted that the value of the property of commercial countries bears a relation of thirty to one of their currency. It follows, therefore, that if one commercial nation becomes indebted to another, under an implied understanding that the debt is to be paid in produce or property, and the creditor, instead of receiving produce, demands and receives gold and silver, the effect will be to diminish the value of the property of the debtor nation thirty times the sum of the payment thus demanded. It is the duty of Congress to so "regulate commerce with foreign nations" as to protect us, as far as possible, from such a contraction of our currency. Will an ad-valorem duty do this? It does the very reverse. Take the case of railroad iron—say that the price is sixty dollars per ton, the duty will be twenty dollars. In case of a pressure in the London market, and iron falls to thirty dollars per ton, then the duty is but ten dollars. It needs no argument to prove that there would be no such reduction in price were it not for some contingency creating an extraordinary demand for bullion in the bank of England, and such sales, at this reduced price, would not be made, were it not for the purpose of shipping our specie. The effect would be that we would save fifty dollars in the price of a ton of iron, and lose twelve hundred dollars in the depreciation of the value of property. I refer you to Mr. Calhoun's speech upon the currency, where he admits that the value of the property of a commercial nation is thirty times the sum of its currency; and if we assume this datum to be correct, I have demonstrated that an ad-valorem duty is not only unwise, but most unjust, and utterly inconsistent with the duty imposed upon Congress by the "power to regulate commerce with foreign nations."

The coalition between Mr. Clay and Mr. Adams adopted as the basis of their party organization a high tariff and internal improvement—a high tariff to collect a large surplus revenue, levied upon the commerce, paid for chiefly by Southern exports, to be expended by combinations chiefly in the North and West. This, the South said, was unequal and unjust, and unconstitutional because it was unequal and unjust, and tending to corrupt legislation. You will, I am sure, admit that there is a palpable distinction between a tariff levied for the purpose of creating a large surplus revenue, to be expended by Congress on local works or internal improvements, and a tariff intended to so "regulate our commerce with foreign nations" as to prevent those periodical contractions of our currency which have caused such ruinous depreciations of the value of property, and each and all of which can be traced to the extraordinary demand for bullion, and the measures adopted by European bankers, coercing the shipment of specie. I spent the greater part of 1842 and 1843 in London, my chief purpose being to study for myself the operations of trade between England and the United States. I knew that the theory of free trade is, that commerce is a reciprocal exchange of the products of labor, and I wished to know why a demand for bullion in the bank of England necessarily produced a ruinous contraction of our currency. I became satisfied that, as ours is the weaker part of the British financial system, a financial crisis in England, whatever might be its cause, whether produced by overtrading, a bad harvest, speculations in railroad shares, or Spanish American bonds, or South American or Mexican mines, was always made to explode here; and its worst effects were transferred to us. I will give a few facts by way of illustration.

The refusal of Congress to recharter the bank of the United States compelled the shareholders to accept a charter from the state of Pennsylvania.

This made it necessary to withdraw the branches located in other states; this was mostly done by sales of the assets in the branches, which were chiefly paid for in the notes of local banks. Had the bank of the United States demanded specie, most of the local banks would have suspended; the directors of the United States bank therefore made large advances on state bonds, and for cotton and tobacco, and sent Mr. Jaudon with the bonds to London, and Biddle and Humphries to Liverpool, in charge of the cotton and tobacco.

The bank advanced some five millions in bills upon London, to enable the merchants who had suffered by the great fire to pay their British creditors. When Mr. Jaudon sailed for London, Pennsylvania and Maryland sixes were worth sixteen per cent. premium; when he reached London he could not sell at any price, and I was credibly informed that the bank would have been protested had not Mr. Morrison, at the last moment, advanced the funds, upon an hypothecation of his best securities at ninety five per cent., to enable Mr. Jaudon to protect the credit of his bank.

Do you ask why Mr. Jaudon could not sell his state bonds? I reply that the interest on the public debt of the several European governments, payable the greater part in London, and the greater part of which is controlled by a few bankers, who are the agents of these governments for the sale of these securities, and also of the principal fundholders to receive and re-invest their dividends, amounts to about two hundred and fifty millions of dollars per annum. These bankers said that if Mr. Biddle was permitted to establish an agency in London for the sale of six and seven per cents., in competition with their European three per cents., Mr. Biddle could furnish any required amount of American six and seven per cents., and that the inevitable consequence would have been that many of the holders of European three per cents. would have sold out and purchased American six and seven per cents. It was, therefore, with them a matter of necessity, as well for themselves as for their clients, the monarchical governments of Europe, and these bankers combined to depreciate American credit. They saw that this could most readily be accomplished by breaking down the bank of the United States, and therefore they refused to purchase the state bonds held by Mr. Jaudon.

Do you ask why the bank did not sell cotton and tobacco through their agency at Liverpool, and thus obtain the means of meeting the drafts given to the merchants of New York? I will explain:

Up to that time the commerce between the United States and England was conducted chiefly through the agency of three London houses, known as the three W.'s. The American merchant bought from the British manufacturer on a long credit, and drew a bill upon one of these W.'s. The goods were brought to the United States, and bonds at long dates given for the duties. The goods were sold and American produce remitted, so that the merchant was enabled to place funds in the hands of his London correspondent in ample time to make his payments.

The British financiers saw that Mr. Biddle could protect his credit through the sale of the cotton and tobacco sent to Biddle & Humphries, at Liverpool, and they therefore resolved not only to annihilate our credit, but to destroy our commerce. What I am now about to say I have from the best authority: One of the W.'s, fearing a monetary crisis, wrote to his American correspondents that he could not accept their bills as he had done. The governor of the bank of England called upon him and said that the bank wished to encourage trade with the United States, and by a pledge of aid in case of necessity induced W to recall his letters. The consequence was, that when the time came W. was under acceptance for more than twelve millions of dollars, and, instead of carrying him through the crisis, the bank of England refused to discount any bill drawn on account of the shipment of American produce, and the consequence was that W., who had a positive capital of more than two millions of dollars, became bankrupt, and his brother, who had retired from business, expended even a greater sum in the fruitless effort to save him. Now, why did the bank of England urge W. to aid them in their effort to send a large quantity of British merchandise to the United States? and why did the bank refuse to discount bills drawn on account of shipments of American produce? Do you not see the motive? The time had come when it became necessary for British financiers to so regulate their commerce with the United States as to enable them to regulate the value of our money by contracting our currency. It was not enough for them to refuse to purchase state bonds—they saw that it was indispensable to assail our credit through our commerce. To do this it was necessary to create a large commercial balance against us, and to protect their three per cents. from the competition with our six and seven per cents., it became necessary to so regulate their commerce with us that, instead of selling upon long credits and thus giving us the aid of their capital, they now required cash payments for their manufacturers while they used their credit in the purchase of our produce.

The effect of this new "regulation" of their commerce with us is to enable the bank of England at any time, upon one week's notice, to create a panic and cause a contraction of our currency by exporting our specie.

Was this new regulation of their commerce called for by any failure on the part of our merchants to meet their engagements? On the contrary, by reference to an official report from the Treasury, you will see that the duties paid by our merchants on customhouse bonds, from the year 1789 to 1837 inclusive, amounted to six hundred and ninety-four millions of dollars on bonds having six, nine, and twelve months to run, and that the loss by insolvency, during that period, was less than one per cent.

It follows that the merchants who were so punctual in the payment of duties were no less punctual in the payment of the sums due to their British creditors. Why, then, did the bank of England refuse to aid those who were engaged in the trade with the United States? The new regulation which compelled us to pay in advance, instead of purchasing on credit, shows that the purpose was to enable the bank at will, to so regulate their commerce with us, as to enable the London bankers to export our specie, and by contracting our currency to so depreciate our credit as to prevent a competition between our six and seven per cents. and their three per cents.

What would be the condition of

England and other European nations, if they were compelled to give seven per cent. for money? How long would England continue the war with Russia if consuls were depreciated to forty?

Do not suppose that I intend to charge that the warfare on our credit, or the contraction of our currency by the exportation of our specie, is done wantonly for the purpose of doing us injury. What I do charge is that such warfare is an indispensable part of the British financial system, and will continue to be so as long as our commerce, as regulated by Congress, furnishes to the bank of England the surest and cheapest means of recruiting her bullion. What I would impress upon you and upon Congress is, that as England has reorganized her system of commerce so as to increase the facilities by which the bank of England can transfer our bullion from Wall street to London, and inasmuch as the export of our specie diminishes the value of our property in the ratio of thirty to one of the sum of the diminution of our currency, which must necessarily be much more than the sum of the specie exported, we lose, by the construction of the currency, and consequent diminution of the value of our property, much more than the benefit which accrues from any reduction in the price of foreign merchandise, and it is therefore the duty of Congress to protect us, not against the cheap labor of Europe, but against the measures which foreign bankers have adopted, by which they can create an expansion or contraction of our currency at will. How can Congress do this? I reply, by so regulating our commerce with foreign nations as to regulate the value of money. The power is expressly granted, and the duty is imperative.

Let it not be said that England is our best customer, and that commerce and exchanges will regulate themselves, or that, as we are the greatest consumers of British merchandise, England is interested in promoting our prosperity. Let me ask you to look to Ireland, to India, and to Portugal. Are not Ireland, India, and Portugal, consumers of British merchandise? And who does not know that the wealth and resources of each have been exhausted by the operation of British commerce.

Do you not see that the real issue of the present age is between the monarchies of Europe and their system of taxation, represented by their funded debt, and our republican form of government, and our system of progress, represented by our railroads as the basis of financial and commercial credit? Do you not see that the crises of 1840 and 1854 are attributable to the same cause? In 1840 the competition was between three per cent. consols and six per cent. state bonds. In 1854 the competition is between three per cent. consols and eight per cent. railroad bonds. Which is the best basis of credit? What would be the condition of England if she were compelled to pay eight per cent. interest on her public debt? Why does England send her chivalry —the best blood of her most noble families—to perish before Sebastopol? Is it not because she hopes thereby to maintain her commercial and financial supremacy? And what assurance have you that if she can humble the pride of Russia, she will not then create combinations to arrest our progress, and thus destroy that competition for the trade of India which our possession of California necessarily creates? Do you ask for proofs that such is her purpose? Look at the late insolent interference of the British and French agents at St. Domingo. Look at the concert of England and France in relation to Cuba and the West Indies, and the Sandwich Islands. Do you not see that the coalition between England and Napoleon the Third is the consequence of the necessities which compel them to sustain each other? And do you not see that the same motives which compel them now to make war on Russia may compel them to make war upon us? Is it not, therefore, our duty to leave our sectional strife and bring union, wisdom, and strength to the support of our common country? And instead of laboring to perpetuate the sectional issues which constitute the chief basis of party organization, should we not rejoice to see the North invite the intelligence and patriotism of the South to unite with the North in a movement which, if the South be wise, will consolidate the North and the South for the maintenance of the institutions which are no less indispensable to the welfare and prosperity of the North than of the South?

I reserve further comment for another letter, and remain your sincere friend,

DUFF GREEN.

FROM THE SAME TO THE SAME.

To the Hon. R. M. T. HUNTER:

When on a former occasion, I ventured to address you through the press, urging the impolicy of an indiscriminate opposition to the American party, not being a member of that party, I did not know, and therefore did not understand to explain or to vindicate their purposes or principles.

I saw that it had become a powerful organization—that many of its prominent members were men of influence, and unquestionable patriotism. I thought I saw in the professed objects of that party, the basis of an organization upon which uniting upon a preference for our own government would give a new direction to party conflicts, and tend to lessen, if it did not entirely supercede, the rivalry between the North and the South. For I hold that the chief purpose of the federal government is to so "*regulate*" our intercourse with foreign nations as best to promote the interests and welfare of the people of the United States, and that in the discharge of this duty, the North and South are and should be one people; and that the measures and policy of the federal government, domestic and foreign, should unite, foster, and strengthen their interests as such.

I knew that names are substantial things, and therefore when I was told that the democratic senators in caucus had resolved to denounce and proscribe the *American* party, and that the issue thus to be made, was to be an important part of the machinery of the Presidential election, I ventured through the letters addressed to you to warn the democratic party, and especially the republican party of the South, of the impolicy of such a proceeding. The result of the election proves the truth and force of what I then said.

I did not ask you or the party of which you are so distinguished a member, to recognise or approve of the proscription of any person or class of persons on account of the place of their birth, or of their religion—but I did then urge, and propose now to repeat, that the issue upon which the future peace, welfare, and prosperity of this country depend, is not a sectional conflict between the North and the South, in which the local and sectional interests involved in the question of the tariff and of slavery should be permitted to array the North and the South against each other, but that it is, as it was before the adoption of the federal Constitution, an issue between all the states of the Union, as one people, on one side, and all the world, with whom we have intercourse, as foreign nations, on the other. And I saw, or thought I saw, in the *American* sentiment, which must necessarily be embodied in an *American* party, the basis upon which all Americans, native-born or naturalized, Protestant or Roman Catholic, might, by rallying upon the Constitution, make a united effort to harmonize and reconcile the local and sectional interests which it was the purpose of the Constitution to assert and maintain.

I repeat that the result of the late election proves the truth and force of what I then said. The democratic candidate is elected, but his majority would have been much greater, if the single issue had been, between a candidate uniting all those who are American in principles and sentiment, and who are ready and willing to make common cause in support of the rights and interests which it was the purpose of the Constitution to assert and protect, as well those of the South as those of the North ; and if this be so, it is our duty to promote that harmony of interest and of opinion which will give strength and permanence to such an *American* sentiment. It is a

melancholy and mortifying truth that in the late election, the vote for the anti-slavery candidate was so great, in most of the Northern states as to create, a sectional, political organization of such power and influence as to give great encouragement to the abolitionists. And this is to be regretted more, because there is an influential and increasing party in the South who believe that there is no hope for the South, but in a dissolution of the Union. While there is an influential and growing party at the North who would greatly prefer a Union with the Southern slaveholding states. The public opinion of each section is being trained to the belief, that there is an irreconcilable conflict of interests and of opinions, which will, in time, dissolve the Union ; and it is apparent that the consequences of such a measure, and the manner in which it can or will be done, has become a question of serious consideration.

I repeat : This question is forced upon us, and although it may not appear, it will enter into and give color to the proceeding of the Southern Convention, about to be held in Georgia, of which I am gratified to learn that you will be a member. How is it to be met and disposed of ? I would meet it by showing that there is no cause for a conflict of sectional interests between the North and the South, and that the legislation of Congress in relation to the tariff, and to African slavery, should be such as to *protect* and foster the interests of the North and the South. I do not use the word "*protect*" here in the sense in which it was used by Mr. Clay and the partisans of *his* "American System," for he proposed high duties for the protection of American manufactures, and to create a fund to be appropriated by a corrupt party Congress to sectional internal improvements. I propose that protection, which it is the duty of Congress to give, by such regulation of our commerce with foreign nations, as will *protect* our *currency* from the contractions and expansions, which are now and will ever be the necessary consequences of the contingencies which affect the money market of the Old World, so long as we give them the facilities which they now have to export our specie. I reserve the further explanation of my views for another letter.

Very truly, your friend,

DUFF GREEN.

CHAPTER XXV.

POLITICAL.

I HAVE referred to the fact, that from the commencement of the government there has been a fundamental difference between the Republicans of the South and the advocates of a monarchical government represented by the Elder Adams and "the British party in the United States." The Republicans of the South and the democracy of the North, insisting that the authority of the federal government is limited by the powers given, and the reservations made in the Constitution, while the monarchists, under the name of federalists and such other aliases, as from time to time they have deemed it expedient to assume, although driven from power themselves, have contended for a "strong government," enlarging its power by implication and construction. Such a division of parties is an anomaly in the history of government, and is to be accounted for by the fact, that although apparently a government of the majority, in point of fact, ours was heretofore a government of concurring majorities. The slaveholding states, although a minority, and therefore vitally interested in limiting the powers of the government by a rigid construction of the Constitution, constituting the Southern republican majority, acting with the democratic majorities of the North, maintained a controlling influence in the government, until after the election of Mr. Lincoln, they unwisely abandoned and sur-

rendered the control of public affairs to their opponents. I had noted the progress of events with deep anxiety, and as the questions of slavery and the tariff were made the issues on which designing men endeavored to organize sectional feeling, I endeavored to show, by numerous appeals, through the press, that the question of the tariff was a question of currency rather than of duties, and that the North and the South were alike interested in its proper adjustment.

That the reader may properly understand the issues inaugurating the late war, I reproduce from the National Intelligencer the correspondence between certain persons in Connecticut and Mr. Buchanan, then the President, relative to the proceedings in Kansas, and also from the Pennsylvanian, a communication in reply to the censure of his conduct.

MR. BUCHANAN AND KANSAS.

(From the National Intelligencer, Sept. 4, 1857.)

IMPORTANT CORRESPONDENCE.—We find under this head, in the columns of the official journal of yesterday, the subjoined correspondence between certain distinguished citizens of Connecticut and the President of the United States with reference to the existing dissensions in the Territory of Kansas and the duties deemed incumbent on the general government in regard to their settlement.

We have no disposition to challenge the right of the memorialists to address their petition to the President, a right which the latter has conceded and honored by awarding to it a respectful attention and a courteous answer. To apply to them, therefore, either as individuals or as a body, the injurious designation of the 'Union,' when it styles them 'reverend and impertinent intermeddlers,' seems to us no less disparaging to the President than to the gentlemen thus inculpated, since it places the former in the attitude of paying undue heed to a manifesto which he would, on the theory supposed, have better consulted his dignity by leaving unnoticed.

We may venture, however, to express our regret that the memorialists, in stating their complaints, should have assumed with so much positiveness their own theory, honestly entertained, we doubt not, of the protracted difficulties in Kansas, and manifested so little allowance for any possible difference of opinion which might conflict with their own impressions. Their experience and observation, we think, should have taught them the fallibility of human judgment as in all moral questions, so especially in those involving political prepossessions, and induced them to admit a wider scope for the play of adverse, though equally sincere, convictions of duty in a case of admitted difficulty and embarrassment. The reply of the President, even though it may fail to change their views in the premises, will at least, we doubt not, suffice to vindicate the purity of his motives, and disclose the grounds on which, as a conscientious magistrate, he feels called to take a position quite different from that which they would assign him.

" From the 'Union' of September 3.

" The public had become apprized during the past week that a correspondence of a peculiar character had taken place between a number of clergymen and others of the North and the President of the United States, in relation to political affairs in Kansas. What purported to be copies or extracts from this correspondence having found their way into the newspapers, we deemed it proper that such a publication of it should be made as would relieve all doubt in the public mind as to its genuineness. To this end we called upon the Presi-

dent yesterday, who has furnished us with copies, and kindly consented to their publication.

" To His Excellency James Buchanan, President of the United States :

" The undersigned, citizens of the United States and electors of the state of Connecticut, respectfully offer to your Excellency this their memorial.

" The fundamental principle of the Constitution of the United States and of our political institutions is, that the people shall make their own laws and elect their own rulers.

" We see with grief, if not with astonishment, that Governor Walker of Kansas openly represents and proclaims that the President of the United States is employing, through him, an army, one purpose of which is to force the people of Kansas to obey laws not their own, nor of the United States, but laws which it is notorious, and established upon evidence, they never made, and rulers they never elected.

" We represent, therefore, that by the foregoing, your Excellency is openly held up and proclaimed, to the great derogation of our national character, as violating, in its most essential particular, the solemn oath which the President has taken to support the Constitution of this Union.

" We call attention, further, to the fact that your Excellency is, in like manner, held up to this nation, to all mankind, and to all posterity, in the attitude of 'levying war against (a portion of) the United States,' by employing arms in Kansas to uphold a body of men, and a code of enactments, purporting to be legislative, but which never had the election, nor sanction, nor consent of the people of the territory.

"We earnestly represent to your Excellency, that we also have taken the oath to obey the Constitution, and your Excellency may be assured that we shall not refrain from the prayer that Almighty God will make your administration an example of justice and beneficence, and, with his terrible majesty, protect our people and our Constitution.

" Nathaniel W. Taylor, Theodore D. Woolsey, Henry Dutton, Charles L. English, J. H. Brockway, Eli W. Blake, Eli Ives, B. Silliman, Jr., Noah Porter, Thomas A. Thacher, J. A. Davenport, Worthington Hooker, Philos Blake, E. K. Foster, C. S. Lyman, John A. Blake, Wm. H. Russell, A. N. Skinner, Horace Bushnell, John Boyd, Charles Robinson, Henry Peck, David Smith, J. Hawes, James F. Babcock, G. A. Calhoun, E. R. Gilbert, Leonard Baker, H. C. Kingsley, B. Silliman, Edward C. Herrick, Charles Ives, Wm. P. Eustis, Jr., Alexander C. Twining, Josiah W. Gibbs, Alfred Walker, James Brewster, Stephen G. Hubbard, Hawley Olmstead, Seagrove Wm. Magill, Amos Townsend, Timothy Dwight, David M. Smith."

" WASHINGTON, *August* 15, 1857.

"GENTLEMEN: On my return to this city, after a fortnight's absence, your memorial, without date, was placed in my hands, through the agency of Mr. Horatio King, of the Postoffice Department, to whom it had been intrusted. From the distinguished source whence it proceeds, as well as its peculiar character, I have deemed it proper to depart from my general rule in such cases, and to give it an answer.

"You first assert that ' the fundamental principle of the Constitution of the United States, and of our political institutions, is that the people shall make their own laws, and elect their own rulers.' You then express your grief and astonishment that I should have violated this principle, and, through Governor Walker, have employed an army, ' one purpose of which is *to force the people of Kansas to obey laws not their own, nor of the United States,* but laws which it is notorious, and established upon evidence, they never made, and rulers they never elected.' And, as a corollary from the foregoing, you represent that I am ' openly held up and proclaimed, to the great derogation of our national character, as violating, in its most essential particular, the solemn *oath* which the President has taken *to support the Constitution of this Union.*'

"These are heavy charges proceeding from gentlemen of your high character, and,

if well founded, ought to consign my name to infamy. But, in proportion to their gravity, common justice, to say nothing of Christian charity, required that before making them, you should have clearly ascertained that they were well founded. If not, they will rebound with withering condemnation on their authors. Have you performed this preliminary duty toward the man who, however unworthy, is the Chief Magistrate of your country? If so, either you or I are laboring under a strange delusion. Should this prove to be your case, it will present a memorable example of the truth that political prejudice is blind even to the existence of the plainest and most palpable historical facts. To these facts let us refer.

"When I entered upon the duties of the Presidential office, on the 4th of March last, what was the condition of Kansas? This territory had been organized under the act of Congress of 30th May, 1854, and the government, in all its branches, was in full operation. A governor, secretary of the territory, chief justice, two associate justices, a marshal, and district attorney, had been appointed by my predecessor, by and with the advice and consent of the Senate, and were all engaged in discharging their respective duties. A code of laws had been enacted by the territorial legislature; and the judiciary were employed in expounding and carrying these laws into effect. It is quite true that a controversy had previously arisen respecting the validity of the election of members of the territorial legislature, and of the laws passed by them; but, at the time I entered upon my official duties, Congress had recognized this legislature in different forms, and by different enactments. The delegate elected to the House of Representatives, under a territorial law, had just completed his term of service on the day previous to my inauguration. In fact, I found the government of Kansas as well established as that of any other territory. Under these circumstances, what was my duty? Was it not to sustain this government? to protect it from the violence of lawless men, who were determined either to rule or ruin? to prevent it from being overturned by force? —in the language of the Constitution, to 'take care that the laws be faithfully executed'? It was for this purpose, and this alone, that I ordered a military force to Kansas to act as a *posse comitatus* in aiding the civil magistrates to carry the laws into execution. The condition of the territory at the time, which I need not portray, rendered this precaution absolutely necessary. In this state of affairs, would I not have been justly condemned had I left the marshal, and other officers of a like character, impotent to execute the process and judgment of courts of justice, established by Congress, or by the territorial legislature, under its express authority, and thus have suffered the government itself to become an object of contempt in the eyes of the people? And yet this is what you designate as forcing 'the people of Kansas to obey laws not their own, nor of the United States;' and for doing which you have denounced me as having violated my solemn oath. I ask, what else could I have done, or ought I to have done? Would you have desired that I should abandon the territorial government, sanctioned as it had been by Congress, to illegal violence, and thus renew the scenes of civil war and bloodshed which every patriot in the country had deplored? This would, indeed, have been to violate my oath of office, and to fix a damning blot on the character of my administration.

"I most cheerfully admit that the necessity for sending a military force to Kansas, to aid in the execution of the civil law, reflects no credit upon the character of our country. But let the blame fall upon the heads of the guilty. Whence did this necessity arise? A portion of the people of Kansas, unwilling to trust to the ballot-box —the certain American remedy for the redress of all grievances—undertook to create an independent government for themselves. Had this attempt proved successful, it would, of course, have subverted the existing government, prescribed and recognised by Congress, and substituted a revolutionary government in its stead. This was a usurpation of the same character as it would

be for a portion of the people of Connecticut to undertake to establish a separate government within its chartered limits, for the purpose of redressing any grievance, real or imaginary, of which they might have complained, against the legitimate state government. Such a principle, if carried into execution, would destroy all lawful authority, and produce universal anarchy.

"I ought to specify more particularly a condition of affairs, which I have embraced only in general terms, requiring the presence of a military force in Kansas. The Congress of the United States had most wisely declared it to be 'the true intent and meaning of this act [the act organizing the territory] not to legislate slavery into any territory or state, nor to exclude it therefrom, but to leave the people thereof perfectly free to form and regulate their domestic institutions in their own way, subject only to the Constitution of the United States.' As a natural consequence, Congress has, also prescribed, by the same act, that, when the Territory of Kansas shall be admitted as a state, it 'shall be received into the Union with or without slavery, as their constitution may prescribe at the time of their admission.'

"Slavery existed at that period, and still exists, in Kansas, under the Constitution of the United States. This point has, at last, been finally decided by the highest tribunal known to our laws. How it could ever have been seriously doubted is a mystery. If a confederation of sovereign states acquire a new territory at the expense of their common blood and treasure, surely one set of the partners can have no right to exclude the other from its enjoyment by prohibiting them from taking into it whatsoever is recognized to be property by the common Constitution. But when the people, the *bonafide* residents of such territory, proceed to frame a state constitution, then it is their right to decide the important question for themselves, whether they will continue, modify, or abolish slavery. To them, and to them alone, does this question belong, free from all foreign interference.

"In the opinion of the territorial legislature of Kansas, the time had arrived for entering the Union, and they, accordingly, passed a law to elect delegates for the purpose of framing a state constitution. This law was fair and just in its provisions. It conferred the right of suffrage on ' every *bonafide* inhabitant of the territory ;' and, for the purpose of preventing fraud, and the intrusion of citizens of near or distant states, most properly confined this right to those who had resided therein three months previous to the election. Here a fair opportunity was presented for all the qualified resident citizens of the territory, to whatever organization they might have previously belonged, to participate in the election, and to express their opinions at the ballot-box on the question of slavery. But numbers of lawless men still continued to resist the regular territorial government. They refused either to be registered or to vote ; and the members of the convention were elected legally and properly without their intervention. The convention will soon assemble to perform the solemn duty of framing a constitution for themselves and their posterity ; and, in the state of incipient rebellion which still exists in Kansas, it is my imperative duty to employ the troops of the United States, should this become necessary, in defending the convention against violence while framing the constitution, and in protecting the ' *bonafide* inhabitants' qualified to vote, under the provisions of this instrument, in the free exercise of the right of suffrage, when it shall be submitted to them for their approbation or rejection.

" I have entire confidence in Governor Walker that the troops will not be employed except to resist actual aggression, or in the execution of the laws ; and this not until the power of the civil magistrate shall prove unavailing. Following the wise example of Mr. Madison toward the Hartford Convention, illegal and dangerous combinations, such as that of the Topeka Convention, will not be disturbed unless they shall attempt to perform some act which will bring them into actual collision with the Constitution and the laws. In that event they shall be resisted and put down by the whole power of the government. In performing this duty, I shall have the approbation of my own conscience, and, as I humbly trust, of my God.

" I thank you for the assurance that you will ' not refrain from the prayer that Almighty God will make my administration an example of justice and beneficence.' You can greatly assist me in arriving at this blessed consummation, by exerting your influence in allaying the existing sectional excitement on the subject of slavery, which has been productive of much evil, and no good, and which, if it could succeed in attaining its object, would ruin the slave as well as his master. This would be a work of genuine philanthropy. Every day of my life, I feel how inadequate I am to perform the duties of my high station without the continued support of Divine Providence ; yet, placing my trust in Him, and in Him alone, I entertain a good hope that He will enable me to do equal justice to all portions of the Union, and thus render me an humble instrument in restoring peace and harmony among the people of the several states.

" Yours, very respectfully,
" JAMES BUCHANAN."

From the Pennsylvanian, October 20, 1858 :

(From the North American of yesterday.)

DUFF GREEN TO THE PEOPLE OF PENNSYLVANIA, AND ESPECIALLY TO THOSE WHO PREFER A GOVERNMENT OF LAW AND ORDER TO ANARCHY.

I am encouraged by your past history, my own hopes of the future, and the sympathies created by our common interests, to appeal to your intelligence and to invoke your co-operation in the adjustment of pending political questions ; and I address myself to you because their early and satisfactory adjustment much depends, as I believe, upon the President, a citizen of your own state, and the influence which he can bring to bear upon the deliberations of Congress ; and because, during the canvass which has just transpired, his official conduct and character have been assailed with a bitterness and vituperation seldom equalled in the political discussions of this country ; and because, as the tendency of that warfare will be, as some suppose, to weaken the influence which he ought to exert in your behalf, it therefore becomes your duty now to examine with fairness and candor, and to determine for yourselves, whether his conduct has been censurable, as alleged, and what it is proper for you to do in the circumstances in which he and you are placed.

If the result of that examination is to satisfy your sober and deliberate judgment that he is no longer worthy of your confidence, but merits censure, then let such be the expression of your opinion ; but if a calm and deliberate investigation shall prove that, under the difficult and embarrassing circumstances in which he was placed he has not only had the wisdom to see, but the firmness to recommend, those measures which were best calculated to promote your interests, and to increase and strengthen his influence in the proper adjustment of that issue which is now most pressing, and involves not only the rich man's wealth, but the poor man's daily food, then it becomes your duty to lay aside your prejudice, and to bring to his aid all the power and influence which you, as a people, can give. Let us pause and see what are the charges and what are the facts. The charge is that he was pledged to maintain the principle of "popular sovereignty" in Kansas, and that, in recommending the admission of Kansas under the Lecompton constitution, and the approval of the English bill, he has violated that pledge. It is understood, and I believe I state the issue correctly when I say, that, by "popular sovereignty," his accusers mean that the whole constitution, made at Lecompton, instead of that part which relates to the question of slavery, should have been referred to the "popular vote," and they claim that this has become a fundamental principle in our government.

I meet this charge directly. I deny that, in this or any other sense, "popular sovereignty" is a fundamental principle of our government. I deny that the President was pledged to maintain such "popular sovereignty" in Kansas, and assert that, so far as he was pledged, he has faithfully and truly exerted his power and influence to fulfil his pledges. I assert further that, although with the limited information which I had, I disapproved of his message recommending the admission of Kansas under the Lecompton constitution, and although I was opposed, and had I been a member of Congress I would not have voted for the English bill ; yet, with the lights I now have, I approve of his message and of his approval of the English bill.

I deny the whole doctrine of "popular sovereignty" as held by his accusers, because I believe it to be infidel and revolutionary, subversive of the fundamental principles of religion and of government. I not only admit, but I maintain, that the *power* of our government is vested in the people ; but, nevertheless, it is a government of the *laws* and the *Constitution*, and not of "*popular sovereignty.*" The government is a compact between the people making it, whereby each and all relinquished to representatives the power to make laws, and gave to the government authority to enforce obedience to the laws thus made.

The purpose of the government is to maintain the rights and interests of the weak against the usurpations of the strong—to restrain and check the power of the many when they would oppress the few. Therefore, if this new-fangled idea of "popular sovereignty" means anything more than the proper exercise of the rights and powers of the people, in the manner and forms indicated by the laws and the Constitution, it is *treason, rebellion*, or *anarchy*. That it was treason, rebellion, anarchy, and civil war in Kansas, I am prepared to prove whenever it is expedient. My present purpose is to show to the intelligent, thinking, religious public that it is a heresy fraught with danger to the church and to the well-being of the state.

I repeat that, if by "popular sovereignty" the accusers of the President mean the proper exercise of the power of the people, as reserved and recognized in the law and the Constitution, I take issue with them on the facts. If they mean a "higher law" than this—that the popular will is to be the law of the land, and that party platforms are more potent than the Constitution—that *vox populi* is "*vox Dei*," then I say that, so far from being a fundamental principle of our government, it is *treason, rebellion, anarchy*, and *infidelity. Obedience* to law is the *duty* of man. This new idea of "popular sovereignty" substitutes the popular will as the rule of the law. In the exercise of such "popular sovereignty," Adam and Eve ate the forbidden fruit and lost us Paradise. It was in the exercise of such "popular sovereignty" that his enemies shouted, "Crucify him, crucify him," and slew the Son of God.

Why it was that man was permitted to sin, or why he should be redeemed through the atoning blood of Christ, are mysteries hidden in the inscrutable providence of God. Why false doctrines, errors, strifes and animosities are permitted to enter the church, or why men, zealous disciples of Christ, and anxious for the welfare and happiness of man, are moved by passion, pride and prejudice, no man can say, except that it is the law of our nature, from which no man is free. We are told that what was written aforetime, was written for our instruction, and hence we find that David, the chosen man of God—the man after God's own heart, had his infirmities, as other men. So there was a *Judas* among the twelve, and *Peter* denied his Lord, with an oath !! If David, and Judas, and Peter, being men, had been perfect and without sin, how could sinful men, as we all know ourselves to be, hope to be reconciled to God? The record of the sins of David, of Judas, and of Peter, was written to admonish us of the disease which is within us—of the existence of the law of God, and of the necessity of the mediating grace of Christ. I believe in a special Providence, working through the use of means. When I reflect upon the immensity of space, filled with the manifestations of His power, and see that He has given laws, regulating the movement of the heavenly bodies, which have continued, without variableness or shadow of change, I recognize the infinitude of His power and the duty of submission to His will. When I look back upon the history of man, I find that the organization of government and submission to the law are indispensable to his spiritual as well as his temporal welfare ; and, therefore, I feel it to be my duty, and yours, to unite in resisting a heresy which would refer to the variable, undefined, unascertainable popular will, created by artful appeals to popular prejudice, made by designing demagogues for the promotion of their own personal ends, instead of that matured will of the people, declared, in the laws and the Constitution, to be the proper guide for the conduct of public men.   Do his accusers charge that, in this matter of "popular sovereignty" in Kansas, the President has violated the law or the Constitution? I do not so understand them. As I understand the case, it is that he agreed, with Gov. Walker, that the best means of terminating the Kansas controversy was to recommend that the legislature of Kansas—then elected, at an election which had received the sanction of the preceding House of Representatives, a majority of whom had admitted the delegate to his seat and rejected the Topeka constitution—should pass an act authorizing the election of delegates, to meet in convention, with power to make a constitution, and that that convention ought to submit the constitution, thus to be made, to a vote of the people of Kansas.

Does any one pretend to say that, under the circumstances, the President did not advise that the Lecompton constitution should be submitted to a popular vote? No one says this. But it is said that the constitution was not submitted, and that, by recommending the admission of Kansas, under that constitution, he violated the pledge given to Gov. Walker, and abandoned the principle of popular sovereignty! Let us pause and examine this charge.

The cry of "no more slave states" was brought into Congress upon the application of Missouri to be permitted to organize a state government. Mr. Trumbull, in reply to Mr. Douglas, said, in a late speech in Illinois, that " No

one has ever denied the right of the people of a territory, when they come to organize a state government, to decide the question of slavery or no slavery for themselves," and I recur to this declaration as an illustration of the undue influence of temporary excitement and party prejudice, upon one occupying so exalted a position, to show the necessity of a strict adherence to the law and the Constitution, and to truth and reason as the rule of our action, instead of launching the ship of state into the uncertain sea of popular opinion, lashed into fury by artful and designing men, who make politics a trade, and live by the excitement which they create.

If that honorable Senator had cast his eyes across the Mississippi river, he would have been reminded that slavery existed in Missouri before it was ceded to the United States, and that the right of property in slaves, and the right to be admitted into the Union, upon an equal footing with the original states, was guaranteed by the treaty ; and yet he must know, as we all know, that the admission of Missouri as a state was opposed, under pretence that Congress had power to prohibit, and ought to prohibit, slavery in Missouri.   This claim of power to prohibit slavery in the new states was not only asserted then, but has been the bone of contention ever since then, until it was admitted to be a usurpation, by the opposition in both houses of Congress, during the last session— in the Senate, on Mr. Crittenden's, and in the House, on Mr. Montgomery's amendment.

We are told that we should judge the tree by its fruits. This vote of the opposition in both houses of Congress, and this declaration of Mr. Trumbull, that " No one has ever denied the right *of the people of a territory, when they come to organize a state government, to decide the question of slavery or no slavery for themselves,"* is the fruit of the President's message, recommending the admission of Kansas under the Lecompton constitution ; and, although I did not approve of that message, and had I been a member of Congress would not have voted for the English bill, yet I now maintain that, judging the tree by its fruits, and looking to the principles involved as well as to consequences resulting therefrom, for that message and all that he has done in relation to Kansas, the President, instead of censure, deserves our commendation and support.

To the charge that the Lecompton constitution was not referred to the vote of the people, I reply that the charge admits, and no one has ever denied, that, under the circumstances of popular excitement, it was the President's opinion, and that he authorized Mr. Walker to say that it was his opinion, that the Lecompton convention should submit the whole constitution, and not a part only, to a popular vote. When the President gave this advice he had exerted the whole of his authority in that matter. He did not make the constitution—he was not the convention. The reference of that constitution was not to be his act, but the act of the convention. He had given no pledge that *he* would refer the constitution to a vote of the people. He had no power to refer it, and, therefore, could give no pledge that he would refer it. As he gave no pledge, he could not, by any forfeiture of such pledge, violate the popular sovereignty of the people of Kansas. But, although he could give no pledge that *he* would refer the constitution to a popular vote, he did give a pledge that he

would exert his power to prevent any improper interference with the right of the people to elect representatives who would refer it, when made, to their approval or rejection. Does any one of his accusers charge that he did not, to the extent of his power, fulfil *that* pledge ? No, no one makes that charge ; although it is said that there were frauds at two or more districts, and that a majority of the people refused to vote, and, therefore, the election was illegal.

I refer to these facts because, in passing judgment upon the conduct of the President, they become important, and, therefore, to enable us more properly to understand the real issue I recur again to the history of the case.

Mr. Calhoun, at the time of his death, was the prominent statesman of the South. Mr. Clay had become so much identified with the North, that he did not even pretend to be a Southern man. The South was without a candidate. In the North, there were Mr. Van Buren, Mr. Marcy, Mr. Dickinson, Mr. Webster, Mr. Buchanan, Gen. Pierce, Gen. Cass, and Mr. Douglas, to say nothing of other aspirants, too numerous to mention. Anti-slavery had become a political sentiment so formidable, that it was well understood no candidate could get a Southern vote, who was not fully pledged against that heresy. Hence the compromise of 1850 ; hence the Kansas-Nebraska bill ; hence the platforms of both parties in 1856, and hence the Cincinnati platform. Those who nominated Mr. Fillmore, as well as those who nominated Mr. Buchanan, hoped to get Southern votes, and hence they were pledged to maintain the right of property in slaves.

But there was another party, who raised the cry of " no more slave states "—and who, although they had themselves violated the Missouri Compromise, by refusing to extend the line through New Mexico and California, availed themselves of the Kansas-Nebraska bill, to renew the agitation. The result was a civil war in Kansas, and zealous Christians, pious fathers of the church, did not hesitate to furnish men, money, and Sharp's rifles to be used, in making Kansas a free state. It was in vain that they were told that the question of slavery in Kansas, was a question of climate and population —that Kansas must of necessity become a free state, because prudent slave-owners would not risk their property in Kansas, and because there is an abundance, and to spare, of unoccupied lands, suited to slave labor in the Southern states ; and that, having no slaves to spare for that purpose, we cannot make new slave states, unless we renew the African slave-trade. The cry had been raised—a Northern political anti-slavery party had been organized—a corps of unscrupulous correspondents had been sent to Kansas, who filled a few partisan papers with repeated falsehoods, until the public mind of the North had become so much inflamed, that pious, good, patriotic Christian men, voted for John C. Fremont for President !!!

I ask you to look back upon this delusion—to compare it with the persecution of the witches, the Quakers and Baptists of New England—and then to ask yourselves if it is a matter of surprise that this movement in the North should create a counter movement in the South—or that the South should have been alarmed and suspicious ? or that the people should require pledges for the protection of their rights of property ?

Such were the fruits of the anti-slavery agitation of the North. It was

understood that the admission of Kansas under the Lecompton constitution would affirm the right of the people of a territory, in making their constitution, to determine the question for themselves ; and that the rejection of that constitution would assert the power of Congress to prohibit slavery in the new states. Mr. Buchanan and his friends were pledged to maintain the right of the people as asserted by the South, and he had been not only suspected, but accused of insincerity, and an influential movement had been made for a dissolution of the Union if the Lecompton constitution had been rejected, upon the ground that its rejection would be proof of the existence of a feeling in the North so powerful, and so hostile to the South, that it would be no longer prudent or safe for the South to remain in the Union.

Under such circumstances, the Lecompton constitution came to the President with a request that he should submit it to Congress, and recommend the admission of Kansas as a state. It is not denied that each citizen of Kansas could have voted in the choice of delegates to the Lecompton convention. A majority, it is said, did not vote, but that was in their own wrong ; and because they preferred the Topeka constitution—which had been rejected by the previous House of Representatives, in which the opposition had a majority. The President had fulfilled his pledge to prevent any improper interference in the choice of delegates. He had advised that the whole constitution should be referred to a popular vote. He could not compel the people to vote, nor could he compel the convention to refer the constitution to the people. He had to act upon the case as it came to him, and I congratulate you and the country that he had the wisdom and the firmness to act so as to vindicate and establish the rights of the South; and that this question which has so long arrayed the North against the South; which has excited so much bad feeling, and has so much disturbed the proper legislation of Congress, has been so auspiciously concluded under the administration and the influence of a citizen of your state, who having thus redeemed his pledges to the South—having vindicated and established their rights in this question, so vital to them, may now call upon the South to stand by him in the proper adjustment of that other question, involving no less the interests of the South than of the North, but which, in consequence of the sectional character it has assumed, has become no less a question between the North and the South than the question of slavery itself. I mean the question of the tariff.

The South selected a citizen of your state as their candidate for the Presidency, knowing that he had been and then was in favor of increased duties on imports, and especially on foreign iron. It is natural to suppose that he can and will exert an influence favorable to your interests, and you must see that so far from deserving bitter censure, his conduct in the matter of Kansas has given him new claims to your confidence, and by increasing his power to serve you, calls for your approval and support.

But it is charged that he betrayed his pledge to Gov. Walker. In what? We have seen that, through Gov. Walker, he advised that the convention should refer the constitution to the people; that it was not so referred, was no fault of his—the reference was to be made by the convention, not by him. In this, therefore, there was no violation of his pledge—because he could not, and did not, make such a pledge. But it is said that Gov. Walker was opposed to the acceptance and submission of the Lecompton constitution. In this there could have been no violation of any pledge, because Gov. Walker himself advised the election of the delegates, and the holding of the convention. Both he and the President advised that the convention should refer the constitution; neither could have foreseen or anticipated that it would not be referred; there could have been no agreement between them in reference to it, and therefore there could have been no violation of pledges in relation to it. But it is said that he approved of the English bill. I happen to know personally that Gov. Walker approved and urged the passage of that bill, if he did not aid and advise in preparing it, and therefore it is manifest that the charge of bad faith to Gov. Walker, so pertinaciously urged against the President in this respect is met by the fact that the English bill had sufficient popular sovereignty for the governor. And it seems to me that those who eulogize the governor and condemn the President are not just or reliable—who applaud one and censure the other—both concurring in the support of that bill.

As to that feature of the English bill which, in case of the rejection of the Lecompton constitution, requires a sufficient population to entitle Kansas to one Representative in Congress before it is admitted as a state, I do not understand that the President's accusers assert that it was put into the bill at his suggestion. Nor do I understand that, apart from the peculiar circumstances of the case, they condemn the principle itself. So far from doing this they admit that each territory should have the requisite population before it becomes a state. So far as this provision makes a distinction offensive to the popular feeling of the North it was not only wrong in principle but unwise in policy ; but is it just to make the President responsible for the error of Congress? It is true that he approved of the bill, but he was required to act upon it as a whole, and we should bear in mind the fact that it was admitted, and urged as an objection to the Lecompton constitution itself, that there was not sufficient population to form a state, and therefore many Southern members were willing to vote for that constitutation as a means of getting rid of the agitation, knowing that, even under that constitution, Kansas would be represented in both houses by anti-slavery men, and be an anti-slavery state. Under the circumstances, is it surprising that they should insist that, if the people of Kansas rejected that constitution, they should wait until they had sufficient population? That clause, therefore, should be placed to the excited feeling of Southern men, and is chargeable to their want of wisdom, and not as a fault of the President.

But it is said that the President has made the English bill a party test, and that he has exerted his influence, and the patronage of the government, to enforce it. If it be true that there has been any abuse of executive patronage, I regret and condemn it. I am not the partisan or the eulogist of the President. I wish to be an advocate of truth and justice, and, therefore, I ask, who, and what, are his accusers? Are they seeking power—and, if they get possession of the government, will they dispense the patronage to partisans and favorites? Have they

no favorite candidate for the Presidency? And if they elect him, will they put in no claims for wear and tear of conscience? Is their advocacy of "popular sovereignty" purely disinterested patriotism, or is it a mask to hide their own selfishness? *Par example*, Mr. Haskins claims great merit for his independence. He claims to be a martyr in the cause of "popular sovereignty," and yet, he himself tells us, in his Tarrytown speech, that he could not have been elected to the present Congress if the opposition vote had not been divided on two opposition candidates, and that he is well aware that he had not the least possible chance of re-election unless he could become the opposition candidate. Now, under such circumstances, I can see a controlling motive to avail himself of the English bill, as a means of getting back to Congress as an opposition member, but the facts admitted by himself, deprive him of all claim to independence, and prove that he went over to the opposition, preferring the chances of a re-election by their votes. What claim has he, under such circumstances, upon the President? Or how can he assume to be a political martyr, or to charge that the President makes a corrupt use of the public patronage, because it is not exerted for his benefit?

I repeat that, although at the time I did not approve of his message sending the Lecompton constitution to Congress, he acted wisely and properly ; for, by their votes on Mr. Crittenden's amendment, in the Senate, and Mr. Montgomery's, in the House, the anti-slavery party have conceded all that the South ever asked or contended for. The discussion following it has not only admitted the right of the people of a territory, when they come to make a constitution, to decide the question of slavery for themselves, but it has conceded our right of property in slaves—concessions which fully satisfy the South, and which would never have been made had not the President submitted that constitution to Congress. It is in this view that the proceedings of the last Congress may be taken as a final and satisfactory adjustment of the slavery issue. The contest in Kansas proves, conclusively, that the question of new slave states is a question of climate and population ; and knowing, as we do, that we have no slaves to make *new* slave states, the South are compelled to choose between remaining in the Union as a permanent minority, or to go out of the Union and form a new government. No sane man can believe that, if we dissolve the Union on such an issue, we can make arrangements with the other states for the surrender of fugitive slaves, or for the protection of our right of property in slaves, as satisfactory to us as the guarantees we now have in the Constitution. To dissolve the Union, therefore, is impossible. We have no inducement to dissolve it. We will not dissolve the Union—we will hold the North to their compact, and rely on the Constitution, and not upon "popular sovereignty," for the protection of our rights. And I repeat my congratulations that this healing measure, which leaves us free to examine and dispose of the question of the tariff, has been achieved under the administration of a son of Pennsylvania, under circumstances which strengthen his influence, and give him claims upon the confidence and co-operation of the South, in the adjustment of that other question, upon which, as I believe, more than any other, depend the welfare and prosperity of this country.

Of this I propose to treat in another letter, in which I will prove, from carefully prepared statistics, that it is impossible to give constant employment and remunerating wages to labor unless we have an abundant and cheap currency; and that we cannot have an abundant and cheap currency unless we so regulate our foreign commerce as to maintain a sufficient specie basis for the protection of a legitimate use of so much credit as may be required to give full employment to labor, and transfer the produce of the soil and of labor from the producer to the consumer. I will also demonstrate, by statistics which cannot be questioned, that the idea that we cannot compete in the markets of the world, unless we cheapen the price of labor, is an error. I will show that it is the low price and abundance of money and of credit, and not the low price of labor, which is the source of wealth and prosperity to nations—for money is the measure of the values of property, as the yardstick is the measure of cloth. Labor is the poor man's property. When money is six per cent., the yardstick is three feet long ; when it is twelve per cent., the yardstick is six feet long, and when it is eighteen per cent., it is nine feet in length. To so regulate our foreign commerce that money is worth eighteen per cent., is to compel the poor man to sell his labor by a yardstick nine feet in length, and to purchase the rich man's money by a yardstick one foot in length. I entreat you to unite with me in the effort to bring the public attention, and especially the attention of the President and of Congress, to such an adjustment of the measure of values that the poor and rich may all have one standard yardstick of three feet in length.

DUFF GREEN.

CHAPTER XXVI.

POLITICAL.

THE failure of the Charleston Convention to nominate a candidate for the Presidency — the nomination of Messrs. Douglas, Breckinridge, and Bell at Baltimore, and of Mr. Lincoln at Chicago, verified my worst apprehensions.

I had been requested by the President of Mexico to make an arrangement with our government, by which, instead of sending specie to Mexico to pay the balance on the Mexican indemnity, our government should accept the bills of exchange of that government, payable in New York for the amount. As the arrangement would have saved to each government several hundred thousand dollars, it was approved by General Taylor and Mr. Clayton, then Secretary of State, and the bills of exchange were forwarded to the Mexican minister in Washington, in accordance with the arrangement thus made. The death of General Taylor made Mr. Fillmore President, and Mr. Webster Secretary of State ; and, for reasons which I was at no loss to comprehend, Mr. Webster disavowed the act of his predecessor, and gave the contract for the payment of the indemnity to the Messrs. Baring and their associates. I appealed to Congress, when, for the first time, I ascertained the powerful organization of the Washington lobby. Conversing with a gentleman who had been very successful in measures before Congress, he told me that I could not obtain the sanction of Congress unless I paid the lobby. I asked, " Who are the lobby ?" He gave me a list containing names of some of the clerks in the departments, and of the committees of both Houses of Congress. I was told that they were an organized body, combined with members of Congress, who, under their influence, voted for or against measures, or for or against claims, as arranged by this combination of irresponsible persons, whose business it was to support or to oppose measures or claims pending before Congress, and that they combined to defeat measures and claims on which the parties interested would not pay them a stipulated sum or percentage for their influence ; and united in support of measures and claims upon which the parties interested would agree to pay for their services. I refused to employ them—they combined against me—the proposition of Mexico was defeated, greatly to the loss of our own government as well as of Mexico.

A few days after the nomination of Mr Douglas, I was going from Washington to Philadelphia, a leading Western partisan of Mr. Douglas took a seat by me, and said : " Green, you are a great fool." I replied, " That may be true, but it is not very polite in you to say so—why do you say so ?" " You," said he, " are wasting your time and energies, and in support of Southern railroads—why don't you unite with us in the Central Pacific ? There is money enough in that for us all."

I afterwards read the report of the

committee, and the "Bill to secure contracts and make provision for the more speedy transportation, by railroad, of mails, troops, munitions of war, military and naval stores, between the Atlantic States and those of the Pacific, and for other purposes," and found that the bill provides that,

"There be, and hereby is, granted to William H. Swift, Samuel T. Dana, and John Bertram, of Massachusetts; Moses H. Grinnell, Benjamin Chamberlain, Hamilton Fish, John A. Dix, Daniel C. Eaton, Azariah Boody, Joseph Harrison, George W. Cass, Anthony B. Wofford, Joseph H. Scranton, Morton McMichael, of Pennsylvania; Edmund Pendleton, of Virginia; Benjamin H. Latrobe, Ross Winans, and Thomas Swan, of Maryland; Henry D. Newcomb, of Kentucky; William Case, S. S. l'Hommedieu, and Henry B. Curtis, of Ohio; Thomas A. Morris, Jesse L. Williams, and David C. Branham, of Indiana; Joshua Cobb, of Tennessee; E. O. Grosvenor and William J. Wells, of Michigan; John Wentworth, A. B. Judd, John Moore, and Charles G. Hammond, of Illinois; John How, James H. Lucas, William Gilpin, and Willard P. Hall, of Missouri; Charles Mason, Lucius H. Langworthy, Hugh T. Reid, and Hoyt Sherman, of Iowa; Samuel J. Hensley, T. D. Judah, and Louis McLane, of California; Herman C. Leonard and J. C. Ainsworth, of Oregon, and to such persons as a majority of such grantees shall admit as their associates, every alternate section of land within one mile of such railroad line as such persons may adopt."

Having read this list of names and the bill, I turned to the report of the committee, and found that they gave as

"THE PLAN OF EXECUTION.

"Your committee have found the greatest diversity of opinion as to the mode of accomplishing the object, and for years the inventive genius of men has been directed to schemes for constructing a Pacific railroad. It is generally conceded that government must, in some way, encourage the work, to induce private capital to take hold

of it. After much consideration, your committee have adopted the plan of advancing government thirty-year bonds, bearing five per cent. interest, in payment for telegraph and transportation service, which is to be executed during the progress, and after the completion of the work. To secure the government they are to be advanced only as sections of fifty miles are completed, beginning at each end with what is supposed to be only enough to aid capital; the amount per mile is to increase as the work proceeds from both ends towards the centre of the line, where the expense will be greatest. As a further security, these advances are to be a first mortgage lien on the road and equipment; so the effect is an advance of government credit for thirty years on what would seem to be ample security. We have stated the annual service now required by the government (which could and would be far better performed by a railroad), at five millions of army and navy transports, and one and a half millions of postal service, which, together, amount to six and a half millions. It is proposed to advance, as the work progresses, sixty millions in bonds, which may be increased by accruing interest over service, as the work proceeds, to seventy millions; the annual interest would then be three millions five hundred thousand dollars. The annual service, as above stated, six millions five hundred thousand dollars; so the annual service would exceed the annual interest, three millions of dollars.

"This last sum would remain with the government as a sinking fund sufficient to extinguish the bonds in less than twenty-four years, and, therefore, *before the bonds will become due.*"

I saw that here was an openly avowed purpose, under pretence of a contract for carrying the mails, &c., to divide among the persons named, and to "such persons as a majority of such grantees might admit as their associates," seventy millions of dollars, with an annuity of six millions five hundred thousand dollars, openly and shamelessly advertising the fact that the proposed contract would pay the interest on the seventy millions of dollars and give a surplus of three millions. I saw that as an annuity of one dollar at six per cent. will, in thirty-two years give ninety dollars and eighty-eight cents, the purpose was to distribute among the associates two hundred and seventy-two millions, six hundred and forty thousand dollars, and that it was a solemn and melancholy truth, that there was money enough in the Central Pacific Railroad bill as presented by Mr. Curtis, for all the associates. I was startled at the corruption, and not surprised at Forney's assurance that if they could not elect Mr. Douglas there would be a bargain to elect Mr. Lincoln. I was not surprised at the charge of corruption made by Mr. Dickinson as quoted in my letter to the people of Pennsylvania and New Jersey, nor am I now surprised at the efforts made to prevent the admission to their seats of members of Congress, who, if admitted, would vote against like donations of the people's money to the associates who have two other bills pending before the radical Congress, which, under pretence of building railroads to the Pacific, will, if passed, add so much more to the public debt, and enable the "grantees" to divide among themselves " and such persons as a majority of such grantees shall admit as their associates," several hundred millions more of " public plunder."

Advised, as I was, by the events of the Crimean war, the repulse of the British fleet in their attack on the Russian fort at the mouth of the Amoor river, and the movement of Russian agents in Japan and China, I was at no loss to understand the real motive for the encouragement given by the British goverument, to the construction of the Grand Trunk Railroad of Canada. I saw that although Vancouver's island and Puget's sound, had been the most remote part of the habitable globe to England, so long as the mode of communication was by Cape Horn, a railroad and telegraph from Quebec to the Pacific would so enhance their value that instead of surrendering their claims to their possessions on the Pacific for a sum sufficient to indemnify the Northwest Fur Company, the British government, who had arrested the progress of Russia by the war in the Crimea, would not only favor the construction of the Central Pacific Railroad, in connection with the Grand Trunk Railroad of Canada, by encouraging an advance of the funds required to build it, but would, if it were necessary, advance the sum requisite from their own public treasury. I saw, that the shrewd men who were interested in competing lines in New England, New York, Ohio, Indiana, Illinois, and Iowa, were deeply interested in preventing the control of the Pacific road from passing into the hands of men who would be interested in making the Grand Trunk Railroad of Canada, the GRAND TRUNK of the Pacific Railroad, and I believed that with them the election of members of Congress and a President who would favor their plan of building that road, was much more important than the election of the candidate whom they had aided to put in nomination. With them, the question was not who ought to be elected President, but whose election will enable the association to get the funds from the treasury of the United States to build the Pacific Railroad, and give to them not only the use of the seventy millions of dollars, and the annuity of six and a half millions of dollars, but give the control of the travel and transportation of the Pacific Railroad, and that by control enable them to transfer so much of that travel and transportation as may be transferable to the railroads in which they were interested, instead of permitting it to go East, over the Grand Trunk Railroad of Canada. Alike interested in the construction of the Pacific Railroad, the Canadian and American railroad companies were competitors for the control of the requisite funds, for upon that control would depend contingent profits, of equal or greater value, great as was the bonus asked of the American Congress. With this view of the purposes and motives of those who had nominated Mr. Douglas, I appealed to my friend Gov. Fitzpatrick, and urged him to refuse to serve as their candidate for Vice-President, and exerted my influence to induce the friends of Breckenridge and Bell to unite upon either, and thus prevent the election of Lincoln. With this view I wrote the following appeal to the people of Pennsylvania and New Jersey :

TO THE PEOPLE OF PENNSYLVANIA AND NEW JERSEY.

The pretence on which Messrs. Seward, Lincoln, Sumner, Hickman, and others, urge the election of the anti-slavery candidate for the Presidency is, that there is a conflict between what they term *slave* labor and *free* labor. They, therefore, insist, that the measures and policy, and the power and influence, of the federal government, shall be exerted to confine slavery within the existing slaveholding States ; that by so confining it it may "die out." The pretence for this war upon the South is, that the Declaration of Independence asserts that "all men are born free and equal," and that inasmuch as negroes are men, therefore they should be *free !*

They assume that such was the purpose of the Congress of 1776, and urge, as a duty, a perseverance in that system of measures which will make the slaves free men. Does any one pretend that Mr. Lincoln would have been thought of as a candidate for the Presidency had he not been the opponent of Judge Douglas in 1858, and had he not then urged, as a matter of necessity, the emancipation of Southern slaves—had he not urged that all the States must become *free ?* Let us, for a moment, reason together. Is it true, in principle or in fact, that all men are born *free* and *equal ?* As a fact, we know that it is not true ; for, so far as their birth determines their *status*, many men are born slaves. Nor is it true that they are born *equal*, for we all know that some are born poor and some are born rich—some are born to live in a republic, and some are born to live in a despotism—some are born to possess the blessings of Divine revelation under the influence of the Gospel, and some are born in heathen lands and never heard of a Saviour—some are born with a white skin, and some are born with a black. It is not true, therefore, that all men are born *free*, nor are they born *equal*. What, then, they ask is the meaning of the Declaration of Independence ? We answer that we must look to the interpretation given to their own declaration by the men who made it. They tell us, in the words quoted by Mr. Jefferson, that the negro-slaves were not intended to be placed on an equality with the white man—that they were considered and held to be, and were taxed as *property*. Mr. Lincoln himself is compelled to admit that they are held as property, and so does Mr.

Sumner, and so does Mr. Hickman. The question, even with them, is not whether slaves are property; they admit, all of them, that they are property, and were and ever have been held to be property in the states, recognizing them to be property. Mr. Sumner, in a single lucid moment, exclaims that he has no more to do with slavery in Charleston than he has to do with the slaves in Constantinople, and says further, that if the South will surrender to Mr. Lincoln, and to him, and to their associates, the control of the power and patronage of the federal government, he will not disturb their right of property in slaves. Let us calmly, as men, as Christians, as patriots, and as statesmen, consider the issues involved.

I appeal to you as men, and as Christians, is it not a fact that there is a distinction so marked between the negro and the white man that it cannot be effaced? Is not the difference such as to prevent an *equality* between the two races? Is the negro the equal of the white man? If he is not, who made the negro? Why was he made to be inferior to the white man? Can any one find, in all the scope of creation, anything which was not rightly and fitly made? and were not all things that were made suited to the purpose for which they were made? Who among all the men that live can know what was the purpose of God, when he made the negro? How can we comprehend his purpose? Is it not by an inquiry into the uses to which he has assigned his creatures? Why were not our railroads — our steamboats — our fine houses—our cities—our clothes, and our food, ready made for use? Why was man made subject to sickness, pain, hunger, thirst, labor, and death?

Why is it that man was permitted to know good and evil, and forbidden to "put forth his hand, and take also of the tree of life and live forever? Are not these things hidden in the inscrutable will of the Creator? Wherefore, then, do these men in their pride arrogate to themselves to condemn the owners of slaves? Wherefore do they assume that slavery is sinful — a wrong? Who made them to judge? By what right do they assume that slavery "must die"?—that *"all the states must be slave or all free"*?

I treat this subject in this wise, because I know that many persons in the North have been trained from infancy to believe that slavery is sinful—that it is an evil, and that it is part of a good Christian to wish that the slave may be free; and because this sentiment has enlisted the sympathies of many pious and good persons, so that designing demagogues seek to make that sentiment a means of creating a sectional political party, of such strength as to enable them, by its use, to usurp the powers and patronage of the government. Is it not a strange feature of this delusion that the men, who insist that they themselves, are no better than the slaves (for they say all men are born free and *equal*, and therefore these slaves being their equals should be free, because they are equals). I say, is it not strange that such men should insist that we, the masters of these slaves, are so much degraded by being masters, that we are unfit to participate, as their equals, in the administration of government? We ask no more than to be treated as equals.

I wish to satisfy all, every one, that these men deceive themselves—they do not believe what they assert—they do not believe that the negro is their equal—they know that they are not our superiors—no, in no sense by which the properties or qualities of men are estimated—and yet they would degrade the white master below the black slave, because by assuming to sink themselves to the level of our slaves, they hope to control and govern us.

Were the men who made the Declaration of Independence black or white? Were they slaves or were they free men? Was the Constitution a compact between free and independent states, made by free men—or was it a compact between slaves? Who were the parties to the Declaration of Independence? Who were the parties to the Constitution? Can any one believe that the Southern states will consent to remain in the Union, if the legality of their right of property in slaves is to be made the question on which they are to remain in a government, the sole purpose of which is avowedly to be the promotion of the sectional interests of the abolitionists of the North?

So much as to the *principles* and purposes of the anti-slavery party. Let us turn for a moment to the purposes and principles of the men who nominated Judge Douglas. It is known that the delegation from New York at Charleston and Baltimore nominated Mr. Douglas. Now hear what the Hon. Daniel S. Dickinson said of that delegation in a speech made at the Cooper Institute on the 18th July. He said:

"But the prayer is over, and a band of conspirators took possession of the assemblage, and, instead of a national convention, a great huckstering bazaar is erected—a political trades sales is opened—management inaugurates her slimy and repulsive court, and the office of chief magistrate of this mighty republic is put up like the board of a public pauper, at the lowest bidder. Its proceedings bear evidence of deliberate and long-cherished design, of a combination and conspiracy to tie up minorities against them, and leave those free who were for them, and thus attain, by fraud or force, a particular result, regardless of the popular sentiment or of consequences which might follow. The ruling faction had snuffed up the scent of four hundred millions of spoil, and for them the administration of Douglas was expected to rain milk and honey, snow-powdered sugar, and hail Moffat's vegetable life pills."

Mr. Dickinson then describes the proceedings at Charleston and Baltimore, resulting in the nomination of Douglas, and says:

"A decision so abhorrent to every principle of common fairness—so replete with outrage and usurpation, divided, dismembered, and broke up the convention, as it should have done, and as every sensible man saw that it would do; and I commend with my whole heart the spirit of the president, General Cushing, who refused longer to preside over the tyrannous cabal, and of the delegations who, under the same president, reorganized and placed in nomination Messrs. Breckinridge and Lane. The remaining faction, *made up chiefly of delegates from republican states,* whose delegations were the authors of the great wrong, *deprived of their head and without a democratic body,* proceeded to nominate Mr. Douglas and Fitzpatrick, and as we were informed, amidst tremendous enthusiasm, Vermont, and other New England states, and the whole Northwest were pledged to Mr. Douglas, *subject, of course, to a slight incumbrance, held by one Abraham Lincoln.*"

Proceeding to speak of the disruption of the convention, Mr. Dickinson says:

"The authors of this outrage, whom we should hold accountable, and who are justly accountable with it, were the ruling majority of the New York delegation. . . . . Creatures who hang festering upon the lobbies of state and federal legislation to purchase chartered privilege and immunity by corrupt appliances; who thrive in its fœtid atmosphere, and swell to obese proportions, like vultures upon offal; office brokers, who crawl and cringe around the footsteps of power, and by false pretences procure themselves, or vile tools, places of official trust and emolument, that they may pack and control caucuses and conventions at the expense of the people they defraud and betray, while honest men are engaged in their industrial avocations to earn their bread. Oh, how has the once noble spirit of the democracy fled from such contaminating approaches? Rome, whose proud banner once waved triumphant over a conquered world, degenerated in the pursuit of sensual delights, into a band of fiddlers and dancers, and the democratic party of New York, founded in the spirit of Jefferson, and emulating for many years the noble efforts of a Jackson and a Tompkins, has, in the hands of political gamblers, been degraded by practices which would dishonor the resorts of a Peter Funk in cast-off clothing; cheating the sentiment of the people of the state and nation; cheating a great and confiding party, whose principles they put on as a disguise, for the purpose of enabling them to cheat; cheating the convention which admitted them to seats; cheating the delegations who trusted them; cheating everybody and everything with which they came into contact except Mr. Douglas, their nominee."

Such is the character of the men and of the proceedings which placed Mr. Douglas in nomination, as given by Mr. Dickinson, whose character and standing are known to the people of the United States. What the purpose of the party, who sustain the nomination thus made, is, appears in the following extract from an address published by Messrs. Miles Taylor, Geo. E. Pugh, and Albert Rust, and dated "DEMOCRATIC NATIONAL EXECUTIVE COMMITTEE ROOMS, WASHINGTON CITY, July 18, 1860." They say:

"It remains for us to add, as the sentiment of the Democratic National Committee, and as the universal sentiment of the supporters of Douglas and Johnson, THAT NO COMPROMISE WHATEVER IS ADMISSIBLE. *We desire to ascertain the strength of the national democracy in every state, North and South,* AND WE INTEND TO ASCERTAIN IT. We have made no proposition for a joint electoral ticket in any state, and earnestly exhort you to reject such propositions indignantly whenever and wherever made. If we have any friends in any state, let those friends call a state convention at once, and nominate a full electoral ticket, pledged to the exclusive support of Douglas and Johnson. We can agree to nothing else, because to acknowledge the right of a factious minority to dictate their own terms of co-operation—suffer them to violate the solemn professions of the democratic party, and trample under foot our democratic usages—would be to disband the national organization at once. Do not fail, therefore, to act immediately; assemble yourselves everywhere, by states, by counties, and neighborhoods; take no counsel, listen to no suggestion from those who have shamefully deserted the national democracy. Every vote for Breckenridge and Lane, is a vote, indirectly at least, for Lincoln and Hamlin; a vote for inaugurating an 'irrepressible conflict' between the North and the South, and, therefore, a vote for the disunion of the states. Be not deceived by plausible assertions of your enemies. Breckenridge and Lane have no strength, not the least, in any of the Northern states. They will not receive one electoral vote in the North, and except perhaps in three or four Northern states, will not have even an electoral ticket.

"On the other hand if the Southern democracy should now desert the democracy of the North, it would be an end of the alliance between them. What remains then to the South if we would maintain the Constitution, the Union, and the integrity and usages of the Democratic party, but the cordial support and consequent election of Douglas and Johnson?"

We add one other extract from the

Washington correspondent of the Philadelphia (Forney's) **Press**, admitted to be a special organ of Mr. Douglas. Hear him. He says :

" In that event in case none of the candidates receive a majority of the electoral vote, neither the friends of DOUGLAS, nor those of Bell and LINCOLN will be foolish enough to let the election go to the House. If they permit that the above scheme of the seceders will be carried out to the letter. It would be death to every one of them. Bell, if there are two democratic tickets in the South, will receive a majority of the Southern states. *An arrangement will be made before the electoral college meets, in accordance with which Bell's electoral vote will unite either with Douglas or with Lincoln, provided* that two will have received enough states to elect. Some suggest, perhaps, in that event, Mr. Douglas as President, and Mr. Everett as Vice-President. *The offices could easily be divided. The Union men taking the South, and the other party the North.* The electors would then meet at the appointed time, and cast the vote for their respective states in harmony with the agreement entered into, thus throwing the seceders out of office, and sending them, even in their own states, up Salt river." —[*See Phila. Press, July* 18, 1860.]

Here we have the declaration of Mr. LINCOLN, that ALL THE STATES MUST BECOME FREE, " OR ELSE THEY MUST BECOME SLAVE."

Upon this issue Gov. Richardson tells us that there is no alternative but a war after the manner of John Brown, or purchase. He tells us that no one believes that slavery will be carried into New Jersey or into the territories, and that, therefore, there is no alternative between a war upon the south, or a *mortgage* of the *white man*, that the proceeds may emancipate the *black ;* and yet with this exhibit we are told by Mr. Forney's Press that there is to be an under-

standing that, in case there is cause to fear that Mr. Breckenridge will be returned to the House as one of the three highest candidates, then " Bell's electoral vote will unite either with Douglas, or with LINCOLN, provided that two will have received states enough to elect," and that " some will suggest, perhaps, in that event, Mr. DOUGLAS as President, and Mr. Everett as Vice-President," adding, as matters of course, that " *The offices could easily be divided, the Union men taking the South, and the other party the North"!!!*

Now, is it not strange that, opposed as Mr. Douglas and his leading friends say they are to Mr. LINCOLN's anti-slavery platform, one of the leading papers, in his interest, shall, at this early day, openly avow a purpose to unite with Mr. Lincoln to defeat the election of Breckenridge upon an agreed plan of a "division" of the offices? What position is Mr. Lincoln to take in the new firm? Is he to be Secretary of State and heir apparent? Such a suggestion is preposterous. It is possible that some few of the partisans of Mr. Douglas, and even Mr. Douglas himself, may prefer Lincoln to Breckenridge, but Mr. Bell and his friends never. Mr. Bell is not, and none of his friends can be, a party to such an arrangement. His nomination was made in good faith, as an earnest by the very respectable body who met at Baltimore, that there is a strong and influential body at the North, who, not only disavow and utterly condemn Mr. LINCOLN's warfare on the South, but as a pledge that their influence will be exerted to quiet the apprehensions and to protect the rights of the South. Mr. Bell was selected because he was an eminent Southern statesman, able and fearless in the discharge of his duty, whom no threats could intimidate, and no office could purchase. To suppose that he or his friends will unite in an arrangement with Mr. *Lincoln* and his friends to make Mr. Douglas President, under an agreed division of the offices, argues an utter ignorance of his character, and of the character and purpose of the gallant Southerners, who will rally, in support of the Union and the Constitution, around his name as their candidate. Nor do I believe that Mr. Lincoln and his friends will be a party to such a union. They will, no doubt, willingly accept of such aid as Mr. Douglas and his friends can give them to elect Mr Lincoln. They may even promise to take Mr. Douglas as their candidate in 1864, *if he will get on their platform;* "but they will not go for Mr. Douglas now, for, if what Mr. Dickinson says of the New York delegates be true, or even approaching the truth, Mr. Lincoln and his backers would not accept their guarantee that there would be a fair division of the offices."

But out of the fullness of the heart the mouth speaketh. This proposition for a union with *Lincoln*, to defeat the election of Breckenridge, may be the shadow of events to come. Mr. Douglas and his friends denounce Lincoln as a disunionist. It is admitted that if the friends of Douglas, Breckenridge, and Bell, in New York, Pennsylvania and New Jersey, have each a separate ticket, the vote of these states will be given to Lincoln, although it is known that, as between him and either of his opponents, he would be defeated. To refuse to unite upon a single ticket, therefore, is to give the votes of these states to Lincoln against the known will of the people. Under these circumstances, the friends of Mr. Breckenridge and of Mr. Bell are willing to unite on a single ticket, but Mr. Douglas and his friends refuse to unite in this arrangement, and have selected Southern men, representing slaveholding states, to issue their mandate forbidding it, and wherefore? It is, they say, because Mr. Douglas is the nominee of the regular "organization ! !" Do they wish to kill the *"organization"?* Of what use will the organization be if Mr. Lincoln is elected? They wish, they say, to ascertain the strength of their party in all the states, *and intend to ascertain it*, for what purpose? They cannot believe that they can elect Mr. Douglas. They may believe that they can elect Mr. *Lincoln.* Why should they prefer Mr. Lincoln to Mr. Breckenridge, or Mr. Bell? To refuse to unite on a single ticket is to vote against Mr. Bell as well as against Mr. Breckenridge ! Have the *Southern* partisans of Mr. Douglas agreed to divide the offices with the Northern partisans of Mr. Lincoln? and is this proclamation of this Southern branch of Mr. Douglas's Committee, a performance of their part of the arrangement, by which Mr. Lincoln is to be elected, that he may make them the recipients of the Southern offices? But this proclamation claims that they are the true "organization ! !"

THE ELECTION OF MR. LINCOLN.

The reader who has carefully read the preceding pages must have been impressed with the fact, that from the date of my conversation with Daniel P. Cook, at Washington city, in 1817, when he disclosed to me, the purpose, originating with John Q. Adams, of organizing a Northern party, on the basis of opposition to slavery, as a means of obtaining the political control of the government of the United States, my mind was deeply impressed with the apprehension that the organization of a sectional party for the avowed purpose of emancipating Southern slaves, in violation, of the recognised constitutional rights of the Southern slave-owners, must necessarily create a counteracting, Southern political organization, in defence and for the protection of the rights and interests so assailed ; and that, although I was intimately connected by marriage with Mr. Adams, and at the time of his election occupied a position, social, personal, and political, which would have secured the most cordial and efficient support of Messrs. Adams and Clay and their "*associates*," if I had united with them when urged to do so, in the winter of 1824–25, by my nephew Mr. Cook, and my personal friend J. Scott of Missouri, who, in disregard of the known will of their constituents, were anxious to secure the aid of my pen and my press to sustain them before the people.

I not only refused to unite with them in that conspiracy against "the Union and the Constitution," and devoted my energies and influence in support of the election of General Jackson, but when I saw that General Jackson, in violation of the solemn pledges which he had himself given, and which I had again and again repeated in his behalf, had entered into the conspiracy, inaugurated by Martin Van Buren and William H. Crawford, to exert the whole influence of federal and party patronage, to elect Mr. Van Buren his successor,* I refused to unite with him in that conspiracy, and refused to take his hand in the presence of his Cabinet and of the greater part of the members of Congress, although I well

* See the disclosures made by William B. Lewis in his letters and memoranda given to Parton, and published in the last volume of his Life of Jackson.

knew that the consequence of my refusal would be to provoke his bitterest resentment, and the loss, not only of the printing of Congress, but of the patronage of the government, then worth to me more than fifty thousand dollars per annum.

Why did I refuse to unite in the support of Mr. Van Buren ?

I gave the reason to Gen. Jackson. I told him, that as soon as Mr. Van Buren became satisfied that by the combined influence of the public patronage and the party organization, he could command the vote of the South, he would bid against Mr. Clay for the abolition vote of the North, and it was because I foresaw that the unscrupulous conspirators, who had combined to educate the people of the North into a belief that African slavery was a sin, which it was their duty to abolish, would not hesitate to make war upon the South, if they found it necessary to wage war as a means of maintaining that political ascendency which is necessary to enable them to enrich themselves and their "associates" by jobs and contracts and the plunder of the public treasury. I saw that there was no hope of defeating that corrupt combination, organized for the purpose of public plunder, but in the doctrine of "state rights" in the right of a state to appeal from the decision of the federal government to a convention of the states, the supreme power, reserved by the constitution to the states, of amending the Constitution. We believed that the Constitution created a government of limited and well-defined powers, that the powers and rights reserved to the states were not included in the powers granted to the federal government, and that as the reservations were against the federal government and the executive, legislative, and judicial, were each departments of the federal government, neither the executive, legislative, nor judiciary, nor all combined, were the proper arbiters to decide questions, involving the authority or powers under the Constitution, arising between a state and the federal government. We believed that all such questions, which necessarily must depend upon the proper construction of the Constitution, should be referred to the tribunal, to whom the exclusive control over the Constitution is given, viz.: To a convention of the states, or to the legislatures of the states acting on resolutions passed by the requisite majorities of both Houses of Congress. We did not believe that a state had the right to nullify an act which Congress had power, under the Constitution, to pass; but we did believe that the states, each in the exercise of its reserved powers, may deny the power of the federal government to enforce an act, which, under the Constitution, Congress had no power, or are forbidden to pass; and we believed that in such case it is the duty of Congress to refer the question thus arising between the state and the federal government to the states, as suggested. If the states believe the power to pass the act in question has been conferred by the Constitution, the declaration, that the power has been given made by the requisite majority of states, would be a decision in support of the act. If the requisite majority believe that the power has not been, but ought to be, given to Congress, then the requisite majority of states may confer the disputed power—and if they believe that the power has not been, and ought not to be given, then, for want of a requisite majority of states in support of the power, Congress ought not to

attempt to enforce an *unconstitutional* act. The argument of nullification was met by the declaration, that a state had a right to secede, but that a state could not, at the same time, be in the Union and out of the Union. I saw that nullification was a peaceful remedy in the Union, and that secession would necessarily bring war or disunion.*

With this view of the issue involved, finding that the appeal to the people of Pennsylvania and New Jersey had failed to effect a union on the democratic nominee, I wrote an appeal to the people of the South urging them to unite in support of Mr. Bell as the compromise candidate, but I became satisfied that such a union could not be made, and I, therefore, did not publish it, and reserved my influence to be exerted on Mr. Lincoln in case of his election.

MR. CORWIN.

When Congress met in December, 1860, Mr. Corwin of Ohio was made chairman of the committee of *thirty-three*, to whom the question as between the North and the South was referred. Mr. Lincoln had married the sister of my nephew's wife. I had known him personally when he was in Congress, and hoped that he could be induced to exert his influence, so as to satisfactorily adjust pending issues. I called on Mr. Corwin and requested him to unite with me in a letter to Mr. Lincoln. He refused to do so. I then wrote to a nephew living in Springfield, asking him to ascertain whether Mr. Lincoln could be induced to exert his influence to prevent the secession of the Southern states. I received a reply, saying that

* See the discussion on nullification and secession in the U. S. Telegraph and the Richmond Enquirer and Globe from 1833 to 1836.

my letter had been submitted to Mr. Lincoln, and that he would write to me in a few days. On the same day I was told that the committee of thirteen of the Senate, to whom had been referred the same question, had met, and that Mr. Davis and Mr. Toombs of Georgia, on the part of the South, had declared that if the Northern members would, in good faith, accept Mr. Crittenden's proposition to extend the Missouri compromise line to the Pacific, as the adjustment of the slavery question, it would be also accepted in good faith by the South, and that this proposition had been rejected by the Northern members of that committee ; and believing that there was no hope of an adjustment without the active interposition of Mr. Lincoln, and hoping that I could, by a personal appeal, induce him to come to Washington for that purpose, I resolved to consult President Buchanan, and if he approved, to go immediately to Springfield. On my way to the White House, I met Mr. Corwin, who seemed much excited, and said, " We have resolved to take Wade's speech in the Senate as our programme, and if the South secede, we will, with the consent of England, organize a strong government, including Canada, and the other British American provinces, we will declare a protectorate over Mexico, and make it a refuge for runaway negroes and free blacks, and will wage a war of extermination on the South. You think that you will injure us by secession—you will give us men to fight our battles."

I replied, " I understand you." I called upon the President, who urged me to go to Springfield, and authorized me in his name not only to urge upon Mr. Lincoln the necessity of his coming to Washington, but to assure

him that he would be received with all the respect due to the President elect, and that he, Mr. Buchanan, would most cordially unite in the measures necessary to preserve the Union. I consulted other influential persons, who concurred in the necessity of Mr. Lincoln's interposition. I went to Illinois. I saw Mr. Lincoln, and upon my return to Washington authorized the publication in the New York Herald, of the following letter :

(From the New York Herald.)

INTERVIEW OF DUFF GREEN WITH MR. LINCOLN ON THE CRISIS.

WASHINGTON, *Jan.* 6, 1861.

Since my dispatch of the 4th, I have seen and conversed with Duff Green upon the subject of his visit to Springfield. He speaks of Mr. Lincoln with much respect, and believes that he sincerely wishes to administer the government in such manner as to satisfy the South ; that he will not favor emancipation in the District of Columbia, nor in the forts or dockyards in the Southern states, nor will he favor an interference with the trade in slaves between the Southern states ; but says, that, having resided so long in a non-slaveholding state, Mr. Lincoln has taken an active part in opposing what he terms the extension of slavery into the territories, and believes that this constituted one of the chief issues in the late canvass, and is therefore firmly and unequivocally resolved to make no concession on this point, unless it be adjusted by an amendment to the Constitution. Mr. Lincoln, so far as his views are indicated by the journal supposed to be advised by him, believes that secession is rebellion, and is resolved to use force to suppress and punish it.

In reply to the inquiry of what will

satisfy the South, Mr. Green placed in his hands a copy of Mr. Crittenden's resolutions, and said that he had been told that, although Messrs. Davis, of Mississippi, and Toombs, of Georgia, voted against these resolutions as being unsatisfactory to them personally, they had both said in the Senate's committee, that if tendered by the other side in good faith, as a basis of adjustment, they would accept them for the South.

Mr. Green endeavored to satisfy Mr. Lincoln that the movement in the South is not the result of any personal objection to him, nor of a desire or a purpose to dissolve the Union; but of an earnest belief of the necessity of additional constitutional guarantees for the protection of their rights in the Union.

He said the South believes that the federal government is a compact between independent sovereign states, which, at the time of their acceptance of the Constitution, by refusing to create an umpire with authority to decide questions arising between them and the common government, and reserving the powers not delegated or inhibited to them by the Constitution, had each reserved the right for itself to judge of infractions of the Constitution, and of the mode and measure of redress. That at the time of the adoption of the Constitution all the states held slaves. That the Constitution not only recognized the right of property in slaves, but authorized the continuance of the African slave-trade, and made an express provision for the surrender of fugitive slaves; that no one at that time could have anticipated that the time would come when, having sold their slaves to the South, and received pay for them as property, entitled to the protection of the federal government, the Northern states would organize a sectional majority, and attain the control of the federal government, upon a pledge that the whole influence and patronage of that government will be exerted in a continuous and persistent effort to emancipate the slaves, who have so much increased in numbers and in value; that the Southern states cannot consent to remain as members of a government which is to be permanently under the control of a sectional majority, organized as a political sectional party, on the basis of a warfare on the institutions of the South; that the effect of remaining in such a Union will be the same as if they had been a conquered province; that if they had been conquered by the sword, and held subject to the despotic will of a sectional government, that government could impose no heavier or more disgraceful burdens than can be imposed upon them by the same sectional government which, having conquered them through the ballot box, wields the sword to enforce their will, and compel them to pay the taxes, and to bear the burdens imposed under the forms of laws passed by the same inflexible sectional Northern majority; that such a condition of the government deprives the South of all that is valuable in government, and subjects them to the caprice of the worst possible form of despotism; that he had become satisfied that the members of Congress who had been elected as members of that sectional majority are using the pretence that they are opposed to the extension of slavery in the territories, as a means of preserving their sectional organization, because they see that if they relinquish that pretence, and permit the question of slavery in the territories to be adjusted, then the South will become a part of the United States, and have its due proportionate influence in the government; that it will then be a part of the whole, instead of being, as as it is now and must forever remain, a mere sectional minority, with no rights, or powers, or influence in the government, except to bear burthens and pay taxes, so long as opposition to slavery is made the text of political ascendency. To the suggestion that if the present agitation be quieted by the extension of the Missouri compromise line to the Pacific, the question will be revived by an attempt to absorb Mexico, and to extend the system of slavery into Mexico, Mr. Green urged that since Cain slew his brother the great question of society had been what part of the joint products of capital and labor shall go to capital and what to labor; that this question had resolved itself into two systems—wages labor and slave labor; that Mr. Seward had admitted this truth, and had endeavored to array the North and the wages labor of the North against the South by assuming that there is an " irrepressible conflict" between the two systems; whereas the truth is, that the conflict is not between the systems, but between the capital and labor which constitutes the system of wages labor; and urged that this truth is forcibly illustrated by the effect of wages labor in England and Wales and of slave labor in the South; that after the confiscation of the nunneries and monasteries which, under the Papal system, were charged with providing for the poor, that duty was devolved upon the parishes; and the conflict between capital which gave employment and the wages labor of England and Wales was such (as appears by official

returns to Parliament) that in thirty-eight years, from 1813 to 1850 inclusive, the sum levied in England and Wales alone as poor rates was more than one thousand three hundred and eighty-eight millions of dollars, show-that the "irrepressible conflict" between the capital and wages labor of England and Wales had applied the lash of hunger and nakedness with such force as to reduce the wages so much below the point of subsistence that capital was compelled to levy a tax as poor rates to the amount of more than one thousand three hundred and eighty-eight millions of dollars to prevent their poor from starving; whilst from the commencement of the system until now not one penny has been levied as poor rates to prevent the suffering of the Southern slaves. In England and Wales, when capital pays labor the stipulated wages, labor has no further claims on capital short of the work-house and the poor-rates. In the South, when the slave child is born or the slave is purchased, the law creates a contract between the slaves and the master, and as they are required to labor, so he is required to provide for, to feed, clothe and protect them in infancy and old age, in sickness and in health; and the master who fails to discharge this duty is not only punishable under the laws, but would be put under the ban of public opinion. He urged that the measures and policy of England are dictated by her commercial interests; that her manufactures were the source of her wealth and prosperity; that having a legislative control over parts of Africa and India, she exchanges her manufactures for the tropical products of Africa and India, which products she sells to other European nations, having few or no tropical colonies, and thus collects a tribute in the shape of commercial profits from those who would otherwise be her competitors in the markets of the world. That such being the interests of England, the influence of her pulpit, her press, her schools, her poets, her philosophers, and her statesmen, was exerted in furtherance of her policy, dictated by her necessities. As she had the legislative control over the commerce of parts of Africa and India, and could regulate that commerce so as to monopolize its profits, while having no control over the products of slave labor in Cuba, Brazil and the United States, and therefore could not monopolize its profits, it became her interest to make a war of public opinion against African slavery. New England is a servile copyist of Old England. Having transferred her slaves to the Southern states, it was a natural and easy process for John Q. Adams to organize a sectional anti-slavery party in New England, which, originating in an abstract idea that slavery is cruel, unjust and sinful, although confined at first to a few fanatics, has progressed until it has become a powerful political sentiment, which, availing itself of other exciting causes, has become a majority, not of the whole, but of the Northern States, and having thus placed the power of the government in the hands of a minority of the people, are resolved to enforce the absolute control of this minority by a civil war, under the pretence that they are a majority and therefore authorized to enforce their party platform by the sword. To this he said the South will not submit. She will not become a subject province, conquered by the ballot-box. She will not remain part of a government which is pledged to exert its power and influence to dis-

parage and deprive her of the rights which it is the duty of that government to protect.

In reply and comment on the idea of the excellence of Northern civilization, and of the barbarism and sinfulness of slavery as enforced by Northern schoolmen, philosophers, and partisan presses and pulpits, Mr. Green urged that there is an inscrutable law regulating all created things, which provides that wherever the stronger and the weaker are brought in conflict there is no alternative but war and extermination, or else subjection and protection. For in the beginning the earth brought forth grass and herb yielding seed after his kind, and the tree yielding fruit, whose seed was in itself after its kind; and God created great whales, and every living creature that moveth, which the waters brought forth abundantly after their kind, and every winged fowl after his kind; and God made the earth after his kind, and cattle after their kind, and everything that creepeth on the earth after his kind; and God created man in his own image, and gave him dominion over the fish of the sea, and over the fowl of the air, and over every living thing that moveth upon the earth; male and female created he them; and he blessed them, and said, "Be fruitful and multiply and replenish the earth, and subdue it." Such was the original creation. By man's transgression "came sin and death, and all our woes;" and hence, as all things were created after their kind, the consequence of sin is, that the stronger preys upon the weaker; and thus, when two races of men are brought in contact, there is no alternative but war and extermination, or subjection and protection. He referred to the fact that the aborigines in the North had perished before the march of Mr. Seward's Northern civilization, while the effect of the protection given to the three hundred thousand African slaves by the Southern civilization, had been to increase their numbers in a few years to more than four millions. As a more forcible illustration of this truth he referred to the fact that, instead of waging a war of extermination, as did the Puritans of New England, the Jesuits carried with them into Spanish America the Roman system of subjection and protection, and that the resulting consequence is, that instead of being exterminated by the remorseless progress of Northern philanthropy, there are at this time seven millions of Indians in Mexico—on a territory but little greater than two of the American states. To the idea that the South wish to acquire Mexico for the purpose of extending slavery into Mexico, Mr. Green replied, that the South cannot acquire Mexico without the consent of the North, which consent it is believed the North will not give, unless it be for the purpose—as avowed by Mr. Wade and others—of making war upon the present sytem of labor in Mexico, exterminating the Indians of Mexico as they have exterminated the Indians of New England. Mr. Green read an extract of a letter addressed by him to Lord John Russel in 1858, as follows:

"There seems to be an impression in England, and especially among the creditors of Mexico, that the United States desire to annex Mexico, and some look to annexation as resulting in the payment of the Mexican debt. The United States understand too well what would be the consequence of annexation to permit it, if all the world wished it. We refused to keep Mexico when we had it. We paid for and kept part of her unoccupied territory; we do not want her people. They are unfitted for such a government as ours, and we would not assume the responsibility of governing them if it were gratuitously tendered to us; much less would we pay their debts and bring them into our Union to become a disturbing, if not a controlling, influence in our politics. We would not accept of Mexico upon condition that we should govern them; much less will we pay their debts upon the condition that they are to govern us."

He urged that to force the system of free white labor into Mexico and the Southern states involves necessarily a war of races, to end in the extermination of four millions of slaves and seven millions of Mexicans. That, as to the extension of slavery in the territories, that is necessarily a question of population and of climate, and that the number of slaves and the influence of slaveholders will not be increased by the extension of the line of thirty-six degrees and thirty minutes to the Pacific; that it is not more slave states, but the acknowledgment of their rights and the peaceable enjoyment of them that is required by the South; that the question of slavery shall no longer be made a pretence for the organization of a sectional political party, and that without this concession it is impossible to maintain the Union. From the manner in which these suggestions were received by Mr. Lincoln, Mr. Green believes, although Mr. Lincoln did not say so, that he desires a satisfactory adjustment, and that, although he is opposed to the further extension of slavery and will not himself recommend any measure having that tendency, he will nevertheless not only acquiesce, but rejoice, if the Congress and the states will, by the adoption of Mr. Crittenden's resolutions, restore confidence and avert disunion.

Mr. Green believes that the movement in the South may yet be so modified as to accomplish this, if the people and the legislatures in the Northern states are earnest in their desire to preserve the Union, and instead of attempting coercion and intimidation, will recognize the fact that the whole South insist that the Constitution is a compact between sovereign states, which in case of secession are to be recognized and treated as such ; and that inasmuch as the concession asked by the South is indispensable to the maintenance of their rights within the Union, and therefore vital to them, whereas it will deprive no state of the North of any single right or impair in any wise a single interest, he does hope that there is yet sufficient intelligence and patriotism in the North, sufficient respect for the rights of the Southern states, and sufficient love of the Union on the basis of the original compact between the states, to induce the people of the North to prefer a peaceable adjustment to civil war. The question of peace or war, of union or dis-union, rests with the people of the North. Mr. Green says that he has endeavored to discharge his duty, and despairing of any action by Mr. Lincoln, or by Congress, unless the people impel them by an immediate and forcible expression of their wishes, he declares that upon the people of the Northern states rests the responsibility. All that the South demands is their equal rights within the Union, or independence out of it. They will not consent to be a conquered province, whether that conquest be by the ballot-box or the sword. The leaders in Congress are clamorous for civil war. Mr. Green hopes and believes that the people prefer peace, and will therefore urge the adoption of the amendments to the Constitution, indispensable to the preservation of the Union."

COMMENT.

The candid reader will see, in this statement of my interview with Mr. Lincoln, that my purpose was to arouse the people of the North to a sense of the necessity of giving the guarantee, in the shape of an amendment to the Constitution, which would protect the rights and interests of the South in the Union, and thus prevent secession. Not content with this appeal to the North, I endeavored, with whatever influence I could exert, to arrest the secession movement, by urging upon the members of Congress from the Southern states that Mr. Lincoln was the representative of a minority even in the Northern states ; that there was a majority in both Houses of Congress opposed to the faction which he represented ; and that as the majority of the people and of Congress were with the South, it would be most unwise to abandon the government by withdrawing our Senators and Representatives from Congress. In the folly and delirium of the moment, a few political leaders, impelled by the just resentments of the Southern people, organized the Southern Confederacy. My family and my sympathies were in the South. Deeply regretting the secession movement, and fearing the disasters which seemed to me inevitable unless we could induce the Northwest to unite with the South, I urged upon Mr. Davis the necessity of maintaining the control of the mouth of the Ohio, and of tendering to the Northwest a union with the South. I urged him to permit me to go to Washington and confer with Mr. Lincoln as to the terms of peace, so that I might, in a semi-official form, present an argument explanatory of a plan of adjustment which would be accepted by the Northwest, and thus terminate the war. After some hesitation he authorized me to write to Mr. Lincoln, asking permission to visit Washington. To that letter I received no reply.

MR. LINCOLN'S PLAN OF RECONSTRUCTION.

I was in Richmond when it was occupied by the federal troops, and called upon Mr. Lincoln. He received me with great kindness. I said: "I went to Springfield to urge you to exert your influence to prevent the war. I come now to ascertain upon what terms we can make peace." He replied: "If you desire peace, all that will be required of you is to acknowledge the authority of the United States. If you wish to keep your slaves, vote against the amendments to the Constitution. I cannot recall my proclamations. Whether they are binding or not will be a question for the courts." He said further, that he came to Washington resolved to carry out in good faith the pledges which he had given to me when I was in Springfield; that at his request his friends in Congress had, on the last night of the session, passed the resolution proposing an amendment to the Constitution prohibiting Congress from any interference with the institution of slavery in the slaveholding states; and said that he did not commence the war, and was anxious for peace.

This conversation took place in the presence of Judge Campbell, and it was in consequence of interviews which Judge Campbell and I and others then had with him that Mr. Lincoln authorized the commanding officer, then in charge of the federal army in Richmond, to invite the members of the Legislature to be convened, that by recognizing the authority of the federal government the relations between Virginia and the Northern states should be restored on the basis of the pledges which he had given through General Singleton, who had been some weeks in Richmond, authorized, as he said, by Mr. Lincoln to give assurances that all that he required was for the seceding states to acknowledge the authority of the United States.

After the death of Mr. Lincoln, I addressed to General Singleton a note to which the following is a reply:

WASHINGTON CITY, D. C.,
March 21, 1866.

DEAR SIR: I have received your note of the 19th, and as I am on the eve of starting for my home in the West I shall be compelled to reply with more brevity than is satisfactory to myself.

I was authorized by Mr. Lincoln to say, and did say freely, while in Richmond last winter, that he, Mr. Lincoln, asked no concession from the South, but a cessation of hostilities, and submission to the Constitution and laws of the United States. That if any states in rebellion would cease hostilities, elect their Senators and Representatives to the Congress of the United States, and ask to be recognized as a state of the Union, to enjoy her full rights and immunities as such (non obstante slavery), that he would be in favor of recognizing such states, and of restoring the people thereof, as if no difficulties had intervened. That his proclamation of emancipation had exhausted his authority over the subject of slavery, the legal effect of which, with all other questions growing out of the war, must be left to the determination of the courts.

I have papers and other evidence to establish beyond cavil what I have written; and it affords me great satisfaction to add that Mr. Lincoln's views and wishes on the subject had undergone no change up to the day of his unfortunate and lamentable death.

I am very truly, &c.,

JAS. W. SINGLETON.

Gen. DUFF GREEN.

CONCLUSION.

Upon turning to the resolution referred to by Mr. Lincoln, I find it to be in the following words:

"That no amendment shall be made to the Constitution which shall authorize or give to Congress power to abolish or interfere, within any state, with the domestic institutions thereof, including that of persons held to labor or servitude by the laws of said state."

This resolution was offered by Mr. Corwin, of Ohio, as a substitute for the following, offered by Mr. Adams of Massachusetts:

"No amendment of this Constitution, having for its objects any interference with the relation between their citizens and those described in Section II. of the fourth article of the Constitution, or other persons, shall originate with any state that does not recognize that relation within its own limits, or shall be valid without the consent of every one of the States comprising the Union."

The substitute offered by Mr. Corwin was unanimously adopted on the 3d of March, 1861, by both Houses of Congress, and, as it now appears, upon the recommendation of Mr. Lincoln, as a means of arresting the secession movement. Who can doubt that if he had come to Washington in December, 1860, as I urged him to do, and had then exerted the like influence in favor of the passage of Mr. Crittenden's resolution, extending the Missouri compromise line to the Pacific—I say who can doubt that his influence, if it had then been exerted, could have passed Mr. Crittenden's resolution, which, if it had then been passed, would have prevented the war?

Let the candid reader compare these resolutions and he will see that the concessions proposed by that which under Mr. Lincoln's advice was unanimously adopted by the radicals after the commencement of the secession movement recognized fully the right of property in slaves, and admitted it to be the duty of the government to protect that right of property, and that recognizing that right it nevertheless adhered to their party platform, regardless of the constitutional rights of the South.

I quote the amendment, however, as proof that the purpose of the radical faction was to control the patronage and powers of the federal government; that their sympathy for the slave was a mere pretence, as a cover for the jobs and contracts which would enable the "associates" to plunder the treasury and enrich themselves at the expense of the people; to admonish them that the present public debt is the fruit of the war; that I, for one, believe that a wise use of the public credit, as the basis of an abundant and cheap currency, will soon restore the prosperity of the whole country, uniting the South and the North as one people in the development of our vast industrial resources; and to warn the men who, having profited by the war to enrich themselves, now seek to control the legislation of Congress, that they may continue their onerous system of taxation, and multiply their riches, by converting their paper money into gold; that they of all others are most interested in the early and satisfactory adjustment of pending issues. The South have accepted the terms proposed by Mr. Lincoln. The demands of the radical Congress are a violation of the terms on which our armies and our people agreed to terminate the war; and it is no less the interests than the duty of all, of the rich and of the poor, to unite and make the peace a sincere, real union of all the people, and all the states, in support of a common government and of a common prosperity.

I would warn the fund-holders that Congress has no right to deprive the Southern states of their representation in either House of Congress, and that the continued exclusion of Southern Senators and Representatives may create an issue as to the authority of the radical Congress, which may seriously impair the value of public securities.

THE END.

NATIONAL LABOR CONGRESS,

Baltimore, Md., August 20, 1866.

LETTER AND REMARKS,

BY

BEN. E. GREEN,

SOLICITOR AND GENERAL MANAGER OF BRANCHES

OF THE

AMERICAN INDUSTRIAL AGENCY.

O F F I C E S :

Nos. 40 and 42 BROADWAY, NEW YORK.

PLEASE READ AND HAND TO YOUR NEIGHBOR.

New York:

BENJ. D. BENSON, STATIONER, 17 NASSAU STREET.

1866.

NATIONAL LABOR CONGRESS.

BALTIMORE. 21st August, 1866.

The following letter was submitted by the President:

"AMERICAN INDUSTRIAL AGENCY,
Nos. 40 AND 42 BROADWAY,
NEW YORK, August 20, 1866.

"To the President of the National Labor Convention, Baltimore, Maryland:

"SIR: Allow me to submit through you to the Convention the following suggestions:

"1. In England the compensation of labor (wages) has been reduced so much below the point of subsistence that one-tenth of the whole population are paupers, and the official returns show that they were compelled to add ten per cent. of the whole rental of the kingdom to wages in the shape of *poor rates*, to prevent the suffering poor from starving.

"2. The first savings bank was established in England in 1804 by a woman, who, as a charity, agreed to receive pennies from the laboring poor, repayable at Christmas with five per cent. per annum interest. In 1856 the Savings Fund Commissioners had invested more than $170,000,000 of the savings funds in the public debt of England, paying the depositors less than three per cent. per annum.

"3. The official returns show that in 1865 the deposits in the savings banks of New England and the State of New York were as follows:

	"Sav's Dep'ts.	No. Deps.	Average.
"New England	$115,977,000	527,702	$219
State of New York	115,472,000	460,000	250
Tot. amount savings deposited	$231,449,000		

"4. This large sum is made up chiefly by the surplus earnings (savings) of our laboring classes, yielding them at most four to six per cent. per annum.

"5. The official returns of the census of 1850 and 1860 show that the average profits on the capital invested in 'mining, manufacturing, and the mechanic arts,' were more than fifty per cent. per annum.

"6. Under the management of the savings banks, the labor, which produces and deposits the above-mentioned $231,449,000, receives only from four to six per cent. per annum, while the capital invested in 'mining, manufacturing, and the mechanic arts,' receives more than fifty per cent.

"7. The early restoration of the industrial interests of the South is indispensable to the prosperity of the laboring men of the North; because the South produces the raw material, on which depends the profitable employment of a large part of the capital and labor of the North.

"8. It is by the use of cheap machinery, purchased with cheap money, that capital receives a profit of fifty per cent. per annum.

"9. The great question, as between the more civilized nations of the world who use machinery, is how each can sell their surplus manufactures to the less civilized nations, who do not use machinery.

"10. The great question of civilized society is, what proportion of the joint product of capital and labor shall be given to capital and what to labor?

"11. The great question for the consideration of your Convention is, how to secure for labor its due proportion of the joint product of capital and labor?

"12. The American Industrial Agency has been organized for the purposes—1st, of restoring the prosperity of the agricultural interests of the South, which produces the raw material, on which so large a part of the capital and labor of the North depends ; 2d, of giving to the industrial classes a larger dividend on their surplus earnings (or savings) than they now receive, and at the same time to create an aggregated and accumulative capital, whereby, 3d, to aid the laboring classes, and especially skilled artisans, to become shareholders in manufacturing companies, on which they can realize their due proportion of the fifty per cent. profit of manufacturing, instead of receiving only four to six per cent. on their savings, as under the present system of deposits.

"Thus, say five or more artisans, competent to 'boss' the several branches of any profitable manufacture, requiring a capital of $100,000, associate themselves under a proper charter with other persons competent to manage their finances, and they together can advance $20,000. The American Industrial Agency proposes to advance the additional $80,000 required, with the understanding that, although in case the profits are 50 per cent. on the $100,000, the $20,000 would be entitled to but $10,000 of the $50,000 earned, yet the owners of the $20,000 shall, in addition to the $10,000 dividend on their shares, receive one third of the surplus above 12 per cent. on the $80,000 ; and that the operatives and shareholders of such manufacturing company shall be permitted to purchase the shares of their company held by the Agency at par, in which case the funds received therefor by the Agency can be used for the further encouragement and promotion of other industrial interests.

"13. The large and accumulative fund created by the surplus earnings of the laboring classes, if properly applied, will be amply sufficient, not only to restore the agricultural prosperity of the Southern States, but also to build up a system of manufactures, giving more profitable employment to the laboring classes, and elevating them to the position of capitalists.

"Respectfully submitted,
"BEN. E. GREEN,
"*Solicitor and General Manager*
"*of Branches.*"

NATIONAL LABOR CONVENTION, }
24th *August*, 1866.   }

Mr. GEO. H. SPAULDING, President of the Iron Moulders' Association, Boston, Massachusetts, moved that the communication from the American Industrial Agency, now in the hands of the Committee on Address, be taken from that committee and referred to the Committee on Coöperation, with instructions to report thereon immediately.

Mr. ALEXANDER TROUP, of Boston, Massachusetts, Chairman of Committee on Coöperation, suggested that the communication referred to by Mr. Spaulding was now in the hands of the Committee on Resolutions, who would be prepared to report thereon in a very few minutes.

Mr. ROBERT GILLASPEY, of Baltimore, suggested that there was a gentleman present, who represented the American Industrial Agency, and moved that he be invited to address the Convention for fifteen minutes, which was unanimously carried.

BEN. E. GREEN, Esq., then addressed the Convention :

Mr. President and Gentlemen of the Convention :

I know the value of time, and will detain you but a few minutes. I am a practical man, and come here for a practical purpose. I came "to grind an axe ;" not a private, exclusive axe, but one which is as free to your use as to mine. It is the working-man's axe; and I want your aid to grind it so sharp, that it will cut through the root of that power which has heretofore held the white laboring man of the North as much the slave of capital as the negro ever was of his Southern master.

You have met here for the purpose of considering what are the best practicable means of improving the material, moral, intellectual, and social position of the laboring classes. You disclaim any political purpose, and all connection with political parties, except so far as may be necessary to secure your object.

As I have said in the communication which I had the honor to address to you through your President, the great question of civilized society is, what portion of the joint product of capital and labor shall be paid to capital, and what to labor?

As, in the great struggle of life, the first question is how to obain the means of living in comfort—(the question of mental, moral, intellectual, and social elevation comes next)—so the first question for your consideration is, how to secure for labor its due proportion of the joint product of capital and labor?

For the purpose of securing to the laboring man time to enjoy the society of his wife and children, and to improve his mind, so that the talents, which God has given him, shall not remain "wrapped up in the napkin" of constant and unremitting toil, you advocate the eight hours law.

Suppose you succeed in that, and a law is passed by Congress and by every State Legislature, making eight hours a legal day's work.

Those, who are employed on public works, may not find their wages proportionately reduced, and, so far as they are concerned, you will have accomplished your object. But the great majority of working men are dependent on private capital for employment, and they will then find themselves met with the same old question between capital and labor. The private employer will say : "Very well. You reduce by law the length of time twenty per cent. I

reduce the amount of wages in the same proportion. Where I gave one dollar for ten hours, I will give eight cents for eight hours' labor."

How can you practically meet and decide this question in favor of labor? Strikes are admitted to be a failure.

The only remedy for *labor* is by forming coöperative associations, and by aggregating the surplus earnings of *labor*, so as to form a *capital* to be used in the interests of *labor*, as proposed by the American Industrial Agency.

You ask how the aggregation of capital is to be effected, and where the money is to come from to put these coöperative companies in motion.

I answer that the returns for 1865 show that the amount of deposits in the savings banks of New England and the state of New York alone amounted to the enormous sum of $231,449,000 ; that the number of depositors in the New England states was 527,762, and in the state of New York 460,000 The average of the sums deposited was in the New England states $219 in the state of New York $250. These small sums, $219 or $250, separately avail nothing towards putting into operation the machinery to give profitable employment to the white laboring men of the North. But aggregated— brought together and capitalized—by being deposited in an institution where it will be used in the interests of labor, as proposed by the American Industrial Agency, they will create a power that will do more to benefit the laboring classes than all other devices which have yet been proposed, put together.

This immense sum—two hundred and thirty-one millions of dollars—is made up chiefly by the savings of the industrial classes. At present the depositors get only four per cent. per annum—rarely more. We propose to guarantee six per cent. per annum on deposits, and to use the capital thus aggregated and placed with us—first, to aid in restoring the agricultural prosperity of the Southern states, and, second, to aid laboring men in the formation of coöperative associations by advancing to them the required capital.

The official returns of the census of 1850 and 1860 show that the average profit on the capital invested in "mining, manufacturing, and other mechanic arts," is more than fifty per cent., while the interest received by depositors in the savings banks is rarely more than four per cent.

You, as mechanics, know that the stock taken by the *Agency* in these coöperative manufacturing companies will pay fifty per cent. on the capital advanced ; and we know that money advanced to aid Southern planters to cultivate their lands and increase the supply of cotton and tobacco will pay (in interest on loans, in commissions on sales of produce, in insurance profit and banking profit) at least twenty per cent. We propose to give to depositors who will leave their money with us for six months, or longer, so that it can be thus used to aid in raising and bringing to market the Southern crop, and in aiding skilled artisans to form coöperative companies, a dividend as *quasi* or temporary stockholders of the Agency.

Gentlemen : One of your body, a delegate from Massachusetts, remarked to me in conversation that this immense sum of $231,449,000, although deposited chiefly by the laboring classes, is now used by capitalists in the interest of capital. Suppose that ten per cent. of that large sum, or $23,144,900, was deposited in an institution like ours, where it would be used in the interest of labor, and to aid laboring men to form coöperative companies, as suggested in my letter to your President, would not the first great object be accomplished for those whom you represent?

But, in this matter of deposits, the first consideration for the depositor is *security* and certainty of repayment ; next, to get the largest possible interest on the deposit consistent with safety. You have not time now to examine into our organization or the security which we offer. I do not, therefore, ask you to endorse the organization known as the American Industrial Agency, but only to endorse one of the objects, which it professes to have in view, to wit: to foster the industrial interests of the country. I only ask you to invite the laboring classes to examine the subject for themselves. I will only detain you now to say, that our plan of organization and administration contemplates that no advance of money shall be made without ample security, except in cases of subscription to the stock of coöperative manufacturing companies, and then only after thorough examination and satisfactory evidence of the character of the parties and profits of the business proposed.

Without detaining you further on this point, I hurry on to another of equal, perhaps greater, importance to those whom you represent. I refer to the revival of the agricultural industry of the South, and the necessity for an increased production of cotton. Every branch of labor, the pattern-maker, the moulder, the machinist the shipwright, the house carpenter,—all that immense aggregate of labor which finds employment in producing the agricultural instruments necessary for the culture of cotton, the machinery whereon to spin it, the houses wherein to store, and work, and sell it, the ships and railroads wherewith to move it—all these as well as those who are employed in the cotton mills; the sewing women, the little children, who have enlisted the sympathies I have heard so eloquently and forcibly expressed here; all who find employment in the production of articles either of necessity or luxury; all who wish to buy a cheap shirt or a cheap gown, are directly or indirectly interested in this great question of the abundant supply of cheap cotton. All, who throw impediments of any kind in the way of that consummation so devoutedly to be wished, are the enemies of the laboring classes.

Gentlemen, I have lived in Washington city and studied law here in Baltimore with that excellent man and able jurist, the late John Glenn, and am known to a few of you. Others of you have never heard of me before. I am a Southern man, and represent, in my family and friends, a large capital invested in Southern lands. I have been an iron master, employing at one time over three hundred hands.

The question may arise in your minds why I, the employer of labor, should feel a sympathy with your movement for the elevation of the laboring classes.

I reply, because my experience as a manufacturer of iron has satisfied me that the only true policy, either for the capitalists or the workingmen, is the "live and let live" policy—that that is a defective system in the state, under which the interests of capital and labor are opposed; that the system should be changed so as to make the interests of the employer and the employed as far as possible identical. Therefore, in asking for a charter to organize a company to put our iron works again in operation, we reduced our shares to ten dollars each, intending to give to every employé the privilege of taking shares in the company at par as fast as he could save from his wages ten dollars to pay for one. We expected thereby to interest every employé in the success of the company and in seeing that every other employé did his duty. We also proposed in our prospectus that after declaring a reasonable and proper dividend on capital, inclusive of the shares held by the employés, a reasonable share of the surplus profits should be set aside to be divided as a reward for faithful service among the employés in proportion to their respective length of service and amount of wages earned, as shown by the pay-rolls; and another portion as an invalid and pension fund, and to support schools for the children of the employés.

Another reason why I feel a sympathy with any movement professing to have in view the elevation of the white laboring classes of the North. I have told you that I am from the South. Mr. Jefferson said that "the Democracy of the North were the natural allies of the Republicans of the South." He used that word "democracy" in its political party sense; but in its lexicographical sense, the democracy of the North are the people—the laboring men—the industrial classes, without reference to their organization as a political party. They, the laboring men of the North, were the natural allies of the Republicans of the South.

1. Because the latter were the producers of the raw material, which is the corner-stone of the prosperity of the laboring classes of the North.

2. The industry of the South being almost exclusively agricultural and confined to the production of cotton, the South were not the rivals either of the mechanics of the North or of the farmers of the West; but their best customers.

3. There was another and stronger bond which has not heretofore been understood at the North by the laboring classes. The struggle at the North was between capital and labor; the party of capital struggling to get possession of the government and to legislate so as to throw upon the laboring classes the expenses of government, and to get the longest day's work for the least possible price.

The planters of the South were the owners of daily labor; they were directly interested in keeping up the price of daily wages, and in keeping down the daily cost of subsistence. In this their interests were identical with the interests of the laboring classes of the North. These last were the majority in numbers, but the minority in political influence; because, engaged all day at the plough, the loom, the anvil and the work-bench, they had neither time nor money to contend successfully with capital in the organization of political parties, or the framing of political issues. The party of capital discovered in this identity of interests between the laboring classes of the North and the planters of the South the full meaning of Mr. Jefferson's celebrated apothegm. They realized that this common interest, namely: *to keep up the price of daily wages and keep down the daily cost of subsistence*, made the laboring classes of the North the natural allies of the owners of negro slave labor engaged in the production of cotton at the South. Therefore it was that the party of capital struck at white labor at the North through the now dead body of its natural ally, negro slavery at the South.

Gentlemen, negro slavery has been abolished, and forever. There is no disposition any where in the South to restore it; for all acknowledge that it is now neither practicable nor desirable. Inasmuch as it had been forced upon them against their will, and in spite of their repeated remonstrances, by the *capital* of Old England and New England, which made large profits out of the slave trade; inasmuch as they were not responsible for its origin, and it had become a domestic question of vital importance to them, the South claimed that it was their own exclusive right to determine how to regulate, and whether and when, and in what manner to get rid of it. But these are now all questions of the past. It is gone forever, and you have lost an important element of strength in your contest with *capital*.

Yet there still remains a strong bond of common interest between you and the South. As I have before remarked, you are a minority in political influence at the North, although you have the majority of numbers. The South also is in a minority, and their contest is with that same *party* of *capital* at the North, who seek to govern both you and them, and to throw on you and them the burdens of government. The only salvation of these two minorities is in making common cause with each other, and standing together. That same "party of capital," who have driven you to meet here for your own protection, who seek to get from you the longest day's work for the least possible price, are now seeking, by destructive legislation, to take from your natural allies, the impoverished South, what little they have left at the least possible price. As an illustration: I called on one of that party in New York last spring to aid me in my efforts to restore the cotton planting interests of the South, by advancing money to aid the planters to make a crop. His answer was that *"the time had not yet arrived for investments South; that, since the meeting of Congress, he had become satisfied that the longer the South was 'kept out in the cold,' with their labor system disorganized and unsettled, the poorer they would become, and the cheaper they would have to sell their lands; that Northern capitalists could do better with their money by waiting for another year, by which time they could buy the South at their own price."*

Gentlemen: While the party of capital are arranging *"to purchase Southern lands at their own price,"* they are destroying that industry which is the basis, the foundation, the corner-stone of the profitable employment of the working men of the North. They can make profit by first destroying, then purchasing at destruction prices, and waiting for a new growth. You, and those you represent, cannot wait this tedious process. You, who have to feed your children from day to day, can't afford to wait for a crop of speculation, or peculation, to mature. You want profitable employment—a fair day's wages for a fair day's work, and, you want it now and every day.

Gentlemen: My time has expired. I thank you for your courtesy and attention, and will detain you no longer.

The Congress unanimously adopted the following resolution:

Resolved, As the sense of this Congress, that the speedy restoration of the agricultural interests of the Southern states is of vital importance to the laboring men of the North; and that the aggregation and capitalization of the surplus earnings of labor for the twofold purpose of promoting an increased production of cotton, and of aiding to elevate the laboring classes, as proposed by the American Industrial Agency, is very desirable, and we earnestly invite the attention of the laboring men to the subject.

THE TRUE SAVINGS BANK FOR THE WORKING MEN.

An abundant supply of Southern cotton is as essential to the well doing of the white laboring men of the North as food is to life. The true interest of the producers of cotton in the South, and of the white laboring classes of the North, are identical. Their financial position is analogous. Neither have adequate cash capital. Both want money. Each require the products of the other. Their remedy is *coöperation* for the protection and promotion of their common interests.

The rich lands, vast mineral resources, and abundant water power of the South offer to the white laboring men of the North, and to their children, the most attractive field of operations in the world. The land-owners of the South invite them and look anxiously for their coming. Will they not *coöperate* to preserve this rich inheritance to themselves and their children?

Coöperation is the fundamental principle of the AMERICAN INDUSTRIAL AGENCY. Its purpose is to organize the planters of the South into a coöperative association—to coöperate with each other, and with the industrial classes of the North, and to utilize their joint credit and means so as to command capital for their common benefit.

It has been organized, and its business will be conducted on the basis of *ample security and absolute safety.*

The charter provides that "*fifty per cent. of the capital shall be invested in good securities, and held as a reserved fund, pledged for the payment of any contingent liability which may be created in the course of their business.*"

There can be no better security than bonds, secured by good Southern lands worth twice the sum of the bonds.

We, therefore, propose to permit Southern planters to subscribe to the stock of the branches, and pay in bonds, secured by lands worth double the amount of their subscriptions. These bonds will be held by the State Treasurer, or other suitable trustee, as a security for the safe and prudent management of the business.

The *titles* and *value* of the lands offered as security will be first thoroughly examined, and if found correct, then

To a bond subcription of........ $100,000
Secured by lands worth $200,000
The agency will add cash........ 100,000
                            ——————
Making together a capital of... $200,000

We have then $200,000 worth of lands as security for $100,000 of currency advanced.

It is well known that no business in the United States pays such large profits on the amount of cash capital used, and is at the same time so *safe*, as the cotton factorage business.

As to *safety*, ample security is required for every advance of money in every stage of our operations. In making advances to planters to enable them to make a crop, we have, as security, their shares and their bonds, secured by lands, worth four times the amount advanced, in addition to the crop to be raised. In making advances on cotton ready for market, we get the bills of lading, which give us the con-

trol of the cotton, as security for such advances. The security, therefore, is perfect.

As to *profit*, $100,000 loaned to planters to enable them to make a crop, or advanced on cotton bills of lading, will bring to the produce and factorage department of the Agency, a crop worth from $500,000 to $1,000,000, paying a net commission over all expenses of at least two and a half per centum. We would then have as profits:

Interest on loans 6 to 7 per c. on $200,000 capital stock
2½ per cent. com-
    mission on crop.6¼ " 12¼ "   "   "   "
Add insurance pro-
    fit.............. 5 " 5   "   "   "   "
Add banking profit 5 " 5   "   "   "   "
Makes dividends on
    capital stock....22¼ " 29¼

This is far below the rate of profit made by individuals in the same business; but we propose to do the business at less charge to the planters, and to divide the profits with the planters, who raise the products, which are the basis of the business.

The following estimates of the profit made by individuals in this business has been furnished me by a Southern cotton factor of long experience.

ESTIMATE No. 1.

Amount advanced to planter to raise his crop, say............	$ 2,000
Amount of crop raised on this advance....................	10,000
Profit by this transaction:	
2½ per cent. commission on $2,000 advanced..................	50
7 per cent. interest............	140
2½ per cent. commission on renewal of loan every 60 days...	300
2½ per cent. commission on sale of $10,000 crop..............	250
¼ per cent. insurance on $10,000.	50
	——————
Profit on $2,000 advanced.......	$790

Or 39½ per cent., which does not include expenses of transportation and other charges.

ESTIMATE No. 2.

Upon advances to operators in the interior :
Commission for discount-
ing.................1 to 2½ per cent.
Interest 7 per cent. per
annum equals........$\frac{7}{12}$ to $\frac{7}{12}$ " "
Upon sale of produce con-
trolled by this advance,
commission and insur-
ance.................3 to 3 " "
_____

$4\frac{7}{12}$ to $6\frac{1}{12}$ " "

This operation should close itself in 30 days, giving a profit of $4\frac{7}{12}$ to $6\frac{1}{12}$ per cent. per month, or 55 to 73 per cent. per annum (storage, forwarding and other charges not included.)

The American Industrial Agency is also authorized, by its charter, to receive deposits, and is a savings bank. The Agency will pay interest on all deposits at the rate of six per cent. per annum. But where the deposits are left with them for six months, or longer, so that they can be used in raising and bringing to market the valuable products of the South, those deposits will be treated as *quasi* or temporary stock, and will be allowed a dividend, not exceeding six per cent. in addition to the six per cent. interest; so that, instead of getting only four per cent., as under the present system of deposits, the depositors will get twelve per cent. per annum, which surely is sufficient inducement to those having small sums to deposit. These small sums added together will make a capital sufficient, on the *coöperative* system proposed, to secure the business, which will give to each depositor the increased dividend above mentioned.

It should be mentioned that, although the depositors will receive a dividend as quasi stockholders, they are not stockholders, *nor liable as such for any losses. They will be secured against loss* by the reserved fund, and the planters, who have given their lands and homes as security, and are responsible for any losses that may be incurred, will see that the directors and officers of the several branches are competent, prudent, and reliable men.

The following table shows how rapidly a capital may be accumulated, which can be used to start coöperative manufacturing companies :

If 2,000 laboring men can save $50 each per annum, this would make :

1st deposit...................	$100,000
12 per cent. dividend.......	12,000
2d deposit.................	100,000
End of 1st year...........	$212,000
12 per cent. dividend.......	25,440
3d deposit.................	100,000
End of 2d year...........	$337,440
12 per cent. dividend.......	40,492
4th deposit.................	100,000
End of 3d year...........	$477,932
12 per cent. dividend........	57,351
5th deposit.................	100,000
End of 4th year...........	$635,283
12 per cent. dividend.......	76,233
6th deposit.................	100,000
End of 5th year...........	$811,516
12 per cent. dividend........	97,381
7th deposit.................	100,000
Makes aggregate accumulation in 6 years................	$1,008,897

Here are the means of giving profitable employment to, and elevating the condition of, the laboring classes.

THE
AMERICAN INDUSTRIAL AGENCY.

CENTRAL OFFICES,

Nos. 40 & 42 BROADWAY, New York City,

With corporate powers and franchises more extensive and valuable than those of the CREDITS FONCIER AND MOBILIER of France, will, through branches located at all important points in the United States and Europe, conduct its business under the following departments, viz. :

1st. Produce and Factorage.

2d. { Banking and Loans.
     Trust and Savings.
     Collection and Adjustment of Accounts.

3d. Insurance.

4th. Immigration, Labor, and Lands.

5th. Transportation.

6th. Railroads, Mines, and Manufactures.

Will make Loans and Advances for twelve months, or longer, at legal rates of interest ;

Make liberal advances on consignments of Cotton, Tobacco, and other produce ;

Will take Stock in co-operative Manufacturing Companies, and advance the capital to put them in operation ;

Negotiate Loans and furnish Machinery and Supplies to Railroad, Mining, and Manufacturing Companies, Planters, and others ;

Negotiate sales and leases of land, supply colonists, tenants, and laborers (native and immigrant) ;

Insure Lives, Houses, Goods, and all other property ;

Guarantee payment of notes, bonds, and accounts ;

By issuing life and accident policies to immigrants, who would otherwise be deterred from moving, by fear of leaving their families unprovided for among strangers, and by providing in advance of their moving for their immediate settlement in desirable locations, will secure a better class of immigrants for colonization of Southern lands ;

Receive money on deposit, and guarantee at least six per cent. interest per annum thereon ; and all sums left with them for six months, or longer, will be treated as *quasi* or *temporary* stock, and allowed a dividend not exceeding twelve per cent., inclusive of the six per cent. interest.

WANTED,

Several MOULDERS, FOUNDERS, and MACHINISTS, to revive a Machine Shop and Foundry, favorably located in Georgia, the operations of which were suspended by the war.

ALSO,

Several Turners, Cabinet-Makers, Carpenters, and other workmen, for a Furniture, Sash and Blind Factory, at a good location in Georgia, to revive a business closed by the war.

ALSO,

Several Carriage-Makers, Trimmers, and Painters, Blacksmiths, and others, for a large Coach, Buggy, and Wagon Factory.

ALSO,

Experienced men to take charge of the business of a Cotton Manufacturing Company.

All the above companies to be organized under the General Laws of Georgia, which are very liberal, on the *co-operative* principle ; the employés to be interested as stockholders.

For further information apply to

BEN. E. GREEN,

OFFICE OF THE AMERICAN INDUSTRIAL AGENCY,

Nos. 40 & 42 BROADWAY.